Controversies in
Contemporary Religion

Controversies in Contemporary Religion

EDUCATION, LAW, POLITICS, SOCIETY, AND SPIRITUALITY

Volume 1: Theoretical and Academic Debates

Paul Hedges, Editor

PRAEGER

AN IMPRINT OF ABC-CLIO, LLC
Santa Barbara, California • Denver, Colorado • Oxford, England

Library of Congress Cataloging-in-Publication Data

Controversies in contemporary religion: education, law, politics, society, and spirituality / Paul Hedges, editor.
    volumes cm
    Includes bibliographical references and index.
    ISBN 978–1–4408–0341–3 (v. 1 : alk. paper) — ISBN 978–1–4408–0342–0 (v. 1 : ebook)
    1. Religion. 2. Religions. 3. Religion and culture. I. Hedges, Paul (Paul Michael), 1970– editor of compilation.
BL87.C68   2014
200—dc23   2014005213

ISBN: 978–1–4408–0341–3
EISBN: 978–1–4408–0342–0

18 17 16 15 14   1 2 3 4 5

This book is also available on the World Wide Web as an eBook.
Visit www.abc-clio.com for details.

Praeger
An Imprint of ABC-CLIO, LLC

ABC-CLIO, LLC
130 Cremona Drive, P.O. Box 1911
Santa Barbara, California 93116-1911

This book is printed on acid-free paper ∞

Manufactured in the United States of America

These books are dedicated to my family: Yue, Raphy, and Zaozao.

Contents

Introduction

Paul Hedges

RELIGION AND CONTROVERSY

Religion, it may be suggested, is inherently controversial, and certainly we can find plenty of evidence for this: if we look at a recent global opinion poll we will see that a majority of people in many countries believe it is a source of social division, many wars and conflicts today and throughout history have had religious associations, and many contemporary debates and heated arguments involve religion and religious people (on such issues as ecology, women's rights, homosexuality, even whether religion itself is innately harmful). However, many religious people will suggest that their tradition is essentially peaceful and tolerant, while the same global poll shows the majority of people in other countries believing that religion does promote social cohesion.[1] Whichever side we agree with, and I would suggest it is too simplistic to argue that either side is right or wrong, we can see that religion divides opinions, even as to whether it is controversial or not!

These volumes will look at the arguments and issues behind many of these debates, and examine a wide range of spheres where religion appears such as education, law, politics, society, and spirituality. This, I would suggest, is important because despite claims in the mid to late twentieth century that religion was dying out as non-religious forces (secularism) progressed, the twenty-first century has clearly seen religion resurgent on the world stage in all areas of life and in different global contexts. Therefore, whether one is religious or not, or believes religion is helpful or harmful, it is an issue which it is naïve or ill judged to ignore; it can be suggested that a certain degree of religious literacy is something any informed and well-educated person needs in our world. Indeed, one aim of these volumes is to provide such knowledge around a range of controversial issues to help us better understand the world in which we live, and so we analyze issues such as the rise of fundamentalism, censorship, human rights, environmentalism, sexuality, bioethics, and other questions of widespread interest. This book is intended to provide in-depth context and analysis far beyond what is available in the news or online, enabling readers to understand the nature of and reasons for controversies in current headlines. Moreover, quite a few chapters make important and exciting contributions in areas that have no comparable coverage. I have certainly felt privileged to be a part of this project.

In looking at the issues, the volumes are both global and multi-religious in scope. I have tried to gather contributors from every continent and also to provide coverage of religions in all areas of the globe, as well as looking at both the most prominent traditions, and smaller or lesser-known ones. Obviously, such an ambitious task has not been entirely successful, and I acknowledge that Africa is under-represented, however, the contributor-base includes scholars from Europe, both North and South America, Asia, and Australasia. Beyond the usual "world religions" (Christianity, Islam, Judaism, Buddhism, and Hinduism) there is coverage of such traditions as Daoism, Confucianism, and Sikhism, as well as Indigenous Lifeways and various New Religious Movements. Obviously, it is impossible to provide coverage of every religious tradition and so there are omissions, but I hope that the diversity of religions in the world is represented. Indeed, many chapters try to provide coverage of a number of different religions or contexts, although others focus upon a specific religion or regional context. Of course, no attempt has been made to be deliberately obscure, and so the world's two largest religious traditions, Islam and Christianity, receive the most attention, however, many chapters will add to the existing literature by covering an issue in relation to religions or regions not adequately surveyed (at least not in any form available and accessible to students and general readers).

These volumes do not intend to provide a reader with a detailed understanding of religions in general, but there are plenty of useful texts that will provide the reader with an understanding of the history, background, and practices of such specific traditions as Buddhism, Islam, Christianity, Judaism and Daoism.[2] However, it is expected that the reader needs some basic understanding of these traditions to read and understand this book, for instance knowing the difference between Catholic and Protestant Christianity, or Theravada and Mahayana Buddhism, as such a brief guide to some of the world's main religious traditions is set out at the end of this introduction.

Each of the three volumes has a specific focus. The first volume covers theoretical and academic debates, the second looks at debates in the public square and ethical issues, and the third examines specific issues and case studies. That is, the first volume looks at the kind of questions scholars ask about contemporary debates, and such things as the very definition of "religion", for there are those who will argue the term is deeply problematic and should be abandoned altogether. It will also look at such issues as "identity" and "postcolonialism". It should be stressed, though, that the division between the three volumes is somewhat arbitrary and there are many linkages, and many chapters will mention issues discussed across all three volumes. Moreover, discussion in the first volume provides some kind of underpinning for issues discussed elsewhere, indeed, it is hoped that the accessible introductions here will make clear to a wider audience the reasons why scholars debate what can often seem obscure issues or those that do not grab headlines but may be of deep personal interest to many. The second volume, though, tries to cover issues that are often in the public eye and the media, such as the position of women, human rights, politics, and the so-called New Atheists. These issues are obviously discussed by scholars, and so are part of the scholarly debate but relate to issues often raised outside of academia. The third volume looks at issues within particular traditions or specific case studies, so the background and debates surrounding the so-called 9/11 mosque project is covered, as are New Religious Movements in Japan among other topics. Some issues are more or less likely to be debates in the public eye, such as the position of women in Islamic law, whereas some are heated debates within religious traditions but do not normally surface in the media, such as the use of Asian traditions of meditation in Christianity or the adaptation of Christianity to indigenous customs in Africa.

A NOTE ON TERMINOLOGY

Dates will be given in the format CE and BCE. These terms correspond to the more familiar AD and BC but are preferred by scholars of religion as they do not carry the Christian connotations (AD is short for the Latin *Anno Domini*, "In the year of our lord" [i.e. after the birth of Jesus], and BC stands for "before Christ"). In contrast, CE and BCE stand for "Common Era," and "Before the Common Era." As such other religions are not dated by explicitly Christian terms. We have also used simplified forms of names, such as "*Quran*" rather than "*Qur'an*", and avoided the use of symbols (e.g., to render Indian languages into English various accents and diacritics are sometimes employed, i.e. sloping lines above the "s", or dots or lines over other letters). We have also generally used English language translations in place of terms from the original language except where it is useful to retain the original. For instance, in relation to Islam, sayings of the prophet will be used in place of the Arabic term *hadith*. This is because we are trying to make the work readily accessible even to those without any background in the specific religions (however, we will often provide technical terms in brackets or footnotes). Also, the term God: capital "G" will be used when referring to a specific supreme deity in any religious tradition, whereas god(s) (small "g") will be used to refer to lesser deities or deities in general. Words not generally found in English are in italic as are all book titles.

RELIGIOUS TRADITIONS 101

As stated earlier, we will end with a brief survey of some important religious traditions, setting out some basic facts that anyone reading these texts would find useful (or indeed should be part of the basic religious literacy). It will be impossible to cover every tradition covered in the texts, which runs from Orthodox Judaism to Cuban Santeria, and from Theravada Buddhism to Raelianism, however, some main details of the largest traditions will be mentioned, as well as some other religions encountered.

Buddhism

Buddhism was founded by Siddhartha Gautama, known as the Buddha, who lived somewhere around 500BCE. It is split into two main schools, the Theravada and the Mahayana. The Theravada predominates in Southeast Asia, in such places as Sri Lanka, Thailand and Burma, whereas the Mahayana is found in East Asia, i.e., in such places as Vietnam, Japan, Korea and China. The former stresses a monastic ideal and sees the Buddha as our guide to our own awakening, the spiritual realization that he himself had. The latter tends to speak of Buddhas and Bodhisattvas, believing there to be many, as god-like beings who can aid us in our own spiritual quest or in this life. There are many schools, such as: Zen, a meditation school; the Pure Land, a devotional school that reveres a figure known as the Amida Buddha and is the largest single Buddhist tradition; and, Vajrayana, which is the traditions of Tibet and elsewhere which have a strong ritual and philosophical focus. Nichiren Buddhism, although a relatively small Japanese sect founded by Nichiren in the middle ages, has become influential in the West because of a twentieth-century offshoot called Sokka Gakai. Buddhism's central texts are the *Tripitaka* (meaning "Three Baskets") comprising the Buddha's sermons (*sutras*), philosophy (*abhidharma*), and the monastic code (*vinaya*), which is used by the Theravada and the Mahayana. The Mahayana has a further set of scriptures which contains many works amongst the most influential of which is the *Lotus Sutra*. Buddhists see their tradition as founded on the "three jewels": Buddha (which signifies his spiritual attainment of awakening), *Dharma* (the Buddha's teachings which lead to awakening), and *Sangha* (the Buddhist community, that preserves the teachings).

Christianity

Most Christians believe Jesus of Nazareth, a first-century Galilean rabbi, was in fact God in human form whose death on a cross resulted in human release from sin. Christianity has various major groupings, often called denominations, which are as follows: (1) (Roman) Catholic, those who believe the Bishop of Rome (the Pope) leads the Church as a direct successor of Jesus' disciple Peter, and are the largest Christian denomination with around 1 in 5 of the world's population; (2) (Eastern) Orthodox, whose nominal leader is the Bishop (Patriarch) of Constantinople, and believe they represent the true lineage from Jesus, they are an ancient church with elaborate and formal rituals; (3) Protestantism, which includes churches that broke away from Catholicism in the sixteenth century and afterwards, led by Reformers like Martin Luther and John Calvin, unlike the two previous denominations—who stress both church tradition and the *Bible* as sources of influence—Protestants tend either to see the *Bible* alone as the source of the church's teachings or at least see it as more important, it is also split into various smaller denominations such as Lutherans, Calvinists, Anglicans and Baptists; (4) Pentecostalism, not strictly speaking a denomination, is a twentieth-century movement that stresses God's gifts given in ecstatic worship, most notably the so-called gift of tongues (the ability to speak foreign languages you have never learned or else to speak an "angelic language" which others can interpret), from recent beginnings it now represents (either itself or through the charismatic movement, which is how Pentecostalism is known inside mainstream denominations) at least 10 percent of the world's Christians; (5) Non-Chalcedonian Christians are those who were involved in a split in the church in the fifth century CE and reject the main statement of belief of most other Christians, what is called the Nicene Creed.

The central Christian text is the *Bible*, which contains the *Hebrew Bible* (what Christians call the *Old Testament*) which it took over from Judaism, and the *New Testament* texts written by Jesus' early followers.

Confucianism

Confucianism is an indigenous Chinese tradition, which some argue is not a religion but a humanistic philosophy, however, throughout history it has exhibited what we may call religious aspects or functions. It looks to a fifth-century BCE Chinese thinker named Confucius who codified older traditions and edited the major texts it relies upon. For much of Chinese history over the last 2,000 years until the early twentieth century it formed the state orthodoxy in China and was the basis of the civil service. In the Middle Ages a movement called Neo-Confucianism arose that had a very specifically spiritual core and tried to reform what it saw as the dry and legalistic examination system that had developed. Its texts are known as the Confucian Classics. Since the end of imperial China, Confucianism has predominately existed as a philosophical system, although a ritual practice persisted in

Korea and recently the Chinese government has attempted to use Confucianism as a means to develop social cohesion in mainland China.

Confucianism has been influential in the whole of what may be termed the Chinese cultural world, which includes Korea, Japan, and other countries where a Chinese population has spread. It is often linked to the practise of ancestor veneration, or worship, as well as filial piety—the respect for parents and ancestors, and linked to this a whole set of hierarchical social relations including family and the nation. Confucian thinkers have included both those who are suspicious of the supernatural world as well as those more clearly focused on some divine or deity, often termed Heaven (*Tian*).

Daoism

Daoism is an indigenous Chinese religion that arose as a formal religious movement in the early centuries CE, but that looks back to a legendary figure known as Lao Zi, said to be an elder contemporary of Confucius, who Daoists believe to have written the influential *Dao De Jing*. Two main schools exist today, one of which is monastic and centred in Northern China called the Complete Perfection School, and the other while having temples as centers has a greater emphasis on providing such public rituals and services as exorcism and healing, and is known as the Heavenly Masters School, it is more common in Southern China. A common false division of Daoism in many texts is between what are termed: "philosophical Daoism", seen as an ancient spiritual tradition going back to Lao Zi; and "religious Daoism", a form of corrupt and popular priestly practice. The origins of this common perception are complex but have no basis in actual Daoist history or practice.[3] Daoism has a huge collection of sacred scriptures built up over centuries. Given the diversity of Daoist systems over the centuries it is hard to generalize about its teachings in any meaningful way, but suffice it to say that practise has often emphasized using the body as a means of spiritual transformation, it has generally been more open to women's leadership and spiritual practise than most religions, and that it has a huge pantheon of deities in popular worship who often cross over into the folk religion of the people.

Hinduism

Scholars often argue that Hinduism is best not understood as a single religious tradition, but as a whole family of traditions, or even that it is wrong to see many things labelled "Hinduism" as part of one related tradition.[4] Nevertheless, a set of fairly central schools and texts exist which while often conflicting and contradictory give the notion of "Hinduism" some use as a broad concept. These central features include: a common set of philosophical schools (*Vedanta* and others); several prominent central deities, Vishnu (whose followers are called *Vaishnavas*, and whose worship includes devotion to two of his best known manifestations [*avatars*] Krishna and Rama), Shiva (whose followers are called *Shaivites*), and the Goddess (often known as Devi, but also Kali, Durga and other names, whose followers are known as *Shaktas*), as well as some others such as Ganesh, the elephant-headed god; shared texts, which include the *Vedas*, which though not central to most Hindus are widely revered, the great epics of Indian literature and religion, called the *Mahabharata* and *Ramayana*, as well as various devotional strands of literature; common tenets such as reincarnation and "order" (*dharma*—a term with many meanings), and traditionally caste; certain traditions like devotion (*bhakti*) and ritual/ esoteric currents (*tantra*), and respect for holy people who renounce the world. However, given the disparate nature of Hinduism, there will be traditions that reject parts of this or have vastly different notions surrounding shared elements.

Indigenous Religions

Often spoken of as "lifeways" rather than "religions," this term is used of the religious and cultural traditions (there is generally no distinction) of groups such as North American Indians, Australian Aborigines, and tribal groups in Africa. In the past they were often called "primitive" or "primal" religions; however, this does not do justice to their sophistication or adaptations, for they do not go back unchanged to some imagined "primal" past. They tend not to have texts, and each tradition will have its distinctive nature.

Islam

Founded by Muhammad in the seventh century CE, Islam is the world's second largest religious tradition and is noted for a strict adherence, or surrender (from which the term "Islam" comes), to God (the Arabic term Allah simply means "(the) God" and is used by Arabic-speaking Jews and Christians). Muslims believe that associating anything with God, whether it be worshipping any other being alongside God, or elevating anything to a similar status, is the worst thing you can do. The two main groups are the Sunni, the majority (about 85% of all Muslims) and the Shia, most of the remainder. The division is as much political as religious as it relates to the leadership of the Islamic community. Indeed, in Islam, the politics and religious activities have always been closely linked as have law; indeed, a code of laws (*sharia*) based upon the sacred text, the *Quran*, the sayings of the prophet and his companions (*hadith*), and developments on these, have been central to Islamic societies throughout history. Indeed, in many ways Islam offers a whole way of life.

Jainism

Mahavira is the founder of this tradition which stresses non-violence, so that strict adherents will not kill any living creature. They even brush the path ahead of them to ensure that they do not accidently step on insects, and also strain their water to ensure that even tiny creatures are not consumed.

Judaism

Although it is one of the oldest continuous religious traditions in the world, Judaism as we now know it grew up around the same time as Christianity in the first few centuries CE. This is because the Romans had destroyed the temple and forbidden Jews to enter their sacred city Jerusalem which had, for centuries, been the center of their religious life. Therefore, for almost 2,000 years Jews have envisaged a time when a leader inspired by God, the Messiah, would rebuild the temple and restore them to Israel. The current state of Israel is a complicated aspect in this story. Since the exile under the Romans Jews have been led by teachers (rabbis) in a religion designed to recreate Jewish life without the temple, known as Rabbinic Judaism, whose chief texts are the Books of Moses (the *Torah*, the first five books of what Christians call the *Old Testament*, although their scripture includes the rest of this text, commonly called the *Hebrew Bible*), and a code of laws (*Talmud*), as well as later law codes. Judaism today has three main traditions: Orthodox, who stick to a strict observance of what they see as their ancient tradition, and make little adaptation to the modern world; Conservative, who see tradition as very important but believe that small adaptations to the contemporary world are necessary; and Reform, or Liberal, who argue that tradition developed in a specific context and so has to be modified and adapted (or as they would see it updated) to the contemporary world, often saying the essence rather than the specific literal meaning of any law or tradition should be used. Globally the Orthodox are the largest tradition, though in some countries, such as the United Kingdom, Liberal Judaism predominates. There are also groups of secular Jews who reject the religious worldview but follow the customs and rituals. Notably, in Judaism, ritual and practice have always been seen as more significant than belief, on which a variety of interpretations are allowed.

New Religious Movements

This blanket term covers a whole array of traditions that have developed in recent times. Scholars disagree over what should be included but it often, in Western usage, covers religions originating in the last 200 years, so things such as Jehovah's Witnesses are included. It is also used for religions that may be ancient but are new in their context, such as Buddhist groups in Europe, especially those that seek Western converts. Popularly such traditions are often termed "cults"; however, there is no academic usage for this term in this context.[5]

Santeria

A religion that emerged through the fusion of African tribal religions and Roman Catholicism, and was created by slaves brought under European colonial influence. It is found in Cuba and parts of South America. It focuses on spirits, who have similarities with Catholic saints and who manifest the supreme spirit.

Sikhism

Developed around 500 years ago in Northern India, Sikhism took elements from Islamic spiritual traditions (Sufism) and Hindu devotion (*bhakti*), which formed part of a common tradition at that time (known as the *Sant* tradition), as well as other elements, and fused them through the particular vision of Guru Nanak. It explicitly taught that there were many paths to God who was one, although approached in different ways. Over the next few hundred years, Sikhism developed a military wing which developed in self-defense (of themselves and others) against the ruling Mughal Dynasty, and this became one of its prominent features or groups.

Zoroastrianism

The prophet Zoroaster lived around 3,000 years ago, or maybe more, and developed what is probably the first significant religious tradition with adherence to a single supreme God (monotheism). Over time, though, it developed a belief in two all-powerful deities—one good, one evil—locked in eternal combat. It developed many ideas that would influence Judaism, Christianity, and Islam, especially in relation to the afterlife, monotheism, and a divinely appointed saviour who would lead the final battle where good would overcome evil; this is arguably its greatest legacy—although small and little known, the world's religious landscape would almost certainly be vastly different without it.

NOTES

1. IPSOS Poll, "Is Religion a Force for Good in the World," 2010, http://www.ipsos -na.com/news-polls/pressrelease.aspx?id=5058 (accessed November 22 2011).
2. There are many excellent textbooks: one which has a contemporary focus is Linda Woodhead et al., eds., *Religions in the Modern World*, 2nd ed. (London and New York: Routledge, 2009).

3. An excellent discussion of this, and some reasons, is provided in a lecture available online by the scholar Russell Kirkland, "The Taoism of the Western Imagination and the Taoism of China: De-colonizing the Exotic Teachings of the East," lecture delivered at the University of Tennessee October 20, 1997, http://faculty.franklin.uga.edu/kirkland/sites/ faculty.franklin.uga.edu.kirkland/files/TENN97.pdf (accessed: November 22 2013).

4. The idea that Hinduism is almost entirely a construct of the Western scholarly imagination was strongly advanced in the 1990s and a text titled *Hinduism Reconsidered* advocated this position; however, since then a more balanced approach has been taken, especially influenced by an essay titled "Who Invented Hinduism?" by the scholar David N. Lorenzen which showed that many key traditions can be linked around this term. As Lorenzen put it elsewhere: "What is needed, as is often the case, is an approach that avoids extremes"—see David N. Lorenzen, "Hindus and Others," in *Rethinking Religion in India: The Colonial Construction of Hinduism*, ed. Esther Bloch, Marianne Keppens, and Rajaram Hegde (London and New York: Routledge, 2010), 38.

5. The usage "cult" in popular language tends to mean a religion the speaker/ writer does not approve of, however, there is no clear distinction—almost every religious tradition has, at some time or place, been seen as socially or morally aberrant (Christianity was viewed as such a "cult" in the Roman Empire for some time). In scholarly usage "cult" tends to refer to a specific devotional tradition or focus, for instance scholars may speak of "the cult of the Virgin Mary" in Roman Catholicism, reflecting no pejorative sense, merely that there is a strong devotional focus to her.

1

What Is Religion? Or, What Is It We Are Talking About?

Anna S. King and Paul Hedges

INTRODUCTION

It may seem odd to ask what the phenomenon we call "religion" actually is. Do we not all know what it is? For instance, if asked, most people could reply by naming a number of religious traditions such as Christianity, Buddhism, and Hinduism. Alternatively, they could talk about concepts or practices religions tend to share such as beliefs and rituals. However, for many years, scholars of religion have realized that such answers simply are not adequate and only give rise to further problems. We will explore some of the most important of these, but let us start with three issues that should help us realize there is no easy answer to the question "what is religion?"

First, it is not always clear what we mean by "religions." For instance, scholars argue whether Buddhism and Confucianism are philosophies or religions. Today, you would typically study Confucianism as a philosophy in China but as a religion in the United Kingdom or the United States. Meanwhile, some traditions encompass a whole way of life so that, for example, some people born into a tradition such as Judaism follow the customs and holidays associated with that tradition but define themselves as atheists. Are they still "Jewish" if we define Judaism as a religion? Judaism is also defined as an ethnicity; you are Jewish because you are born to an ethnically Jewish mother (at least traditionally). However, people can convert to (some forms of) Judaism without being ethnically Jewish. Therefore, some scholars suggest such traditions as Judaism, as well as Hinduism and indigenous religions, may be better described as cultures, worldviews, or lifeways.

Second, the defining of any individual "religion" is often contested. Hinduism is a notorious example as the term "Hindu" came from a geographic designation meaning "beyond the [River] Indus" and was used to encompass both the religious and cultural traditions of the people of India. This means it actually covers what some see as a very diverse, or even conflicting, range of traditions. Also, definitions of Hinduism sometimes expand to include all native Indian traditions such as Buddhism, Sikhism, and Jainism.

Third, there is a problem with defining just what a religion is, or even if "religion" is a meaningful term. Most of our definitions emerge from a Christian cultural background, which shapes the way "religion" is defined. For instance, we mentioned "belief" earlier as something people would commonly associate with religion. However, for many traditions we have called religions, the idea of a common set of beliefs does not exist. Given this and the other problems we will discuss later in this chapter, some scholars argue that we should abandon the term "religion" altogether.

BACKGROUND AND CONCEPTS

Today, in Religious Studies the category "religion" is ambiguous and contested. Differing definitions have been given over the last couple of centuries by such notable theorists as Emile Durkheim (1858–1917), Max Weber (1864–1920), Mircea Eliade (1907–1986), Ninian Smart (1927–2001), and Clifford Geertz (1926–2006), whereas Wilfred Cantwell Smith (1916–2000) suggested we abandon the term. Some recent scholars such as Russell McCutcheon, Talal Asad, Jonathan Z. Smith, Tomoko Masuzawa, and Timothy Fitzgerald have even critiqued the very notion of "religion" being meaningful at all. We will begin by laying out some basic issues. First, we will consider how scholars have tried to define "religion." Second, we will explore the way that definitions of religion seek to control what religion is and how it should be understood. Third, we will explore some of the history that shapes the way we think about religion.

Defining and Contesting "Religion"

One basic distinction that needs to be made is that "religion" may refer either to specific religious traditions or to a domain of human behavior often assumed to be universal.[1] Although the two are linked, they also need to be considered separately. For instance, we may seek to define broadly what makes something a "religion" or what it means to be "religious," or we may speak about a variety of "religions," such as Christianity, Hinduism, and Sikhism. Although obviously linked, they can be seen as separate areas for discussion, and indeed, we will come to the first part of this discussion shortly, but first let us focus on the second: what is "religion" as an aspect of human behavior?

Definitions of "religion" as a category may be distinguished in various ways. One of these is to give what we will term "simple definitions" or short descriptions; another is to create a typology of the types of things religions do; and a third is to analyze the way the word is used. We will describe each approach. An example of a simple definition would be a dictionary definition, the most minimal of starting points, which is often rooted in a particular historical understanding. The *Oxford English Dictionary* offers this primary definition: "the belief in and worship of a superhuman controlling power, especially a personal God or gods."[2] However, although many religious traditions presume some kind of superhuman reality, not all the traditions we refer to as religions do. Buddhism, for instance, has no creator deity, and although it has traditionally not denied the existence of gods, it is not really helpful to define it in a way that emphasizes a personal God or worship of a superhuman power.[3] We may suggest, therefore, that listing characteristic traits of religions might be more useful. We will look at other examples later, but the most widely used classification is that of Smart, who argues that religions have various dimensions, for example a physical dimension (buildings, objects), a narrative dimension (stories, myths), and so on (we will discuss his typology later on). Perhaps the most straightforward approach, though, to defining religion is the third, and this could involve applying the philosopher Ludwig Wittgenstein's (1889–1951) insight that words have meaning only within the contexts in which they are used, hence Wittgenstein's use of the term "language-game" (*sprachspiel*) to refer to simple examples of language use and the actions into which the language is woven. "Religion" has no meaning apart from the way it is used—that is, we need to look at what people mean when they speak of "religion," especially the way it is related to other words. However, this only tells us how we use the term, not whether it is actually a useful term, and critics such as McCutcheon and Fitzgerald complain, as we will see, about the usage.

Another approach divides these definitions into substantivist and functionalist perspectives. Substantivist theories focus on the internal dynamics of religions and the meaning the traditions have for people. Functionalist definitions focus more on social or psychological aspects. They are sometimes termed, respectively, "essentialist" and "reductionist" because the former often assume that there is an essence behind the religion, its "real" form, whereas the latter "reduce" them to something outside the religious system, that is, to society or the mind. We will briefly examine some examples of each before moving on. Substantivist theories typically assert that traditions hold important values and make the world comprehensible for devotees. Those scholars (e.g., Paul Tillich, Rudolph Otto, Mircea Eliade) who see religion as irreducible to something else (*sui generis*) argue that it is a unique phenomenon. Here, we understand religion at least in part as a universally experienced phenomenon that results from the human impetus to know "truth" or "ultimate reality." Religion is seen in terms of "sacred," "divine," "ultimate concern," or the spiritual quest of individuals. This quest may be defined in terms of the transcendent or the search for truth or even the realization of illusion. Although some substantivist scholars stress some reality behind religion, some suggest we do not need reference to supernatural beings or powers, as experiences of the sacred, divine, or ultimate can come from any source in the world. From this perspective, it is the nature of the devotee's internal experience, not any supposed source of that experience, which gives us the reason to define something as "religious." When we discuss functionalist approaches later, we will see that these two approaches are not necessarily opposed although we can contrast them.

Functional theorists focus on religion's social or psychological functions. Religion is viewed as an aspect of culture and a by-product of complex social, political, economic, historical, and psychological factors; in strong forms, functionalism simply reduces religion to nothing but this, and so is reductionist. Scholars committed to understanding human institutions and knowledge as in some part influenced by such factors as gender, class, and race "are interested in discarding the notion of *sui generis* religion as the first step toward conceiving of religion as but one aspect of human culture, to be studied in the same way in which we study other aspects of culture."[4] This approach to defining "religion" is common among social scientists and is indebted to Karl Marx (1818–1883), who theorized religion as deadening the oppressed's sense of pain and outrage, and to figures such as Durkheim and Weber. Another influential figure in this social-scientific approach to religion is Geertz, whose work emphasizes the interpretation of symbols, which provide meanings and order in societies and to individuals, describing culture as "a system of inherited conceptions expressed in symbolic forms by means of which men communicate, perpetuate, and develop their knowledge about and attitudes toward life."[5] In an essay titled "Religion as a Cultural System," he formalized a definition of religion that has been widely employed, which looks at the way religion guides and forms life, although there is no need, in his terms, for deities or much of the usual institutional organization we associate with religions.[6] We will return to his definition later.

We should note that this distinction, though often used, is rather crude as there are many differences between various figures in the substantivist and functionalist camps. Moreover, a scholar such as Geertz can be read in different ways, either as a functionalist searching for general laws to explain religion away as some functionalist approaches do or as emphasizing interpretation and exploring the ways humans use symbols to explain and make sense of their world.[7]

Controlling Religion: Definition as Power

Whether the definition of religion is substantivist or functionalist, it is never entirely neutral and objective; it often holds all sorts of hidden assumptions. Some of the best-known definitions of religion are ideological or tactical definitions, which gain their power from their essential simplicity.[8] These definitions are often explanations advanced in support of a single overriding thesis, and as Sharpe points out, many are aphorisms, or epigrams. Sharpe notes that the tendency is to make "religion" mean neither more nor less what a person chooses that it should mean.[9] Thus, Sigmund Freud (1856–1939) found that all religion reduces to neurosis. Marx wrote that religion is "the opium of the people." Friedrich Schleiermacher (1768–1834), a liberal Christian theologian, defined religion as "a feeling of absolute dependence." The philosopher Georg Hegel (1770–1831), on the contrary, defined religion as "the Divine Spirit becoming conscious of Himself through the finite spirit." Max Müller (1823–1900), a linguist, argued that we should define religions along linguistic lines, whereas the anthropologist Edward Burnett Tylor (1832–1917) in *Religion in Primitive Culture* (1871) famously defined religion as simply "the belief in spiritual beings," which he believed was common to all societies. In each case, the definitions of religion are not simply descriptive but often serve a specific end, and we will now look at a few more in detail.

To take an example of a substantive religious definition, we may turn to the Christian theologian Paul Tillich (1886–1965), who offered us one of the most famous of all definitions. For him, faith is "the state of being ultimately concerned." For him, religion is the substance, the ground, and the depth of human spiritual life. Tillich was influenced by the early nineteenth-century Protestant theologian Friedrich Schleiermacher's "feeling of absolute dependence." He writes:

> Religion, in the largest and most basic sense of the word, is ultimate concern.... Manifest in the moral sphere as the unconditional seriousness of moral demand[,].... In the realm of knowledge as the passionate longing for ultimate reality[,] ... in the aesthetic of the human spirit as the infinite desire to express ultimate meaning.[10]

Tillich here wanted to assert that at the very basis of all our concerns and aspirations is the quest for meaning, which, for him, is ultimately a quest for God or the highest reality. Influenced by contemporary existential philosophy, Tillich was not concerned whether we expressed ideas in terms of Christian doctrine as he wanted to show that all human effort reveals this quest.

Although most definitions have come from Christian contexts or Western scholars, some come from elsewhere, and so we may note the late-nineteenth-century Hindu reformer Vivekananda (1863–1902), who considers Hinduism not simply as another religion but as the supreme religion:

> Ours is the universal religion. It is inclusive enough, it is broad enough to include all the ideals. All the ideals of religion that already exist in the world can be immediately included, and we can patiently wait for all the ideals that are to come in the future to be taken in the same fashion, embraced in the infinite arms of the religion of Vedānta.[11]

In Vivekananda's definition, therefore, we come to the idea that religion is supremely encompassed or summed up in one universal religion, or more accurately, one interpretation of this particular religious tradition: his own. The attempt to define religion is therefore an attempt to define truth.

Turning to ideas of nonreligion or atheism, we can see that definitions from this perspective also seek to define "truth." The philosopher Ludwig Feuerbach (1804–1872), for instance, was sympathetic to religion, but he argued that "God" was actually a projection of the idea of human nature perfected or a form of wish fulfillment that would help us cope with life's struggles. The study of God is therefore the study of humanity: "Consciousness of God is self-consciousness, knowledge of God is self-knowledge. By his God thou knowest man, and by the man his God; the two are identical."[12] However, he also saw it as a form of alienation from the self: "Religion is the disuniting of man from himself; he sets God before him as the antithesis of himself. God is not what man is—man is not what God is."[13] His definition of religion, therefore, as a human projection is a reflection of his own lack of belief in a deity—although this is not to dismiss any such attempt to explain religion as merely a reflection of the researcher. We should also note that for nearly all the theorists we will discuss here, when a critique/definition of religion is offered, it is, because of their cultural context, primarily (if not entirely) a critique of Christianity (in the form, or forms, they knew it).

Meanwhile, we see various functionalist theories competing to give contrasting definitions of the origins of religion. Throughout his life, Freud, the founder of psychoanalysis, endeavored to understand religion, declaring in *The Future of an Illusion* that religion is a universal obsessional neurosis.[14] Turning to Marx, we may note that he critiqued Feuerbach's approach to religion as being simply concerned with ideas and mentalities rather than with social and economic conditions, and he may well have thought the same of Freud, although the two are often seen as allied in their attempts to dismantle or deconstruct religion. For Marx, religions, especially Christianity and Judaism, were products of the social system, and he regarded them as products of capitalism and therefore tied into systems of alienation and exploitation:

> The religious world is but the reflex of the real world. And for a society based upon the production of commodities, in which the producers in general enter

into social relations with one another by treating their products as commodities and values, whereby they reduce their individual private labour to the standard of homogeneous human labour—for such a society, Christianity . . . is the most fitting form of religion.[15]

We can also find other aspects of this assertion of domination today, for example with the New Atheism, which has often argued that religion is "dangerous" or "harmful," represented by authors such as Richard Dawkins, Sam Harris, Daniel Dennett, and Christopher Hitchens (see Volume 2, Chapter 5). All this has a relation to the way religion is understood and defined by the interpreter. We can see, therefore, that definitions of religion tend to be related to a particular ideology or worldview that seeks to classify and therefore control what religion is thought to be and so how it is interpreted. This is another factor that makes any attempt to search for a definition of religion more difficult.

The History of "Religion"

In Religious Studies, a key debate of the late twentieth and twenty-first centuries has been over the history of the idea of "religion" and the challenge to the common-sense notion that it refers to a universal feature of the world. Much analysis has been devoted to showing that the term is itself the product of historical development. Its use for many contemporary scholars becomes a form of cultural imperialism, which involves the imposition of Western academic classifications.[16] Scholars have pondered the following questions:

> If a culture does not have the concept, can we study "their religion"? Should scholarship only employ concepts local to the group under study? Is the thing to which our word points shared by all people, regardless [of] their [sic] self-understandings (as Shakespeare wrote in "Romeo and Juliet," "a rose by any other name would smell as sweet")? Is using our local term as if it were a universal signifier an act of cultural imperialism?[17]

As most non-Western religions lack words that correspond in meaning and intention to "religion," to what extent are we justified in using religion as a universal, cross-culturally useful signifier? We will set out some of these issues.

The first scholar to really challenge the term "religion" was Wilfred Cantwell Smith in the 1960s in an influential book called *The Meaning and End of Religion.* Cantwell Smith had three main arguments that are useful to us here. First, he pointed out that, as we have mentioned earlier, most languages do not have a word that means the same as the English word "religion." That is, although in modern English we use the term to mean a range of fairly similar systems relating to some special part of culture (i.e., areas associated with gods, transcendence, and phenomena beyond the physical world), it is simply impossible to find a similar word in many other languages.[18] Therefore, we can ask whether the term is simply part of our system of classifying the world rather than referring to something that actually exists in reality. Cantwell Smith also argued that the term "religion" has changed its meaning in the Western Christian tradition. From meaning "faith," it has come to signify a system or set of systems of beliefs. The very idea of there being a range of religions is therefore, he argued, very modern! (We shall see this is itself debatable.)

Second, Cantwell Smith showed that the naming of the religions, as we discussed in the introduction, was also part of this modern Western classification system. Islam's name, meaning "submission [to God]," is derived from its own system, but the names by which we know other "religions" were all more or less inventions that were meaningless to non-English practitioners of those religions. We have already noted that "Hinduism" derives from a geographic term originally applied by Persians to the people of India. That it has become normal for Hindus in the West and in India to recognize and label themselves as such is very much part of the cultural dominance of the English language and the way Hinduism has become part of a global culture in the twentieth century. However, many "Hindus" still prefer to refer to their tradition by the terms *sanatana dharma*, which means "eternal tradition/teaching," or *Vedic dharma*, either because they may not want to accept a Western-imposed name or because they wish to differentiate themselves from mainstream Hinduism.[19] As another example, what we call Confucianism, naming an "ism" after someone seen as a founding figure, is also an imposition. Traditionally, in China the term "tradition [or family] of the scholars" (*rujiao* [*rujia*]) would have been used. Indeed, Confucius himself, who gives us the name "Confucianism," is not understood to be the tradition's founder. This affects the way we understand the tradition.

Finally, as religion became increasingly a matter of personal choice in Western culture, religious attitudes (meaning primarily Christian) were increasingly sidelined. Cantwell Smith argues that from the seventeenth century the name "religion" came to be given increasingly to the system of *ideas* with which people of faith were confronted.[20] The rationalism of the eighteenth-century Enlightenment period came to focus on the intellectual aspects of religion. This meant that ideas of belief or doctrines became central to what "religion" was said to be. To sum up, the very concept of a religion has a history that can be seen as a scholarly construct or device, which in many cultures and societies makes no sense.[21]

Later scholars have built on and extended Cantwell Smith's critique of religion and have followed him in advocating that we abandon the term altogether. The idea that we should abandon the term "religion" altogether is, though, highly debatable, and we will offer a critique of some of Cantwell Smith's ideas in what follows as we discuss the development of arguments.

SURVEY OF ARGUMENTS

In this section, we will consider several related issues. First, we will engage critically with current debates on the use of the term "religion." Second, we will go back to the question of definitions and ask how useful definitions of religion actually are. Finally, we will look at some controversies that affect the way we understand the term and its usage today as well as shaping ways it may be used in the future.

The Invention and Deconstruction of "World Religions"

We begin by considering contemporary debates about the term "religion" and whether we should abandon it. Historical patterns of understanding have shaped how we think, and so in universities and schools "religion" is often (some would say arbitrarily) divided up into geographically and culturally determined religions of the world. These classifications owe much to the European colonial past, to American cultural dominance, and to the lecturers and teachers who have internalized this paradigm. The familiar classification into "world religions" has also been strengthened by the rise of interfaith and peace organizations that aim to develop relationships between members of the world's most influential religions. Thus, the religions most frequently taught at the college and university level are still usually understood as the five (with possible additions) "great" religions of the world (or "world religions"): Christianity, Judaism, Islam, Hinduism, and Buddhism (extras often include Sikhism, Jainism, Daoism, and Confucianism). This pattern is seen in one of the subject's most influential textbooks, *The World's Religions* (originally titled *The Religions of Man,* 1958), by Huston Smith, who has sections on Hinduism, Buddhism, Confucianism, Daoism, Islam, Judaism, and Christianity and one chapter on "primal religion." We find something like this repeated in almost every book published and course taught. This, of course, supposes that we know what religions are. A question we will discuss later is where the limits of "religion" lie, because such ideologies as Marxism, Humanism, and nationalism have been classified as quasi-religions by some scholars.

Two questions come up here. First, assuming we keep on working with the term "religion," how can we meaningfully categorize religions? Second, despite its popular persistence, should we abandon the term "religion" altogether? As for the first, one of the most recent scholars to deconstruct the "invention" of world religions is Tomoko Masuzawa (2005), who ambitiously examines the birth trauma of the nineteenth-century world religions discourse and relates it to the formation of modern European identity and the retention of European power against a background of Orientalism and colonialism (for more on these terms, see Volume 1, Chapter 11).

Masuzawa argues that the discourse of world religions perpetuates Christian theological universalism and a Eurocentric view of the world. In particular, she shows that the way we divide religion into different categories was often politically motivated or served specific ends. To look at one case, in the nineteenth century a familiar division was drawn between religions seen as universal (seeking to attract converts) and those that were ethnic or cultural (do not evangelize). Examples of the former, often termed universal or universalizing religions, are Christianity, Islam, and Buddhism; examples of the latter, often termed ethnic or cultural religions, are Judaism, Shinto, Hinduism, Confucianism, and Daoism. This kind of polarization has broken down largely as a result of migration and greater knowledge about individual traditions. "Hinduism," for example, though not considered directly missionary, has in fact been very influential through gurus who have travelled worldwide, techniques such as yoga, scriptures such as the Bhagavad Gita, and active missionary groups such as ISKCON, Self-Realization Fellowship, Transcendental Meditation, and Siddha Yoga. (It is also debatable if it was ever correct or useful to regard the Hindu traditions as non-missionary!)

Another common distinction, still widely used today, is between "Eastern" and "Western" religions; Hinduism, Buddhism, Daoism, and Sikhism are often listed as the former, and Judaism, Islam, Christianity, and Zoroastrianism as the latter. Not only is this a problem because almost every religion is now global, but many religions have been so for centuries. Christianity has been present in India for at least 1,500 years and possibly much longer, and in China since about the seventh century CE, while Islam spread to India and beyond. Likewise, Buddhism spread from India to Central Asia and beyond in the centuries following its birth and has been present throughout East Asia for more than 2,000 years. Therefore, the classification of "world religions" is always problematic, as is revealed by the constant debates as to what it means or should include. This is especially the case when we focus on what are called Indigenous Religions—African traditional religions, indigenous American religions, and so on. These were largely ignored by scholars for centuries, but it is increasingly recognized that to understand religion globally, they are important.

Scholars have also gone radically beyond Cantwell Smith in calling for an abandonment of the notion of "religion" altogether. Recent scholars have argued that terming a specific practice as "religious," as opposed to cultural, political, or social in nature, is problematic—there is simply not even a clearly religious realm (something Cantwell Smith did not challenge).[22] An American scholar, McCutcheon, has argued that not only should we abandon the term "religion" altogether, but that we should even stop having a separate discipline dedicated to studying religion (whether it is called Religious Studies, the History of Religions, or the Study of Religion). J. Z. Smith has contended that as religion is nothing but an arbitrary demarcation of an area of culture and that all study of "religion" should simply become part of Cultural Studies. In other words, there is no such thing as "religion" beyond the classification system of the last few hundred years, which we should now abandon. In his introduction to *Imagining Religion*, he denies the possibility that there is a common essence or core to all religions:

> . . .while there is a staggering amount of data, phenomena, of human experiences and expressions that might be characterized in one culture or another, by one criterion or another, as religious—*there is no data for religion*. Religion is solely the creation of the scholar's study. It is created for the scholar's analytic purposes by his imaginative acts of comparison and generalization. Religion has no existence apart from the academy. For this reason, the student of religion, must be relentlessly self-conscious. Indeed, this self-consciousness constitutes his primary expertise, his foremost object of study.[23]

Nicholas de Lange, professor of Hebrew and Jewish Studies at Cambridge University, reflects that the notion of religion has developed from a Western Christian background and has therefore shaped what it sought to find:

> The comparative study of religions is an academic discipline which has been developed within Christian theology faculties, and it has a tendency to force widely differing phenomena into a kind of strait-jacket cut to a Christian pattern. The problem is not only that other "religions" may have little or nothing to say about questions which are of burning importance for Christianity, but that they may not even see themselves as religions in precisely the same way in which Christianity sees itself as a religion.[24]

Another contemporary critic of the term "religion," the British scholar Timothy Fitzgerald, has argued that the notion of "religion" as a separate area of life is embedded in the assumptions of the Western world over the last 200 years. Looking back historically, he finds that in the medieval world there was no separation of politics, culture, and religion; they simply existed as part of a vast tapestry or panorama of life. In a world where the king was God's agent on earth, where priests and churches were part of the legal system, and where an archbishop might become Lord Chancellor or chief minister, the separation of private spheres of life such as religion and public spheres of life such as politics and economics would make no sense. Fitzgerald's argument is that far from there being a clear and natural separation of these areas (i.e., secular and religious spheres), it is simply the modern Western worldview to see them as such. He thinks that one reason why the Western world today has such a problem with Islam is because it is still often rooted in a world where this natural fusion of politics, economics, law, and the sacred go hand in hand. For scholars such as Masuzawa, McCutcheon, Fitzgerald, and J. Z. Smith, the word "religion" is loaded with so many meanings from history and culture that its continued use will always distort.

Many scholars have sympathy for at least parts of this thesis, and indeed, it cannot be denied that wherever and however we seek to define "religion," it comes with a whole set of cultural baggage. However, as we noted earlier, "religion" persists as a term. Indeed, the hard-line notion that because there are problems with our usage we should abandon the term is generally rejected. Rather scholars have argued that (a) it is unrealistic to reject a term that is so widely embedded in our society—it will simply make scholars of religion unable to communicate with the world around them; (b) it can be used strategically and with full awareness of its cultural and ideological baggage; (c) it is actually quite a useful term, because it helps us bring certain phenomena into focus in a way other terms do not, and it has been noted that the critics discussed earlier still need to invoke terms such as "sacred" or "transcendence" to speak about this particular dimension of culture.

Hedges, in particular, has launched a robust defense of the term "religion" while recognizing its problematic nature. He has argued against J. Z. Smith's suggestion that it is simply an arbitrary modern classification on the grounds that what we now term "religions" have been relating to each other throughout history. This shows that long before Western scholarship created a specific category the actual practice of different religions relating to each other was already happening:

(1) Islam came to regard both Zoroastrianism and the Hindu family of faiths as "religions of the book," indicating it found them comparable to Christianity and Judaism.[25]
(2) Sikhism was founded from the Sant tradition, which drew from Islamic and Hindu roots, showing unities of ideas and origins.
(3) The fiercest debates Buddhism had in entering China were with the Daoist tradition as its nearest rival.
(4) There is a tradition of equating the gods of different religions stretching back in the ancient Middle East of the last three millennia BCE, where "religion appears to have been the promoter of intercultural translatability. . . ."[26]

We argue therefore that the traditions we call "religions" have in fact been encountering and debating with each other for centuries, if not millennia, without any need for modern Western scholars to tell them that they all share some common characteristics. Although it cannot simply be said that what we call "religions" existed and defined themselves as we do now, the broad traditions have related to each other in a variety of ways, which shows that they are aware of each other as similar areas of activity.

Moreover, the notion that the "religions," as we now know them, are modern inventions because of our Western classification system is also something to be questioned (this was a key part of Cantwell Smith's argument and has been taken up by many later figures). For instance, although "Confucianism" is a Western name, it does equate very largely to the Chinese native term "tradition of the scholars." Therefore, although the Western name suggests it is a tradition created by or about Confucius (which is not accurate), it does not simply make up a new tradition of its own imagining. Likewise, while Buddhism is a Western name, various Asian languages have long had terms that equate to it, whether this be what literally suggests "Buddha teachings" (*Buddha dharma*) in India or "Buddha tradition" (*Fojiao*) in Chinese. We could equally suggest that the Indian or Chinese names for Christianity mean they have "invented" a new tradition because these are not ones that would make sense to Western Christians! For instance, the Catholic and Protestant traditions have different names in China and are regarded, officially, as two separate "religions." Linguistic cultures need to make new terminology when they encounter new traditions, and it is too simplistic to suggest that this equates to the creation of something new.[27]

It is also unclear what we would substitute if we gave up our present terminology. Fitzgerald, who proposes that we abandon "religion" altogether, still argues that we need a term such as "the sacred" to refer to the area we would otherwise call "religious."[28] Meanwhile, McCutcheon's argument that we should use "culture" instead is open to exactly the same critique that he places in front of the term "religion"; it is a term that has changed definition over time and inherits historical meanings from a Western (Christian) past, and therefore merely replaces one problematic term with another.[29]

A final point to note is that we should not just think of the process of finding, labeling, and defining religion and religions as one of "invention." Instead, we may better think of it as "discovery." As explorers and scholars went beyond their own culture, they did not "invent" a new world out there (although there is evidence to show that their interpretations reflected their own ideologies and involved invention) but that they actually encountered living cultures and traditions that existed and so came to discover a range of "religions." This relates to our last point about names; Western scholars did not "invent" Confucianism but rather Western culture "discovered" it and then simply gave it a name in our own language (just as Indians and Chinese gave a name to Christianity or Islam when they were "discovered" by their culture). Indeed, the argument of such figures as Masuzawa, Fitzgerald, and McCutcheon that Western scholars imposed their own ideas on the external world ignores the fact that the encounter with the external world actually challenged and disrupted Western notions and ideas.[30]

For instance, Cantwell Smith argues that before the modern period, the terms "faith," "religion," and "Christianity" were all related, so for a medieval European to use any of these terms the others were also implied—that is, to have faith was to have Christian faith. Today, though, we recognize that faith is not just Christian, and religion refers not just to Christianity but to many traditions. It is, in this context, inadequate to simply say that Christian terms have been used to make sense of non-Christian religions, because we can also see that the understanding of these terms has changed and been challenged; that is, religion now means more than simply Christianity, and to use the term, we do not think of just one tradition but many. We can say, therefore, that the "Christian" understanding of these terms has been challenged. Of course, this is not to deny that this process involved, at least initially, viewing other religions through Christian lenses—that all religions have a God or gods and certain key beliefs. However, increasingly it is understood that religion must be understood in other ways.

It can therefore be argued that while "religion" is a term with a particular cultural history, and while many definitions and assumptions with it are problematic, we should not abandon it as it does seem to be meaningful. Of course, this then raises the question of whether there is a good definition, to which we now turn.

Problems with Definitions of Religion

We will now proceed to outline four attempts to define religion that either are widely used or are recent definitions that have sought to improve the way we use the term. We will ask how helpful these are.

First, one of the most widely used definitions of religion is that of Geertz, who conducted fieldwork in Indonesia:

> (1) a system of symbols (2) which acts to establish powerful, pervasive and long-lasting moods and motivations in men (3) by formulating conceptions of a general order of existence and (4) clothing these conceptions with such an aura of factuality that (5) the moods and motivations seem uniquely realistic.[31]

Critics of Geertz have raised various issues. They have argued that his definition is a functionalist or reductionist account, which assumes that religious beliefs are false. Geertz says, for example, that the "conceptions" are clothed with "an aura of factuality," implying, of course, that there is no factuality. He has therefore been accused of an inbuilt prejudice (for more on such issues, see Volume 1, Chapter 2). (However, a more positive reading would claim that Geertz is focused on interpretation,[32] and rather than "reducing" religion to a set of symbols, he is exploring how religious traditions use symbols to make sense of their world.) Talal Asad raises other issues: first, Geertz's account assumes that belief is a basic grounding factor for religion, whereas not all religions see a set of beliefs as central; various studies have shown that activity, whether it be a specific ritual or social interaction in some form, may be said to have a prior role. Therefore, Asad argues that Geertz's prioritization of symbols as forming beliefs is problematic. Second, Asad contends that the model assumes a fairly static idea of religion and does not address the dynamics of symbols changing their meaning over time. Criticisms by Asad and other scholars mean Geertz's definition is no longer so widely employed; nevertheless, it still has its defenders (who would suggest Asad's critique is somewhat unfair).

A more recent definition comes from the British scholar of Hinduism Gavin Flood, who defines religion as follows: "I broadly understand religions to be *value-laden narratives and behaviours that bind people to their objectives, to each other, and to non-empirical claims and beings.*"[33] This primarily functionalist definition manages to avoid being reductionist as Flood does not say that religions simply are the narratives or behaviors. We also see here that he avoids the issue of emphasizing belief that Asad criticized in Geertz,[34] while he also stresses the fact that religion builds on ways of understanding the world, or narratives. Problems arise, however, with Flood's notion of the nonempirical, or, as we could say, not-physical. It is not entirely clear what this means. Marxism, for instance, makes nonempirical claims that history is moving us toward a future where capitalism will give way to socialism. This is based on a particular interpretation of the world and history that is not simply gained from looking at the world. As we mentioned earlier (and will discuss later), some scholars would quite happily include nationalism or Marxism as religious worldviews. It is, though, broadly successful in summing up aspects common to many traditions we label as religions. However, others suggest we need a definition that can be more usefully employed as a tool to examine religion.

Ninian Smart argued that the search for an essence in religion ends up in vagueness but that, despite the variety, it is possible to discern some patterns in the world's religions and subtraditions, and he gave us nine dimensions of religion: the ritual, experiential or emotional, narrative, ethical, social, institutional, material, political, and economic.[35] Smart argues that in any particular religion one dimension may be weak or virtually nonexistent. Nevertheless, he claims that this multidimensional portrait is adequate enough to obviate the need for further definition. Smart consistently included secular worldviews and ideologies in his analysis because they fulfill religious functions and help express the various ways in which human beings conceive of themselves and act in the world. Indeed, Smart even wrote a text titled *Worldviews* in which he argued that any ideology, whether it be Christianity, Marxism, humanism, forms of nationalism, Daoism, Islam, or whatever, could and should all be studied alongside each other as related phenomena.[36] Far and away, Smart's has been the most widely used and employed definition of religion, still found in textbooks and academic works today. Nevertheless, it is not uncontroversial. The fact that it includes other "secular" worldviews has disturbed some and may be taken to indicate that actually "religion" has no particular meaning: "Try as he might, it seems that Smart cannot effectively maintain a distinction between a religious and a non-religious worldview."[37]

The family resemblance model—that a set of similar characteristics makes something a religion—has also been criticized, although the criticism seems to suggest that it is attempts to use it rather than the method itself which is at fault.[38] Others have raised issues with the fact that Smart's definition is very much a scholar's view and is not something that would be meaningful to religious actors themselves. Certainly, the fact that no mention is made of some form of transcendent that goes beyond the empirical world seems odd in attempting to define religion, and people have argued that this is also where Smart falls down in including other worldviews; just because something looks or acts like a religion does not mean that it is.[39]

Our final theory could be seen as a modification, or refinement, of Smart's paradigm; however, the author suggests it also seeks to go beyond it and offer a different standpoint, termed a "religious orientation typology."[40] Like Smart's classification, the typology offers a family resemblance approach, where if at least three or four of the factors are present then a tradition can be defined as a religion, yet it differs from Smart in attempting to look at concepts that would make sense from within a religious tradition. In this sense, it has an orientation toward the "transcendent," a term that is left somewhat open by the author but is given content by the factors. In an attempt to escape the way that many definitions have come from a Christian or Western perspective, examples are drawn from various religious traditions. There are six factors:

(1) Belief in a spiritual power or being(s)
(2) Interest in the afterlife
(3) Guiding societal and ethical norms
(4) It is transformative
(5) Methods or procedures for prayer or meditation
(6) Explanations of the human and natural situation

Each of these needs a bit of unpacking, and they are described as follows:

(1) *Belief in a spiritual power or being(s):* Belief in (perhaps) a supreme God, in some form of spiritual power pervading the universe, or in lesser deities or spiritual beings. The core of this factor is a belief in something

that transcends the purely physical or phenomenal universe. It is not just a belief that something directs or guides the course of phenomenal events, but is itself phenomenal. It suggests that there is another "transcendent" layer to the universe.

(2) *Interest in the afterlife:* Teachings on what happens after this life, suggesting that individual human existence is not the end. Teachings may offer rewards or punishments for our behavior in this life. Normally, the continuity involves a fixed "soul" that links the "I" in this life with the "I" in the next, but not always.

(3) *Guiding societal and ethical norms:* It provides a "way of life." This may be guidelines for the individual, or social and cultural systems into which the individual is bound. In different settings, and at different times, the same religious tradition may function in both ways. This way of life will be determined by the other factors, such as belief in deity, the afterlife, and the way to transformation. This factor, perhaps, shows most fully where the "religious" impinges on the "secular," although, often, this impinging will mean the secular becomes "religious" (we will discuss this later).

(4) *It is transformative:* The reorientation, or transformation, of the devotee is sought. Generally, it is recognized that the way we live, or our essential nature, is impure or not correctly aligned or adjusted. Therefore, a solution is offered to orient the devotee in a manner determined by the other factors. Exactly how this happens can vary within traditions. Three aspects exist: (1) forms, (2) timescales, and (3) types. Forms: "weak" transformation is where the devotee decides to follow the religious path; however, he or she is not inherently changed except by commitment. "Strong" transformation fundamentally alters the devotee, perhaps, with direct "mystical" contact with the divine; he or she is "reshaped" or "reformed." In the former, the devotee follows the religious path because it is required; in the latter, once transformed, the devotee follows the religious path because that has become his or her nature. Timescales: before and after death. Types: "sudden," where the devotee is catapulted by an "instant experience" into a new state; "gradual," where the devotee has an ongoing process of alteration. Each of these is not necessarily exclusive of any other; some traditions seeing various transformations happening at different times or in different ways.

(5) *Methods or procedures for prayer or meditation:* Apart from ethical behavior, the devotee shows his or her orientation through "religiously oriented actions." These behaviors may include giving adoration or thanks, making petitionary intercessions, seeking to "attune" oneself with the divine, community festivals, pilgrimages, and so on. In seeking to orient the devotee toward that which the religion sees as the most important within life, it must be placed in relation to factors 1, 2, and 4.

(6) *Explanations of the human and natural situation:* Teachings describe where the devotee is and what she or he should do in this situation.

Explained in terms of other aspects of the religion's orientation, it may discuss the causes or origin of such things as the world and human suffering. Some cosmotheologic questions may be described as beyond human knowing or simply not important.[41]

Although this typology may be said to answer some criticisms made of other definitions, and possibly avoids either an essentialist or a reductionist approach, it is not immune from criticism. One criticism could be that it focuses on major institutional religious traditions and may not be so useful in describing a range of phenomena from Indigenous Religions, to what is sometimes called everyday religion or implicit religion (which we will discuss later). Therefore, it has a focus on elite traditions, which assume that religion makes sense as part of a cohesive system, whereas studies of popular religion have shown that many ordinary believers do not live in a system where all the parts join up or make sense. Hence, there may not be the systematic cohesion it suggests. Another criticism is that rather than seeking to question the way we construct the term "religion," it starts with the assumption that we are right in categorizing the major religious traditions as religions and then builds its definition up from this. Nevertheless, it may succeed in showing there is something distinctive about "religions," which means we are right to single them out as a distinct category.[42] Yet it does not deny that there are functional similarities to other worldviews or ideologies and that such systems as Marxism and humanism can usefully be studied alongside them. It should also be remembered that the typology was not designed to show that there is some essence called "religion"; rather it had a twofold purpose—first as a teaching tool to help students think about the subject matter termed "religions," and second to counter claims that the term "religion" was entirely meaningless and essentially arbitrary. If we can define a set of factors that apply to religions and make sense to religious people, then we can say that there is something distinctive about this area of culture (it does not seek to provide a substantivist definition of religion as something *sui generis* but rather to argue that the category is not arbitrary and that we have a distinct area of culture). Indeed, the typology only claims to be a tool rather than a definition of the "essence" of religion.

Religion: Social or Private

One major issue that stirs debate today is whether religion is essentially a private and individual matter or whether it is essentially social. The former assumption is one that operates in much public debate, and legislation, in countries such as the United States and the United Kingdom. In countries such as the United States and France, a constitutional divide is made between religion and the state. That is, you can believe what you like as long as it does not interfere with the way you act and behave in official and public spaces; contrarily, however, in the United States it is normal for religion to occupy quite a high profile in the way figures such as politicians define themselves and in various national debates. Some countries that distinguish the private and public role of religion have tried to ban religious symbols from public spaces; there are huge controversies on such matters in the United States, whereas in Turkey and France bans have been implemented on wearing the *hijab* (traditional headscarves for women) in various spaces or while undertaking certain jobs such as teaching or medical care.[43] This is tied into an interpretation, or definition, of religion that has become dominant in modern times and is exemplified in a very important text, *The Varieties of Religious Experience,* by the psychologist William James, in which religion is defined as "...the feelings, acts and experiences of individual men in their solitude, so far as they apprehend themselves to stand in relation to what they may consider the divine."[44] However, it is not clear that this is the only, the most obvious, or even the best way of discussing religion.

Emile Durkheim was one of the first sociologists to emphasize that religion is not simply a private belief, it is "something eminently social." In *The Elementary Forms of the Religious Life,* he defines religion as "a unified system of beliefs and practices relative to sacred things, that is to say, things set apart and forbidden—beliefs and practices which unite in one single moral community called a Church, all those who adhere to them."[45] In general terms, Durkheim thought religious rituals helped unite the group, producing a sense of some higher power; however, he ascribed such experiences to nothing but society as a collective beyond the individual. In traditional Islamic societies, it was not just personal belief but collective social norms that were crucially important; behavior was based in part on traditions of the Prophet, and the ordering of society as a whole by the application of *sharia* law. Islam gave regulations on banking (you should not charge interest on loans), public welfare (through almsgiving, *zakat,* a common purse was provided to help the weak in society), criminal punishments, food regulations, and marriage. This raises questions about whether we define religion in terms of beliefs, practices, or social codes.

It is useful in this context to consider that definitions of religion have expanded to include concepts of civil religion. The phrase "civil religion" was employed by Jean-Jacques Rousseau (1712–1778) in *The Social Contract* (1762) but was given scholarly usage in the twentieth century particularly by Robert N. Bellah and Martin E. Marty. Bellah defines civil religion as a "transcendent universal religion of the nation," which shares much with the religion of Jewish and Christian denominations but is distinct from them.[46] Bellah saw civil religion as an "objective social fact"[47] in a way that echoes Durkheim.

Religions and Nonreligions

We come now to a somewhat different issue, but one that will help us deepen our understanding of some of the themes we have discussed so far, the relationship of religious and nonreligious, or atheist, ideologies. There has been debate as to whether it is meaningful to talk of atheism or humanism as spiritualities or even as religions or quasi-religions, perhaps dedicated to abstract principles or ideals rather than a personal deity, and characteristic of the eighteenth-century and the French Enlightenment with its emphasis on reason. Scholars argue that Marxism and ideological liberalism have their own dogmas, scriptures, priests, theologians, and heresies and so have functioned as religious systems for millions of individuals. Some humanists, skeptics, or atheists argue that they seek spiritual experiences as much as anyone else. Such experiences could include a sense of vitality, connectedness, transcendence, and meaningfulness.[48]

Moreover, some atheists have suggested that religion may also be useful. There have always been skeptics who nevertheless value religion for various reasons: its art, music, ritual, values, and rites of passage. Terry Eagleton points out that many signed-up atheists have believed that religious beliefs are false, but underpin civilized life,[49] and he looks at the contemporary philosopher Alain de Botton as an example. In a recent book, de Botton has argued that atheists need a form of religion (which reflects an earlier attempt by a nineteenth-century French atheist philosopher, de Comte, to create an atheist church to give rituals to live by), such as secular versions of various ceremonies with originally religious import such as the Jewish Day of Atonement, the Catholic Mass, and the Zen Buddhist tea ceremony. According to Eagleton, "De Botton does not want people literally to believe, but he remains a latter-day Matthew Arnold, as his high Victorian language makes plain. Religion 'teaches us to be polite, to honour one another, to be faithful and sober', as well as instructing us in 'the charms of community.'"[50] As such, there is no clear distinction between atheism and religion as we see religious forms of atheism. Meanwhile, we see today atheist religious communities and theologies, such as the Christian Sea of Faith Network and humanistic Judaism. The latter encourages humanistic and secular (i.e., atheist) Jews to embrace Jewish identity through celebrating Jewish holidays and life-cycle rituals. The former is an atheist movement within Christianity in the United Kingdom that counts a good number of priests and theologians among its members and whose Web site is headed by the words: "exploring and promoting religious faith as a human creation."[51] The boundary between a "religion" and atheism or nonreligious worldviews is not always clear. Useful to consider here is Edward Bailey's notion of implicit religion, which refers to areas in everyday life that are not traditionally described as "religious" but nevertheless seem to hold some aspect of inherent religiosity.[52]

Boundaries and Definitions of Religious Traditions

Although we still tend to speak of religions as clear and distinct traditions which we can label "Christianity," "Islam," and "Buddhism," we have already noted that this usage is problematic. This idea of what scholars term "monolithic religious traditions" (i.e., that each tradition is clearly separate and distinct as a unique whole) has been radically destabilized by the increasing recognition that religion is a fluid cultural entity, that religious traditions are internally diverse, and that they have always been mutually influential. Hedges points out that the merging of cultures and meeting of religions is unavoidable in a world marked by global population movements and exchange of ideas.[53] Syncretism and cross-fertilization have always been aspects of all religious cultures and ideas, but the crossing and transgression of boundaries is particularly visible today. The fact that we can refer to Islam, Judaism, and Christianity as "Abrahamic" religions, or traditions which look back to the figure of Abraham, helps show that they share a common heritage and background. In India, Buddhism and Jainism developed at very much the same time as Hinduism, often influencing each other and sharing many commonalities and overarching concepts. There is not a single religious tradition that has not developed in dialogue with other traditions, adapting its words, rituals, or ideas. In Nepal, Buddhist and Hindu religious syncretism is a matter of pride, whereas in China and Japan, multiple religious identities are normative, so that people often attend Shinto life-cycle rites and Buddhist funeral rites while having a value system based on Confucian ethics. Although these ideas about multiple religious identities seem new, or even shocking or strange, to many Westerners, they are normal elsewhere. Figures such as Thomas Merton, Abhishiktananda, Bede Griffiths, and Aloysius Pieris have aroused great theological interest in the West, yet elsewhere in the world such dual religious identity is unremarkable (see Volume 1, Chapter 10). This, therefore, challenges the way we speak of religions.

There are also issues about who gets to define the limits or terms of any one religion. Ninian Smart noted that even though we use labels such as Christianity, there are multiple varieties of Christianity, and some movements that would identify themselves as Christian, for example the Church of Latter-Day Saints or the Unification Church, are denied this label by others. Those within the movement see themselves clearly as followers of Jesus and so as being Christians; other Christians, however, often see them as breaking with essential elements of the tradition and so as having left Christianity. Also we do not just see the boundaries of a specific religion being contested, but the boundaries of religion itself. Some movements that clearly have religious elements are not always defined in this way. Falun Gong, for instance, which observably has religious elements, does not define itself as a religion.[54] It exists in a context where only certain religions are recognized by the government and so would have problems seeking this label, whereas it is branded as an "evil cult" by the Chinese government (see Volume 3, Chapter 6). Another tradition where debate rages as to whether it is a religion or not is Scientology; as in the case of Falun Gong, it is not simply an academic debate but one that involves governments and the law as traditions recognized as religions often have certain rights or privileges.[55]

We have already argued that religion itself often has no clear boundaries with nonreligious traditions. Moreover, although religion is often contrasted and differentiated from magic and superstition, the boundaries are diffuse. Indeed, whereas many atheists and skeptics argue religion and superstition are similar, members of many religious communities would insist on a sharp distinction. This takes us back to our initial discussion about power and definitions and the rhetorical use of labels; religious people may want to distance themselves from superstition, which generally has negative connotations, whereas the reverse may be true for atheists. Scholars, meanwhile, will often contest the grounds and criteria by which such distinctions are made.[56] This brief mention of contested borders should nevertheless make it clear that definitions are, as we have argued earlier, always controversial. Moreover, definitions may be made on theological, legal, political, or academic grounds or criteria (indeed, these often intersect).

Meanwhile, the Internet and the new social media are radically changing how we perceive and "perform" religion. Rachel Wagner's book *Godwired* (2011) explores the intersection between the "two other-worlds known to human beings; the supernatural world of the spiritual, and the virtual world created by on-line communication technologies."[57] Wagner argues that although utterly unlike traditional religious practice, there are religious aspects to the way we approach virtual reality, and so it can be interpreted as a form of religious activity. Heidi Campbell also explains how different religious communities are negotiating complex relationships with the new media in light of their history and beliefs.[58]

Spiritual but Not Religious

In contemporary popular culture, increasing numbers of people define themselves as spiritual but not religious, meaning that they do not need organized religion to follow a spiritual and ethical path that is right for them. Spirituality is seen as the giver of meaning, religion as the giver of rules.[59]

Whereas "spirituality" was previously regarded as an integral aspect of religious experience, the term "spiritual" is now frequently used in contexts in which the term "religious" was formerly employed and has tended to overtake the use of the term "religion" in its inclusiveness. Anna King has explored the idea of spirituality as it has evolved within the countercultures of many Western societies and the diverse ideas conjured up in the popular mind by the term "spirituality":

> If "religion" is seen in terms of inherited structures and institutional externals . . . spirituality has become a term that firmly engages with the feminine, with green issues, with ideas of wholeness, creativity, and interdependence, with the interfusion of the spiritual, the aesthetic and the moral.[60]

Taylor, developing this argument, points out that spirituality can be seen as related to an inner truth of religions rather than something in opposition to them. He sees it as getting to the heart of what traditional religions teach—in this sense, it has some correlation to the traditional meaning of the term that comes from Christian usage.[61] It is, moreover, a term that gives some "religious" or "transcendent" meaning to activities we may see as nonreligious, or secular, such as psychotherapy, political activism, and even working life.[62] As King argues:

> The term spirituality as currently used, indicates both the unity at the heart of religious traditions and the transformative inner depth or meaning of those traditions. . . . It supplies a term which transcends particular religions and it suggests a non-reductionist understanding of human life. It is more firmly associated than religion with creativity and imagination, with change, and with relationship. It is less associated in the popular mind with hierarchies of gender, race or culture. It indicates an engagement with, or valuing of human experience and expression through art and music, through a response to nature and to ethical ideals as well as through the great religious traditions. It can embrace secular therapies and cosmologies as well as concerns with the environment. Thus it seems to include both sacred and secular, and to enable a fundamental rethinking of religious boundaries. Its very ambiguity and flexibility suggests a richness and texture which allows traditional religious maps to be redrawn and minorities to find a voice [and this also] makes it a more flexible concept than religion and encourages the user to reflect and to challenge institutionalized thought.[63]

Malory Nye argues that for many people in the West, religion has become spirituality—that is, deinstitutionalized and individualist religion.[64] Linda Woodhead and Paul Heelas argue that we are living through a "spiritual revolution" in which "traditional forms of religion are giving way to new forms of spirituality." Their research suggests that spiritualities that people see as relating to personal experience are experiencing success compared to traditional religions with demands of doctrinal conformity. Woodhead and Heelas explain these developments by suggesting our wider culture is increasingly concerned with sensitivity to people's inner life and well-being rather than conformity to rules and obligations.[65] Heelas argues that the language of spirituality has become a major feature of the sacred dimensions of contemporary modernity.[66]

Modern definitions of spirituality often emphasize the experiential and individual aspect of religion and are not necessarily linked to concepts of the supernatural or metaphysical; therefore practices are often detached from their particular traditional belonging, notably things such as yoga and meditation, and seen as spiritual and capable of benefit even without any religious rationale. Spirituality in this context may be seen as about harmony and well-being, although some have suggested that certain religions such as Buddhism have much in common with this.[67]

CONCLUSION

Religion and the way we define it have shifted through the centuries and are shifting still today. The distinction made between "religion" and "spirituality" discussed earlier is one such instance of transformation. Moreover, this is an age in which "religion" has reasserted itself nationally and internationally, becoming a matter of public discussion, a major source of daily news, and a marker of identity and source of resistance.[68] The movement of populations and information around the globe, together with the World Wide Web and the growing influence of popular culture (particularly film and music), is transforming religious traditions. This affects the way we understand religion as a marker of identity (see Volume 1, Chapter 7, for more on this), notably with the growing awareness in the West of what are termed dual or multiple religious identities, where someone belongs to, or practices within, two (or sometimes more) religious traditions at the same time. It is unclear what factors such as the migration of populations and increased interreligious encounters (see Volume 1, Chapter 8) and conflicts (see Volume 2, Chapter 12) will do to our understanding of religion in the decades and centuries to come, but the way we define and set the boundaries of the term and the traditions we associate with it is bound to change.

GLOSSARY

Civil religion: discussed at length by Rousseau in 1762, it was used by late-twentieth-century scholars to speak about religious ideas and traditions shared within a society.

Essentialist/essentialism: to see religion as having some fundamental core or essence by which it may be defined.

Family resemblance model: the attempt to define a set of characteristics shared by some group, whereby they may be identified.

Functionalist: in the study of religion, the perspective according to which religion is explained in terms of its social, psychological, or cultural functions.

Implicit religion: the term "implicit" directs attention to areas of human behavior usually seen as simply secular; "religious" is applied here because it is holistic and exemplifies commitment.

Reductionist: religious reductionism generally attempts to explain religion by analyzing it in nonreligious terms, so that religion is "reduced" to nothing but that nonreligious aspect; that is, it may be said to be a product of society or mental neurosis.

Sanatana dharma: Sanskrit Hindu term meaning roughly "eternal teachings/tradition/law," used by many Hindus to describe their tradition.

Substantivist: in relation to the study of religion, definitions or approaches that assume there is some "reality" behind religion so it cannot be explained in terms of society or something else.

Sui generis: literally "of its own kind (or genus)," meaning that it is a specific thing that cannot be reduced to something else.

World religion: a term often used to refer to what is defined as "major" religions; however, there is no clear means to make such a classification which includes some traditions and not others.

NOTES

1. Malory Nye, *Religion the Basics* (London and New York: Routledge, 2003), 18.
2. http://oxforddictionaries.com/definition/english/religion.
3. In Buddhist thought, the various gods are beings who will die and be reborn like humans, dogs, or other creatures. Therefore, a definition emphasizing this aspect misses out a huge aspect of what Buddhism means. Arguably, though, it may apply to Mahayana Buddhism; however, this is not a debate we can enter into here.
4. Russell McCutcheon, "Introduction," in *The Insider/Outsider Problem in the Study of Religions: A Reader*, ed. R. McCutcheon (London and New York: Cassell, 1999), 71.
5. Clifford Geertz, *The Interpretation of Cultures* (New York: Basic Books, 1973), 89.
6. Clifford Geertz, "Religion as a Cultural System," in *Anthropological Approaches to the Study of Religion*, ed. S. Banton (London: Oxford University Press, 1966), 284–338.
7. A more nuanced approach might therefore suggest that we place Geertz, and others, in a third school, an interpretivist one; however, to provide a general outline here, we will just refer to these two approaches.
8. Eric J. Sharpe, *Understanding Religion* (London: Gerald Duckworth and Co Ltd, 1983), 34.
9. The discussion between Humpty Dumpty and Alice in Lewis Carroll's *Through the Looking-Glass* (1872) illustrates this point.
10. Paul Tillich, *Theology of Culture*, ed. R. C. Kimball (New York: Oxford University Press, 1959), 7–8.
11. Swami Vivekananda, *The Complete Works of Swami Vivekānanda*, vol. 3, ed. Mayavati Memorial (Calcutta: Advaita Ashrama, 1964), 251–2.

12. Ludwig Feuerbach, *The Essence of Christianity (Das Wesen des Christentums)*, trans. George Eliot (Marian Evans) (New York: Harper & Row Publishers, 1957 [1841]), 12.

13. Feuerbach, *The Essence of Christianity*, 33.

14. Freud devoted much time to discussing religion in works such as *Totem and Taboo* (1913), *The Future of an Illusion* (1927), *Civilization and Its Discontents* (1930), and *Moses and Monotheism* (1938).

15. Karl Marx, "Selection from Karl Marx, *Capital*," in *The Marx-Engels Reader*, ed. Robert Tucker (New York: Norton, 1978): 319–29, accessed July 16, 2013, http://faculty .washington.edu/cbehler/teaching/coursenotes/Texts/MarxselCapital.html.

16. Sharpe, in *Understanding Religion*, notes that some history goes back to ancient Roman times when the term was disputed. The Latin word *religio*, from which "religion" derives, has strong overtones of a political and moral nature. Cicero derived *religio* from the verb *relegere* (to re-read), whereas Lactantius derived *religio* from *religare* (to bind fast). For the pagan Cicero, this meant that *religio* was about following the rituals of one's ancestors (to re-read; i.e., to repeat customs), but for the Christian Lactantius *religio* was about the bond between a human and God. Cicero and others drew a firm distinction between *religio* and *superstitio*—a distinction that in a confused form is still with us. Moreover, *religio* referred to the due reverence that it was the duty of every Roman citizen to pay to the official deities of the state, and it could be used to refer to an oath or any other sacred duty, to personal piety, or to any of the rituals and customs that have to do with the worship of the gods. Therefore, Lactantius, as a Christian, wanted to show it had another meaning, and this sense of personal piety became dominant. Sharpe points out that during the long period of Latin Christianity, the word continued to be used in broadly the same sense, and that the word "religion" occurs seldom in either the Old or New Testaments, but where it does in English translations it always means a living relationship to God within the terms of a "covenant" or "testament." In the ancient world, therefore, "religion" was a matter involving not only the individual's inward experiences of the holy but the attitudes, rituals, and moral conventions on which a particular society and culture rested.

17. See Russell T. McCutcheon, "Religion," in *New Dictionary of the History of Ideas*, ed. Maryanne Cline Horowitz (New York: Charles Scribner's Sons, 2004), accessed August 6, 2013, http://www.as.ua.edu/rel/pdf/rel237definitionofreligion.pdf.

18. The Indian Sanskrit term *dharma* and the Arabic word *dīn* may seem equivalent. However, *dharma*, for example, cannot be easily rendered into English but may be interpreted as a way of life based on universal values, whereas the Buddhist usage (Pali: *dhamma*) signifies particularly the teachings of the historical Buddha summed up in the Four Noble Truths and the Eightfold Path. Similarly, the term *dīn* means something other than "religion" to both mainstream and reformist Muslim writers. In the Quran, the act of submission to God is always referred to as *dīn*, whereas in general it means an all-encompassing way of life. However, the globalization of religious traditions and the fact that they are now often in close proximity means that in the contemporary Anglophone world many English-speaking non-Christians use the word "religion" happily, and some scholars argue that it has become a useful way of describing how people talk about their experiences. In India, for example, English has become something of a lingua franca and can liberate low castes in particular from the negative associations of Sanskritic or Hindi religious terminology. Words such as *sanatana dharma* or *Vedic dharma* can carry all kinds of hierarchical implications.

19. The issues behind the labels people wish to give themselves are often complex, and we cannot discuss this at length here (see, however, Volume 1, Chapter 7).

20. Wilfred Cantwell Smith, *The Meaning and End of Religion* (London: SCM, 1978 [1964]).

21. Simon Coleman (2009) comments: "People living in the West tend to have a clear idea of what religion should look like: it tends to take place in a building set aside for the purpose (a church, synagogue, mosque, temple etc.), revolves around appeals to a higher, all-powerful deity and involves the articulation of beliefs (often set down in texts) to which the general population may or may not subscribe. Anthropologists have studied such religions, but they have also examined contexts where religious practice looks very different. In many cultures and societies, the idea of a single God may not be present, and the notion of reading a sacred book like the Koran or the Bible would seem very strange, not least because writing and reading may not play any part in people's lives. Even the western notion of 'belief' does not make much sense in contexts where ideas about gods and spirits are taken for granted, and are not challenged by other faiths or the conclusions of the natural sciences," accessed August 23, 2013, http://www.disco-veranthropology.org.uk/about-anthropology/specialist-areas/anthropology-of-religion .html.

22. Russell T. McCutcheon, *Critics Not Caretakers: Redescribing the Public Study of Religion* (Albany: SUNY Press, 2001).

23. Jonathan Z. Smith, *Imagining Religion: From Babylon to Jonestown* (Chicago: University of Chicago Press, 1982).

24. Nicholas de Lange, *Judaism* (Oxford, England: Oxford University Press, 1986), 3.

25. Of course, the fact that many Muslims have also argued that Hinduism is idolatrous, again shows that they are relating to it in essentially "religious" terms.

26. Paul Hedges, *Controversies in Interreligious Dialogue and the Theology of Religions* (London: SCM 2010), 74.

27. This would be true of, for instance, the name "Confucianism," as what is termed the "scholar's tradition" in China does not see Confucius as a founder; however, he is acknowledged as an important interpreter of that tradition. Perhaps, to use an analogy, if we imagined that a Chinese explorer came to Europe and encountered Judaism for the first time and named it the "Moses tradition," we could not say that he had invented a new religion; however, we would have a new name for it.

28. Timothy Fitzgerald, *Discourses on Civility and Barbarity: A Critical History of Religion and Related Categories* (Oxford: Oxford University Press, 2007).

29. See Tomoko Masuzawa, "Culture," in *Critical Terms for Religious Studies*, ed. Mark C. Taylor (Chicago: University of Chicago Press, 1998), 70–93. An accessible account of the changes of meaning can also be found in the BBC Radio 4 series "The Value of Culture," especially episodes 1 and 2, http://www.bbc.co.uk/programmes/ b01pmg02/episodes/guide.

30. The intellectual history of this debate is argued in James J. Clark, *Oriental Enlightenment: The Encounter between Asian and Western Thought* (London: Routledge, 1997), while the way in which notions of religion challenged Western Christian thought and altered its perceptions is argued in Paul Hedges, "The Old and the New Comparative Theologies: Discourses on Religion, the Theology of Religions, Orientalism and the Boundaries of Traditions," *Religions* 3, no. 4 (2012): 1120–37.

31. Geertz, "Religion as a Cultural System," 42.

32. Clifford Geertz, "Thick Description: Toward an Interpretive Theory of Culture," in *The Interpretation of Cultures: Selected Essays*, ed. Clifford Geertz (New York: Basic Books, 1973), 5.

33. Gavin Flood, *Beyond Phenomenology* (London: Cassell, 1999), italics in original; more recently, he has offered the following definition: "Religions are ways of being in the world which make strong claims and demands upon people and while they are concerned with socialization they primarily function to address questions of ultimate meaning at a bodily and temporal level in which human beings make sense of their experience. In other words, religions are responses to the human encounter with what is beyond us, to the encounter with mystery, paradox, and the overwhelming force and wonder of there being anything at all. Religions cannot be reduced simply to beliefs or propositions about the world but are visceral responses to the human condition and expressions of what might be called the will to meaning," in Gavin Flood, *The Importance of Religion: Meaning and Action in Our Strange World* (Chichester: Wiley-Blackwell, 2012), 2.

34. Geertz also stressed behavior in his discussions of religious traditions and cultures.

35. The first six are found in Ninian Smart, *The Religious Experience of Mankind* (New York: Charles Scribner's Sons, 1969), 15–25; the seventh was added in Ninian Smart, *The World's Religions: Old Traditions and Modern Transformations* (Cambridge, England: Cambridge University Press, 1989); and the eighth and ninth were included in *Dimensions of the Sacred: An Anatomy of the World's Beliefs* (London: Fontana, 1996).

36. Ninian Smart, *Worldviews* (New York: Charles Scribner's Sons, 1983).

37. Bryan S. Rennie, "The View of the Invisible World: Ninian Smart's Analysis of the Dimensions of Religion and of Religious Experience," *Bulletin CSSR* (63, 28, 1999), 3. He goes on to suggest that Smart's distinction between religion and magic could lead us to "begin to construct a common understanding of religious experience as an awareness of the otherwise 'invisible world' of the determinants of our actions and expressions. Whether those determinants are characterised as 'God', 'the laws of physics', or 'the unconscious mind' is a ramified expression dependent upon the culturally conditioned worldview of the subject" (ibid.).

38. Certainly various scholars have done something similar.

39. John Shepherd, "Introduction: A Critical Analysis," in *Ninian Smart on World Religions*, ed. John Shepherd (Aldershot, England: Ashgate, 2009), xxi–lxxv, lv.

40. This has been set out in Paul Hedges, "Defining Religion: A Religious Orientation Typology," Part 1, *Interreligious Insight* 4, no. 3 (2006): 9–15; "Defining Religion: A Religious Orientation Typology," Part 2, *Interreligious Insight* 4, no. 4 (2006): 34–42; "Can We Still Teach 'Religions'? Towards an Understanding of Religion as Culture and Orientation in Contemporary Pedagogy and Metatheory," in *International Handbook for Inter-Religious Education*, ed. G. Durka, L. Gearon, M. DeSouza, and K. Engebretson (New York: Springer Academic Publishers, 2010), 291–312; and *Controversies*, 64–87.

41. Hedges, *Controversies*, 78–80.

42. Craig Martin, *A Critical Introduction to the Study of Religion* (Sheffield, England: Equinox, 2012), 2.

43. Turkey is deeply torn on such issues, and the riots in Istanbul and other cities, often cited as being related to constructions of a park in the media, are related to issues concerning the extent of Islamic influence in government and society.

44. William James, *The Varieties of Religious Experience: A Study in Human Nature; Being the Gifford Lectures on Natural Religion Delivered at Edinburgh in 1901–1902* (London: Longmans, Green, 1902), 31.

45. Emile Durkheim, *The Elementary Forms of the Religious Life*, trans. Karen E. Fields (New York: The Free Press, 1995 [1912]), 39–44.

46. U.S. civil religion is "an institutionalized collection of sacred beliefs about the American nation," which is symbolically expressed in the United States's founding documents and presidential inaugural addresses. It includes a belief in the existence of a transcendent being called "God," an idea that the American nation is subject to God's laws, and an assurance that God will guide and protect the United States. These beliefs in the values of liberty, justice, charity, and personal virtue are concretized in, for example, the words *In God We Trust* on both national emblems and the currency used in daily economic transactions.

47. Ronald C. Wimberley and William H. Swatos, Jr., "Civil Religion,"in *Encyclopedia of Religion and Society*, ed. William H. Swatos, Jr., accessed November 8, 2012, http://hirr.hartsem.edu/ency/civilrel.htm.

48. One of the most commonly described experiences of spirituality involves a sense of one's interconnectedness to others and a dissolving of self–other boundaries (see http://www.atheistrev.com/2008/01/atheist-spirituality.html). At the World Humanist Congress in 2002, an updated Amsterdam Declaration was adopted which emphasized not only the ethical but the spiritual nature of human beings: "Ethical humanism unites all those who cannot any longer believe the various creeds and are willing to base their conviction on respect for man as a spiritual and moral being."

49. During the eighteenth-century Enlightenment, some atheists thought that ordinary people should still be instilled with religious beliefs as this would keep them in check and promote morality and social order, and certainly such a strain, perhaps influenced by Marx's views of the way religion was a tool of oppression, has had similar thoughts. Notably, though, similar views could be found in some classical Chinese thinkers.

50. Terry Eagleton, "Religion for Atheists by Alain de Botton—Review," *The Guardian*, January 12, 2012, accessed November 30, 2012, http://www.guardian.co.uk/books/2012/jan/12/religion-for-atheists-de-botton-review.

51. http://www.sofn.org.uk/, accessed August 5, 2013. The movement owes much to the British theologian and priest Don Cupitt, who himself is inspired in part by Feuerbach, whom we discussed earlier.

52. Edward I. Bailey, *Implicit Religion in Contemporary Society* (Leuven, Belgium: Peeters, 1997).

53. Hedges, *Controversies*, 6, 47.

54. On its religious elements, see Benjamin Penny, *The Religion of Falun Gong* (Chicago: Chicago University Press, 2012).

55. See Owen Bowcott, "Scientology Case Has Judges Debating the Meaning of Religion," *The Guardian*, July 18, 2013, accessed August 23, 2013, http://www.theguardian.com/world/2013/jul/18/scientology-case-judges-religion.

56. H. S. Versnel, "Some Reflections on the Relationship Magic–Religion," Numen 38, no. 2 (1991): 177–97.

57. Rachel Wagner, *Godwired: Religion, Ritual and Virtual Reality* (London: Routledge, 2011).

58. Heidi Campbell, *When Religion Meets New Media* (London: Routledge, 2010). Campbell suggests a wealth of examples of the religious-social shaping of technology, such as the Christian evangelism movement, modern Islamic discourses about computers, and the rise of the Jewish kosher cell phone, which demonstrate the dominant strategies that emerge for religious media users as well as the unique motivations that guide specific groups.

59. Diarmuid O'Murchu, *Consecrated Religious Life: The Changing Paradigms* (Maryknoll, England: Orbis Books, 2005), 95.

60. Anna S. King, "Spirituality: Transformation and Metamorphosis," *Religion* 26 (1996): 345.

61. On a variety of usages, see Philip Sheldrake, *A Brief History of Spirituality* (Oxford, England: Blackwell, 2007).

62. Bron Taylor, "Earth and Nature-Based Spirituality (Part I): From Deep Ecology to Radical Environmentalism," *Religion* 31 (2001): 176.

63. King, "Spirituality," 345.

64. Nye, *Religion*, 205.

65. See Linda Woodhead and Paul Heelas, *Religion in Modern Times: An Interpretive Anthology* (Oxford: Blackwell, 2000); and Paul Heelas, Linda Woodhead, Benjamin Seel, Bronislaw Szerszynski, and Karin Tusting, *The Spiritual Revolution: Why Religion Is Giving Way to Spirituality* (London: Wiley-Blackwell, 2005).

66. Paul Heelas, *Spirituality in the Modern World: Within Religious Tradition and Beyond* (London: Routledge, 2011).

67. The Dalai Lama teaches that human survival has depended and will continue to depend on basic goodness. *Ethics for the New Millennium* presents a moral system based on universal rather than religious principles. Its ultimate goal is happiness for every individual, irrespective of religious beliefs. A Web site offers this definition of contemporary spirituality: "Spirituality exists wherever we struggle with the issues of how our lives fit into the greater scheme of things. This is true when our questions never give way to specific answers or give rise to specific practices such as prayer or meditation. We encounter spiritual issues every time we wonder where the universe comes from, why we are here, or what happens when we die. We also become spiritual when we become moved by values such as beauty, love, or creativity that seem to reveal a meaning or power beyond our visible world. An idea or practice is 'spiritual' when it reveals our personal desire to establish a felt-relationship with the deepest meanings or powers governing life." From Robert C. Fuller, "Spiritual, but Not Religious," accessed November 3, 2012, *beliefnet.com*.

68. Rosalind I. Hackett, "Anthropology of Religion," in *The Routledge Companion to the Study of Religions*, ed. John R. Hinnells (Abingdon: Routledge, 2005), 144.

FURTHER READINGS

Fitzgerald, Timothy. *Discourses on Civility and Barbarity: A Critical History of Religion and Related Categories.* Oxford, England: Oxford University Press, 2007.

Flood, Gavin. *The Importance of Religion: Meaning and Action in Our Strange World.* Chichester: Wiley-Blackwell, 2012.

Hedges, Paul. "Discourse on the Invention of Discourse: Why We Need the Terminology of 'Religion' and 'Religions,' " *Journal of Religious History*, 38: 1, 2014, 132–48.

Masuzawa, Tomoko. *The Invention of World Religions.* Chicago: University of Chicago Press, 2005.

McCutcheon, Russell. *Studying Religion.* London: Equinox, 2007.

Nye, Malory. *Religion: The Basics.* 2nd ed. London and New York: Routledge, 2008, pp. 7–21.

Smith, Jonathan Z. *Imagining Religion: From Babylon to Jonestown.* Chicago: University of Chicago Press, 1982.

Smith, Wilfred Cantwell. *The Meaning and End of Religion.* London: SCM, 1978 [1964].

2

Is the Study of Religion Religious?
How to Study Religion, and
Who Studies Religion

Paul Hedges and Anna S. King

INTRODUCTION

Who understands religion best: the devoted believer who regularly worships and acts out his or her religious life, or the objective and neutral scholar who dispassionately stands back and observes? Surely, we may suggest, the answer depends on what we mean by "understanding" here. If we want to know what it means to live out and act within a religion, then the believer is placed in a position to "know" things about what it means to *be* part of that religion that the scholar never will know. On the other hand, the scholar can take a stance that does not require certain presuppositions and can maybe make informed comparisons between believers in different religions. However, have we misconceived the question or oversimplified the issue?

In this chapter, we will explore some of the debates and controversies surrounding how religion is studied and why any simple division between scholar and devotee is untenable. In particular, we will focus on what is called the insider/outsider debate, which examines the way that those inside religious traditions ("insiders") and those looking from the outside ("outsiders") approach issues in different ways, and also why stark divisions often do not work. We will also look at the ways that religion can be studied from theological and religious studies perspectives, and at some variety of stances found within both. As we will see, there is not any single or simple division between these two, while the way the division is managed varies from country to country.

HISTORICAL BACKGROUND AND CONTEXT

The development of the study of religion as a separate area from confessional theology (where the study of religion is tied to a specific religious tradition or denomination) can really be said to have its beginnings in the nineteenth century. At this time, various scholars sought to formulate what was often then termed the scientific study of religions, comparative theology, or comparative religion as a new science. However, many of these early and foundational figures, such as the German professor Friedrich Max Müller, who spent most of his career at the University of Oxford, United Kingdom, were Christians, and in many ways their understanding and interpretation of different religions was fitted into a framework linked to their religious views. (We develop this later in this chapter as well as in Volume 1, Chapter 1.) This makes it hard to draw a clear break between the study of religion as a secular and neutral subject and previous theological approaches, which are often seen to be best expressed in the words of an eleventh-century Christian theologian and Archbishop of Canterbury, Anselm, who famously described theology as "faith seeking understanding."[1] Increasingly, however, under terms such as "religious studies," "the study of religion," or "the history of religion," this field of study came to be understood and taught in many Western universities, colleges, and schools in what are often claimed to be nonconfessional, cross-cultural, and interdisciplinary ways, utilizing methods and concepts from disciplines such as history, political science, geography, sociology, anthropology, philosophy, psychology, postcolonial literature, and cultural studies. For the sake of simplicity, we will use the term "religious studies" to refer to nonconfessional approaches that seek to study religion from an academic perspective. (We should note that "theology" may be studied in a university context through academic modes and a non-confessional approach; however, we will use "theology" here to mean confessional theology.[2]) Its advocates insist that religious studies has always had an inclusive approach with varying styles and methods. The concept of religion is generally analyzed from a cultural perspective and discussed as a reality embedded in life and custom and embodied in institutions, texts, and images. However, in recent decades, various perspectives including feminist, Marxist, and postcolonial have contributed importantly to scholarly reassessment and transformation. We will discuss these further as we proceed. Contemporary key themes include globalization, gender issues, religion and cognition, and the ways in which religion responds to modernity, science, popular culture, and national politics. In the section that follows, we will explore some aspects of this development as well as engage with debates about how religion can and should be studied.

KEY TERMS, PEOPLE, AND DEBATES

The Insider/Outsider Debate

One of the most significant debates in religious studies is the insider/outsider issue, which in turn relates to the two terms "emic" and "etic." These latter two terms were coined by linguistic anthropologist Kenneth Pike (1912–2000) in his work studying the significance of language in the study of human societies. Both terms apply to the scholar studying a society from the outside; however, they refer to two different ways of seeking to understand and explain it. For an anthropologist taking an emic approach, the key question will be to use perspectives of those within the culture being studied to undertake analysis—that is, the anthropologist would use the language and terms with which those inside that group would explain themselves. In contrast, when taking an etic approach, the anthropologist would specifically be using her or his position as an external observer to try and make sense of the behaviors and beliefs of a society or group. This would appeal to the specific terms and language of an academic discipline to explain or describe the "other." Within anthropology and elsewhere, this distinction is seen as part of the basic toolkit that makes up the way the discipline is approached. It should be clear that this distinction works well within the study of religion, analogous to the study of any other society or group. It should also make clear why, at times, students of religion will find themselves not merely observing a religious group as "outsiders" but seeking empathetically to enter the devotees' world as "insiders" (an emic approach). Just as an anthropologist must enter into the thought world of a group, culture, and society if she or he is not to remain forever exterior, so the scholar of religion will likewise seek to understand what terms mean within the thought world of those within it. Indeed, within the anthropological field, it is suggested that emic understandings can help inspire and bring new insight into etic description, even to assess its appropriateness. Indeed, it would be expected that new concepts or principles beyond those known to the insider group would be uncovered.[3] By analogy, in the study of religion, this originally anthropological distinction suggests that an emic, or theological, approach is justified as something which the external scholar of religion may seek to understand. We should bear in mind, however, that this exercise in empathetic imagination is contested and that within the study of religion some scholars find it deeply suspect. Should the study of religion be primarily aimed at explaining the meaning and origin of religion and belief from entirely external perspectives? Certainly, some scholars such as Pascal Boyer and Russell McCutcheon have suggested so.

Before taking this discussion further, we now turn to the pair of distinctions with which we introduced the idea of emic and etic approaches—the notion of "insider" and "outsider" perspectives. Whereas both *emic* and *etic* refer to scholarly modes of discourse and enquiry, the insider/outsider debate asks questions about how the ways of knowledge of the scholar, an "outsider" perspective, differ from those of devotees or believers within a religious tradition, an "insider" perspective. Clearly this has links to the notion of emic and etic perspectives, and the discussion has come about, at least in part, through thinking through such issues. Indeed, the debate raises the question of how far an emic approach is attainable—can the outsider ever stand in the shoes of the believer? One important figure in the study of religion, the British scholar Ninian Smart (1927–2001), has suggested that we should, wherever possible, seek to walk in someone else's moccasins. However, we can ask if vicarious moccasin walking is ever possible. We will turn in the next section to debating this question further, where we discuss an approach called phenomenology; however, our aim is first to start to address some issues that complicate the whole debate.

As we saw in our historical survey earlier, the separation of the study of religion from the confessional activity of theology has often been seen as one of its main aims and part of its rationale; however, the separation is, in some ways, not so clear. Let us present one important challenge to this neat division. Many scholars of religion are themselves believers and practitioners, either within the religious tradition they study or within another. Should we label them insiders or outsiders? Scholars can, of course, engage in etic reflection on their own tradition, that is, applying standards and questions that come from elsewhere, as well as engaging in confessional theology and praxis. Indeed, their work as scholars in the etic framework may even affect their own insider confessional theology and approach—they may come to new understandings, interpretations, and applications of their religious beliefs and rituals. An example here would be the Christian philosopher of religion John Hick (1922–2012), best known for his work on religious pluralism (see Volume 1, Chapter 8), whose historical and critical studies of the *Bible* led him to conclude that Jesus never claimed to be, nor thought of himself as, divine—such ideas would simply make no sense to a first-century Galilean rabbi. Hick then adjusted his theological position to argue for a Christianity in which Jesus is seen simply as a human being, although more open to God (or the "Real," to use one of Hick's terms in his philosophical and pluralist writings) than most others.[4]

Of course, many scholars are atheists or agnostics, so another question that may arise is who is better placed to study and understand a religious tradition. If we accept the argument found in anthropological study that to be able to work in both emic and etic modes can provide richer insights, then may it not stand to reason that the insider can extend the emic position even further? However, this contradicts what may seem fairly clear common sense that insiders will never be able to remove themselves from a position that endorses their own agenda and so cannot look impartially at the facts. Of course, we must admit that atheist scholars will also bring their own presuppositions, and so they may well be said to not look impartially at the facts either. However, here we are only touching the edge of the complications that arise.

To examine the issue deeply, we also need to realize that to think that the terms "insider" and "outsider" refer solely to religious belonging is misleading. We are all beings composed of intersecting and multiple identities, and the way we may understand other people, empathize with them, or be linked to them occurs in a multitude of ways and at various levels. Variables such as gender, ethnicity, region, class, and other matters all play a part. For instance, a Western scholar who seeks an emic understanding of the religious culture of a Hindu (ex)-untouchable, or Dalit (one of the lowest castes within the social strata that traditionally make up Indian society), will find himself or herself an outsider not only on account of religion but also in terms of class and ethnicity, to name but two factors. As human beings, we are always insiders to various discourses but outsiders to others. If we consider a movement such as Santeria, a fusion of Roman Catholicism and African traditional religions developed and practiced by black slaves in the Caribbean, we may find that many insiders within Roman Catholicism, for instance Italian Roman Catholic priests, may experience greater difficulties relating to and understanding this system than many others, perhaps those who share the cultural and social origins that gave rise to Santeria even if they do not practice it (i.e., descendents of black slaves). Indeed, the history of religions tells us that disputes within and between religions can be as sharp and bitter as attacks from the outside.

Another interesting complication may occur when we are discussing new recruits into a religion. Recent converts are, of course, now insiders; however, we may ask if they are as deeply aware of the belief system they now hold as someone who has lived and been brought up in it all their life.[5] This raises the question of whether there are levels of being an insider (and also of course of being an outsider). For example, Buddhist converts from Christianity will have levels of what we may term "insiderness" and "outsiderness" in relation to each. They may identify with the new tradition but retain perhaps a deeper rootedness in their old tradition. In a similar fashion, an outsider scholar may have more theoretical knowledge than an insider within a tradition, but the understanding may be of a different type. Yet what if they are themselves converts from the religion that they study? The British Buddhist scholar Paul Williams is one example. Williams was brought up as a Roman Catholic but converted to Tibetan Buddhism, becoming an insider to that tradition for over 20 years, a tradition in which he is also an internationally renowned scholar. More recently, he has converted back to Roman Catholicism.[6] It will be difficult if we seek to understand to which tradition he is an insider or outsider; certainly, we could not simply quantify it and ask whether he has a higher level of insiderness or outsiderness to either tradition, and when such a change occurred. Also, we can ask what happens when he thinks in emic or etic terms about each tradition as a scholar, or even if this makes sense. Moreover, presuming that many conversions are a process rather than an event, we may ask where someone such as Williams stood one week, or one month, before he formally converted back from Buddhism to Catholicism. Of course the process may be one of many years during which questioning of both traditions finally leads to conversion. To which tradition was Williams, as our example, an insider and an outsider during the period leading up to his conversions? As another example, the noted atheist Richard Dawkins has described himself as a "cultural Anglican," suggesting that although he has no religious belief, he lives within the world that appreciates the music and language of a religious tradition. Again we see insider and outsider boundaries being crossed, or transgressed even, in complicated ways; can an atheist have some form of religious insiderness? If, as we have suggested earlier, we all have many levels to our identities, then the answer is clearly "yes." Indeed, in some ways these may be said to be relatively straightforward examples; some people profess multiple religious identities (see Volume 1, Chapter 10).

We could certainly write more about these issues and controversies, and certainly they will keep recurring as we discuss the ways we should approach and study religion. What is clear so far is that simple ideas about studying a religion from either inside or outside are not are straightforward as they might at first seem.

The Observer as Subject

Scholars analyzing the study of religion, indeed academic thought as a whole, have increasingly come to a realization that knowledge has been constructed within a particular context, and largely by male, white, and Western scholars, often of a particular social class. This raises issues in relation not only to gender (see Volume 2, Chapter 1) but also to our relation to the rest of the world. What is termed postcolonial theory has explored the ways in which our descriptions of ourselves and others are located in a complex network of understandings and representation (see Volume 1, Chapter 11). This has implications for the study of religion, as we discuss later in the chapter.

The insider/outsider debate and the controversy over Orientalism are tied together. *Orientalism* is a term coined by Edward Said (1935–2003), a scholar of comparative literature, who argued that the Western world has always misinterpreted the East (he specifically wrote about Islam, but scholars since then have employed the term more widely to look at India and Hinduism, for example). Said contended that we create an image of ourselves when we write about the Other, but a "dark" side, so that we can provide a "light" side when we portray ourselves. For example, he suggests the West portrays itself in positive terms as rational, democratic, and advanced, and so the rest of the world is portrayed as the flip side of this: irrational, authoritarian, and backward. This is related to an exercise of power where the West (today predominantly the United States, in the past predominantly Europe) explains the rest of the world in its own terms. Both the insider/outsider debate and Orientalist discourse put a spotlight not only on the object of study but also on the one studying, and ask about our agenda and how we shape that which is being studied.

Both the insider/outsider and Orientalist theories seek to demonstrate that when scholars write about "the other," they are often writing about themselves and defining themselves by means of stereotyped portraits of the other. The terms *insider* and *outsider*, for instance, are always polarized. McCutcheon claims that Said's Orientalism is not so much about the Muslim world as it is about the way in which European writers and scholars traditionally attempted to distinguish and define their own cultural and national histories. David Hufford argues that disinterest, or neutrality, is impossible in the study of belief systems (including religion) and that calls for neutrality actually betray the effort on the part of one group to construct and justify their power over another group, that is, the powerful, uninvolved observer versus the powerless, passive subject. Hufford sees what is termed the reflexive turn, when applied to the study of religion, as enabling scholars not only to identify those moments when they have overstepped their self-created authority but also to distinguish between their scholarly and their personal voices. This reflexive turn is about the self-reflection of scholars and their own inbuilt prejudices and assumptions:

> Reflexivity is a response to the egocentric predicament, and it parallels responses to awareness of the ethnocentric predicament. Both risk mere self-justification, but both have the potential to reveal the culturally-situated, human quality of all knowledge.[7]

Hufford writes that a reflexive account of our knowledge-making work can give us a more accurate sense of where we are because it will always require us to tell how we got there:

> Reflexivity should also free us from the stultifying fiction that our every belief and active can and should dissolve us from our scholarly training, or else be suspect. And most importantly, it should help it to relieve some of the awful asymmetry that currently exists in our field as we apply to our informants and their institutions culturally and psychologically based interpretations from which we exempt ourselves.[8]

To put this in other terms, we need to realize that there is no point of view from nowhere, that all academic reflection on religion involves the presuppositions of the scholar, which are located in her or his own gender, social class, and national identity. Scholars such as Hufford and Gavin Flood have called for us to be reflexive, that is, to be aware of our own biases and prejudices, because otherwise our attempts at scholarship will always be distorted in ways of which we are unaware.[9] This awareness has been spoken of as the reflexive turn in academic study—the idea that our ways of knowing and ideas are not neutral but based in a specific cultural and historical heritage.[10]

Ways of Studying Religion

As we have discussed earlier, religious studies is multidisciplinary, which is to say it uses the tools of many different approaches and disciplines, such as sociology, phenomenology, philosophy, feminism, postcolonialism, and psychology, to inform its understanding. Here, we will look at the implications of some of these for studying religion. Our aim is not so much to describe these approaches and how they are used but to explore what they mean for the study of religion.

Functionalist Approaches

Functionalism (more strongly reductionism—described later) emphasizes areas such as the social or psychological in analyzing religion. That is, religion is viewed as a dimension or form of culture, and all human practices as by-products of complex social, political, economic, historical, and psychological factors of which the insider is not necessarily aware. Such approaches are "functional" because they investigate the way religion works, or functions, in relation to society or something else:

> ...scholars committed to understanding human institutions and knowledge as in some part, influenced by such factors as gender, class and race, are interested in discarding the notion of religion as a common universal category as the first step toward conceiving of religion as but one aspect of human culture, to be studied in the same way in which we study other aspects of culture.[11]

Because this approach seeks to describe religion in nonreligious terms, it is often termed reductionist, as it reduces the meaning or explanation to other causal explanations. So a sociologist may analyze religion as a projection of human society and the way it structures our relationships, whereas a psychoanalyst may analyze religion as a product of the mind. In the view of Sigmund Freud, it is a collective form of mental illness or neurosis (see also Volume 1, Chapter 1).[12]

Functionalism builds from figures such as Karl Marx, who interpreted religion as deadening the sense of pain and alienation of the oppressed, and Emile Durkheim, one of the fathers of modern sociology and an important figure in what can be termed the functionalist school in sociology and anthropology.[13] Durkheim maintained that society was an "organismic analogy of the body, wherein all the parts work together to maintain the equilibrium of the whole," and "religion was understood to be the glue that held society together."[14] Lincoln comments that "Insofar as this model stresses the continuity and integration of timeless groups, whose internal tensions and conflicts, turbulence and incoherence, permeability and malleability are largely erased, it risks becoming a religious and not a historic narrative: the story of a transcendent ideal threatened by debasing forces of change."[15]

Another important theorist whom we may describe here as a functionalist thinker[16] is Max Weber (1864–1920), who, like Durkheim, recognized religion's strong social aspects, but differed by insisting that religious ideologies actually had an effect on the society and its development. This is best known through his classic work *The Protestant Ethic and the Spirit of Capitalism.*[17] Also significant in this social-scientific approach to religion is Clifford Geertz, who suggested that specific beliefs are not significant as it is the way religion organizes our life and world (Geertz's definition is discussed further in Volume 1, Chapter 1).

Functionalist approaches tend to focus on the role and function of religion and what it means. They tend to emphasize outsider perspectives and etic approaches; although, especially in anthropology, as it developed in the twentieth century, it was increasingly realized that emic approaches would be needed to balance this emphasis. Having said this, the scholars we have described have very different approaches to religion and are more or less sympathetic to it. We should also not see functionalist approaches as dismissive of religion in a straightforward way as even figures such as Marx or Freud, who saw religion as in some way essentially "false" or "negative," were nevertheless impressed by its power. Weber and Geertz were primarily concerned with the way religion constructed society and the often subtle ways it helped people interpret the world.

Phenomenology of Religion

Although functional or social-scientific accounts are very significant, religious studies as a whole is associated with the philosophical form of phenomenology, which draws its name from the study of phenomena. This approach aims to eliminate subjectivity from the inquirer's process of thought by the suspension of judgment (*epoché*) and gaining a sense of things as a whole (eidetic vision). Also, especially in religious studies, it is associated with an empathetic, emic approach to the groups studied.

As a school of thought, phenomenology dates back to the earliest twenti-eth century and a philosopher called Edmund Husserl. However, the phe-nomenology in religious studies is indebted to theorists who developed it in new ways,[18] especially in developing techniques for "non-critical, empa-thetic descriptions of human behaviour" to bridge the divide between insider and outsider.[19] Some commentators therefore critique religious studies as a quasi-religious undertaking because it inherits the strategy of "methodologi-cal agnosticism" associated with the work of Ninian Smart and the empa-thetic approach of bracketing out truth claims and judgments favored by phenomenologists.

This controversy goes back in part to the roots of religious studies, which emerged from previous theological approaches before developing its own distinctive place as a more neutral academic discipline. In discussing this, it is useful to go back to the theologian Rudolf Otto, who was strongly influ-enced by the philosophy of Immanuel Kant and whose influential work in this area focused on the "wholly other"[20] and the nature of "religious experi-ence." Indeed, Otto's most famous work, *The Idea of the Holy*, is still often part of a set of classics texts studied by students in the area. Exploring reli-gious experience, drawing especially on the Christian tradition and the *Hebrew Bible* (the Christian *Old Testament*), Otto described the encounter with the divine by three Latin words, *mysterium, tremendum,* and *fascinans*. These can be thought of various ways, but here we may use a standard dis-tinction of seeing them as two parts: a terrifying mystery (*mysterium tremen-dum*) and an awe-inspiring, fascinating mystery (*mysterium fascinans*). Otto described the human encounter with these mysteries by the term "numi-nous." A numinous experience is regarded as unique in kind and irreduc-ible—it cannot be reduced to culture or society. We see here a distinction between a reductionist account and Otto's theological one. Whereas we may have phenomena, that is, what we encounter in the world, which can be explained in functional terms, religion is held to go beyond this. Indeed, drawing on the work of Otto and also Mircea Eliade (1907–1986), who we will discuss next, phenomenology in the study of religion suggested that the simple raw social data or phenomena of religion did not explain what religion was. Religion must therefore have some transcendent meaning. It should be noted, though, that although two of the great founders of religious studies, Ninian Smart in the United Kingdom and Wilfred Cantwell Smith in the United States, were keen to distinguish religious studies as a discipline from a theological phenomenology like that of Otto, nevertheless Otto's work remains an important part of studying religious experience. Indeed, part of the reason his approach remains useful is because we need to consider the meanings the practitioners give to their own experiences.

In the development of religious studies, Eliade also played a significant part, and in his method, which is primarily phenomenological, he also understood religion as unique and autonomous. It could not simply be discussed in reductionist terms. Eliade, perhaps the preeminent interpreter of world religions in the twentieth century, was one of the last scholars of religion who attempted to find universal, cross-cultural patterns and unities in religion.[21] For Eliade, religion, or the sacred, was an important focus of human life and experience; we have a longing for the real or the sacred. He believed that as a species the religious desire formed the core of what we are and that a universal spiritual desire or quest marked us out. Therefore, he used the term "homo religiosus"—the "religious [hu]man"—to describe us:

> Whatever the historical context in which he is placed, *homo religiosus* always believes that there is an absolute reality, *the sacred*, which transcends this world but manifests itself in this world, thereby sanctifying it and making it real.[22]

Although Eliade has been hugely influential and his work has proved inspirational for a whole generation of scholars, criticism has largely focused on his notion that religion is an absolute category that is not definable in other terms, or what is called "essential" (i.e., there is a pure core or essence to religion), as well as his selective use of ethnographic data and quasi-religious stance. Many scholars of religion have rejected Eliade's approach for an uncritical and unscientific methodology, as well as for being selective and inattentive to history.[23] Some have also objected to his political stance, as he was for a while a supporter of fascist groups in his native Romania— it is debated as to whether this should or not affect how we read him as a philosopher or theorist of religion. Roger Corless, Russell T. McCutcheon, and Jonathan Z. Smith in particular have called for the end of the Eliadean era. However, Eliade still has defenders, such as Bryan Rennie, who argues that Eliade's universal humanism is one of the elements that makes him a precursor of our contemporary outlook.[24]

Although phenomenology, like Eliade himself, has fallen out of favor among a considerable number of scholars, there is no clear replacement, and so it remains something of a default position in religious studies. Moreover, some scholars, notably James Cox, a professor at the University of Edinburgh, United Kingdom, have argued that a viable contemporary form of phenomenology can not only be found but is also essential for religious studies to ground itself as a solid academic discipline.[25]

The Ethnographic Approach

Within religious studies, various subdisciplines contribute significantly. Among the most important is social anthropology, which combines an interpretative approach with sociological analysis. Its importance to the study of religions lies predominantly in its methodology, which offsets the tendency to study texts rather than people. The foundations of contemporary anthropology of religion owe much to theorists we discuss elsewhere who influenced all the social sciences, such as Marx, Weber, Freud, and Durkheim. However, anthropology has a strong sense of descent from a specific group of theorists.[26] There is as a result no single, uniform anthropological theory of religion or common methodology—anthropological methods and theories[27] are part of the wider context of social sciences and applied to the study of religions. Anthropological analyses tend to be "thick," secular, and naturalistic (a "thick" account is one which is strong on local detail and context). They account for religions as products of human culture and human nature. The hallmark of twentieth-century anthropology lay in the advocacy of firsthand participant observation and/or fieldwork.[28]

Thomas Hyllan Eriksen notes that anthropology has, historically, had great success in overcoming racial prejudice and biological determinism, in making us see the world in new ways, and in "making the exotic familiar and the familiar exotic," to paraphrase Malinowski. It offered scholars "the possibility to raise fundamental philosophical questions while simultaneously engaging with the world of real existing people...."[29] However, Eriksen believes that the discipline today is marked by a timidity in the face of theoretical self-questioning, although it has brought a maturity, and anthropologists of religion today are highly self-reflexive and self-critical, questioning categories such as belief, culture, ritual, and religion itself.[30]

Although Eriksen fears that anthropology could become "an anachronism from the 20th century," Rosalind Hackett is optimistic. She points out that anthropology of religion remains indebted to the early monographs produced by Edward Evans-Pritchard, Durkheim, Mary Douglas, and Geertz, but that

> ...the postmodern and postcolonial turns, compressions of time and space with globalization, and rise of "multiculturalist" issues, have occasioned some significant rethinking and realignment. Determining the general provenance or parameters of religion in "exotic" small-scale societies has ceased to preoccupy contemporary anthropologists. Some now see their contribution as being rather to reconsider modern, secular society as symbolically and culturally constituted, and as much based on the religious impulse as on reason. ... In sum, as stated at the outset, anthropological theory and method appear increasingly well positioned to respond to such pressing social and cultural issues as identity, difference, conflict, and livelihood as they are mediated by religion(s) in our globalizing world.[31]

Gender, Sexuality, and Feminist Theory

The contributions of feminist critical perspectives to the study of religion have in the last half-century transformed the subject. Many recent debates in the discipline have focused on gender, sexuality, feminist theory, and the complex relationship between religion and gender (although another chapter is devoted to this topic, it is of such importance that we must also address it here; see Volume 2, Chapter 1). Feminist perspectives have addressed not only the problem of male-dominant God language and religious experience, and the patriarchal nature of many scriptures and religious traditions, but the biases inherent in the discipline itself. Linda Woodhead argues that developments of recent decades mean discourse about "patriarchy," or male domination, should be replaced as it is clear that many factors oppress and exploit women (and others) related to issues such as ethnicity, race, gender, and class and that we must deal with this complexity:

> Under the towering influence of Michel Foucault many writers dismiss the idea of power as a possession which is unequally distributed in society, above all between men and women, in favour of a picture of power as constantly negotiated in the small, ceaseless, real-time interactions between individuals. There is, however, a countervailing move by others who believe that the stress on "capillary" rather than "arterial" power has gone too far . . . , and that talk of "differences" must not be allowed to mask the massive and consolidated inequalities of power which still structure contemporary societies—including, pre-eminently, that between men and women.[32]

Although strongly embedded, Woodhead believes that gender is not yet securely part of all religious studies. Nevertheless, the gender balance is shifting in universities with more women lecturers and professors. Change in the wider society is also important, and gender is also a significant factor in public discussion about such matters as homosexuality, abortion, Islamic veiling, calls for "traditional family values," religiously inspired terrorism and violence, and ecology.[33]

Theological Approaches

As we have seen earlier, theology has a complex intersection and history with religious studies, and even where we find religious studies scholars strongly insisting that what they do is not theology, and is even radically different, it nevertheless remains the case that, for many, theological approaches remain part and parcel of religious studies, at least as an emic category. Here we look at various aspects of the relationship.

First, we should consider the geographical issue that is involved here because the nature and relationship of theology as an academic discipline to religious studies varies. Let us start in Germany. Here, traditionally, theology departments in universities have been tied to a confessional standpoint so that they are either a department of Catholic theology or a department of Protestant theology (and, interestingly, many universities have both, which exist as entirely separate and self-contained units each running their own courses, normally without any connection). Given their allegiance to a particular denomination, they do confessional theology within those boundaries, although there is, potentially at least, more scope for freedom in Protestant departments because of the range of potential affiliations, namely Lutheran, Calvinist, Anglican, and so on.[34] In this context, religious studies, which is often called history of religions (the common term for the discipline across mainland Europe), exists again as an entirely separate and distinct department within universities. It tends to see itself as a "science" and focuses on functionalist approaches, generally eschewing emic approaches or the phenomenology associated with Eliade. To mark its place as a social-scientific study, there tends to be no connection to theology. There are changes, though, and the University of Potsdam (just outside Berlin) is integrating Jewish theology into its offerings in the study of religion, although as separate from its core teaching for the training of rabbis. In this sense, Jewish theology will stand as some type of counterpart to a Catholic or Protestant theology department, but its affiliation is with a religious studies department.

If we turn to the United States, we find a somewhat similar picture. Many universities with a religious foundation or affiliation tend to have departments that do some form of confessional theology. In contrast, secular universities tend to have a department that does religious studies. Of course, some universities have both, and so Harvard has both a Divinity School, which does confessional theology and is geared toward training people for the Christian ministry, and the Study of Religion as a separate area within the Faculty of Arts and Sciences. However, they are not clearly demarcated despite being institutionally separated, and so there is crossover in research and teaching. Indeed, the Divinity School houses the Center for the Study of World Religions. Within this, there are plans for training for Buddhist ministry to parallel the teaching of Christian ministry. Such crossovers between religious studies and theology are not the pattern across the whole United States, but they indicate that the division is not so deep. A similar area of encounter can be seen in the way that the American Academy of Religion (AAR) and the Society of Biblical Literature (SBL), between them the United States' primary scholarly networks for religious studies and biblical studies (if not all theology), have traditionally held their annual meetings together. Although there are some tensions over this, and for a while they split, there is certainly a sense that together they generate a size and momentum that is beneficial to both (indeed, the size of the United States and the number of departments that exist there, along with the finances behind this, make the AAR [this runs as the headline name] annual conference the largest and most important international conference for religious studies globally).

If we turn to the United Kingdom, we find a different picture. Here, for historical reasons, theology has been taught in all the older universities

stretching back to medieval times. This has, naturally, been Christian confessional theology (primarily Anglican). As we discussed earlier, though,
moves to begin a new "science" of religion that became religious studies were
underway from the nineteenth century and really saw fruit at the beginnings
of the twentieth century. The first professorship of religious studies was at
Manchester, where John Nicol Farquhar (1861–1929) was appointed.
Farquhar was, however, a former missionary and, although an able scholar
of Hinduism, often took a sectarian position; we have discussed some of this
combined history.[35] By the late twentieth century, separate departments of
religious studies were growing up; however, many of these were placed
within existing theology departments as their natural homes. As part of
developments through time, under the British system all universities are
considered secular institutions (some have religious foundations and certainly continue to have chaplains and chapels but do not belong to any
Christian denomination), and so theology departments are not confessional
in the way that they are in Germany. Therefore, the development of departments of theology and religious studies arose without any overt issues about
the teaching of any particular system as "true" or "correct" as confessional
theology requires. This can pose problems as theologians of particular
denominations teach about Christian theology, bringing presuppositions
about the correct way to teach it. At the same time, there are also atheist theologians of no religious affiliation (i.e., people who teach, study, and research
theology as academics but with no religious belief or background). It can
appear then that, at times, theology in British universities is simply religious
studies about Christianity, whereas religious studies is the study of non-
Christian theologies and practices. This, of course, oversimplifies, and many
theologians would be unhappy with this distinction. As in the United States
and Germany, there are also various particular strands and interpretations of
the correct way of doing things, whereas theologians and religious studies
scholars exist in greater or lesser harmony in different places and at different
times.

These three sample cases show us that there is no simple, one-size-fits-all
answer to the question of how theology and religious studies relate as
academic disciplines. Indeed, while at times harmony exists between them
as complementary ways to study religion such that, especially in the UK context but also elsewhere, it is possible for someone to consider himself or herself to be both a theologian and a scholar of religious studies; this is not
always so. Some religious studies scholars regard theologians as something
"Other," at best as subjects to be studied and at worst as people not doing
proper scholarship or academic work because they are bound by confessional presuppositions and doctrines. Likewise, some theologians regard
religious studies and its practitioners with suspicion, seeing them as not
engaging with what is essential about religion, and argue that religious

studies should in no way inform theology or the way it is practiced (this is, in some ways, quite odd because many of these theologians will quite happily say they should use insights from disciplines such as sociology, psychology, and business studies to inform their understanding but reject outright the contention that the subject which most explicitly studies religion has anything to say to their own discussion of religion!). Part of the dispute is, of course, political and territorial and relates to the way scholars in each area seek to claim their space within academic departments and research environments (because of its nature, many people studying religion are often deemed to have a partisan agenda, and so religious studies scholars are often at pains to show they are not doing anything "theological," and likewise theologians want to show that they have a rightful place in academia and are not just a subset of broader studies in religion).

Comparative Religion

Perhaps one of the most contentious issues for religious studies today is the status of comparative studies in religion. As already mentioned, one of the first names for the nineteenth-century attempts to create a new form of scientific study was comparative religion. However, at that time it was little more than a concealed attempt to prove Christian superiority by using preselected terms and categories. It was then developed by scholars such as James Frazer (1854–1941), whose magnum opus *The Golden Bough* (1890) is a comparative study of mythology and religion that attempted to show a progression from magic to religion to science. Eliade also advocated a form of comparative religion; however, his interest was oriented to revealing what he believed was the core essence of religious phenomena—the sacred—by seeking to demonstrate universal patterns of belief, myth, symbol, and ritual across history and cultures. Later scholars have critiqued Frazer and Eliade for emphasizing commonalities rather than differences and employing ethnographic or historical data out of context. Therefore, "comparative religion" has become somewhat associated with what are seen as old and problematic assumptions in the study of religion. Moreover, as across academia generally, increasing specialization means that scholars tend to focus on more localized areas or specific traditions, and so today there are few scholars like the giants of the past such as Eliade, Ninian Smart, or Wilfred Cantwell Smith who were accepted as experts across all "world religions" (indeed, the very notion of "world religions" is problematic, an issue discussed in Volume 1, Chapter 1). Scholars today who show too much expertise across a range of traditions are liable to be classed as "generalists," a derogatory term. This is a regrettable turn of events in some ways as it means that many potentially exciting developments happen in isolation, and scholars often are unaware of useful comparative endeavors.

Comparative studies in religion are not, however, altogether dead, and especially in some geographical regions they remain the normal way of doing business. Indeed, some would even argue that the failure to seek common patterns of ritual, belief, or symbol is to some degree an abrogation of a scholar's responsibility to try to make sense of and classify religious phenomena. Indeed, the authors of this chapter would concur with a phrase coined by one of the founders of the modern discipline, the nineteenth-century linguist F. Max Müller, that "to know one, is to know none." Coming from his background in linguistics, Müller realized that just as a deeper understanding of the structure (grammar, syntax, etc.) of your own language was gained when you studied another language, the same was true of religion as well. Too much specialization leads to a narrow tunnel vision. Indeed, there have even been calls for a new comparative religion after the reflexive turn, and Gavin Flood has done some pioneering scholarship in this regard.[36] Such moves are also very much in accord with the new discipline of interreligious studies, which we will discuss later.

SURVEY OF ARGUMENTS

The Study of Religion(s)

We will now take stock of all our preceding arguments and see what we can make of them. A pragmatic approach is to argue that religion is whatever is studied under that name in university departments of religious studies and colleges.[37] However, even, or particularly, here, we find complexity.[38] Religious studies has two principal meanings. It can mean very generally the all-embracing study of religion, which includes theological and confessional teaching, or it can be more narrowly defined as excluding a god-centered or confessional approach (theology). Theology in the latter sense is an alternative path that centers on the cumulative historical tradition preserved within a single religion, whereas religious studies takes a global view of humans and engages with their practices and beliefs. The confessional approach studies religions from a faith perspective and generally assumes the truth or value of one religious tradition (although it can be far more open and inclusive, and perhaps the Center for the Study of World Religions in the Harvard Divinity School is indicative of this). Religious studies in contrast is predominantly the study of religion as culture.

Although members of the general public may discuss the phenomenon of "religion" and feel that they know what it means, many contemporary scholars avoid the term and speak only of *religions*, regarding the singular usage as encouraging essentialism. (Our discussion here will cover some ground debated elsewhere but raises important issues; see Volume 1, Chapter 1.) Some go further, arguing that the concept of religion itself should be abandoned. Jonathan Z. Smith, in his introduction to *Imagining Religion*, denies the possibility that there is a common essence or core to all religions:

> . . .while there is a staggering amount of data, phenomena, of human experiences and expressions that might be characterized in one culture or another, by one criterion or another, as religious—*there is no data for religion*. Religion is solely the creation of the scholar's study. It is created for the scholar's analytic purposes by his imaginative acts of comparison and generalization. Religion has no existence apart from the academy. For this reason, the student of religion, must be relentlessly self-conscious. Indeed, this self-consciousness constitutes his primary expertise, his foremost object of study.[39]

According to Timothy Fitzgerald, there is no coherent nontheological theoretical basis for religious studies as a separate academic discipline; he claims that liberal theological beliefs about a universal essence of religion lie behind much religious studies (we have discussed this earlier in relation to Eliade and his legacy, and other aspects are discussed here and in Volume 1, Chapter 1).[40] Russell T. McCutcheon also offers a powerful critique of traditional religious studies scholarship, including Eliade, the notion of "world religions" (see Volume 1, Chapter 1), and the notion of "religion" as a universal and single phenomenon (the *sui generis* argument).[41] Instead, he argues, religion can only legitimately be seen, in religious studies, as a manifestation of human culture, and therefore the data we bracket as "religion" are merely arbitrary distinctions within the whole continuum of secular human culture, society, and behavior.[42] Lincoln recommends that students of religion should engage in critical *inquiry* rather than *advocacy*. When we fail to do this, when "one permits those whom one studies to define the terms in which they will be understood . . . we have ceased to function as historian or scholar."[43] Employing Bakhtin and Ricoeur, and seeking to relate more broadly to other disciplines in the social sciences and humanities, Flood also challenges the view that religious studies is about the human quest for the sacred.[44] He challenges the view that religions are privileged objects of knowledge and presents an argument for the nature of inquiry into it as involved in dialogue and increasing understanding when it rejects a *sui generis* approach. Such approaches suggest that the study of religion should begin with language and culture, and indeed this is broadly in line with much contemporary movement within religious studies as a whole.

Interreligious Studies

In something of a contrast to the approaches we have just discussed by scholars such as McCutcheon and Fitzgerald, who form a powerful voice within the contemporary study of religion, the late twentieth century and especially the twenty-first century have seen moves toward a study of religion that engages both practitioners of religion and scholars. Often going by the name of interreligious studies, advocates argue that it is artificial to demarcate sharp boundaries not only between disciplines but also between theology and religious studies. Although used in various ways, the term *interreligious studies* suggests that the purely functional and etic perspective does not provide a case for advocacy of important causes . For example, many scholars (whether they come from within a religious tradition or not) feel that religions should have a voice on the current environmental crisis (on religion and the environment, see Volume 2, Chapter 7). Again, interreligious studies is often involved in areas such as peace building and social cohesion as well as interreligious dialogue, and its advocates argue that there should be an active engagement between scholars, devotees, and other stakeholders in bringing people together in dialogue and common understanding (for more on the relations between religions, see Volume 1, Chapter 8, and Volume 2, Chapter 12, on issues in religion and social cohesion). This is what Oddbjorn Leirvik refers to as the "space between."[45]

Although interreligious studies is still a young and developing disciplinary area (a small but growing number of professorships and postgraduate courses take this name) and those affiliated come from different backgrounds (with significant numbers from theology, religious studies, and sociology), it would be useful to note some typical features:

> . . .it is often seen linked to the term Intercultural Theology . . . emphasis[ing] moves . . . towards dialogue with the religious Other. In this context . . . it may carry a theological tone where study between religions for mutual enrichment is key. However, . . . it may refer to the study of different religions in meeting, encounter and activism. Here, a more "secular" than theological concern may be involved. . . . Another area that may be of concern in Interreligious Studies . . . is . . . Interreligious/Interfaith Dialogue. . . . Interreligious Studies often tends to imply more than simply a study of two or more religions, but is about studying the dynamic encounter and interaction between them. This may involve hermeneutics, dialogue, historical encounters or other areas, moreover there is normally an interest in the meaningful growth, enrichment and benefit gained in this. Much of its focus will be on modern and contemporary issues, however, for particular scholars historical studies may be the focus.[46]

Meanwhile, Leirvik's influential study advocates what he terms a "relational" approach, employing theorists such as Martin Buber and Emmanuel Levinas as well as his own personal involvement with dialogue to argue for a new approach to the study of religion that has regard for the Other.[47]

CONCLUSION

Religious studies in the Western world often seemed at its most exciting (and exotic) in the second half of the twentieth century when students were introduced to a range of religions and movements that they had not previously encountered, and when phenomenology and anthropology were at their most confident. Since then, knowledge and understanding of different religious cultures have grown exponentially, and with them the rejection of any trace of "exoticism," "othering," or attempts to create a grand narrative explaining all religion. Various perspectives including feminism, postcolonialism, Orientalism, and rejection of world religion paradigms (see Volume 1, Chapter 1) have led scholars to reflect deeply on how they can and should represent religion. This has often led to hesitation and self-doubt about what to say and how to say it. The scholar as subject has become a central focus of attention, along with the importance of reflexivity in redressing the over-extension of academic authority. Ideas of collaborative research, cocreation, hospitality, and guest-hood have come to characterize the position of the scholar as participant observer. There is an insistence on greater transparency in, voicing our own personal convictions and views.

To return to our earlier discussion on insider/outsider debates, we can see that these are always complicated disputes and that the stance people take across a spectrum of positions affects the way they study and think about religion. There is also no definitive answer as to which has greater strengths or benefits, and although some scholars may strongly argue for one approach or the other, it is likely that several may be useful. Today, most scholars are reflexive about their own position and prejudices and seek as far as possible to be aware of their own standpoint. Therefore, it may be said that a reflexive phenomenology characterizes much religious studies today as a default position when scholars are not explicitly employing approaches from disciplines such as sociology, psychology, history, or any of the other methodologies that enrich the interdisciplinary subject area.

Academic discourse about religion is in reality an ongoing conversation pursued through the generations and across time and space, sometimes arid and sometimes catching the spirit of the times. Scholars joining the conversation continually attempt to define and redefine theories in the hope that a more rigorous critical voice develops. As a result, the very real achievements of past scholars have sometimes gone unrecognized, and with them the contributions of the different disciplines that come under the aegis of religious studies. It cannot be denied that some of the greatest figures of the recent past have also been seen as great myth-makers, quasi-religious figures who have excited thought and mapped new directions in scholarly research. Today, the emphasis is on "discussing the temporal, contextual, situated, interested, human, and material dimension of those discourses, practices, and institutions that characteristically represent themselves as eternal, transcendent, spiritual, and divine."[48] We also argue that there is a place for the development of a critically engaged study of religions that makes research and writing relevant to pressing global problems. The scholarly ideal has often been of a disengaged discipline that does not make value judgments or take a political or moral stand, but the reality is that we are all engaged. Perhaps more attention needs to be paid to the tensions between the cultural and religious specificities and the universal values that we encounter in our work, along with greater discussion of what commitment to social justice and peace building might mean for the study of religions.

GLOSSARY

Confessional: as used in relation to the study of religion, a confessional approach is to teach or study within the worldview of a particular tradition (or confession). So, for instance, to do Lutheran theology is to follow the teachings and ideas of a specific Christian denomination and its assumptions about doctrines such as the Virgin Birth or the divinity of Jesus.

Emic/etic: terms adopted from anthropology, which mean, respectively, to study a religion with a sympathetic eye and in terms that make sense within that system, and to study a religion with a critical eye and to use terms that come from external, scholarly worldviews. Both are seen as outsider approaches (see later).

Essentialism: in the study of religion, essentialism is to assume that there is an essence within religion. That is to say either that certain ideas define what a particular religion is or that all religions share some common central core. This is seen as problematic as historical studies show that the beliefs of every tradition change over time and that different interpretations within religions will emphasize different aspects.

Functionalist/reductionist: approaches to the study of religion that examine religion through the lens of disciplines such as sociology or psychology and so explore the "function" religion plays either in society or as a category of thought. At its strongest level, such theories are called reductionist as they "reduce" religion to anthropology or to a function of society or the mind.

Insider/outsider: terms to define whether someone is a devotee/believer in a specific religion (an "insider") or a scholar who is not a devotee/believer (an "outsider"). In practice, though, there is no clear distinction, and a spectrum of "insiderness" and "outsiderness" exists in all of us and is open to many intersecting levels of identity (gender, social class, race, culture, etc.).

Numinous: a term that refers to an experience of the divine/God that is wholly different from what we experience in this world. Most commonly associated with Rudolf Otto and his terms *mysterium, tremendum,* and *fascinans* (mystery, tremendousness/awe, and fascination), it looks back to the eighteenth-century philosopher Immanuel Kant who distinguished between things in this world, or phenomena, and a world beyond it which we cannot directly experience, the *noumen* (roughly, the divine).

Orientalism: a theory (or ideology?) associated with Edward Said that argues that Western attempts to define the East (the orient) have acted to control or distort it.

Arguing that all interpretation is political and an act of power, Said argued that Western interpreters painted negative images onto the other while portraying themselves in a positive light. It is part of postcolonial theory and has been heavily criticized for taking some excesses of Western interpretation as a basis for an entire theory.

Patriarchy: a system that favors men or is led by men. Much used in feminist thought to characterize many of the world's religions. It is now often seen as too simplistic an analysis of society or religion (notwithstanding that a strong male bias, to say the least, exists in many religious traditions).

Phenomenology: a philosophical method or theory to study the world (phenomena). As used in religious studies, it refers to an attempt to gain an empathetic understanding of a religious worldview and to study objectively the facts (phenomena) as found. Especially because of its foundational thinker, Edmund Husserl, it is often portrayed as an attempt to explore phenomena "neutrally" and without bias, and so has been critiqued in light of the reflexive turn. Nevertheless, it remains a common standpoint, in nuanced ways, in religious studies, and attempts to reform it as a suitable twenty-first century methodology have also been undertaken.

Reflexive turn: associated with a late-twentieth-century philosophical and social movement known as postmodernism, as well as postcolonialism and feminism, it involves questioning (being reflexive) about the way the scholar is not neutral or objective but has inbuilt assumptions from his or her own culture, upbringing, and beliefs. It especially questions the way dominant patterns of knowledge have been historically (and still often are) set in place by elite, white, Western males.

Sui generis: when applied to religion, literally meaning "of its own kind (genus)," it is a belief that religion is a unique category that cannot be reduced to society, the mind, philosophy, or anything else. It is a unique and absolute thing in and of itself. Common up until the late to mid-twentieth century in religious studies, it is now recognized as having problematic theological assumptions and is also open to criticism from historical arguments that show there is no "essence" in all religions (see "essentialism" earlier).

NOTES

1. For a discussion of what he meant by this, see Thomas Williams, "Saint Anselm," *Stanford Encyclopedia of Philosophy* (2007), 2.1, accessed August 6, 2013, http://plato.stanford.edu/entries/anselm/#FaiSeeUndChaPurAnsThePro.

2. The exact relationship between academic theology and confessional theology is far from clear and the distinction varies from place to place and age to age.

3. Marvin Harris, "History and Significance of the Emic/Etic Distinction," *Annual Review of Anthropology* 5 (1976): 329–50.

4. See John Hick, *The Metaphor of God Incarnate* (London: SCM, 1993).

5. Although the reverse may also be true, a new convert may be much better informed at least technically.

6. Paul Williams, *The Unexpected Way: On Converting from Buddhism to Catholicism* (Edinburgh, England: T&T Clark, 2002).

7. David Hufford, "Reflexivity in Belief Studies," in *The Insider/Outsider Problem in the Study of Religion: A Reader,* ed. Russell T. McCutcheon (London and New York: Cassell, 1999), 297–98.

8. Ibid., 309.

9. Gavin Flood, *Beyond Phenomenology: Rethinking the Study of Religion* (London: Cassell, 1999).

10. The term "postmodern" is often used of this; however, this term, while much used in the 1980s through the 2000s, has now become less widely used. This is partly because people have realized that despite some claims that we had reached a new period in intellectual history (the postmodern, which replaced the modern), most are now suspicious of such a notion, and terms such as late modern or hyper modern are used—showing that the reflexive turn (postmodernism) just marks a new awareness within modernity (which is variously dated from either the late sixteenth century as the Medieval period ended or the eighteenth century and the Enlightenment). Indeed, the way we shape our own knowledge was a key claim of one of modernity's, or more accurately the Enlightenment's, greatest thinkers, the philosopher Immanuel Kant (1724–1804).

11. Russell McCutcheon, "Introduction," in *The Insider Outsider Problem in the Study of Religion*, ed. Russell McCutcheon (London and New York: Continuum, 1999), 71.

12. This is discussed further in Volume 1, Chapter 1, but largely goes beyond the interest of these volumes with its focus on contemporary controversies as Freud's theories belong to debates in the early twentieth century and are no longer seen as viable in credible scholarship.

13. Marcel Mauss, Paul Fauconnet, Célestin Bouglé, and Lucien Lévy-Bruhl, and later thinkers, such as Maurice Halbwachs, Talcott Parsons, Alfred Radcliffe-Brown, and Claude Lévi-Strauss, were all strongly influenced by him.

14. Swatos Christiano, Kevin Kivisto, and Peter Willian, Jr., *Sociology of Religion: Contemporary Developments* (New York: Rowman & Littlefield Publishers, 2008), 36.

15. Bruce Lincoln, "Theses on Method," *Method & Theory in the Study of Religion* 8 (1996): 225–27; also cited in *The Insider Outsider Problem in the Study of Religion*, ed. Russell McCutcheon (London and New York: Continuum, 1999), 396.

16. We could classify both Weber and Geertz, who we discuss next, as interpretivist thinkers, who stress the way religion (or culture) helps shape how we interpret the world around us. However, for the sake of simplicity, we will assess them under this broader category.

17. Weber wrote that modern capitalism developed partly as a result of the Protestants' worldly ascetic morale. His main focus was not on developing a theory of religion but on the interaction between society and religion, while introducing concepts that are still widely used in the sociology of religion.

18. For instance, Pierre Daniël Chantepie de la Saussaye, William Brede Kristensen, and Gerardus van der Leeuw.

19. Russell T. McCutcheon, "General Introduction," in *The Insider Outsider Problem in the Study of Religion*, ed. Russell McCutcheon (London and New York: Continuum, 1999), 3

20. *"Ganz andere."*

21. In his work on the history of religion, Eliade is most highly respected for his writings on alchemy, shamanism, yoga, and what he called the eternal return—the implicit belief, supposedly present in religious thought in general, that religious behavior is not only an imitation of, but also a participation in, sacred events, and thus restores the mythical time of origins.

22. Mircea Eliade, *The Sacred and the Profane: The Nature of Religion*, trans. Willard R. Trask (New York: Harcourt, Brace and World, 1957), 202.

23. Douglas Allen, "Eliade and History," *Journal of Religion* 68, no. 4 (1988): 545. See also Douglas Allen, *Structure and Creativity in Religion: Hermeneutics in Mircea Eliade's Phenomenology and New Directions* (The Hague: Mouton Publishers, 1978).

24. Bryan Rennie, *Reconstructing Eliade: Making Sense of Religion* (New York: State University of New York Press, 1996). Rennie argues that this universal humanism makes Eliade a precursor of the "postmodern" rather than himself a typical modern. Explaining this debate takes us beyond the limits of this chapter; however, in brief, Rennie's case is that although modern functionalism looked just at the local, Eliade has gone beyond this to show that humanity has categories that are common to us all and not just particular or definable by local cultures and societies.

25. James Cox, *An Introduction to the Phenomenology of Religion* (London and New York: Continuum, 2010).

26. These include Edward Burnett Tylor, Franz Boas and Marcel Mauss, Bronislaw Malinowski, A. R. Radcliffe-Brown, E. E. Evans-Pritchard, Claude Lévi-Strauss, Mary Douglas, Arnold van Gennep, Victor Turner, and many others.

27. For example, versions of Marxism, structuralism, hermeneutics and phenomenology, and structural functionalism.

28. The continued importance of ethnographic fieldwork is beyond questioning: "What passes for qualitative data in sociology is a weak soup indeed, compared to the thickness of the ethnographic stew—consisting of an elephant of empirical stuff and a rabbit of theory, to use Godfrey Lienhardt's metaphor, but cooked in such a way that the taste of the rabbit comes through in every spoonful." (Thomas Hyllan Eriksen, "The Perilous Identity Politics of Anthropology," keynote lecture, 21st Century Anthropology, University of Oxford, June 28–29, 2007.)

29. He continues, "Is the party over? Anthropologists of my generation were somehow given the distinct impression that early-to mid-20th century anthropology was sparkling with magic. It held a confident belief in its huge intellectual task. . . .Through most of the twentieth century, anthropology took much of its intellectual power from its ability to draw bold comparisons and making surprising contrasts, thereby creating a sense of wonder and strangeness (Verfremdung) in the wider world. . . . It was, after all, the ability to juxtapose the Western life with that of remote, usually small-scale societies that gave anthropology its identity in the wider world, and it contributed in no small degree to the intellectual confidence of its practitioners" (ibid.).

30. Ibid.

31. Rosalind I. J. Hackett, "Anthropology of Religion," in *The Routledge Companion to the Study of Religion*, ed. John R. Hinnells (London and New York: Routledge, 2005), 157.

32. Linda Woodhead, "Gender Differences in Religious Practice and Significance" (n.d.), 2–3, accessed August 6, 2013, eprints.lancs.ac.uk/id/document/4385.

33. The term "ecofeminism" is often used here; see Woodhead, "Gender Differences."

34. While Protestant departments tend to be Lutheran dominated, certainly in Germany, they allow staff from any Protestant denomination, which they understand as including Anglicans.

35. Nevertheless, Farquhar also wrote some excellent books, and his *Modern Religious Movements in India* (1915) remains an important sourcebook and study of Hindu reform movements of the late nineteenth and early twentieth centuries.

36. Gavin Flood, *The Ascetic Self: Subjectivity, Memory and Tradition* (Cambridge, England: Cambridge University Press, 2004).

37. Religious studies can mean very generally the all-embracing study of religion that includes theological and confessional teaching, or it can be more narrowly defined as excluding a god-centered or confessional approach (theology). Theology in the latter sense is an alternative path that centers on the cumulative historical tradition preserved within a single historical tradition, whereas religious studies takes a global view of humans and engages with their practices and beliefs. The confessional approach, whether exclusivist, inclusivist, radically pluralist, or particularistic, studies religions from a faith perspective and generally assumes the truth or value of one religious tradition. Religious studies in contrast is predominantly the study of religion as culture.

38. In fact, the situation is more complex than this because in the United Kingdom and the United States, departments often combine theology and religious studies, and modules from both count toward degrees and awards. The relationship of theology and religious studies is also undergoing change. "Theology" today still tends to mean Christian theology, although this is changing gradually. There is also a relatively new discipline, comparative theology, whose trailblazers are theologians such as Francis X. Clooney and James Fredericks. In the late 1980s, they proposed that comparative theology should entail the interpretation of the meaning and truth of one's own faith by means of a critical investigation of other faiths. Generally, comparative theology is a confessional enterprise, unlike the nonconfessional enterprise that is part of the general academic study of religion, but it does proceed dialectically and interreligiously. Comparative theology is to be distinguished from theology of religions. It asks what Christians should think about the other religions of the world: Hinduism, Buddhism, Judaism, Islam, Zoroastrianism, Jainism, Daoism, Sikhism, and Shinto.

39. Jonathan Z. Smith, *Imagining Religion: From Babylon to Jonestown* (Chicago: Chicago University Press, 1982), xi.

40. Timothy Fitzgerald, *The Ideology of Religious Studies* (Oxford and New York: Oxford University Press, 2000).

41. Russell T. McCutcheon, *Manufacturing Religion: The Discourse on Sui Generis Religion and the Politics of Nostalgia* (New York: Oxford University Press, 1997).

42. Ibid., 18–19, 107, 127ff.

43. Lincoln, "Theses on Method," 398.

44. Flood, *Beyond Phenomenology*.

45. Oddbjorn Leirvik, "Interreligious Studies: A Relational Approach to the Study of Religion," *Journal of Interreligious Studies* 13 (2014), accessed March 30, 2014, http://irdialogue.org/journal/interreligious-studies-a-relational-approach-to-the-study-of-religion-by-oddbjorn-leirvik/.

46. Paul Hedges, "Interreligious Studies," in *Encyclopedia of Sciences and Religions*, ed. Anne Runehov and Lluis Oviedo (New York: Springer, 2013), 1176–1177.

47. Oddbjorn Leirvik, *Interreligious Studies: A Relational Approach to the Study of Religion* (London: Bloomsbury Academic, 2014).

48. Lincoln, "Theses on Method," 395.

FURTHER READINGS

Chryssides, George, and Geaves, Ron. *The Study of Religion: An Introduction to the Key Ideas and Methods.* London and New York: Continuum, 2007.

Cox, James. *An Introduction to the Phenomenology of Religion.* London and New York:
    Continuum, 2010.

Fitzgerald, Timothy. *The Ideology of Religious Studies.* Oxford, England: Oxford
    University Press, 2000.

Flood, Gavin. *Beyond Phenomenology: Rethinking the Study of Religion.* London and New
    York: Cassell, 1999.

Hinnells, John, ed. *The Routledge Companion to the Study of Religion.* 2nd ed. London
    and New York: Routledge, 2009.

Martin, Craig. *A Critical Introduction to the Study of Religion.* Sheffield, England:
    Equinox, 2012.

McCutcheon, Russell T., ed. *The Insider Outsider Problem in the Study of Religion.*
    London and New York: Continuum, 1999.

Nye, Malory. *Religion: The Basics.* 2nd ed. London and New York: Routledge, 2008.

Partridge, Christopher, ed. *Introduction to World Religions.* 2nd ed. Minneapolis, MN:
    Fortress Press, 2013.

Rodrigues, Hillary, and Harding, John. *Introduction to the Study of Religion.* London and
    New York: Routledge, 2009.

Woodhead, Linda. "Gender Differences in Religious Practice and Significance." Accessed
    August 6, 2013, eprints.lancs.ac.uk/id/document/4385.

3

Charisma, Scriptures, Revelation, and Reason: Sources of Religious Authority

Paul Hedges and Christina Welch

INTRODUCTION

For many Western Christians, in Europe, America, or Australia, for instance, the answer to religious authority may seem very simple: you look in the book. The *Bible* is often assumed, particularly for Protestant Christians, to be the mainstay and inspiration for everything they do and believe. However, things are never really this simple. Why, for instance, if this is so, are there many different churches, and why do different Christians, even in the same church, believe different things? There are numerous reasons for this; for one thing, of course, the *Bible* is not just one book but many books written over thousands of years by multiple authors and then translated by multiple scholars. Therefore, it does not just have one simple, easy-to-understand message giving an answer to every question, and that is why, when faced with a problem, Christians will often go to their priest or pastor to interpret it. Here we come to the big issue that we do not simply read the book, we interpret it, and so the authority of the book actually comes from human ideas, reason, prejudices, and traditions. And this is only the tip of the iceberg. For most of the world's Christians, the *Bible* is not simply the only source of authority; for Roman Catholics and Orthodox believers, the tradition of the church is at least as important as the text itself—we only have the text because it has been passed down to us through a community, and that community also tells us how we should correctly interpret it because, ideally understood, it represents an oral tradition—word-of-mouth teachings—passed from the time of Jesus and his disciples to the present day and supplemented by inspiration from the Holy Spirit and the community itself. So far, of course, we have only talked about Christians, and only some Christians, and only some issues faced by some Christians. When we think about how important religious authority is—what do we believe or do, why do we believe it or do it—it is clear that controversies will naturally abound, especially as authority is linked to issues of power and control.

Here, we will look across the globe at a range of religious traditions, at a variety of things that form the sources of religious authority, and the disputes and debates that surround this. We will start by examining some key concepts associated with authority in religion in both historical and contemporary contexts before moving on to look at some specific examples and debates in more detail in relation to a range of contemporary contexts focusing on what are termed New Religious Movements (or New Religions) and Indigenous Religions (or Lifeways).

KEY TERMS

We will begin by looking at some key terms that scholars and members of religious traditions use to talk about sources of authority in different traditions. These terms will include scripture, reason, tradition, experience, charisma, gender, interpretation (hermeneutics), and revelation. Finally, we will mention the authority of the individual.

Many religions have specific books that they look to as the source of their authority, and in general terms these books are referred to as scripture. Christians have the *Old* and *New Testaments*, which make up their *Bible* (although notably different Christian traditions have different sets of books in each of these!); Judaism has the *Hebrew Bible* (the Christian *Old Testament*) as well as the *Talmud*; Islam has the *Quran* and sayings of Muhammad (*hadith*); Hinduism has the *Vedas*; and so on. However, as we mentioned in the introduction, although in various ways devotees within each tradition will go to these books as sources of authority, it is never (or rarely) simply enough to look at the book as a simple answer as to where the authority comes from; even if a book claims to have a special meaning, it takes a community of people to treat it as such for it to have authority, and it also depends on how it is read. In other words, a sacred text is only a sacred text because people treat it as such, and how that works in practice depends on how it is used, interpreted, and employed. For instance, different parts of the texts are given different value or interpreted in different ways. For instance, when Christians come to read the *New Testament* texts, they will find the following two passages: "Men of Israel, hear these words: Jesus of Nazareth, a man attested to you by God with mighty works and wonders and signs which God did through him in your midst, as you yourselves know" (*Acts* 2: 22[1]) and "Jesus answered them, 'My Father is working still, and I am working.' This was why the Jews sought all the more to kill him, because he not only broke the Sabbath but also called God his own Father, making himself equal with God" (*John* 5: 17–18). Now, most Christians will give priority to the second quote; that is to say that, following what became orthodox Christian belief that Jesus was God, they will fully accept the idea that Jesus made himself equal to God and so ignore the literal meaning of the first quote that Jesus was simply a human being through whom God worked. This first passage will be interpreted to mean that here it is only Jesus in his human form and not in what is believed to be his divine nature that is being talked about. In this sense, we may say that the meaning of one passage has more "authority" than the meaning of another. Now, we could ask all sorts of questions about this. For instance, historians are quite clear that most of *John's Gospel* include words that do not go back to Jesus himself but is instead the ideas of the early church put into Jesus's mouth (we should not interpret this as being lying or deceitful—this is a matter we will come to shortly), and so the clear consensus of almost every single reputable biblical scholar or historian is that Jesus never claimed to be divine.[2] Indeed, the passage from the *Acts of the Apostles*, which we quoted first, is quite possibly a much earlier recording of teachings about Jesus from the earliest layers of tradition before the developments that see the movement coming to view Jesus as divine. This may seem a shocking idea to many, but scholars know that such a belief was widespread among the earliest followers of Jesus (indeed, if *John's Gospel* is not included, it is very hard to find any *New Testament* text, read in the Jewish context from which Jesus and his earliest followers came, which implies that Jesus was divine) and lasted for centuries. Moreover, Christians who have sought to read the biblical text have for several hundred years come to the same conclusion—it is not simply the way modern historians have come to interpret it to attack Christian faith![3] The interpretation of Jesus is not, though, our main concern here; what is important is the way that authority texts are interpreted based on various factors—they do not stand alone as providers of doctrines and beliefs even when religious devotees say this is how they use them. Therefore, things such as interpretation, the use of reason, and tradition come into play.

Various other aspects of talking about scripture are also important. One is what "scripture" really means. The meaning and use of scripture very clearly changes between traditions. In Islam, for instance, the *Quran* is understood to be the word of God in a very real sense. Muslims came to understand that the *Quran* existed eternally with God and that in its Arabic form it could not be translated because every sound was part of the divine revelation it contained (we will come back to this word "revelation" shortly). For a Confucian, however, the scriptures he or she uses are texts written by ancient sages and kings but then edited by Confucius into their current form. Therefore, there is no complete and final form, and human activity is seen as part of their creation. Christian views vary, with some Christians insisting that the *Bible* is revelation, or God's word sent to humanity, whereas others suggest that revelation is the person of Jesus and that the *Bible* is simply a human record of God's dealing with humanity. Indeed, although the former view is very strongly advocated by many Protestants, it can be said, within the theology of the Christian tradition, to be a form of false belief, and therefore to be a heretical interpretation because a book is placed in the position that only Jesus should hold. Meanwhile, in Hinduism, although it is often asserted that the *Vedas* are their main scriptures, they are far less central to the lives of most Hindus than many other texts. Like the *Quran*, they are written in a sacred language (in this case Sanskrit) and are generally said to lose their meaning or power in translation. However, for most Hindus, they are inaccessible because of this, and various other texts or stories that speak about the specific gods they revere will be more important. Indeed, the two most important texts are the *Ramayana* and the *Mahabharata*, epic poems that tell the stories of heroes and gods, most significantly Rama in the former and Krishna in the latter—both of whom who do not appear in the *Vedas*. It is debated as to whether these great epic poems should be called scripture, but they are certainly treated as such by most Hindus![4] We can therefore see that "scripture" cannot have one single meaning across different religious traditions but is used to refer to texts that are of some divine or special significance. In this regard we should note that it is also not clear that we should refer to the Confucian texts as scripture—they are the central texts of that tradition but do not have a divine mandate as such, yet they do instruct people how to follow what is termed the Way of Heaven. In each tradition, we need to seek to understand how the texts are used.

On the question of scriptures, one final point remains, which is that those who are often termed *fundamentalists* are people who take their scriptures literally—but what does this mean? As we saw in our example about Jesus's divinity in the *Bible*, only one passage was—indeed could be—taken literally without contradiction. Also, almost all scriptures contain poetry and other elements. To take another Christian example, also from *John's Gospel*, Jesus speaks about being the true vine, and God as the vinedresser, and his followers as branches (Chapter 15). Obviously no one takes this literally: Jesus and Christians are not understood as products of viticulture! Again, in a Hindu example, even Hindus who claim to take their scriptures literally will admit that allegory, poetry, and imagery should not be. A notorious example, partly because Christian missionaries used it to attack the morality of the tradition, is the example of the god Krishna who appears as a handsome young man and through the beauty of his flute playing entices the young cow girls from their husbands to come and play with him. Some of the imagery of the texts can be quite sexually charged; however, Hindus have always insisted that what we read is not to be taken literally: the cow girls represent human souls, the husbands are their entrapment with worldly pleasures, and Krishna and his flute is the call of the divine to bring people to loving devotion of that divine. Therefore, the texts are not understood as examples of human morality; rather it is language to help us understand the power and love of god in calling humans into relationship.[5]

We have mentioned revelation earlier, and again this is a term used in various ways. In its general sense, it speaks of a message of the divine to the human, and obviously this, in many ways, can be taken as the ultimate claim to power. Therefore, almost every religious tradition will make some claim of this type. As mentioned earlier, for Muslims the *Quran* is seen to fulfill this role as a text that is literally God's word to humans, whereas for Christians Jesus as both God and human is seen to be the greatest expression of revelation. Hinduism has various forms of revelation in these terms: the *Veda*s are taken to be, like the *Quran*, a direct transmission of the divine word to humans, whereas figures such as Krishna, like Jesus, are held to be a manifestation of God in human form. More recent religions likewise often claim revelation. A recent religious grouping, the Brahma Kumaris, see their founder as having had revelations from God in the form of visions, which revealed a new message that should be spread.[6] However, from a scholarly perspective it is necessary to ask what role is played by claims to revelation. Obviously, at one level, it is the assertion of an absolute, or new, teaching. So, for instance, the Brahma Kumaris grow out of Hinduism; however, to make their particular claims for reinterpreting the tradition the claim to revelation is central. Islam is also interesting because one claim is that it is not a new religion at all, but rather the original religion! In Islamic thought, God has always been revealing himself (indeed, the term revelation comes from a term that means "to reveal" or "make known" but that as time has passed people have lost, forgotten, or distorted the message. Therefore, Muslims claim that the teachings Muhammad proclaimed was the same message taught by Adam, Abraham, Moses, Jesus, and many other prophets across all nations (this is discussed further in Volume 1, Chapter 8). Muhammad's revelation, however, is known as the final revelation because Muslims believe that this one alone has not been, and will not be, corrupted, and that all aspects of the teaching are revealed to humanity. The Islamic claim to revelation is therefore not a unique claim against other religions but places Islam in continuation with other religions while making a special claim for its own supremacy.

Having talked about scripture and revelation, we should also note that although these are central aspects of almost every single major religious tradition, there are many traditions that do not claim to have either. Buddhism, for instance, at least in the Theravada tradition, understands its tradition to be founded on a realization of the historical Buddha himself, not a revelation from a God. Meanwhile, scripture, obviously, only plays a part in cultures that are literate, and not all literate cultures see their texts as scriptural. We have already mentioned Confucianism as an example. Another interesting case would be the ancient Greeks and Romans, who had written stories about their gods, but the texts had no special meaning; therefore, we can say they had no scripture. Certainly, many traditions would see other things as more important. Again, looking at Buddhism, although it was born into a culture that was highly literate, it prized the spoken (oral) tradition above writing and was very suspicious of putting ideas down in some written form as it would be meaningless without the oral teachings and the experience that went along with it. Later, however, the scriptures it developed would become very important but would never attain the significance scriptures generally have within Islam or Christianity. Indeed, the Zen tradition of Buddhism is famous for the notion that it is a tradition outside of scripture, a phrase attributed to the semi-legendary founder Bodhidharma, because it always emphasizes that truth is essentially an experience, not something encountered through reading or thinking. Likewise the Daoist tradition in China, despite having one of the largest scriptures of any tradition, has always emphasized experience and direct teaching of master to disciple as important, and many of its texts are often felt to be meaningless without this. We encounter here two other aspects we have mentioned earlier, tradition and experience, which we will discuss next.

Tradition is a word that is often called upon in a religious context and that can strongly polarize opinion. For critics of religion, because it relies on tradition, religion is often seen as old-fashioned, behind the times, or incapable of change (we see these kind of criticisms made by many of the so-called New Atheists, such as Richard Dawkins and Christopher Hitchens, who are discussed in Volume 2, Chapter 5). On the contrary, religious people may defend their religion precisely because of tradition as it is seen to provide a secure and well-tested system and is not simply wavering with every new idea or concept. However, tradition is also contested within religions. The development of Protestantism within Christianity was essentially a rejection of tradition because it was believed that various false ideas and corruptions had crept in; instead Protestants sought to go back to the origins of Christianity, especially scripture. Indeed, many debates in this period, and still today between rival Christian factions, are based on the weight and importance given to scripture and tradition as rival or complementary sources of authority.[7] Similar debates occur within other religions, and also between religions.

Experience, likewise, is highly contested and also very controversial. By experience we are referring here to what may be termed "religious experiences," or a direct encounter with the divine or reality in some way. Clearly, for any religious institution this can be dangerous because if religious experiences are available, then anyone can rise up and claim a new revelation or teaching. Indeed, as we have discussed with the Brahma Kumaris earlier, it is the claim of new visions that forms the basis for its challenge to various traditional aspects of Hinduism and is one reason why it is now generally seen as a separate religious tradition. Therefore, in many religions, experiences are controlled or denied in various ways. In Roman Catholicism, for instance, the church takes upon itself the role, either at a local level through priests and spiritual directors or higher up within the Vatican, of deciding whether experiences are legitimate. When the daughter of a poor miller in nineteenth-century France started to have visions of the Virgin Mary, her claims were at first treated with suspicion by the local priest; however, gradually through a belief in miracles, the church came to accept that the visions had taken place, and the young girl was made into a saint. We refer, of course, to the famous St. Bernadette and her visions at what is now the famous pilgrimage site of Lourdes. Likewise in Hinduism, many people, especially spiritual aspirants, will have a spiritual guide, or guru, who will help train and explain their experiences to them. Of course, to some degree all religion has experience at its heart: the Buddha's experience lies at the heart of Buddhism; Jesus's sense of being called by God and his disciples' experience of his resurrection for Christianity; Muhammad's visions that became written down as the *Quran* for Islam; and so on.

Our earlier discussion leads us naturally to the next term, charisma. The term has a particular origin in Christian usage as a spiritual gift and is described in Paul's letters (see, especially, *1 Corinthians* 12); however, it has a particular usage in the study of religion to refer, as in general usage, to the special character or magnetism of people, and it was used in this way by the sociologist Max Weber. According to Weber, the individual who exercised some special form of holiness, heroism, or character had, because of this, a specific authority or power. The term is often used to speak of the founders or leaders of new traditions to explain their appeal. Of course, it is very hard to pin down what exactly charisma might be or how it manifests and operates, and the exact cultural context that makes someone charismatic in a specific setting is important—most religious leaders have episodes in their lives and careers when they attract some followers and/or supporters but are virulently opposed by others (charisma is not universal!). Despite its somewhat imprecise meaning, it is a useful term to describe movements where a particular figure appears as the primary source of attraction, either by personality, teaching, or reputation. Obviously, Jesus and Buddha are two historical examples of leaders who inspired by charisma and whose movements grew out of this. However, Weber also suggested that charisma could be held by virtue of a specific role or else could be inherited. Many religions obviously continue after the founder, and the charismatic leader is either a successor in a role or a hereditary heir.

Reason has a complicated role in relation to religious authority. Today, as in the example of the New Atheists we mentioned earlier, there are those who would argue that reason and rational thought lead one against religion; the suggestion is that because religion relies on things such as tradition or experience the role of reason is reduced or minimal in religion and belief. However, this is far from clear, so let us look as some instances and examples. In almost every culture throughout human history, the primary educated and literate group have been religious professionals, and very often education has been entrusted to them. For this reason, much development in science, mathematics, architecture, and almost every other sphere has a deep connection to religious traditions. Indeed, the phenomenal developments in science in the Western world over the last few hundred years came from deeply religious roots: the foundations of science in the ancient Greeks were preserved and developed by the Islamic civilization of the Middle East, which developed algebra, optics, and many other fields, and this was passed to Europe around the period we call the Renaissance (roughly the fifteenth through sixteenth century in Western Europe). Here, Christian scientists believed that because God had created the world it was essentially rational and ordered started to refine the scientific method, and figures (all Christians, but many famous scientists were also Jewish or of other religious backgrounds) such as Francis Bacon (1561–1626), Rene Descartes (1596–1650), Isaac Newton (1643–1727), Tycho Brahe (1546–1601), developed what became modern science. Now the specific debate about science and religion is not our concern (see Volume 2, Chapter 2), but this just helps show that reason and religion are not natural enemies. Indeed, the person often seen as the greatest Christian philosopher of the Middle Ages, Thomas Aquinas (1225–1274), argued that reason brought you to God, not away from him. Notably, the development of philosophy has often been part and parcel of religion; whether in Christianity, Buddhism, Islam, or other religions, there have been traditions that developed rational systems to describe and explain faith, to argue their particular interpretation, and so on. Indeed, the world's oldest university, Nalanda in India, was a Buddhist institution, while the great universities of Europe such as Oxford, Cambridge, and Paris all had Christian religious faith and teaching as their foundation. In general, then, we may say that religions, especially the major global traditions, have used reason to seek to explain their worldview and concepts. However, since at least the eighteenth century in Europe, the relationship between reason and religion has become more strained. This is not the place to discuss the history of this development, but in various ways many religions in the contemporary world, to some degree at least, accept that reason, while potentially a friend, is also an enemy and stress tradition and experience over and against it. We should note, though, that while there have often been cases where tension has occurred (parts of early Christianity show this tension), it is generally speaking an exception to see them in conflict, although many traditions will always stress that reason on its own is not

enough—the Zen Buddhist example we discussed earlier is indicative—and that study or knowledge even of the scriptures is not the actual religious experience that is sought and will not get you there.

Gender may seem like an odd point to bring up: does authority arise from being male or female? The answer, though (and this will come as no surprise to anyone who has studied feminism), is that it is significant, and deeply so. Although we should always beware of generalization, in almost every religious tradition throughout recorded human history the main figures of authority have been men: they wrote the scriptures, they interpreted the scriptures, they defined reason, they decided which experiences counted and which did not, and they shaped the traditions. Therefore, for most people throughout history gender has been, arguably, the primary factor in deciding where authority lies. Of course, many religions argue that gender is not important to being "saved" (however that is interpreted) or to having a relationship to God, reality, or the divine (again, diversely understood). Nevertheless, the words and traditions that have shaped the religions have typically been male ones. There are, of course, notable exceptions: it is almost certain that the earliest Christians had female priests and leaders; various Daoist lineages have had female leadership, and it is even suggested women may have advantages in spiritual development; women have had roles as visionaries, shamans, and prophets in various traditions. Nevertheless, the mainstream has gone against this: most Christian traditions historically and today do not allow female priests or bishops; in Buddhism monks had a higher status than nuns; Islam has reserved the status of religious-legal experts to men; and we could continue.[8] For feminist scholars, unraveling the way that patriarchal, or male-dominated, societies have fed into and oppressed women is seen as an important part of analyzing these traditions (for more discussion on these issues generally, see Volume 2, Chapter 1). In terms of authority, it is important to note that gender has been central.

HISTORICAL BACKGROUND

For the remainder of the chapter, we will explore some contemporary forms of religion; before discussing them, however, it will be useful to discuss some background of these traditions and terms associated with them.

"New" in the designation New Religions is a somewhat contentious term as many of these so-called New Religions are not recent in terms of their establishment, and indeed often draw on ancient religious texts. However, it must be noted that even "recent" is a contentious term, as some scholars suggest a religion being established or brought to the West after 1945 makes it "new", while others suggest 100 to 150 years makes a religion recent in terms of scholarly study.[9] Clearly adherents to these so-called New Religions do not necessarily agree with the scholars' definitions. Examples of New Religions that draw on ancient text include the Jehovah's Witnesses, which was established in 1879 and takes the *Bible* as a central text. It may be "recent" in that it was founded less than 150 years ago, but it sees itself as re-traditionalizing Christianity. Soka Gakkai International (SGI), which is based on Nichiren Buddhism, whose founder was born in 1222, is another New Religion. Founded in 1930 by Tsunesaburo Makiguchi in Japan, chanting the title phrase from the *Lotus Sutra* (*nam-myoho-renge-kyoi*) and studying the writings of Nichiren mean that, for many of its followers, terming SGI as a New Religion is problematic. Other more recent religions utilizing ancient texts include the Nation of Islam, founded by Wallace Dodd Ford in the United States in 1930, which draws on the *Quran*, and the International Society for Krishna Consciousness (ISKCON), which was brought to the West in 1965 by His Divine Grace A. C. Bhaktivedanta Swami Prabhupada. ISKCON is based on the teachings of Sri Caitanya Mahaprabu (c. 1486–1533) and is firmly rooted in Hinduism.

There are, however, more recent New Religious Movements such as Raelianism, which was founded in 1974 by French racing car driver Claude Vorihon after alien encounters; Scientology, which was inaugurated in 1954 by Lafayette Ron Hubbard; and modern or new/neo-Paganism, which can largely be traced back to the writings of Gerald Gardiner in the 1950s. Just from these few examples, it is clear that the term New Religions covers a wide gamut of faiths and spiritualities, as well as covering both traditions less than 100 years old and those dating back to the thirteenth century or before.

Although all the religions noted earlier have been established or popularized by men, it should be noted that there are a number founded by women, notably Christian Science, established by Mary Eddy Baker who wrote the central text *Science and Health* in 1875, which boasts churches in more than 70 countries worldwide. This is important to emphasize that one way of exploring religions is through looking at their founders and/or leaders and followers in terms of gender; Elizabeth Puttick's book *Women in New Religions*[10] includes a chapter on female spiritual leadership and a section on female leaders in male-originated religions, and it is useful as a starting point to examine this topic further. Largely, though, religions (new and traditional) have been established by men, and this does often have an impact on issues of authority, as we shall explore shortly.

DEBATES AND ARGUMENTS

Controversies

Although most New Religions are no more controversial than more mainstream traditions, there are some that have proved highly controversial. Often new and alternative religions are associated with authoritarianism and totalitarianism, especially in regard to issues around religious conversion and coercion. Anthony and Robbins examine these issues, particularly around brainwashing, which, as they note, has received a "disproportionate amount of . . . research and related theorizing."[11] However, they argue that even devotees of "highly authoritarian and somewhat manipulative movements which aspire to discipline and control over their adherents . . . [are not] helpless, brainwashed 'cult victims.'" Indeed, they argue "there appears to be little evidence that people are confined in . . . [new religious] groups against their will."[12] Asserting that brainwashing is a popular cultural myth,[13] they do, though, "tentatively suggest" nine characteristics that appear to be shared by a number of New Religions, such as separatism, deference to strong leaders, a concern with proselytization and consequentialism, and the use of doctrinal correctness to ensure appropriate behavior.[14]

While the main thrust of Anthony and Robbins's argument is correct, there are a small number of religions where, although members are not brainwashed, the encouragement to remain within the group does impact their ability to exercise free will. To explore this in more detail, the two so-called suicide cults of Heaven's Gate and The Peoples Temple will be examined in further detail later in this chapter.

There are other so-called New Religions where issues of authority lie more in a rejection of a hierarchical structure, or even a rejection of any form of authority beyond the self. The Pagan umbrella of religious/spiritual traditions and the New Age movement fall into this category. On the whole, as Chryssides notes, the New Age characteristically rejects "institutional religion . . . [that claims to have] found the absolute final truth."[15] Often with a tendency for spiritual bricolage, the mixing and matching of aspects of several established religious traditions, New Agers see themselves as their own figure of authority in forming their spiritual path, and whether outsiders see this as "a harmonious medley of world religious ecumenism, or . . . a hotchpotch of inconsistencies" typically matters very little to them.[16] In terms of contemporary Paganism, again many Pagans tend to see themselves as the final authority figure and like New Agers tend to reject canons of scripture, although as Harvey notes, "there are books which are important to Pagans."[17] Similarly, while there are priests and priestesses in some Pagan traditions, these are people recognized by their peers as capable of leading ceremonies appropriately; there is no innate authority in what they do as typically Pagans tend to be skeptical, "even cynical about leaders."[18]

As regards Indigenous Religions (and it is important to consider these in any work exploring religions in a global context, although they are not common in university curricula, for not only are they significant for those living them but exploring them academically adds many dimensions to the study of religion), authority is determined contextually, depending on the peoples and their lifeways. To class Indigenous Religions as religions *per se* would not be entirely accurate for typically they are more of a way of life than something that can be separated into specific areas to study as is common in the comparative study of religion; Smart's dimensions being one such approach. However, the same can be said of observant Judaism or Islam, for example, and as such the scholar of religion does need to be careful with terminology. Thus, it may be more accurate to term these as Indigenous Lifeways, for rarely do they have texts or charismatic founders. Often tradition is oral (and this has remained the case even into modernity)—transmitted through stories, art, dance, and music—and important information is held by significant individuals able to communicate with authoritative other-than-human persons.[19] Further, knowledge is often transmitted in an apprentice mode; knowledge is being passed on, or gifted, according to the recipient's needs, abilities, gender, and age. In reality, this is often little different from what is found in many "world religions," but the anthropological study of religions differs from a theological approach, and the latter tends to dominate the discipline. What is different, though, is that the knowledge may come from an other-than-human person through dreams and visions, as well as through a medicine man or woman/shaman who, like a priest, rabbi, or imam, is a teacher with specialized knowledge of spiritual matters who is held as a figure of authority within his or her own community.

Debates

When it comes sources of authority, as the title suggests, there are a number of issues to explore as authority does not lie in one place only; indeed as previously mentioned, authority can lie in text, in traditions, and/or in a charismatic person. Further, it must be noted that authority in whatever form is not necessarily adhered to, for religion is often more about correct practice than correct belief, and lives are complex, played out in a variety of sociocultural and historical contexts. Authority too, in whatever form, is often multilayered and rarely static. What follows are a few examples that highlight the complexity of sources of authority in regard to the study of religion.

In exploring New and Alternative Religions that have an authoritative text, the Church of Jesus Christ of Latter-Day Saints (LDS) can provide a useful example. Founded by Joseph Smith (1805–1844), for members of the LDS church (commonly known as Mormons), authority lies in text. The *King James Bible* (KJB) is considered authoritative but works alongside several texts by Smith to ensure correct Mormon living. The KJB was revised and amended by Smith, and his version is generally used to ensure correct interpretation of the *Bible*; the Mormon version is called the *Inspired Version* (IV) or *Joseph Smith Version* (JSV). Alongside the *KJB* or Smith's revised version are three other texts written by Smith, *The Book of Mormon*, *Doctrine and Covenants*, and *The Pearl of Great Price*; these contain a creation story, a set of doctrinal revelations, and the articles of faith. Further to these texts are the church presidencies. The First Presidency is made up of a senior president assisted by two counselors (although Brigham Young, the leader of the church after Smith, had eight); next comes the Council or Quorum of the Twelve, and the president of this group is recognized as second in charge to the president; all are men in the Melchizedek priesthood,[20] and all are termed apostles. The overall president is considered a prophet and seer able to receive and interpret divine revelation (see D&C 28: 2, 6–7); he also clarifies existing doctrine. However, any new revelation must be accepted by the Council of the Twelve. Thus, the texts remain authoritative, but there is some room for amendments and additions.

With the leadership of the LDS church and thus the authority of the church firmly in the hands of men, the issue of feminism within the church is an interesting topic. This is especially so because men are also the authority figures within the family to the extent that a boy over the age of 12 has authority over any woman regardless of her age; in effect, "gender is theologically important."[21]

A study by Lori G. Beaman[22] has explored Mormon women's diverse responses to LDS authority. She found that some women are content with their role as homemakers. Often termed Molly Mormons by those within the church, these women are the archetypal good Mormon mother. They are happy with their role as a mother and understand motherhood as equivalent to male priesthood at least in terms of responsibilities to the church. Indeed, it could be argued that there are some analogies between the priesthood and motherhood in the church via teaching and support; however, there is an issue in that biologically not all women can be mothers, but religiously all men can be priests, and the LDS emphasis on spiritual fulfillment through motherhood can be problematic for the single Mormon woman. However, for LDS mothers, the pressure to be a Molly Mormon can be overwhelming, and some women find that while they can celebrate their Mormon tradition and heritage, the limitations imposed on them in regard to religious participation even as a mother can leave them feeling resentful of church authority.[23]

But Mormon feminists do exist and have done so from the church's earliest days. In 1843, Smith announced the doctrine of polygamy (a policy brought to an end in 1887 by the Edmunds-Tucker Act that prohibited multiple wives in the United States). Smith's wife, Emma Hale Smith, is believed to have been firmly opposed to plural marriage despite accepting her husband as a prophet.[24] Notably, when she, with her eldest son as first president, formed the Reorganized Church of Jesus Christ of Latter-Day Saints (RCLDS) in 1860, after the death of her husband in 1844, polygamy was not part of doctrine. Although accepting the same overall church structure and sacred texts, the RCLDS (now the Community of Christ) has continued to interpret doctrine in a more female-friendly manner, and since 1984, both men and women are able to be ordained as members of the priesthood.

As we can see, women in the LDS church have not always happily accepted total male authority (both in the church and in the home), and from examples in the Beaman article, we can find a number of coping mechanisms, including exercising "agency in their interpretation of church doctrine"[25] via reading church doctrine through a particular lens, typically one where feminist issues such as equality in all matters is marginalized in favor of an "equal, but different in the eyes of the church and God" reading. However, in one of the studies participants felt that LDS patriarchy was cruel and demeaning[26] and that no interpretive reading could be sufficient to provide women with equal status.

In terms of the status of women and figures of authority, a brief mention of the Osho movement is necessary. Chandra Mohan Jain (1931–1990), later known as Bhagwan Shree Rajneesh and then Osho, established his first ashram in 1974 in Poona, India, after several years of teaching. With a controversial understanding of renunciation based not on the material but on one's past and cultural conditioning, and with a pro-sex stance, he rapidly gained an international audience. In 1981, he moved with most of his disciples to Oregon, United States, where this ranch, Rajneeshpuram, became infamous—largely for his fleet of 93 Rolls Royce cars while disciples worked 12-hour days and lived in primitive conditions.[27] Many of these disciples or renouncers (*sannyasin*) were women.

Osho's understandings of women and discipleship have received a good deal of academic attention, notably by Elizabeth Puttick. Puttick notes that, according to some texts at least, the Hinduism concept of renouncer is only for men in their final stage of life; Osho altered this concept to be available to anyone at any stage of life, provided they wore orange robes, wore around their neck a mala with a locket containing a picture of Osho, changed their name, and did at least one daily meditation.[28] Women, Osho believed, made better disciples due to their feminine qualities of devotion, love, receptiveness, warmth, intuition, and nurturing nature. These he suggested could be developed in men; although he did feel that women could be like men at times in terms of aggression. Osho grounded his perception of women as ideal devotees on a connection between women, holism, and embodiment, with his method of achieving enlightenment drawing on body-based techniques, particularly sexual techniques such as tantra; Osho was often known as a sex guru.[29] Women in the movement were encouraged to practice a free-love ethic, with marriage and children discouraged, and while some female devotees found the movement spiritually liberating with Osho functioning as a father figure,[30] others found the movement abusive.[31]

In terms of authority and the potential abuse of power, it is not only women who can be understood to be as a focus of critical attention, for as Palmer and Hardman[32] note, children too can be subject to a range of experiences in New Religions. In their edited book *Children in New Religions*, they detail a range of explorations into the issues surrounding children born into, and brought up in, New Religions, but there are a number of biographies that sit alongside this work to give a firsthand insight—although of course these need to be understood as having a certain, often negative, bias. In *My Life in Orange* (2004), Tim Guest details his life in various Rajneesh/Osho communes after his mother converted when he was six years old. As a young child, his figures of authority extend beyond his mother's guru to his mother, and thus any understanding here needs to examine the sociology of New Religions and living outside mainstream society in general.[33] Largely brought up by carers who were often unable to really care properly for young children, Guest highlights in his book the many issues related to a nonnormative childhood, from an education without official qualifications on one side to a childhood with immense freedoms on the other. Children never really get the opportunity to choose their upbringing, but when it sits well outside what is deemed normative in any society, issues of authority and abuses of power can be pronounced; children brought up in movements such as the Children of God and the Branch Davidians[34] stand as examples here with allegations of child sexual abuse in both cases at various times in the history of the two groups.

A Christian-based New Religion that emphasizes authority in text is Christian Science. As with the LDS church, the *Bible* is a central text, but again the writings of the founder ensure Christian Scientists live correctly. However, what is notable is that the central text, *Science and Health with Key to the Scriptures*, almost acts as the mouthpiece of the founder, Mary Eddy Baker (1821–1910); indeed, it, along with the *Bible*, is understood as the church's pastor. Healed, miraculously as she understood it, by reading the biblical accounts of Jesus's ministry and healing, and without recourse to medical intervention, Baker asserted that the *Bible* was her "only authority [and] only textbook" and that it contained "the recipe for all healing" and was "the chart of life" (*S&H*: 126, 110, 406, 24). Therefore, the *Bible* and her key to it act as the primary forms of authority for Christian Scientists. Further, *Science and Health* does not just keep her memory alive, but her written words effectively ensure that she remains physically present within her church. Given that a central tenet of Christian Science is that death is an illusion, this is perhaps unsurprising.

There are of course issues that arise from these two texts being ultimately authoritative. Those in the church who hold fast to the teachings have, like Baker, sought healing without recourse to medical science, and this can be problematic when a child dies through having been denied medical treatments that may have saved his or her life. There are a number of notable cases including *Commonwealth v. Twitchell*. Initially convicted of involuntary manslaughter of their two-year-old, the Twitchells' verdict was overturned in 1993 because of the United States' Freedom of Religion Act.[35] Such cases, however, extend beyond Christian Science to Jehovah's Witnesses (especially regarding blood transfusions) and Scientologists (via their Dianetics technique[36]); faith healing is largely connected with Christianity. A current prominent case concerns parents in the Unleavened Bread Ministry who lost their 11-year-old daughter to diabetes in 2008 and were brought to trial for not seeking medical aid for their child. However, under the 1996 Child Abuse Prevention and Treatment Act in the United States, parents who do not seek medical care for their children for religious purposes are exempted from prosecution. Although convicted of reckless homicide, the parents, who appealed this decision, have yet to serve any of their sentence, and the case is still rumbling on with arguments both for and against faith healing; a final verdict is expected in late 2013.[37] It must be noted, though, that for many Christians the authority of text is not always unquestionably accepted, and any exploration of religion needs to examine religious practice as well as religious belief.

But text and its interpretation is not the only place to find authority within a religion, for some emphasize tradition, such as in Indigenous Lifeways. It is easy to generalize, but often storied knowledge combined with experience is crucial in alternative religions, especially those that derive from Indigenous Lifeways. In Cuban Santeria, the practitioner will typically seek the aid of a specific Orisha (a spirit reflecting an aspect of Olodumare, the supreme being) depending on the issue that needs addressing. Each Orisha has a known area of expertise and influence, and appropriate offerings are made for assistance in everyday matters. However, for more major concerns, aid is sought through the Babalowa (a ritual specialist). As an authority figure steeped in the knowledge of tradition and the ways of the many Orisha, carefully following his instructions is believed to ensure a successful outcome.[38] Like most Indigenous Religions, Santeria is engaged more in this-world rather than next-world issues, and because the effects of rites and rituals are immanent rather than transcendent and are visible in a relatively short timescale, it is clear whether accepting the authority of a Babalowa or a particular Orisha has been effective.

As can be seen in Santeria, authority is often enhanced through the testimony of others who can authenticate whether a ritual has worked, and this can be seen also in regard to indigenous shamans. Shamans are men or women (depending on their cultural context) who, through certain experiences, are able to communicate with those beyond the limits of everyday humans—mostly other-than-humans and the dead. Although much is culturally specific, there are some commonalities in shamanic practice such as engaging in reciprocal and respectful relationships with spirits, animals, plants, rocks, and other other-than-human persons. Communication is often done in a trance state using music, dance, or psychotropic plants or comes through dreams and visions. Korean shamans are a case in point. An indigenous folk practice operating in an increasingly industrialized country that values the practice for its cultural heritage, shamans are largely marginalized in Korean society. Working with individual clients and in dramatic public performances, the authority of the shaman lies predominantly with the real-life effects of her work. If a client is satisfied, then the shaman will be recommended and her authority in working with her spirits endorsed, and she will gain new clients.[39]

Charisma

Suicide cults provide an example of charismatic authority figures, although it must be noted that these are extreme examples. Charismatic authority figures are indicative in religion, and indeed all founders of new religious traditions must have been charismatic individuals to persuade people to leave their established ways of life for the one they promoted, often rejecting social norms in the process. The study of New Religions has provided insight into the phenomenon of charismatic leadership, but it would be incorrect to assume charisma is easily identifiable, for what one person finds charismatic is not necessarily the same as for another. Further, just having charisma would not necessarily be enough to sustain a growing movement over a long period. Therefore, charisma needs to go hand in hand with a way of living (tradition- and/or text-based) that appeals to followers; again, this will vary between individuals, across time periods, and throughout cultures.

In brief, we will explore two Religions in terms of charismatic leaders and the effects they have had on their followers. The Peoples Temple (short for the Peoples Temple Full Gospel Church) was established in 1956 by a charismatic preacher, Jim (James Warren) Jones.[40] Active in politics as well as religiously evangelical, Jones established a multireligious socialist church in the United States at a time of racial segregation and anticommunist fervor. He adopted children of different races and started what he termed his Rainbow Family. Initially, he was courted by local politicians for his inclusive social policies, but over time and with the onset of anticommunist McCarthyism in the United States, alongside the influence of prescription medication, Jones became increasingly controlling of his church members. Setting himself up as the main authority of his movement (even over the *Bible* that he fervently preached), reports suggest that he became increasingly paranoid and even sexually predatory and sadistic. After moving his church from its initial home of Indianapolis to Redwood California, and then by 1975 to San Francisco, Jones's increasing involvement in politics led to increasing media scrutiny, and in 1977 an inquiry by the Internal Revenue Services for fraud was conducted. In the summer and fall of that year, Jones moved almost 1,000 people to his agricultural project that became known as Jonestown, Guyana.

Set up and publicized as a utopia, Jonestown shortly became a virtual prison camp with forced labor carried out to the relentless sound of Jones's sermons broadcast by loudspeakers throughout the area. Although Jonestown was shut off from the rest of the world, concerned relatives managed to arrange a visit from Congressman Leo Ryan in 1978. Initially there appeared to be little in the way of discontent, but when a small number of members left Jonestown with the congressman, Jones had them, Ryan, and the news reporters who accompanied him shot dead as they boarded their plane. He then ordered the remaining members at Jonestown to carry out what was termed a White Night, a well-practiced mass suicide. What followed was no attempt, though, but an enforced suicide/murder where church members drank a lethal mix of narcotics with a flavored drink (similar to Kool Aid; hence the popular American saying "drink the Kool-Aid," meaning to blindly follow[41]), and 909 men, women, and children died; only a few managed to escape.[42]

Heaven's Gate, classified now as a suicide cult, similarly did not start off with this outcome in mind. Founded by Marshall Herff Applewhite (1931–1997; later known as Do, among other names) in the late 1970s with Bonnie Nettles (1927–1985; later known as Ti, among other names), around understandings of the Book of Revelation, notably 11:3, the religion had a strong connection to UFOlogy. With an emphasis on androgyny, celibacy, and a separation of members from the wider world, in 1997 Applewhite and 38 members of his religion swallowed a lethal dose of phenobarbital, vodka, and applesauce to board the UFO they believed was hiding behind the Hale-Bopp comet, which would take them to what they understood as the "Level Above Human"—their afterlife. Although obedience to Applewhite and Nettles was expected as part of the religions ethics and practice, members were free to leave at any stage, and indeed, from the videoed farewells and various documents left behind, none were coerced into taking their lives.[43] Therefore, while obedience and authority continue to be issues raised in connection with New and Alternative Religions, it should not be considered an overriding concern.[44]

However, there are two New Religions of particular current interest in terms of authority: the Unification Church, where authority rested with recently deceased founder, Sung Jung Moon (1920–2012), and the Gulen

Movement, where the founder, Fethullah Gulen (b. 1941), is in increasingly poor health.

The Unification Church (the Holy Spirit Association for the Unification of World Christianity) was founded in 1954 in South Korea and is largely based on the *Bible*, as interpreted through the church's theological textbook, *Exposition of the Divine Principle*, combined with Korean folk beliefs. The church is probably best known for its international mass weddings where couples, typically unknown to each other and often not from the same country, culture, or language group, were paired by Moon and his wife in matrimony. By taking part in the wedding ceremony, the couple would be spiritually and symbolically reborn, "offered to God as newly created beings, pure and free of past sin,"[45] and their children would be understood as immaculate.[46] However, since Moon's death it is unclear as to the church's position on this and other aspects of Unification doctrine and practice. The death of any charismatic leader will typically have a dramatic effect on the future of the movement, and it will be interesting to see how the Unification Church develops without their founder.[47]

The Gulen Movement is currently not understood as a New Religion as it is firmly founded in Islam.[48] However, with the teachings of Fethullah Gulen, the Turkish Sunni Muslim founder, central to the movement, we argue it can indeed be understood in these terms. Gulen, whose own writings are based on the work of the Turkish reformist theologian Said Nursi (1878–1960), charismatically leads a worldwide community of traditionalist but moderate Muslims based on the ideals of *Hizmet* (service) and peace building. Although loose in structure, the movement is heavily influenced by the thoughts and writings of Gulen, with his latest lectures and speeches taking precedent over his earlier philosophies.[49] Although there is undoubtedly a hierarchy in the movement, evident through the organizational structure of the many local and regional groups of businessmen and the various foundations such as the Journalists and Writers Foundation, the charity Kisme Yok Me, and the interfaith-based Dialogue Foundation, it is unclear what will happen after Gulen's death. In self-imposed exile in the United States, Gulen is known to be ill enough to restrict visits to his compound,[50] yet given that he does see himself as a spiritual leader in the Sufi tradition despite his teaching being largely Sufi in its concepts,[51] it is very unlikely that there will be any announcement on a successor. With the clear leadership of and wealth of published material from Gulen, it is highly likely he can continue to lead from the grave (much like Mary Eddy Baker and Christian Science), and with the loose organizational structure and worldwide reach, the movement clearly has the groundswell of support and the momentum to continue even when Gulen passes on.

CONCLUSION

Clearly, authority is a central issue in contemporary debates around religion: on what basis do we accept a religious authority? How do religions justify their power structures? What happens when a religion "goes wrong"? As we have seen, it is not clear that there is any single answer to these questions; the particular matrix of factors that constitute authority within any religion tends to be unique and always subject to change and development.

GLOSSARY

Babalowa: a ritual specialist in Santeria.

Hizmet: a Turkish term meaning "service," which the followers of the scholar Fethullah Gulen use to define their movement, which is generally called the Gulen Movement in English. The notion of service, though, sums up their aims to help society, their nation, and humanity.

Lotus Sutra: an important Mahayana Buddhist scripture.

New Age: a term for the loose movement of spirituality that grew up in the late twentieth century that suggested that each individual should find his or her own path and that often blended ideas from many different traditions.

New Religious Movements: a term scholars use for recent religions; this can mean either those which are of recent origin (often the last 200 years or so) or are new in their context (i.e., various Asian traditions in Europe and America).

Orisha: a spirit reflecting an aspect of Olodumare, the supreme being. Each Orisha has a known areas of expertise and influence, and appropriate offerings are made for assistance in everyday matters.

Other-than-human persons: used in relation to Indigenous Lifeways and shamanic tradition to refer to things such as plants and animals that are treated as sentient beings who can be engaged with.

Renouncers (sannyasin): in Hindu traditions, a term referring to those who renounce worldly life and become ascetics or monastics in a particular spiritual lineage. Normally male, there are some female renouncers as well.

Santeria: a dynamic blend of African Yuruba traditions and Catholicism.

Shaman: men or women (depending on their cultural context) who, through certain experiences, are able to communicate with those beyond the limits of everyday humans.

Spiritual bricolage: the blending, in a pick-and-mix style, of various spiritual and religious traditions to create your own spirituality.

NOTES

1. Biblical references here and elsewhere are from the Revised Standard Version.

2. For a recent summing up of this, see Mark Allan Powell, *Jesus as a Figure in History: How Modern Historians View the Man from Galilee* (Louisville, KN: Westminster John Knox Press, 2013), 244–46. Powell's book, we should note, includes quite a number of

conservative scholars (some of whom should probably be seen as taking a more faith-based than historical account) and misses off some more radical liberal theologians as well as some more clearly historical-critical scholars, and so that it still has to conclude that mainstream scholarship takes this view is indicative of the strong weight of evidence.

3. Probably after the early centuries, the first reassertion of belief that Jesus was only human came in the sixteenth century when Protestants starting reading the Bible in translation and some radical thinkers came to this conclusion but were rigorously persecuted. Groups such as the Quakers who maintained such a view still continue today. More widespread support, though, came from the eighteenth century as the scholarship of historical analysis started to support such a view. The concept that Jesus was only human and never claimed to be divine has been held by both atheists in attacking Christianity and Christians seeking to be true to their own heritage; for the latter groups, one of the most recent attempts to make sense of what this means can be found in John Hick, *The Metaphor of God Incarnate* (London: SCM, 1993).

4. Kim Knott, *Hinduism: A Very Short Introduction* (Oxford, England: Oxford University Press, 1998), 42ff.

5. An interesting text of Krishna's exploits can be found in Wendy O'Flaherty, trans., *Hindu Myths* (London: Penguin, 1975), 228–31.

6. Frank Whaling, *Understanding the Brahma Kumaris* (Edinburgh: Dunedin Academic Press, 2012).

7. Alistair McGrath, *Christian Theology: An Introduction*, 4th ed. (Oxford, England: Blackwell, 2007), 138–40.

8. For a deeper discussion on this and examples, see Leona Anderson and Pamela Dickey-Young, eds., *Women and Religious Traditions* (Oxford, England: Oxford University Press, 2004).

9. G. Chryssides, "Defining the New Spirituality," CESNUR 14th International Conference, Riga, Latvia, August 29–31, 2000, accessed June 25, 2013, http://www.cesnur.org/conferences/riga2000/chryssides.htm.

10. E. Puttick, *Women in New Religions: In Search of Community, Sexuality and Spiritual Power* (Basingstoke, England: Macmillan, 1997).

11. D. Anthony and T. Robbins, "Conversion and 'Brainwashing' in New Religious Movements," *The Oxford Handbook of New Religious Movements*, ed. J. R. Lewis (Oxford, England: Oxford University Press, 2004), 243. Also see L. L. Dawson, ed., *Cults and New Religious Movements: A Reader* (Oxford, England: Blackwell, 2003).

12. Anthony and Robbins, "Conversion and 'Brainwashing,'" 264–65, 287.

13. For more on this, see E. Barker, *The Making of a Moonie: Choice or Brainwashing?* (Oxford, England: Blackwell, 1984), and "New Religions and Mental Health," *Psychiatry and Religion: Context, Consensus and Controversies*, ed. D. Bhugra (London: Routledge, 1996), 125–37.

14. Anthony and Robbins, "Conversion and 'Brainwashing,'" 269–70.

15. George Chryssides, *Exploring New Religions* (London and New York: Continuum, 1999), 316.

16. Ibid., 317. For more on this topic, see S. Sutcliffe and M. Bowman, eds., *Beyond New Age: Exploring Alternative Spirituality* (Edinburgh, UK: Edinburgh University Press, 2000).

17. Graham Harvey, *Listening People, Speaking Earth: Contemporary Paganism* (London: C. Hurst and Co., 1997), 212.

18. Ibid., 213.

19. Other-than-human persons are relational beings; sometimes they are object persons, sometimes other traditionally sentient beings. The notion operates in terms of a semianimate universe where other-than-humans communicate with humans. For a fuller description, see K. M. Morrison, "The Cosmos as Intersubjective: Native American Other-Than-Human Person," in *Indigenous Religions: A Companion*, ed. G. Harvey (London: Cassell, 2000), 23–36.

20. This is the higher of the two LDS priesthoods. Melchizedek priests are typically over 18 years of age. This level of priesthood allows a man to preside over his family and to give blessings and healings to his wife and children. The Aaronic priesthood is for boys aged between 12 and 18 years and allows for the administering of the sacrament and some teaching in the home.

21. L. G. Beaman, "Molly Mormons, Mormon Feminists and Moderates: Religious Diversity and the Latter Day Saints Church," *Sociology of Religion* 6291 (2001): 69.

22. Ibid., 65–86.

23. Ibid., 73, 75, 76.

24. Linda K. Newell and Valeen T. Avery, *Mormon Enigma: Emma Hale Smith* (Chicago: University of Illinois Press, 1994), xx.

25. Beaman, "Molly Mormons," 70.

26. Martha in ibid., 75.

27. E. Puttick, "The Osho Movement," in *Encyclopedia of New Religions: New Religious Movements, Sects and Alternative Spiritualities*, ed. C. Partridge (Oxford, England: Lion, 2004), 191–93.

28. Ibid., 191. In Hindu practice, however, people became renouncers at almost any stage in their life, while it was not always limited to men. Despite this, Osho still simplified and altered the concept for his purposes.

29. Puttick, *Women in New Religions*, 80, 113–16.

30. Jacobs in ibid., 44.

31. E. Puttick, "Sexuality, Gender and the Abuse of Power in the Master–Disciple Relationship: The Case of the Rajneesh Movement," *Journal of Contemporary Religion* 10, no. 1 (1994): 29–40.

32. S. J. Palmer and C. E. Hardman, eds., *Children in New Religion* (London: Rutgers University Press, 1999).

33. C. E. Hardman, "Children in New Religious Movements," in *The Oxford Handbook of New Religious Movements*, ed. J. R. Lewis (Oxford, England: Oxford University Press, 2004), 386–416.

34. D. A. Halperin, "Cults and Children: A Group Dynamic Perspective on Child Abuse within Cults," in *Groups Therapy with Children and Adolescents*, ed. P. Kymississ and D. A. Haperin (Washington, D.C.: American Psychiatric Press, 1996), 353–66.

35. See J. J. Jurinski, *Religion on Trial: A Handbook with Cases, Law and Documents* (Santa Barbara, CA: ABC-Clio, 2004).

36. Scientologists were engaged in touch healing in Burma shortly after the 2008 Cyclone Nargis and Haiti 2010 earthquake; the media have been skeptical about the effects of their healing work.

37. M. Anderson, "Marathon Co. Faith Healing Case: 5 Years after Kara Neumann's Death," accessed June 25, 2013, http://www.wsaw.com/home/headlines/Marathon-Co -Faith-Healing-Case-5-Years-After-Kara-Neumann-Died-199960551.html.

38. M. A. De la Torre, *Santeria: The Beliefs and Rituals of a Growing Religion in America* (Cambridge, England: Eerdmans, 2004).

39. C. Kim, *Korean Shamanism: The Cultural Paradox* (Aldershot, England: Ashgate, 2003).

40. In 1955, the precursor to the movement was founded—the Wings of Deliverance.

41. http://mentalfloss.com/article/13015/jonestown-massacre-terrifying-origin-drinking-kool-aid.

42. There are a number of reports held by various organizations including audio tapes broadcast at Jonestown (see http://archive.org/details/ptc1978-11-18.flac16) and the medical examiner report (see http://archive.org/details/JimJonesMassacre). The Jonestown Memorial site holds witness testimony and the story of relatives (http://www.jones-town.org/video.html). To place the Peoples Temple in the context of other new religions with a violent history, see J. R. Hall, with P. D. Schuyler and S. Trinh, *Apocalypse Observed: Religious Movements and Violence in North America, Europe and Japan* (London: Routledge, 2000). See also J. R. Hall, "The Apocalypse at Jonestown," in *Cults and New Religious Movements: A Reader*, ed. L. L. Dawson (Oxford, England: Blackwell, 2003), 186–207.

43. W. Davis, "Heaven's Gate: A Study of Religious Obedience," *Nova Religio* 3, no. 2 (2000): 241–67. See also Hall, *Apocalypse Observed*, 181.

44. For more information, see "Are New Religions Harmful?" on the INFORM site (Information Network on Religious Movements), accessed June 26, 2013, http://www.inform.ac/node/14.

45. H. Spurgin and N. Spurgin, "Blessed Marriage in the Unification Church: Sacramental Ideals and Their Application to Daily Marital Life," in *New Religious Movements: A Documentary Reader*, ed. D. Daschke and W. M. Ashcraft (New York: New York University Press, 2005), 148–63, 155.

46. S. Yoshihide, "Geopolitical Mission Strategy: The Case of the Unification Church in Japan and Korea," *Japanese Journal of Religious Studies* 37, no. 2 (2010): 317–34, 326–27.

47. J. Saliba, *Understanding New Religious Movements* (Oxford, England: Rowman & Little Publishers, 2003).

48. B. Park, "The Fethullah Gulen Movement," *Global Politician*, December 31, 2008, accessed June 26, 2013, http://www.globalpolitician.com/default.asp?25355-fethullah-gulen-turkey.

49. See http://en.fgulen.com/ for his works and weekly broadcast of lectures.

50. M. Rubin, "What Happened When Fethullah Gulen Dies?" *Commentary*, June 5, 2012, http://www.commentarymagazine.com/2012/06/05/what-happens-when-fethullah-gulen-dies/.

51. See http://en.fgulen.com/about-gulen-movement/4063-is-the-gulen-movement-a-sufi-tariqa.

FURTHER READINGS

Green, Garrett. "Hermeneutics." In *The Routledge Companion to the Study of Religion*, ed. John Hinnells. London and New York: Routledge, 2005, pp. 392–406.

Holm, Jean, and Bowker, John, eds. *Sacred Writings*. London: Francis Pinter Publishers, 1994.

Lewis, J. R., ed. *The Oxford Handbook of New Religious Movements*. Oxford, England: Oxford University Press, 2004.

Martin, Craig. *A Critical Introduction to the Study of Religion*. Sheffield, England: Equinox, 2012, especially chapter 6.

Mcguire, Meredith. *Lived Religion: Faith and Practice in Everyday Life*. Oxford, England: Oxford University Press, 2008.

Nye, Malory. *Religion: The Basics*. London and New York: Routledge, 2008, especially chapter 3.

Puttick, E. *Women in New Religions: In Search of Community, Sexuality and Spiritual Power*. Basingstoke, England: Macmillan, 1997.

Stoller, Paul. "Rationality." In *Critical Terms for Religious Studies*, ed. Mark C. Taylor. Chicago: University of Chicago Press, 1998, pp. 239–55.

4

Religion and Embodiment: Religion and the (Latin American) Bodies That Practice It

Renée de la Torre[1]

INTRODUCTION

This chapter considers the increasingly discussed issue of the way that bodies and embodiment are central to the study and understanding of religion. For some, this is controversial because the focus moves away from beliefs and doctrines as central or defining of what religion is about, to looking at the way practice or ritual is key to the formation of religious identities and believers. To examine this, the study presented here uses as an example of the role that the body has started to assume as a locus for the experience of newer forms of popular religion in Latin America. Through the qualitative analysis of four manifestations of religious fervor, it is shown not only that these are representative of an ever-increasing number of new tendencies in popular religion but also that they conform to a trend of becoming more and more deinstitutionalized and subjectified. They are also ever more emotional in nature and are creating new social bonds, which come of shared experience, instead of merely formal ones. The role of the body is highlighted as the location of a living experience of the sacred, and as the legitimizer of contemporary credibility, in the emotional religions of Latin America.

In Latin America, the rites and symbols that make up popular religion (recognized for the power it has to unite differences in a single blend—its syncretic nature) are charged with identity, history, and memory. They therefore provide points of reference to help with the uncertainties that come with what is termed *postmodernity*; popular religion helps people displaced by mass movements of human beings to put down roots and come to terms with the anonymity characteristic of the industrial age, making stark spaces into places for meeting and sharing an identity, bringing a sense of ownership and links back to communities, and regenerating continuity over the constant changes and ruptures that are provoked in the current age. Thus, the first part of this study addresses the question of understanding the part played historically by a syncretic type of popular religion in the construction of a sense of identity for Latin America. In the second part, the main concepts used to structure discussions of contemporary culture are reviewed, and their effects on the study of religious changes are noted, leading to the observation that there has been a dismantling of religious institutions along with the emergence of a subjectified religiousness. To understand the religious phenomenon in terms of sociological and anthropological traditions, these disciplines will provide a frame of reference for studying the body and religious experience. The final discussion concerns the directions likely to be taken by this relationship between the body and religious experience in the middle of contemporary postmodernity.

Four manifestations of religious change currently experienced in Latin America were chosen for the study: (1) the Charismatic boom: emotion and embodiment; (2) the New Age: the recovery and invention of native religions; (3) magic, shamanism, witchdoctor healing, and miracles in the neo-esoteric market; and (4) portability and the anchorages brought by popular religion to transit and mobility.[2]

In the study of these four tendencies, the new part being played by the living experience in the body of the sacred is seen, and there is a discussion of the new functions popular religion has acquired with domesticating, confronting, and responding to the effects of uncertainty, anonymity, and deterritorialization that have been created by the general changes in contemporary society.

HISTORICAL BACKGROUND AND CONTEXT: POPULAR RELIGION AS A FEATURE OF A COMMON IDENTITY IN LATIN AMERICA

Latin America is a region that projects an *imagined community*,[3] and the term is used as though it were a continent (though in fact it is only part of the continent of America). Still it stands for a territory that offers a historical and cultural identity to its inhabitants because, in the first instance, it has a shared history of Iberian (Spanish and Portuguese) colonization, and second because the inhabitants have in common a utopian outlook. For this reason, in spite of the great distances separating many members of the population who are scattered in the countries of the North as a result of all the migration, and in spite of the racial and linguistic diversity of its inhabitants, the term *Latin America* is still the best for reflecting on a particular contemporary social reality. For example, if we consider ourselves to be Latin American, this is a way to distinguish ourselves from the countries of North America (Canada and the United States), not only because their history is of colonization by English speakers but also because subsequently these nations came to represent the spirit of capitalism and liberal imperialism. Although it is true that the designation of this part of the continent as Latin America is an effect of the project of domination by the French,[4] it is also separate from the rest as a result of having been denied the right to belong to the same entity as the inhabitants of the North, as the English-speaking country across the border assumed the title of the continent to itself: "The United States of America means America and its American inhabitants, to the exclusion of the rest of the region and its inhabitants. The other America will have to be called Spanish, Iberian, Latin or Amerindian."[5] Nevertheless, the adoption of a Latin American identity was something that developed and acquired historical meaning as a result of the inner need for emancipation from colonial domination. Replacing *Iberoamerican* or *Hispanoamerican* with the term *Latin American* implied making a break with the original colonization by Spain and Portugal, and by the end of the nineteenth century, Iberian Europe not only ceased to be the reference for identity but became a reference for the differentiation that was required for building independent nations. Thus,

> Over the years, identifying with Latin America also became a banner for independence and an anti-colonial anti-Yankee ideology, which went to make up an imagined political and cultural unity in a territory stretching from the North to South America, whose principal common features are the language, and the Catholic religion, and which sought to generate a cultural movement and a Latin American political thinking, that would make a break with the inertias of economic dependence on the capitalist countries.[6]

There is no doubt that the key aspect of this distinction was the religious factor: between the English-language speakers (of Protestant culture) and the Romance-language speakers (Catholics).

However, making distinctions to create identity—to define the complexity of the Latin American region—has not been an easy task. This is largely due to the fact that it has no inner unity (of a racial, cultural, social, or linguistic type). A solution tried by the nation-states was to speak of the *mestizo* to make up for the lack of cultural unity, but although there is a *mestizo* layer of the population, generalizing the use of the term standardizes and unifies the internal differences between the peoples of this part of America unjustifiably.[7]

A second problem is that the presence of Latin Americans is not limited to this territory, because—as García Canclini says—"Latin America is not complete in Latin America. Her reflection reaches her from mirrors dispersed through an archipelago of migrations."[8] The enormous emigration flows within the continent and between continents, make Latin American an identity that people can relate to more than anything else and not an identity of belonging to a particular place. It is a relative type of identity that is made real in ritual practices, with relating to others to allow common features of identification to be expressed without denying the differentiation of other cultures. These rites take place both in the part of the continent that is called Latin America and in other territories, especially in the United States and some European countries. We can even think, as Renato Rosaldo points out, that there may be a Latin American cultural citizenship in the United States.[9]

As the Catholic religion is one of the main shared cultural features, it should be noted that this differs from European Catholic religiosity through having a markedly syncretic style and through the popular development of rites. This way of practicing Catholicism and giving it meaning has been called "popular religion."

Historically, popular religion in Latin America has been, so Christian Parker tells us, the fermenting agent of culture in America. Although it is sometimes synonymous with popular Catholicism, it is a syncretic expression of the cultural clash between Catholicism, introduced by the conquistadores, native (indigenous) cosmologies, and later the religions of African origin that came over with black slaves.[10] Thus, a particular feature of popular Catholicism is that it flourished through a syncretic way of operating and therefore functions as a matrix for diverse beliefs. As Pierre Sanchis notes, in the case of Brazil, it is:

> . . .a faith in the form of a religion. And that is why, when it sets up in a space
> dominated by previous religious institutions, it tends to operate by means of
> transmutations of what it might be possible to assimilate and resemanticize
> in a synthesis of its own. Conceiving of itself as a "totality", as "Catholic", pre-
> disposes it to adopt this strategy, as it has a stronger vocation to phagocytize
> than to exclude.[11]

It should be remembered that one of the Latin American intellectual movements from which the theory of dependency grew developed as an understanding from inside Latin American theology—this being the Theology of Liberation,[12] which reached its peak in the 1970s and 1980s and managed to join political wills and to share utopias in a considerable part of the subcontinent. Popular religions continue today to be a practice generating a mixture of various religious systems: indigenous family devotions with magic, witchcraft healings, animism, and "paganism"; this is mixed with Catholicism, the articulator of devotion to saints and virgins, miracles, and ritualism, and also with New Age spirituality and neo-esotericism. The latter two are also molds for constructing meaning that take pieces of traditions seen to be exotic (from East to West, from Patagonia to Tibet) and are a sign of the religious spirit of the age of globalized culture, as they tend to make universal claims about historical religions, with their esoteric traditions and exotic nativisms, along with pseudoscientific beliefs, in a blend that creates a juxtaposition of amalgamated fragments. Popular religion still continues to be the mold for giving meanings to the new. A number of countries in Latin America have recently experienced a tendency toward religious diversity, which is weakening the Catholic monopoly and opening the way for different Christian denominations to spring up, of a Charismatic and Pentecostal type; these have been taken up by Latin American popular religion, and ethnic versions of the same have been produced.

The nations of Latin America continue to suffer a primary tension between:

> The unitary will ... and the plurality founded on this interethnic encounter with the other ..., with the structure of these relations providing a language or a model to incorporate other distinguishable components into the nation as a whole—as for example, the presence of collectivities formed around particular religious options.[13]

Staying with the same writer, but considering her reflection on the role of the nation with respect to ethnic diversity, we can speculate that with regard to religious diversity, it is popular religion that incorporates diversity into itself through the impression of profiles and values that are found in the syncretism that already exists. This means that although religions of Protestant and Pentecostal origin have arrived on the scene from English-speaking countries, these are given fresh contents that have local meaning and have come to represent particular social groups while also providing an answer to concrete regional needs. So it is, as several anthropologists have pointed out, that there are processes of taking on ethnic identity in Pentecostalism.

It might seem that the religious panorama and the elements composing it are suffering from profound changes in Latin America due to various factors, such as the growing abandonment of the church by members of the Catholic flock, who choose to make their religion a personal one ("in my own way") or decide to convert to other Christian denominations and assemble an individual spirituality. Nevertheless, crisscrossing this change is the persistence of established religious traditions, which accompanies the process of creating new cults and serves as an enclave basis for them, as the new cults come up with new signs while also referring to the symbolic and ritual signs of popular Catholicism (e.g., pilgrimages, visions, mass sanctuaries, collective rituals, miracles, magic, healing, animisms, and cases of possession).[14] Hence, as Latin Americans, we have wondered whether we might not be witnessing a continuation of the same creative capacity of popular religion, but now "with more modern vestments."[15]

As mentioned initially, in the case of Latin America, a feature of the cultural wealth and the permanence of religion has been its syncretic character, balancing between the local and European cultures. For this reason, the Charismatic versions of Christianity, the neo-esoteric offerings, and the New Age sensibility not only follow their own track but also link up with popular religion. This gives them the characteristic of being postmodern, or neotraditional—that is, combining elements of what is new with older patterns of belief and tradition, which builds on the cultural conditions of a deep syncretism between the traditions of resistance and modernity. Although we cannot ignore the fact that Catholicism tried to derail the religious practices of the indigenous societies, calling their ancient cults idolatry and dismissing their knowledge as superstitions and the practice of witchcraft,[16] all the same the creativity of native peoples in their re-creation and popular taking over of Catholicism made a historical resistance to the colonial project possible. The same creativity continues to be dynamic in anticipating responses to contemporary modernity.

We therefore propose that popular religion be studied as the main point of tension produced by the taking on of a native culture, and the reason it continues to be valid derives from the permanent dynamics between assimilation and rejection of modernity and between the cultural resistance of the traditions and their response to contemporary modernization, which is not just one of adaptation but also something that is performed. Some years ago, Rostas and Droogers noted that in popular religion there is a permanent negotiation of the processes of redefinition and reinterpretation of the practical sense of religion; there is a confrontation between the relations of domination and resistance, both between the official church and the believers and between classes:

> The users of (popular) religions are not much concerned about the origins of
> their beliefs and practices, but they are concerned about the efficacy of their
> version of the religion. They appropriate symbols and apply them or reinter-
> pret them in particular situations with the aim of helping themselves (to solve
> financial problems or to recover from an illness). The users of popular religion
> have no scruples about mixing elements or incorporating them in order to sat-
> isfy their needs, without regard as to whether these are spiritual or material.[17]

We consider that it is in the rites of popular religion (accepted, tolerated, or rejected by the Catholic establishment) that the collective sense of the new religious forms is constructed, as is the space that serves as a reference for anchoring a legitimating authority for a tradition that offers a principle of social identity and the possibility of incorporation into a community of believers.

KEY DEBATES: THE BODY AND RELIGION IN POSTMODERN TIMES

Religion and the Body

There are distinct theories showing the importance of the "body" to the study of society. One approach is that of the functionalist-structuralists, who regard the body as a place where power is colonized. From this point of view, the body is seen as an object that is receptive of the assaults of modernity and political domination. According to Bryan Turner, "our bodies are regulated and administered for the benefit of the social order."[18] This approach led to important debates on delicate subjects, which then became social, political, and citizenship agendas, with respect to the right to be different and to nondiscrimination. This resulted in what has been termed *biologization*, whereby inherited ideas about the body have been related to scientific ideas to create a sense of truth and authority for various interpretations. At the same time, increasing biological and medical technologies and understanding have meant that biologization has become a natural part of our understanding of ourselves and our bodies.[19] However, the body has also been a part of ways of knowing that have resisted this.

Turner synthesizes this position with the argument that "The body is a target for modern rationalization, which turns it into an object of power and of knowledge."[20] The most important classifications of the differences operating in the colonization of the body (i.e., the way that social and political forces control the way we understand the body) were gender (which imposed male dominance and excluded women from the political and economic systems of society)[21] and race (a codification of differences between conquerors and conquered, on the basis of which a different biological structure was assumed, one that left the latter in a natural condition of inferiority with regard to the former).[22] There are also other biologizing classifications with which to colonize the domination of bodies, such as, at various times, "normal" versus "abnormal," complexion (i.e., skin color, which would exclude dwarves and giants, the obese, and the handicapped) and age (which has given priority to adults and currently holds the aged in contempt), among other regimes of social and political classification on the basis of the body. In so far as religion consists of a measure of moral values that conditions rules of behavior, it has been studied without abandoning this line of approach.

An idea that comes from these studies is that which looks at the way we divide the body and soul and also genders and looks back to the philosopher René Descartes. In this system, woman equals nature, but man equals nurture. These notions have developed in an interesting way in Latin American postcolonial projects. The best example is that of the Peruvian sociologist Aníbal Quijano, who proposes that race and gender were very astute historical constructions, invented as they were to colonize power over non-European bodies and thereby legitimate domination over them and exploitation of them. The author favors the analysis of power through the supposedly scientific creation of "superior" bodies; he also explains that a notion of reason stemming from Europe was imposed that reduced the body to nature while its faculty of "reasoning" was taken away by encouraging the theological doctrine of a "soul" as the only faculty capable of reasoning.[23]

Against such a division of "body" and "reason," when we refer to embodiment, we also mean thinking processes that relate to bodily sensations, and we do not see limits based on ideas of reason or ideologies. Embodiment values emotional experiences as ways of knowledge and for perceiving the position of the individual in society and looks to academic discussions about phenomenology and perception and to a developing anthropology of experience:

> In phenomenological terms it suggests the preobjective character of bodily being-in-the world and likewise suggests two possible consequences of objectification, that is the individuation of the psychological self and the instantiation of dualism in the conceptualization of human being.[24]

The anthropology of religion has recently taken an interest in the body as a place of knowledge, what may be termed *cognitive interiorization*, and also as a place where social action takes place—the performative actions of the norms that direct a society. Of particular note have been the studies of dreams, visions, ecstatic rituals, and charismatic experiences. Clearly this position was developed on the basis of theories of the body centered on experience, as the place of interiorization (where we look inward) but at the same time as the place of cultural transformation.

The study of religion, based on embodiment, can be seen as an heir to phenomenology and picks up the validity of thinking of the body (and not just of language) as the place from which a way of being in the world is experienced. Phenomenology, whose chief exponent was the philosopher Merleau Ponty, showed that the consciousness of being, and of being in the world, comes through the body.[25] Within this tradition, the body predates language (making it a preobjective consciousness but nonetheless a cultural act). It is through the body that the individual has self-awareness and awareness of his or her surroundings (self-identity) and that he or she relates to space, to the world, and to the other. One of the principle representatives of embodiment has undoubtedly been Thomas Csordas, a contemporary sociologist, who has promoted a methodology based on embodiment for the study of healing and religion (especially in his comparative studies of the Charismatic Catholic Renewal and the Navajo). Csordas combines phenomenology with the concept of *habitus*, proposed by Pierre Bourdieu. For Bourdieu, *habitus* is at the same time the socialized human body and the socialized human mind. The *habitus* places an emphasis on the interiorization of social structures, whose effectiveness is action and depends on their dwelling in the consciousness and the will of the agents. This is how the *habitus* directs the practices and their representations in accordance with society's rules of the game, through practical dispositions to represent, value, and act.[26]

Csordas encourages attention on the body, but not as a biological place, rather as a methodological tool that he calls the paradigm of embodiment. His methodological proposal leads to the study of bodily social structures, that is, ones that have been subjectified, individualized, and experienced, through which subjects become aware of their place in the world, and thence interiorize society—that is, make its rules and norms part of their own thinking. Therefore, he constructs the notion of embodiment as something destined to interpret, as it is something that both is created through culture but, as a human being, at the same time contemplates what is experienced in the encounter with society. In the study by Csordas, the relevance of what is said (what is transmitted through language and text) loses its sense of being the ultimate point of reference when compared to the study of the way meanings, values, and social norms are manifested in gestures, movements, or postures because it is not just words but also our bodies that govern the way we as individuals experience the world. It is through the lived body (the act of experiencing one's own body and that of others) that a sense of being in the world is created. As noted by Barsalou and colleagues:

> Embodied knowledge appears central to three aspects of religious experience: religious visions, religious beliefs, and religious rituals. In religious visions, the process of simulation offers a natural account of how these experiences are produced. In religious beliefs, knowledge about the body and the environment are typically central in religious frameworks, and are likely to affect the perception of daily experience. In religious rituals, embodiments appear central to conveying religious ideas metaphorically and to establishing them in memory. To the extent that religious knowledge is like non-religious knowledge, embodiment is likely to play central roles.[27]

Following the anthropologist Clifford Geertz,[28] if religion is thought of as a symbolic system with the power to provoke and establish powerful states of mind through which conceptions (whether imaginary or probable) of general order are made legitimate as though they were real or "effective," one is forced to ask how we come to describe an object which is not what it is in itself (the law of the symbol being that it never is the same as what it symbolizes) but whose value is found in what it is able to evoke. Due to the cultural charge that religion has as a symbolic system through which it aims to give answers to fundamental questions about things and ultimate reality,[29] we should keep in mind the role that is played by the bodily nature of religious lived experiences. It is bodily experience that gives things the creative capacity of feasibility, credibility, and legitimacy that comes with transmitted beliefs. Belief in that which is beyond the world, whose existence and functioning cannot be proved scientifically (i.e., God, miracles, soul, spirit) is lived as something real, not because it is "provable" but because it generates strong states of mind, which are able, as Rudolph Otto says, to generate experience of the sacred.[30] It is through the religious experience—which is the object of study of religion—that the sacred expresses that which transcends this world but also assumes a specific interior manifestation, which is in turn shared by the group.

The Body in a Postmodern World

As well as emphasizing the part played by the study of the body in religious experience, we should ask what the new role is that the body has assumed in the contemporary world. I shall highlight three aspects that seem to me to be important in characterizing the changes that have impressed a new cultural sense on the body: (1) the mobility of globalization; (2) the position of the individual in postmodern times; and (3) the value of the body in a consumer society, in the communications media, and in the virtual reality of cyberspace.

Today the relation of the individual to the world is perceived through new technological, informative, and communicative mediators that are changing the situation of being in the world profoundly in response to readjustments to the scales of space and time. In a world that is intensely globalized through information flows, technologies, means of communication, transnational corporations, and worldwide exchanges of merchandise, it is worth highlighting the impact of mobility on the configuration of new ways for us to relate to ourselves, to each other, and to the world.

To start with, advances in the technologies of communication and information have transformed the nature of the processes of social interaction, multiplied the channels for cultural production and transmission, repositioned the individual on the scale of interactions covering the globe, broadened our conceptions of the world, and shortened the distances between here and there. The bodily consciousness of being in the world is mediated more and more by the communication technologies and through interactive experience on the Internet and social networking sites: images, objects of desire, and virtual worlds are creating novel ways of self-representation and location in the here and now, mediated more and more through the experience of simultaneous relations at a distance and by exposure to virtual realities that begin to be present in everyday interactions. It should also be noted that the perception of the individual in the world is also influenced by the simulation of virtual reality and the fictionalization of reality by the mass media.

Second, various philosophers suggest that currently we have left behind the civilization of modern times, characterized by rationality and a specialization of spheres of activity, and that the world culture has, as its seal, the horizon of postmodernity (which is not to deny that it is experienced unevenly in terms of the relation to cosmopolitan centers and their margins). A contemporary sociologist, Zigmunt Bauman, has even coined a metaphor for this effect as liquid modernity. This metaphor not only speaks to us of the crisis of the grand narratives and institutions but also points to the new role of superficiality among the containers of culture, the lightness of individual constraints, and the return of "nomadism":

> During the whole of the solid period of the modern era, nomadic habits were badly regarded. Citizenship went hand in hand with being sedentary, and the lack of a "fixed abode" or not belonging to a "state" implied exclusion from the law-abiding and law-protected community, and law-breakers were frequently condemned to legal discrimination, if not prosecution. Although this is still the way the "sub-class" of the homeless are treated, by being subjected to the old techniques of panoptic control (techniques no longer used to integrate and discipline the majority of the population), the period in which the sedentary is unconditionally superior to the nomadic is tending to reach an end.[31]

Bauman points out four fundamental changes: emancipation from the institutional and fixed supports of modernity; the tendency toward individualism mediated to a large extent by the cultural freedom of the consumer; the new ways of experiencing space and time that create new distances, accelerate lived time (impressing on people the logic of the instant and the permanent present), and effect a deterritorialization of history and culture that makes the solid transitory; and finally, the deregulation of labor and the weakness of the nation-state.

In his turn, anthropologist Marc Augé states that the features that best define the form in which we perceive the world of *supermodernity* are an excess of individualism, an excess of incidents, and an excess of speed.[32] These three excesses provoke a dislocation in our conventional ways of conceiving and experiencing our being in the world where the causality of time and space is continually being modified.

With regard to religion, there are several works that observe the way in which these changes modify it profoundly. The most important contribution is undoubtedly that of the research directed by Hervieu-Lèger, who claims that religion is undergoing a transformation called religious dissemination, which shows up in the process of moving from institutions as sources of religious authority, accompanied by the individualizing of modes of belief, recognized as "a la carte religions." However, she also distinguishes the role of the return of the religious quest, because in a world where the threads of memory are fragmented and the grand narratives have been reduced to crumbs, religion, as a system of beliefs, offers individual and collective senses of recomposition (even though through invention) of the continuity of their belonging to particular lineages of believers.[33]

At present, provoked by the states of mind associated with uncertainty and defenselessness against the new challenges and threats of an overflow of modernity, far from vanishing or weakening, religion is flourishing, with the human need to resituate memory and the continuity of tradition, to seek solutions to those vital problems that neither the sciences nor the technologies have been able to resolve, and to sacralize the new human experience.[34] In the Latin American case, eurocentrism persists even in postmodern times, and along with that:

> Kept systematically outside the benefits (technical capacity, free association, enrichment of the needs system, etc.) that this modernity had insistently promised them in exchange for abandoning their cultural dysfunctionality (especially in religion), the peoples on the periphery find they are obliged to return to the one refuge left, which they were on the point of giving up: their archaic identity, as the crystallization of a survival strategy validated on so many occasions in history.[35]

Considering that religious legitimation, as it was called by Peter Berger, offers to relate humanly defined reality to sacred, universal, and ultimate reality, the intrinsically precarious and transitory constructions of human activity receive the appearance of a definitive security and permanence.

Finally, we should consider certain reflections on the new role and significance of the body in contemporary society. Mardones, for example, suggests that the present tendency to see various aspects of life and society as distinct realms (what he terms the Weberian atomization of the spheres of life) has contributed to secularizing the body—that is, the body is seen as related to things such as biology or social care rather than religion—each one being seen as a separate realm. This secularization gives the body freedom with respect to religious controls (based on assumptions of the superiority of the soul and the conception of the body as the basis of sin) and promotes sexual liberation, the care of the body, and the health of the body as a way of relating to spiritual well-being. Overall, the perceived needs of the body have been placed above what is seen as the body-denying ethic imposed by historical religions (especially Christianity and Islam). But at the same time, due to the seduction that accompanies publicity and consumerism, the body has become an object for the increasing sense of the hedonistic desires characteristic of a consumer society being seen as having some kind of religious value (being sacralized).[36] The Spanish author concludes that we are seeing an emotional type of religion supplanting the rational religion that the sociologist Max Weber would say was the principal feature of modernity. On the other hand, sociologists of religion agree that one of the symptoms of contemporary changes is the freedom from institutions in relation to religion, which makes religiosity become understood and legitimate more and more in terms of individual experiences. This is where the tendency toward an emotional type of religion arises, as a feature of the individual search for experience of the sacred and its legitimation in contemporary society.[37]

Taking these changes into account, this chapter will provide examples of new expressions of Latin American religion to try to answer the questions: in what way is the body being transformed in religious experience? What place does bodily experience (where the body is an object to consecrate or colonize and a place for the religious experience) hold in the recomposition of religion? What are the contemporary needs, and how do they model the role of religious embodiment? What impact do they have on the new experiences that are mediated by mobility, consumerism, virtual reality, postmodern disenchantment, and individuality?

To this end, we shall revise four phenomena that are representative of contemporary religious change in Latin America.

ARGUMENTS AND EXAMPLES

The Charismatic Boom: Emotion and Embodiment

In Latin America, the cultural impact of the Protestant missions from English-speaking countries has been studied since the 1970s. The missions, such as those of Jehovah's Witnesses, the Assemblies of God, the Mormons, the Seventh-Day Adventists, and the Evangelical or Pentecostal churches, were very well received in Central America and in some South American countries. They were originally defined by various sociologists of religion as a strategy for cultural and religious colonization and imperialism directed against Latin America. However, by the 1990s, Pentecostalism had become the principal factor in the religious transformation of Latin America. The element of this religion that stands out the most is that it is a charismatic-emotional version of Protestantism that arose among the sectors most discriminated against in the United States (the blacks, the poor, the Hispanics), as it values the experience of charismatic gifts and receiving the Holy Spirit above an intellectualized reading of the Bible. It is a movement that cuts across the historical denominations, including Protestantism (Baptists, Presbyterians, Anglicans), new national Pentecostal denominations[38] (in Latin America, the main examples are *La Luz del Mundo* [Light of the World][39] and, from Brazil, the Universal Church of the Kingdom of God,[40] both of which have had considerable success and have spread worldwide), as well as the Roman Catholic Church (Renovation Movement).[41]

An essential characteristic of Pentecostalism, and one that distinguishes it from other religious expressions, is the centrality given to the relation between body and spirit, in prayer, in praise, in song, and in dance. It is the interior living experience corporealized, where the Pentecostals experience in their own flesh the presence of the Holy Spirit (gifts and charismata) or the presence of demons (exorcism). As they proclaim, the body is the living temple where the grace of the Holy Spirit is manifested, through its expression in gifts and charismata, such as the power to speak in divine languages (glossolalia), the healing of the body and spirit, exorcism, prophecy, understanding, and so on. It is the bodily living experience where faith in the divine is verified in one's body. It is the experience of ecstasy where the senses perceive and verify the supreme power, but it is also in the body of the believer that the forces of evil shelter, and where they have to be expelled from through acts of exorcism. As noted by Csordas,[42] weeping, laughing, feeling heat or pain, enjoying happiness or peace, and even losing one's senses and falling to the ground are acts that are lived as subjective, in an interiorized way, but are objectified through corporeal techniques, by means of which they are classified and identified as symbols of good or evil. Pentecostalism plays an important part in the healing of the spirit and body through faith healing. For the Pentecostals, healing comes from God, and the individual, and his or her body, are the instruments through which the Lord works to heal.[43] This belief, when brought to living bodily experience, verifies the miraculous power of the Holy Spirit and confirms that every individual who receives his gifts is "one of the chosen."

At first, the Protestantizing or Pentecostalizing of the continent was seen as a cultural threat that would weaken, replace, and end up by destroying the traditional and local identities. Now the phenomenon of Pentecostalization is spoken of as a sign of globalization, as it has managed to expand worldwide (America, Asia, and Oceania), and that is why it is regarded as an emblem of globalized religion.

Nevertheless, it is not a globalization that takes the traditional route of colonizing missions, but in a special way crosses in the opposite direction, from South to North, from the colonies to the centers of colonization, from Africa to Europe, and from Mexico to the United States.[44] This new horizon rules out addressing the phenomenon in the way that David Stoll does when he asks "Is Latin America turning Protestant?"[45] Rather, as David Martin noticed early on, Pentecostalism can be considered a symbol of what is termed *transnationalized religion*, as it has achieved worldwide expansion (in America, Asia, and Oceania, but also as noted earlier up into Europe from the South), which is due in large part to the fact that it is such a malleable spirituality that can adapt to different cultures.[46] Following this line of thought, what is being claimed currently is that Pentecostal Protestantism is actually becoming ethnic. Many of the evangelical churches have been recultured and have even become ethnic and put down roots in Latin America. The main example is the translation of the *Bible* into native vernaculars and the changes of the charismatic cults, which, because of their emotional charge and miracles, are recognized as a therapeutic source of healing. To this extent, the ecstatic rituals of Pentecostalism are more and more often linked to indigenous shamanism and to the cases of possession that are treated in the cultures of descendants of Africans.

Also, the charismatic experience based on the interior manifestation of the Holy Spirit to individuals, provoking ecstasy, speaking in tongues, or experiencing miraculous healing shares a frame bridging[47] with the animism that is still present in popular religion (the system of witch doctors or natural healers, cleansings, protections against the evil eye, and spells) and is based on the soul and spirits (or "animas"), which are able to transmigrate and shelter or manifest temporarily in different bodies. In this way, the Holy Spirit can become manifest in the bodies of Christians and perform magic cures (through the laying on of hands and the receiving of extraordinary gifts) similar to those conducted by witch doctors.

In the Amerindian world, according to Francisco de la Peña,[48] indigenous shamanism produces a "voluntary, active and self-induced trance thanks to which one can get into the other world." With regard to the devotions inherited from Africa and their Latin American versions, such as Santeria, Candomble, and Voodoo, these are cults in which possession by spirits predominates, as they incarnate in the bodies of the practitioners. Although Pentecostalism regards these devotions as demonic, it also respects them, as Luiz Eduardo Soares showed:

> Pentecostalism requires doctrinal purity and rejects practices and beliefs that popular strata cultivate especially in Umbanda, in Quimbanda, and in Candomblé. They invoke the presence of Exú or of Pombagira in their exorcism rites . . . In other words, the mimetic veracity of the belief is not put into doubt, the reality of the spiritual entities that inhabit the Afro-Brazilian religious imaginaire is admitted, the plays on language and the corporeal

performances of incorporation ceremonies continue to be valid and are exercised on the stage of the temple.[49]

Currently, Catholicism finds itself in a similar situation. For example, it is well known that there has been a revival both in Guadalajara and in Vera Cruz (Mexican cities) of mass exorcism rituals. Formerly the practice of exorcism was reserved for special cases, and those who were recognized as exorcists were just a few priests. However, along with the gifts and the charismata received in the Charismatic movement, priests with no ecclesiastical training in this practice are being recognized as exorcists. It has been reported in Guadalajara recently that every Tuesday thousands of the faithful attend a ceremony with members of the family who have been "possessed by demons"; for the most part, they are teenagers whose tutors say they have rebellious and disobedient attitudes, and at the ceremony, the demon is revealed and the spirit of evil is taken out of them. According to a more critical priest, participating in such rituals leads to the opening of doors (which ought to have remained shut) through which the devil gets in. As in the paradoxical situation described by Soares, Catholicism seeks to destroy something that manifests itself in the performance, which it regards as real.[50]

The New Age: Recovery and Invention of Native Religions

In Latin America, religions linked to native populations and ethnic groups, whose identity and religion predated the conquest and the modern construction of nations, have been kept up. Although for most of the time these devotions were practiced under syncretic forms in popular Catholicism, historically they had been closely connected to racial aspects and the local cultures of certain indigenous populations or groups of African origin. For example, Latin American Afro-religions such as Santeria in Cuba, Candomble in Brazil, and Voodoo (Vodun) in Haiti,[51] and also neo-Indian movements such as Mexicanism or Indian ritualism in Mexico. In fact, these religions were the cultural and identity matrix for nationalist, ethnic, and racial movements. However, in the 1950s they started to be reformulated in processes of styling linked to spectacles of the exotic and to the recovery of national folklore, which had the effect of unhooking their practices from the medium they originated in and spreading them to other strata of national societies.[52] These religions have been transnationalized (there is Candomble in Argentina and Santeria in Miami, Paris, and Mexico). Also, the rituals of Mexicanism (based on practicing the ritual dance as a way of knowledge and therapeutic experience of the body and the soul, as well as the sacred baths of the *temascal* and the vigils) have been taken up by networks of alternative spiritual seekers from Spain, France, Japan, and Germany, to mention some of the cases studied.[53]

Mexicanism has even been incorporated into the *Chicano* movement as its emblem and as a way to bring awareness and a sense of belonging to the imagined *Chicano* nation.[54] To a great extent, this is a result of the migratory movements and the massive exile that make the inhabitants of particular places take their beliefs and rituals with them to their destinations, but it is also due to the importing of "exotic" cults, which hybridize the native religions, as the practitioners are new and not necessarily the subjects who historically kept these traditions linked to ethnic, national, class, and racial values.

Every day there are more *mestizos*, and even "foreigners" (usually Europeans), who dance and think of themselves as being Aztecs, or consult the spirits of the Santeria and Candomble movement (known as *orishas* or *orichas*) and join a ritual family of the Santero movement. Previously, these practices were circumscribed to Cuban Santeria or Brazilian Candomble and were regarded as valued "Afro" cultural objects, but now we can think of the experiences of Africanization that the whites or Europeans, and even the orientals, are having by getting involved in the rituals of drumming, initiation ceremonies, and being adopted into a ceremonial family. The biological and territorial frontiers that united Aztec, Afro-Cuban, or Brazilian religions to the race and culture of the nation have been transcended. In this situation, it is common to question the authenticity of a German, a Japanese, or a Spaniard who has affiliated to an Aztec line of transmission and claims to be the heir of the culture of "our forefathers." However, according to what I have found, it is the body, altered by New Age narratives, that remits to a new way of repositioning the inheritance and membership of a ritual lineage.

I have conducted my study through experience of the Aztec dance as an activity through which an ancestral lineage is reinvented and which contributes to creating imagined transnational communities and nations. For the neo-Mexicanists, it is not only a living experience of the sacred but also the medium through which connections are experienced between the dancer's body and a cosmic identity—the memory of which lay dormant but is reactivated by the movement of the dance—which was labeled by one of the major New Age exponents, José Argüelles, as "vibrational resonance."[55] According to the definition by Csordas, the body is not only a biological entity but a cultural entity through which ways of being in the world can be studied. One needs to be very attentive to the ways in which cosmic identities settle and become rooted in bodies and to the living experience that produces the consciousness, the memory, and the sense of belonging to an ancient ancestry that people have in the ritual. These identities seek to put down roots through the ritual anchor of tradition, whereas shared and subjective experience of the rituals weaves the thread of belonging to a historical-genealogical tapestry into the emotional life that can find reference to an imagined lineage.

An interpretative mold that allows neo-Indianism to be appropriated as the practice of the spiritual ancestors of an ancient lineage is that of the New Age, which is to be found in the seeking and the recovery of native cosmological visions. This mold, based on the self and the holistic amalgam of unity with the whole, spreads a new sensibility, with the experience of a syncretic ritual performed in the framework of popular Catholic devotion as though it were a healing practice, through which individuals attain an interior balance between mind, body, and spirit ("we are connecting the left hemisphere of the brain to the right," say the practitioners). They also interpret the rituals as a school for gaining knowledge of the cosmos and for experiencing a connection to nature and the universe. New Age spirituality encourages seeking for a state of inner peace that produces harmony with the universe, and practitioners aim to gain this state through relaxation exercises (e.g., yoga, tai chi, and the circular dance), introspection and reconciliation therapies (e.g., family relations, meditation, and hypnosis), techniques for balancing or harmonizing energies (e.g., Feng Shui and Reiki),[56] natural nutrition (to keep the body healthy), alternative medicine (natural, vegetarian, and holistic), and contact with creatures of light (channeling and connecting with angels), for example. Today, many of these New Age attributes, which were once found in oriental religions and techniques, are practiced in sacred circles formed around the Aztec dance. This syncretism has produced interesting metaphors for the neo-Indian dance ritual, which is thought of as "yoga in movement" or valued as "Reiki for Mother Earth." The holistic concept of bodily spiritual therapy is also applied to the cosmos, which is regarded as a sacred body, and the steps of the dance are supposed to help with the spiritual cleansing of the channels (*nadis* and *chakras*, from terms in Indian philosophy) of Mother Earth, which have been injured by the environmental abuses of contemporary industrial society.

Therapy for New Age followers links the unit to the whole, the body to the spirit, health to beauty, inner awareness to universal awareness, the alignment of the physical chakras to balancing cosmic energy flows, and the healing of the human body to Mother Earth (identified with *Gaia*, a term from ancient Greece used for a mother goddess). New Age is an individualized religion, but it promotes awareness of inhabiting the cosmos and awareness of being universal.

Magic, Shamanism, Witch Doctor (and Natural) Healing, and Miracles in the Circuits of the Neo-esoteric Market

A number of traditional healers, shamans, or witch doctors (*brujos*) have been co-opted by the esoteric industry, and they have joined the new crowd of parapsychologists adopted by the mass media, who see in the esoteric field a market to exploit, and who give it a lucrative character.[57] The "esoteric nebula"[58] has incorporated symbolic elements from esoteric traditions, parapsychology, divinations from various traditions, astrology, occult sciences, fortune telling, and shamanism from the East and West, and created a supply of universal esoterica for sale. The traditional knowledge of medicinal herbs, and knowledge linked to Latin American popular Catholicism, has to share space with new merchandise brought over from the East: little Buddha statues, pentagrams, and Egyptian pyramids. There has also been an increase in sales of industrially produced magic articles from Venezuela and Mexico, sold as objects "charged" with power, such as sprays, soaps, essences, and candles, which are bought by the witch doctors to conduct "works" of "high magic" or by consumers to protect themselves from "bad vibrations" or to generate positive energy. At the same time, the language used in certain oriental therapies has been taken up to explain traditional practices; for example, "cleansings of (problems caused by) the evil eye" started to be referred to as "protection from blocks in the aura," and a cleansing was equated to aligning the chakras; Catholic prayers, and even the repetition of dance movements, are thought to be the equivalent of oriental mantras, or sacred words and phrases, and evil spirits are interpreted as negative energies. To cite an example, briefly, that is taken from my fieldwork notes at a neopagan ritual for charging energy on the Spring Equinox at the pyramid of Ixtépete (located in the municipality of Zapopan, Jalisco): every year tens of thousands of celebrants arrive to charge themselves with solar energy. Particular healers and shamans meet at this archaeological site. One of them, who is the owner of an esoteric shop called Afrodite, in the city of Guadalajara, conducted a ceremony to visualize and channel the energy of the body through the chakras:

> Bring the color up to the thyroid, there in the throat, make it turquoise blue, the color of harmony, the color of the sky and of the macrocosm. Everyone's body is a microcosm that we are connecting to the macrocosm. There is no magic wand. Excalibur is in the mind, and that is where we have the power to change the microcosm; we are part of it. Now we shall chant a mantra: Uuuuuuuh.[59]

This ritual shows how a living physical experience is made to have a connection with the sacred map of the body (chakras) and to an idea of universal (macrocosmic) energy perceived by the senses, with both the physical, close at hand, and the remotely imagined, seen as having value in a holistic relation where individuals believe they are part of the universe and at the same time they have the energy of the universe (macrocosm), which they can feel "inside." Exploring the body through sensations and visualizing it in colors is clearly an experience of embodiment, in so far as embodiment is to situate abstract concepts in the here and now. Meanings and beliefs acquire the status of existing because it is in the body that the "holistic" idea of consecrating the individual and the cosmos, the inner self and God, interior energy and planetary energy, is lived. The physical experience places magic and energy inside the subject. In the words of Csordas, experience of the "majestic other" is lived and transforms into the idea of the "intimate other," as what gives the "self" sacred value. The new supply of esoteric goods has found a place to cohabit with traditional cultures, sharing rituals and knowledge and forming new hybrids in contact with the traditional popular practices of herbalism, spiritism (the practice of channeling is much used) of the Catholic religion, and magic-religious practices.[60]

Neo-esoteric magic endows witch doctors and healers with miraculous power and does the same to objects (turned into amulets). Both the magicians and the amulets are understood to possess special powers that can change the nature of things, cure, mend broken bonds, redirect one's destiny, and provide protection against the perils of daily life. In magic, we find again that the body expresses a need, as "the place for believing in miracles."[61]

The Body and the Portability of Popular Religion: Migration, Uncertainty, and Places of Transition

Today, the saints and virgins for whom ceremonies typical of popular religion in Latin America are enacted are providing a function of some relevance through giving symbolic protection, company, and rootedness to the faithful. In Mexico, the Virgin of Guadalupe is worshipped with considerable fervor. She is linked to the myth of her appearance to a native, recently canonized as Saint Juan Diego, making her both Catholic and Aztec, Guadalupe and Tonatzin, and Spanish and Native at the same time. Recently, there has been quite a fever of miraculous apparitions of the Virgin of Guadalupe in the most unlikely places, where she is worshipped. The "apparitions" tend to be oval-shaped stains created by leaking water that appear on various surfaces (e.g., floors, walls, and windows). The faithful see in these stains the oval surrounding the Virgin of Guadalupe, and they interpret it as a message from heaven—an appearance made by the Virgin in different places. Television and other mass media have broadcast this phenomenon of recent appearances. Between 1997 and 1998, the number of appearances of the Virgin Mary in Mexico broadcast by the mass media reached 62.[62] From the end of the 1990s onward, just before 2000, there was a widespread belief in Mexico that appearances by the Virgin of Guadalupe had started again: in the subway (1998); on a car windshield; on a public telephone stand (December 2000); on a kitchen pan for heating tortillas (Sayulita, October 2000); and on a stone slab in the mountains of

Mazamitla (La Manzanilla). Every one of these places soon became a shrine where the faithful brought candles, votive offerings, and their prayers. Some of them disappeared as fast as they appeared. But others have become sanctuaries for pilgrimages. A recent case is the appearance of an outline of the Virgin of Guadalupe in a microwave oven. First noted in Mazatlán, news of the appearance spread rapidly on television and through the Internet, and thousands of housewives found their microwaves were shrines where the Virgin would appear to them. There was a myth that proved the visions; it was said that John Paul II had appeared in a dream to Pope Benedict XVI and told him that the Virgin would be appearing on microwave dishes.[63] In Guadalajara, the apparition was observed in several households, restaurants, and shops. In most of these new popular cults, we find the need to endow anonymous spaces, where a large part of the daily life of a good number of passers by is spent, with a sacred reference. Marc Augé has enabled us to think of the accelerated transformations suffered by space and time in the present period, which he characterized as *supermodernity*, through a new term referring to social life: nonplaces.[64] These are both the installations required to speed the movement of persons and goods (highways, crossings, airports) and the means of transport themselves as well as the big shopping malls and anonymous public services. It is a fact that the pace of life for contemporary people is less stable and rooted in a particular location than ever, so also is there a need for modern people to have physical points of reference that serve as anchors to their identity. The cases of appearances of the Virgin of Guadalupe show the relevance of the Catholic tradition for responding to the need people have to create new founding myths based on traditional forms of symbolic appropriation of the territories of life, which work as points of reference for the collective sense, where the velocity of living in an itinerant way fragments the possibility of continuity in the social interactions of daily life. The shrine, the miraculous image, and the cult of a virgin, a saint, or a Christ (generally associated with individual holy objects), which are the founding symbols of traditional communities in Mexico and elsewhere in Latin America, are the product of practices that popular culture has used (and that continue to be used when cultural validity allows it), to make anonymous territory (whether microwave ovens or highways or subway stations) a place with meaning and to consecrate more diverse and even unorthodox worlds than that of the official position on life of the church; to endow the place with a reference for the sense of community where people move at massive speed; and to regenerate anonymous encounters (whose specific quality is not being permanent and having little continuity) in a community lived in and shared in through a symbol consecrating the very condition of itinerancy.

In some countries in Latin America, there are rituals for profane or secular figures of veneration who have been unofficially made into saints (outside the church structure) by popular sectors of society. One example is that of Santa Muerte (Holy Death, or Saint Death) in Mexico, whose cult has spread among the most stigmatized sectors of society such as convicts, prostitutes, street vendors, and in general people suffering from moral stigmas; another is Santo Malverde (patron of drug traffickers in the north of Mexico); and another, Juan Soldado ("Johnny Soldier"), a saint on the Mexico-U.S. border, who is asked to intervene and provide protection for the illegal crossing. In Guatemala, there is Santo Maya, who stands for duality, and "is capable of personifying both aspects of Maximón" (the best and the worst). "Those who wish evil to their enemies also have recourse to him because he has a reputation for repairing injustices."[65] Even Ekeko (Andean god of abundance and fertility) or Gauchito Gil (the Gaucho referring to a people of skilled horsemen), who is the guardian saint for drivers and highways in Argentina, find new worshippers. Many of these saints have in them the duality of good and evil or of justice for rich and poor. Shrines are erected for them, sanctuaries are built, and they are asked to intercede in a miraculous way to resolve difficult situations, although they often suffer from the contempt of society and the church. Usually these saints receive a gift from those who pray to them, which might be money (dollars), alcohol (local brews), cigarettes, gold ornaments, and marijuana. They are thought to be very powerful and agree to fulfill what they have been asked to do, as long as their followers remain faithful, complete the ritual, and do not stop trying to keep them pleased, because they can be vengeful. The duplicity of the power of vengeance and compensation at the same time reaffirms the ambivalence of holiness proposed by Rudolph Otto, because they exercise fascination and also attraction. Due to their tremendous power, they produce feelings of awe, fear, and obligation.[66] The power of these saints, like that of the Catholic saints, in a way that is analogous to the religious system of relics, is reactivated through merchandise that makes them portable: they can be transported and set up anywhere. Thus, the saints, purchased as souvenirs but converted into little figures, small prints, medallions, CDs, or stickers, are moved from place to place and exchanged, keeping the faithful company on their migration routes and movements. These commercial products that are commonly acquired at ceremonial events are charged with the miraculous power of these saints and therefore not only accompany the faithful on their journeys but are later placed in other locations (normally through setting up home altars), and this implantation in other places reproduces their devotion in a flexible fashion on a scale of multiple locations. To cope with the deterritorialization impressed on the faithful by their constant mobility, the symbols, charged with history and identity, are able to bring back the new emotional anchors put down with reterritorialization.

In addition, consecration is also found with the idols of mass culture: singers, football players, or political leaders, who generally personify the possibility for a low-income person of managing to scale the heights of success. One of the strangest cases is the cult of the football player Maradona, whose church was founded in Argentina 10 years ago. It now has 80,000 followers and has expanded rapidly to Spain and Brazil and to Mexico, where there are 7,000 members. The idea might seem to be frivolous, but as researchers into religion we should pay attention to a movement that is built up as an analog to a church and proclaims that football is a religion, making Maradona the forward, who had the number 10 (*Diez*) on his shirt, a metaphor for the word God (*Dios*) (written "D10S"). His two world cup goals in the quarter final against England in Mexico, 1986, four years after the Falklands War, one of which he attributed to "the hand of God" and led to Argentina winning the World Cup, are recognized as miraculous (cf. the film *Maradona*, by Kusturika). This unlikely cult has its feast days and rituals, its temples are the stadiums where Maradona played, and it also has a DVD calendar starting in 1960, when Diego Maradona was born. The church has already celebrated marriages, and the only requirement for joining was to fill in a form on their Web page. Although it is true that this idiosyncratic church does not seek to supplant the other religions, it is nevertheless a challenge to understand the motives of its followers for identifying with it and becoming members and even taking part in its rituals.[67]

CONCLUSION

Surveying some of the new forms of Latin American popular religious practice (Charismatic Pentecostalism, neo-esotericism, neo-Indian New Age, and the cult of images through which to colonize anonymous territory) has enabled us to establish that there is a move toward making the body central and consecrated. Faced by the assaults of postmodernity and globalization, which bring with them uprootedness, uncertainty, the anonymity of nonplaces, and the disenchantment with promises of progress, the new popular religions emerging now share the characteristic of being emotional. Always less focused on institutions and based on subjective experiences, though not necessarily individualized as they all engage in collective practices, they generate new social bonds of an emotional type with other participants, with the space they occupy, and with objects that provide anonymity. They are forms of colonizing the new spatial and temporal dimensions of the times.

Taken as a whole, these expressions of contemporary religion gain their legitimacy through the way of experiencing the sacred in the body. God, the cosmos, the macrocosm, the Holy Spirit, all find a base in living experience. This feature is present in all four cases. Although there might be some competition among the religions in which one disqualifies another, a common denominator of the new searches for experience of the sacred is the living experience in the body of the sacred. The body also appears as a frame bridging between contemporary religions and the long-standing traditions, between daily life and the media industries, between the transitory nature of intense flows caused by mobility, the daily journey, and the need to reterritorialize existence and identity. The body has become the mediator of intimate, sacred, or transcendental experience. But at the same time it appears to offer the possibility of creating a global, cosmic consciousness, which is itself promoted in the promised land of consumerism: through beauty, the sculptured body, well-being, physical health, and tranquility, for example. The body itself is the place consecrated to consumerism; it is the promise, made by advertisers to consumers, of attaining perfect happiness and personal transcendence, and its values are ever more hedonistic and individualistic as a result of the overvaluation of aesthetics, comfort, and pleasure. Transcendence and the supernatural are not to be found outside the body but in it, and at any rate they are assimilated and experienced by the body. And in popular religion the body continues to give devotional practices a new therapeutic function. Religious practice is not to get to the beyond but to heal the body and the spirit alive on this earth.

To sum up, we can conclude that today the body is the last bastion of culture. It is the basic unit of cultural location. It is also what allows cultures in movement to be relocalized and what makes it possible for the universalizing to be particular, one's own, and exclusive. It is the place where the unity of the secular and the religious, the sacred and the profane, the aesthetical and the ethical, and the spirit and the flesh are experienced emotionally. For this reason, the bodily dimension of religion will continue to claim our attention and require further studies.

GLOSSARY

Deterritorialization: one of the effects of global flows that put into circulation symbols, actors, and practices that have been extracted and uprooted from their traditional contexts (territorial, cultural, "racial," or "ethnic"). The dynamic of deterritorialization makes "people and things to be more and more out of place." The factors provoking it are waves of migration (rural-urban, inter-urban, and from southern to northern countries). The ideological and artistic exchanges it generates offer religious cultures to a much wider public through the essentially mercantile activities of the cultural industries and social interactions mediated by technologies of information and communication. See Kali Argyaridis and Renée de la Torre, "Introducción," in *Raíces en Movimiento: Prácticas Religiosas Tradicionales en Contextos Translocales,* ed. K. Argyriadis, R. De la Torre, C. Gutiérrez Zúñiga, and Aguilar Ros (Mexico: El Colegio de Jalisco/CIESAS/IRD/CEMCA/ITESO, 2008).

Habitus: according to Pierre Bourdieu, habitus is composed of "[s]ystems of durable, transposable dispositions, structured structures predisposed to function as structuring structures, that is, as principles which generate and organize practices and representations that can be objectively adapted to their outcomes without presupposing a conscious aiming at ends or an express mastery of the operations necessary in order to attain them."[68]

Holistic: the term *holism* comes from the Greek *holos*, meaning *whole, entire*, or *total*. It is the "tendency in nature to form wholes that are more than the sum of the parts, by ordered grouping" (C.O.D.); it means in effect that a whole formed by parts ordered in a particular way can perform functions that none of the parts on their own or organized in a different way can. In New Age spiritualities, the holistic view of spirituality is alluded to when therapeutic or healing techniques establish a connection between the individual and the universe. It is suggested that there is a connection between the individual, the collective, and the cosmos, on the basis of the belief that the parts contain the whole and the whole determines how the parts behave.

Magic, shamanism, witch doctoring: evolutionist anthropologists had linked magical systems together as a phase of religion proper to archaic societies. However today magic not only survives but, with the failure of modernity, is undergoing a renaissance. Shamans and witch doctors are referred to as specialists in magical or miraculous healing. Mircea Eliade described a typical practitioner thus: "he is believed to cure, like all doctors, and to perform miracles of the fakir type, like all magicians. . . . But beyond this, he is a *psychopomp*, and he may also be a priest, mystic, and poet." See Mircea Eliade, *Shamanism: Archaic Techniques of Ecstasy* (Princeton, NJ: Princeton University Press, 1964), 3–4.

Mestizo: (Originally Spanish or Portuguese, half-caste). Cultural *mestizaje* (or mixing) is the result of a fusion between two cultures, but the term is not neutral and does not refer to a simple synthesis between two different cultures. Because one of the cultures dominates over the other, syncretism in Latin America becomes the battlefield of tensions between different projects. In Mexico, Guatemala, Bolivia, and Peru, Catholic syncretism links Hispanic Catholicism to indigenous cosmologies and ceremonies, which have lasted till now though subjugated and prohibited. In countries with a larger population of African descent whose ancestors were brought over as slaves to Latin America, religious syncretism shows up in religions with African roots and Catholicism, producing syncretic versions such as Candomble and Umbanda (Brazil), Santeria and Rule of Ocha (Cuba), and Voodoo (Haiti).

Neo-esotericism: historically, esotericism was reserved for members of secret societies or circles with restricted systems of initiation. The prefix *neo* is applied to a set of heterodox religiosities with blurred limits which incorporate elements of nineteenth-century European esotericism that are combined with oriental and nativist influences to make New Age interpretations. Unlike historical esotericism, neo-esotericism is exhibited, spread abroad, and offered to customers on a massive scale through cultural industries. See José Guilherme Magnani, "O Circuito Neo-Esoterico a Cidde de Sao Paulo," in *A Nova Era No Mercosul*, ed. María Julia Carozzi (Petrópolis, Brazil: Vozes, 1999).

New Age: refers to a spiritual movement with no church, no dogma, and no central authority; it arose in the United States in 1960s, and its principal beliefs are the coming of a new astrological age in which life on Earth will be under the influence of the constellation of Aquarius, and as distinct from the Age of Pisces that came before it, the new era will be marked by all the cultural traditions of the world living in harmony with each other and with nature; and a belief in the universe as a system of energies in which every element is connected to the rest, so the individual acquires a new responsibility on a cosmic scale for the management of his or her own energy. Personal transformation based on self-knowledge and the healings offered by the various traditions are valued by New Age practitioners as a means of effecting deep social and cultural change. María Julia Carozzi, "Ready to Move Along: The Sacralization for Disembedding in the New Age Movement and the Alternative Circuit in Buenos Aires," in *Civilisations* no. 1–2 (2004): 139–54.

Pentecostal: according to Martin, Pentecostalism refers to the Protestant churches that experience the gifts of the Holy Spirit, which are demonstrated in powers of healing and speaking in tongues. The name comes from the word *pentecost* in the Bible, described in the Acts of the Apostles as the day on which the disciples received the gifts of the Holy Spirit. This current started in the United States at the beginning of the nineteenth century and came to Latin America with the return of migrants in 1920s, and it expanded through the missionary work of Pentecostal congregations.

Phenomenology: the German philosopher Husserl developed the phenomenological method, which proposes the description of the objects we find before us and grants validity to knowledge of representations and social significations.

Postmodernity: the French philosopher Lyotard named the state of culture after the transformations that affected the rules of the game for science, literature, and the arts from the nineteenth century onward the "postmodern condition." Postmodernity is defined as a time that appears to have left permanently behind instrumental reason and faith in linear progress as the center of social life and to have the characteristic of being incredulous as seen in meta-accounts, eclecticism, paradox, chaos, nonlinearity, symbolism, and plays on the language.

Reterritorialization: refers to symbolic elements that were circulating in the context of globalization and are now finally transplanted, appropriated, and practiced according to the cultural framework of the places and territories they have moved to, generally creating new religious hybrids between the so-called popular cultures (magic, Santeria, nativism, paganism) and the hybrid cultures or cultures of supermodernism (orientalisms and neo-Indianisms, pseudoscience, information technology and mass culture, fictionalized ancestries, neomagic and neo-esoterica, therapeutic and personal betterment techniques, contact with extraterrestrials, etc.). See Argyaridis and de la Torre, "Introducción."

Syncretism: "The union (or attempted fusion) of different systems of thought or belief (especially in religion or philosophy)." In Latin America, syncretic religions were generated because of the fusion of Catholicism and native American religions, and afterward of Catholicism and African religions. Through popular Catholicism, beliefs and rituals of the original religions have kept going, and they continue to be practiced these days under a syncretic modality of Catholicism.

Transnationalized religion: refers to the spread, on a smaller scale, of congregations and religious movements moving in the opposite direction to that of globalization or the worldwide expansion of the great religions promoted by the imperialist nation-states, which traveled from North to South, as the direction taken now is from the colonized countries to the colonial centers, from the geographical peripheries to the metropolitan centers, and so on. See Thomas J. Csordas, ed., *Transnational Transcendence. Essays on Religion and Globalization* (Berkeley and Londres, England: University of California Press, 2009).

NOTES

1. Translated by Nicholas Barrett.

2. These tendencies are explored at greater length with the presentation of empirical cases in Renée de la Torre, *Religiosidades Nómadas. Creencias y Prácticas Heterodoxas en Guadalajara* (Guadalajara, Jalisco, Mexico: CIESAS, 2012).

3. Imagined communities, which is what nations and the subcontinental identity are, are those in which numbers of individuals who do not know each other personally, and never will, establish imaginary links that form them into a communion through the knowledge that they are part of a larger community that allows them to share ceremonies, values, and symbols through which is represented as a whole. See Benedict Anderson, *Comunidades Imaginadas. Reflexiones Sobre el Origen y la Difusión del Nacionalismo* (Mexico: Fondo de Cultura Económica, 1993).

4. The term *Latin America* was invented to extend the dominion of the French Empire and to legitimize the invasions by France of the Spanish and Portuguese colonies. At the beginning of the nineteenth century, under the rule of Napoleon III, the Latin identity in American territory would provide a cultural unity for France to extend its commercial and cultural hegemony. See John Phelan, "El Origen de la Idea de Latinoamérica," in *Ideas en Torno de Latinoamérica*, ed. V. Tomo (Mexico: UNAM, Coordinación de Humanidades, Unión de División de América Latina, 1986), 441–55.

5. Leopoldo Zea, "Latinoamérica, Milenarismo en la Utopía," in *Hacia el Nuevo Milenio*, ed. Tomo II (Mexico: Universidad Nacional Autónoma de México, 2000), 46.

6. Renée de la Torre, "El Catolicismo Popular: Un Lugar Donde se Negocia la Identidad Latinoamericana," in *Union Latine La Latinité en Question* (Paris: IHEAL/ Union Latine, 2006).

7. Although Spanish and Portuguese are the majority and dominant languages, it should not be forgotten that there is a diversity of idioms and dialects among different regions and nations (the Spanish of Colombia is not the same as that of Argentina or Guatemala), with different pre-Hispanic roots (Mayan, Nahuatl, Quechua, etc.) or crossed with other transterritorial cultures (e.g., the Spanglish of Latin populations in the United States, where they are referred to as Hispanics). Latin America does not encompass a single totality but is inhabited by a multiplicity of national cultures with different histories and utopian aspirations, which might or might not consider themselves circumstantially as part of what is Latin American. There are also enormous differences of a regional, local, and even ethnic type within each nation.

8. Néstor García Canclini, *Latinoamericanos Buscando Lugar en Este Siglo* (Buenos Aires, Barcelona, Mexico: Paidós, 2002), 20.

9. Renato Rosaldo, "Ciudadanía Cultural en San José, California," in *De lo Local a lo Global*, ed. Nestor García Canclini et al. (Mexico: Universidad Autónoma de México-Iztapalapa, 1995), 66–87.

10. Christian Parker, *Otra Lógica en América Latina: Religión Popular y Modernización Capitalista* (Santiago de Chile, Chile: Fondo de Cultura Económica, 1993).

11. Pierre Sanchis, "Cultura Brasileira e Religião ... Passado e Atualidade ...," *Cuadernos CERU* 2, no. 19 (2008): 71–92, 82.

12. Theology of liberation, or liberation theology, also known as Latin American theology, refers to a theological movement developed by Catholic bishops and priests in Latin America from 1960s onward. Its originality consisted in interpreting the Bible from a Marxist perspective, from which an alternative understanding of the faith was

developed on the basis of a preferential option for the poor, which would continue to incorporate the points of view of the weakest members of society: the rural population, the urban poor, the indigenous people, and most recently women. Unlike European theology, liberation theology does not arise from an abstract intellectual concern but is the result of a Catholic program of action and social commitment, which is reflected and systematized in theology. This line of thought had social repercussions in the continent, through the formation of ecclesiastical base communities that worked through the method of "See, Judge, Act" from which different social and political movements developed in Latin America. See Renée de la Torre, "Vigencia de las Teologías Latinoamericanas," *Boletín de la Biblioteca del Congreso de la Nación* no. 124 (2009): 31–48.

13. Rita Laura Segato, *La Nación y sus Otros: Raza, Etnicidad y Diversidad Religiosa en Tiempos de Políticas de la Identidad* (Buenos Aires, Argentina: Prometeo, 2007), 183.

14. See, for example, the case of evangelists in Guatemala who continue to practice the cult of Max Simón, a syncretic Mayan saint. Silvye Pédron Colombani, "El Culto a Maximón en Guatemala: Entre Proceso de Reivindicación Indígena y de Apropiación Mestiza," *TRACE* 54 (2008): 31–44.

15. Deis Siqueira and Renée de la Torre, "Presentación," Sociedade e Estado. Dossier Diversidade Religiosa na A. Latina. Brasilia, Departamento de Sociologia da Universidade de Brasília 23, no. 2 (2008): 221.

16. Parker, *Otra Lógica*.

17. Susanna Rostas and André Droogers, "El uso Popular de la Religión Popular en América Latina: Una Introducción." *Revista Alteridades* 9, no. 5 (1995): 81–91, 87.

18. Bryan S. Turner, *The Body and Society* (London: SAGE Publications, 2008), 15.

19. An excellent theoretical review of this subject is provided by Turner, in *The Body and Society*.

20. Turner, *The Body and Society*, 15.

21. So the only way to understand this particular form of domination is to move beyond the forced choice between constraint (by forces) and consent (to reasons), between mechanical coercion and voluntary, free, deliberate, or even calculated submission. The effect of symbolic domination (whether ethnic, gender, cultural, or linguistic) is exerted not in the pure logic of knowing consciousness but through the schemes of perception, appreciation, and action that are constitutive of *habitus* and that, below the levels of the decisions of the consciousness and the controls of the will, set up a cognitive relationship that is profoundly obscure to the conscious mind. Thus, the paradoxical logic of masculine domination and female submissiveness, which can, without contradiction, be described as both spontaneous and extorted, cannot be understood until one takes account of the durable effects that the social order exerts on women (and men), that is, the dispositions spontaneously attuned to that order which it imposes on them. See Pierre Bourdieu, *Masculine Domination* (San Francisco, CA: Stanford University Press, 2001 [1998]), 37–38.

22. Aníbal Quijano, *Colonialidad del Poder, Eurocentrismo y América Latina* (Buenos Aires, Argentina: Antropologías Latinoamericanas, 1999), 202.

23. Ibid., 224.

24. Thomas J. Csordas, *Embodiment and Experience: The Existential Ground of Culture and Self* (Cambridge, England: Cambridge University Press, 1994), 7.

25. Maurice Merleau-Ponty, *Fenomenología de la Percepción* (Barcelona, Spain: Editorial Altaya, 1999), 15.

26. Pierre Bourdieu, *Le Sens Practique* (Paris: Les Éditions Minuit, 1980).

27. Lawrence W. Barsalou, Aron K. Barbey, W. Kyle Simmons, and Ava Santos, "Embodiment in Religious Knowledge," *Journal of Cognition & Culture* 5, no. 1–2 (2005): 14–57.

28. One of the most accepted definitions of religion in the academic world of cultural anthropology is that of Clifford Geertz: "Religion is (1) a system of symbols (2) which acts to establish powerful, pervasive and long-lasting moods and motivations in men (3) by formulating conceptions of a general order of existence and (4) clothing these conceptions with such an aura of factuality that (5) the moods and motivations seem uniquely realistic." Clifford Geertz, *La Interpretación de las Culturas* (Barcelona, Spain: Editorial Gedisa, 1987), 89.

29. Peter Berger, *El Dosel Sagrado: Para una Teoría de la Religión*, 2nd ed. (Barcelona, Spain: Kairós, 1981), 4.

30. Based on the coincidence of numinous experiences and experience of the *mysterium tremendum*, a mixture of fascination and fear at the same time, see Rudolph Otto, *Lo Santo, lo Racional y lo Irracional en las Ideas de Dios* (Madrid, Spain: Alianza, 1995).

31. Zygmunt Bauman, *La Modernidad Líquida* (Mexico: Fondo de Cultura Económica, 2002), 18.

32. Marc Augé, *Hacia una Antropología de los Mundos Contemporáneos* (Barcelona, Spain: Gedisa Editorial, 1995).

33. Daniele Hervieu-Léger, *Le Pèlerin et le Converti: La Religion en Mouvement* (Paris: Flammarion, 1999).

34. Renée de la Torre, "Los Nuevos Milenarismos de Fin de Milenio," *Revista Estudios del Hombre* 11 (2000): 57–78.

35. Bolívar Echeverría, *Las Ilusiones de la Modernidad* (Mexico: UNAM/El Equilibrista, 1995), 65.

36. José María Mardones, *Para Comprender las Nuevas Forma de la Religión* (Estella, Navarra, Spain: Editorial Verbo Divino, 1994), 99.

37. Francoise Champion, "Persona Religiosa Fluctuante, Eclecticismo y Sincretismos," in *El Hecho Religioso: Enciclopedia de las Grandes Religiones*, ed. Jean Delumeau (Madrid, Spain: Alianza Editorial, 1995), 705–37.

38. Following David Martin, "Latin America where the first explosion of Pentecostalism (and Evangelical Protestantism) took place in the sixties and even earlier." This author reports that there are 40 to 50 million Evangelical Protestants in Latin America. David Martin, *Pentecostalism: The World Their Parish* (Oxford, England: Blackwell Publishers, 2002), 71–81.

39. This denomination started in 1964 in the city of Guadalajara, where they have their world headquarters. According to figures from the National Institute of Geography and Statistics (INEGI; *InsitutoNacional de Geografía y Estadística*), in 2010 it had 188,326 followers in Mexico. According to their own pronouncements, they had around 1.5 million members in Mexico in 2000 and over 5 million followers in all. It is a church that has transnationalized, having established missions and temples in 45 countries: 263 in the Americas, 12 in Europe, 1 in Oceania, 2 in Asia, and 7 in Africa. Most of the faithful reside in Latin America (mainly Mexico, Colombia, and Venezuela) and in the south of the United States, with a big presence among Latin migrants. See Renée de la Torre, *Los Hijos de la Luz* (Guadalajara, Jalisco, Mexico: CIESAS/ITESO/Universidad de Guadalajara, 2000).

40. The Universal Church of the Kingdom of God (UCKG) started in Brazil and developed thanks to the use of the mass media for its missionary work (especially programs on television). It has managed to establish itself as a multinational church with a presence in 80 countries and has recruited 2 million adherents. It is commonly known as "Pare de sufrir" (stop suffering), as its temples are announced with this successful phrase. It is also recognized as the principal promoter of the theology of prosperity. This church has worked successfully at restoring big cinemas, where activities are held every day of the week, specializing in daily prayers to solve current problems, such as financial problems, incurable diseases, family trouble, exorcism and liberation, love therapy, and prosperity. See A. Corten, J. Dozon, and A. Oro, *Les Nouveaux Conquérants de la Foi: Léglise Universelle du Royaume de Dieu* (Brésil) (Paris: Éditions Karthala, 2003).

41. In his study, Carranza reports that there are approximately 40 million followers of the Charismatic Renovation Movement, with 270,000 prayer groups spread over 140 countries, and 30 percent of them in Latin America. See Carranza, cited in Eduardo Gabriel, "Catolicismo Carismático Brasileiro en Portugal," *Debates do NER* 10, no. 16 (2009): 101.

42. Thomas J. Csordas, "The Stirling Award Essay: Embodiment as Paradigm for Anthropology," *Journal of the Society for Psychological Anthropology* 18, no. 1 (1990): 5–47.

43. Thomas J. Csordas, *Language, Charisma, and Creativity: The Ritual Life of a Religious Movement* (Berkeley: University of California Press, 1997).

44. André Mary, "Politiques de Reconquête Spirituelle et Construction des Imaginaires Transnationaux," in *Religions Transnationales des Suds: Afrique, Europe, Amériques*, ed. K. Argyriadis, S. Capone, R. de la Torre, and A. Mary (Louvain, Belgium: Editorial d´Academia-L´Harmattan/ANR/IRD/CIESAS, 2012).

45. David Stoll, *Is Latin America Turning Protestant?* (Berkeley: University of California Press, 1990).

46. David Martin, *Tongues of Fire: The Explosion of Protestantism in Latin America* (Oxford, England: Basil Blackwell, 1990).

47. The term *frame bridging* helps to understand the way in which two different frames of interpretation integrate, fuse, or mix, like schemata of interpretation that enable individuals to locate, perceive, identify, and label occurrences within their life space and the world at large. The authors propose to use the term *frame bridging* to denominate "the linkage of two or more ideologically congruent but structurally unconnected frames regarding a particular issue or problem." See David A. Snow and E. Burke Rochford, Jr., "Frame Alignment Processes, Micromobilization, and Movement Participation," *American Sociological Review* 51 (1986): 464–81.

48. Francisco de la Peña, "Cuerpo, Desorden Mental y Cultura," in *Cuerpo, Enfermedad Mental y Cltura*, ed. Francisco de la Peña (Mexico: Escuela Nacional de Antropología, 2009), 11–30.

49. Luiz Edoardo Soares, cited in Segato, *La Nación y sus Otros*, 205.

50. See Victor Turner, *The Anthropology of Performance* (New York: PAJ Publications, 1987).

51. Latin American Afro-religions, such as Santeria, Candomble, and Voodoo, refer to religions of African origin that came out of syncretism with Catholicism and were practiced by African populations that had been brought to America as slaves. One feature of these religions is the syncretism found in its cults, as they could keep up their devotions to their African deities, known as orisha, while appearing to be venerating Catholic

saints. Very common in these religious expressions are magic, the experience of trance, and spiritism—elements that are appreciated by neo-esoteric circuits.

52. Kali Argyridis and Renée de la Torre, "Los Tiempos Inestables de las Neoreligiones," in *Los Retos de la Diferencia: Los Actores de la Multiculturalidad en México y Colombia*, ed. Odile Hoffman and María Teresa Rodríguez (Mexico: IRD-CIESAS-IDYMOV, 2007), 471–508.

53. See Renée de la Torre, *El don de la Ubicuidad: Ritualesétnicos Multisituados* (Mexico: CIESAS, 2012).

54. Renée de la Torre, "Alcances Translocales de Cultos Ancestrales: El Caso de las Danzas Rituales Aztecas," *Revista Cultura y Religión* 1, no. 1 (2007), http://www.revistaculturayreligion.cl/index.php/culturayreligion/article/view/214.

55. Renée de la Torre and Cristina Gutiérrez Zúñiga, "La Neomexicanidad y los Circuitos New Age: ¿Un Hibridismo sin Fronteras o Múltiples Estrategias de Síntesis Espiritual?" *Archives de Sciences Sociales des Religions* 56, no. 153 (2011): 183–206.

56. Feng Shui is a technique and at the same time an art, originally from China, for balancing energies in physical spaces and is very fashionable among architects and interior designers, whereas Reiki is a technique of physical healing from Japan, conducted through the laying on of hands by the practitioner, who channels universal energy. Both Oriental techniques are highly valued in neo-esoteric circles for holistic healing.

57. Renée de la Torre and José Manuel Mora, "Itinerarios Creyentes del Consumo Esotérico," *Imaginário* 7 (2001): 211–40.

58. Francoise Champion, "Persona Religiosa Fluctuante, Eclecticismo y Sincretismos," in *El Hecho Religioso*, 705–37.

59. Fragment of fieldwork notes during the equinoctial ceremony in Ixtépete, 21 March 2005. The complete description and analysis of the ceremony can be found in Torre, *Religiosidades Nómadas*.

60. Csordas, *The Stirling Award Essay*.

61. José María Mardones, *Para Comprender las Nuevas Formas de la Religión: La Reconfiguración Postcristiana de la Religión* (Navarra, Spain: Editorial Verbo Divino, 1994).

62. *Público*, February 21, 1998 (Guadalajara, Mexico).

63. The first appearance occurred in the city of Mazatlán, Sinaloa, and news of the event was propagated from February 8, 1996, in a regional newspaper called *Noroeste*. Later massive cover was given to the appearance by news programs on Aztec television and in "documentary" broadcasts by Jaime Maussán and Giorgio Bongiovanni (who make programs about sightings of extraterrestrials) on the program De fiesta con Kristy y Óscar. See http://cortedelosmilagros.blogspot.mx/2006/02/la-virgen-en-el-microondas.html.

64. Marc Augé, *Los no Lugares: Espacios del Anonimato—Una Antropología de la Sobremodernidad* (Barcelona, Spain: Gedisa, 1993).

65. Sylvie Pédron Colmbani, "El Itinerario de San Simón Entre Guatemala y Estados Unidos: Procesos de Reapropiación de un Santo Popular Guatemalteco," in *Variaciones y Apropiaciones Latinoamericanas del New Age*, ed. Renée de la Torre, Cristina Gutiérrez, and Nahayaelli Juárez Huet (Mexico: CIESAS, 2013).

66. Rudolph Otto and Lo Santo, *Lo Racional y lo Irracional en las Ideas de Dios* (Madrid, Spain: Alianza, 1995).

67. Diego Borinsky, "7,000 Adeptos en México, Llegó la Iglesia Maradoniana," *Supplement of Milenio* (2007): 67–71.

68. Pierre Bordieu, *Outline of a Theory of Practice* (Cambridge, England: Cambridge University Press, 1977), 69.

FURTHER READINGS

Barsalou, Lawrence W., Aron K. Barbey, W. Kyle Simmons, and Ava Santos, eds. "Embodiment in Religious Knowledge." *Journal of Cognition & Culture* 5, no. 1–2 (2005): 14–57.

Csordas, Thomas J. *Embodiment and Experience: The Existential Ground of Culture and Self.* Cambridge, England: Cambridge University Press, 1994.

Csordas, Thomas J., ed. *Transnational Transcendence: Essays on Religion and Globalization.* Berkeley and Londres, England: University of California Press, 2009.

De la Torre, Renée. *Religiosidades Nómadas: Creencias y Prácticas Heterodoxas en Guadalajara.* Mexico: CIESAS, 2012.

Engler, Steven, Anatilde Idoyaga Molina, Renée de la Torre, Pablo Barrera Rivera, and Silvia Marcos. "Religious Studies in Latin America." In *Religious Studies: A Global View*, ed. Gregory D. Alles. London and New York: Routledge, 2007, pp. 270–300.

Parker, Christian. "Christianity and the Cultural Identity of Latin America on the Threshold of the 21st Century." *Social Compass* 39, no. 4 (1992): 571–83.

Rostas, Susanna, and André Drogers. "The Popular Use of Popular Religion in Latina America: Introduction." In *The Popular Use of Popular Religion in Latin America*, ed. Susanna Rostas and André Drogers. Amsterdam: CEDLA, 1993, pp. 1–16.

Steigenga, Timothy J., and Edward L. Cleary, eds. *Conversion of a Continent: Contemporary Religious Change in Latin America.* New Jersey: Routgers, 2007.

Turner, Bryan. *The Body & Society: Explorations in Social Theory.* Los Angeles, CA; London; New Delhi, India; Singapore: SAGE Publications, 2008.

5

Religion, Commodification, and Consumerism

Vineeta Sinha

INTRODUCTION

Scholars have noted that consumption is a dominant social practice, often using the term *consumerism* to denote its excesses. Some have described the contemporary consumer as being on a "consumption treadmill," caught in a vicious cycle of "overwork and overconsumption."[1] These observations have led scholars to examine points of contact between the processes of commodification, consumption, and the overwhelming dominance of consumerist tendencies in late capitalism. Questions have also been raised about the effects of such practices, and emerging responses are often framed in highly moralistic terms. In an edited volume, *Commodifying Everything*, Strasser asks if there are limits to commodification and if everything is necessarily and inevitably commoditized. Part of the answer is present in Strasser's collection itself, which includes evidence of commodification of medical services, health care, coffins, human hair jewelry, pet business, gifts, Chinese nationalism, and so on, suggesting that it would not be inaccurate to state that potentially "everything is for sale."[2] Students of religion have wondered if religion might be the exception to the rule. Putting forward the commonsense view, Heelas writes, "Religion would appear to be the very last thing that can be consumed,"[3] but empirical evidence, both historical and contemporary, suggests otherwise. Social science scholars of religion and theologians alike have reflected on the effects of commercializing and commodifying forces on the sacred. This chapter offers a selective sampling of these deliberations.

A *consumer society* is defined as one where everyday life has been dominated by a concern with the need to utilize and possess material goods and services that are acquired in the marketplace. According to John Benson, in *The Rise of Consumer Society*, consumer societies are those:

> ...in which choice and credit are readily available, in which social value is defined in terms of purchasing power and material possessions, and in which there is desire, above all, for that which is new, modern, exciting and fashionable.[4]

David Lyon avers that "Consumer culture, dependent as it is on the electronically mediated signs and images that restlessly circle the globe, is in constant flux. More like a screen saver than a movie, it is always altering into new configurations."[5] He adds, "Consumerism, that is lifestyles and cultures structured around consumption, is a defining feature of the postmodern."[6] Echoing earlier pronouncements about the overwhelming and pervasive reach of market and commercial forces, Lyon makes the following observation about postmodern consumer society:

> Its effects are felt well beyond the store and the market, as more and more institutions—schools, hospitals, museums, government departments, universities, libraries, and so on—see their users as consumers, and their members and users respond as such. "Will it sell?" and "Can I buy it?" have become metaphors commonly used in all sectors of life, including religion. Nothing is non-marketable.... Just as the impact of McDonaldization is felt throughout the world, and in diverse contexts, so that of which it is a sign, consumerism, leaves no area of life untouched.[7]

Social scientists and historians have noted the ubiquity and inevitability of commodification processes. The *Oxford English Dictionary*'s definition of commodification has constituted the starting point for numerous scholarly inquiries on this topic,[8] and indeed for Strasser's volume as well. It is included here in the same spirit:

> ...the action of turning something into, or treating something as, a (mere) commodity; commercialization of an activity, etc., that is not by nature commercial.[9]

There is an explicit recognition in this articulation that it is possible to identify a category of acts and things that are by nature "not commercial," and the rendering of these into commodities is problematic and detrimental. Philip Sampson notes that the "culture of consumption is quite undiscriminating and everything becomes a consumer item, including meaning, truth and knowledge."[10]

Markets and marketplaces certainly precede modernity, but recently, students of religion have prioritized questions about the relationship between religion and market forces. Scholars of religion have queried *not if, but how* commodification processes and the allied practices of consumption and consumerism have impacted religions and religiosity itself. Of the numerous and complex responses offered, rational choice theorists have argued that in a world dominated by market forces, religion itself has become a commodity, speaking of a "religious marketplace" where various religious options exist for individuals as "consumers of religion." Working across a range of religious traditions, others have highlighted the rise of an industry for religious paraphernalia (material objects), for religious personnel and expertise, for religious practices (rituals, festivals, and processions), for religious spaces (pilgrimage sites and holy places), and marginally to more symbolic religious notions (blessing, charisma, spirituality, efficacy, piety, and devotion)—all of which are treated as commodities, mass produced, and further subjected to branding, packaging, and merchandising techniques. Numerous examples through history and across varied religious traditions affirm the existence of intimate links between religious spheres and commercial, worldly concerns. The commodification and commercialization processes have been noted for Roman Catholicism,[11] Islam,[12] Buddhism,[13] Hinduism,[14] and New Age religiosity.[15] An elaboration from the Hindu case is instructive. Historians have noted that in medieval India, Hindu temple complexes were integrated with a system of trade and commerce, something that was essential for their perpetuation.[16] Historical data attest to the presence of artisans, craftsmen, and traders who created and produced various objects that were required for worship in the temples. Thus, commercial activity was not by any means alien to the functioning of temples and worship within Hinduism, and it was certainly not introduced by an industrial capitalist system of production and consumption.

Cross-cultural examples further demonstrate that the spiritual and material do not represent ideological polarities but have been historically tangled in complex ways.[17] An excellent example comes from Kaufman's discussion of the Catholic tradition, where it is noted that the "spiritual and material have always been entwined at sites of pilgrimage."[18] Lamb observes that "Protestants, Jews and Muslims typically reject the concept of sacred objects, although in everyday actuality, many members of these traditions do hold material things in reverence,"[19] contrasting this position with that of Roman and Orthodox Catholic denominations and Hinduism, where the association of the divine with materiality is not a problem theologically. He further notes that "the Muslim concept of *shirk* (literally, association) specifically prohibits its followers from identifying anything created with the transcendent glory of Allah."[20] Nonetheless, he highlights that in practice, Muslim denominations do hold objects, texts, and buildings in reverence, a point confirmed through concrete ethnographic data in Starrett's work on religious commodities in Cairo.[21] Further evidence is offered in the convoluted intersections of religious domains within the realms of popular culture, material culture, visual culture, and various technological and communication modes including print and digital media and the Internet.

Religions continue to thrive with a vibrancy and dynamism that would no doubt both astonish and intrigue nineteenth-century European social thinkers, who anticipated the eventual end of religion in an age dominated by capitalist markets, modern science, and technology. Drawing inspiration from such logic, secularization theorists of the 1960s and 1970s boldly sounded the death knell for religion, but clearly neither institutionalized religion nor private religiosity have been laid to rest with the rise of rational, modernist tendencies. Instead, religious traditions of all varieties have demonstrated a capacity to morph themselves to ever-changing social, cultural, political, and material circumstances and to be conspicuously visible, not to mention relevant and meaningful, to millions of believers. Warner notes that "The religious market is shifting towards the pragmatic, experiential, de-traditionalized, post-denominational and therapeutic,"[22] where, in a diverse marketplace, the "preeminent authority of consumer choice" prevails. Consumers prefer participatory, individualized religion, so religion becomes provisional and optional.

CONSUMER CULTURE AND COMMODIFICATION OF RELIGION

Unpacking the relationships among religion, commodification, and consumerism takes us back to a puzzle as old as sociology itself. In the late nineteenth century, European classical sociologists, led by the likes of Max Weber and Emile Durkheim, theorized the fate of religion in the midst of foundational economic, social, political, and cultural transformations ushered by the arrival of modern society. Responses to the question of what would happen to religion under conditions of modernity included firm pronouncements about the irrelevance and erosion of religious sentiments, practices, and institutions. Theorists anticipated the eventual demise of religion, assuming the dominance of scientific, technological, and rational logic, which was seen to be incompatible with and hostile to religious worldviews. To some extent, the commodification and consumption of religion also challenge claims of secularization theory itself.

The concept of consumption has commanded scholarly engagement from social scientists in the classical and modern periods, an interest that has persisted in reconstituted modes into the present. The field continues to be vibrant, and it has rightly been noted that while consumption is "a somewhat nebulous concept,"[23] it is nonetheless a dominant social practice of our times[24] and worthy of sociological analysis. It has been associated with the complex process of industrial-capitalist development starting in the seventeenth century but is seen to have intensified especially in the highly consumer-oriented society of the twentieth century. Assuming a historical perspective, Warde has noted two dominant strains in interpreting consumption: the first carries negative connotations, conjuring images of destruction and wastefulness, of taking things in and devouring them; the second, a more impartial usage, views consumption as one of the processes of an emergent capitalist society in the eighteenth century.[25] He argues that the former tendency was twinned with an explicit critique of capitalism and of consumer society in general and had emerged from a focus on the "instrumental aspects of consumption."[26] These observations have not been neutral but are embedded in assumptions about the natural definition of commerce and religion as alienated, hostile, and incommensurate spheres. The latter emanate from ethical, moral, elitist, and neo-liberal critiques of consumerism and "excesses" of consumption. The rich and nuanced literature produced in debates from these two camps continues to be scrutinized by students of religion, and the final word on the value of consumption is yet to be resolved. It is beyond the scope of the present project to either survey or assess this body of scholarship in its entirety. Rather, the intention here is to articulate some strands in this complex discourse about religion's location in a consumerist culture where consumption is a dominant social practice.

Yet although critiques of material consumption are aplenty by now, the discourse is far from unified. Agnew presents the scholarly tensions in the field of commodification studies as follows:

> Should we look at the rise of modern market culture, as some historians encourage us to do, as a colonizing, not to say, disciplinary regime? Or should we rather see it as a liberatory resource for the reenchantment of the world...? Or shall we say that it is not so much a matter of interpretive choice as of historical necessity?[27]

Much of the discussion on consumption is focused on these underlying "norms, values, and meanings" of consumer culture, which are often judged as promoting greed, profit, desire to acquire, and so on. Ritzer and Jurgenson rightly note that:

> Instead of focusing on the structure of consumer society, the notion of consumer culture draws our attention to the norms, values, and meanings associated with a society dominated by consumption.[28]

In the 1980s, some expressed the view that consumption is not necessarily about hedonistic self-indulgence and narcissism and that consumers are not passive, apathetic, helpless recipients of market forces. In contrast, a more positive assessment of consumption emerged, for example, in de Certeau's writings, suggesting its emancipatory potential as a political force and a mode of resistance.[29] These alternative formulations hint that consumption could be an imaginative and creative process, involving the participation of active agents—the consumers—who appropriate goods and commodities for their own specific, meaningful purposes. Avoiding economistic conceptions of consumption, I concur with Hefner that "Consumption, then, is not the economist's inscrutable act of shapeless desire. On the contrary, consumption is implicated in identity and is socially communicative as well as technical or material."[30] This allows us to disconnect the functional utility of things from the process of consumption and to approach the latter using a different conceptual terminology and motivation.

Certainly, as demonstrated in the previous section, the religious domain is not immune to the workings of the market, before or after the advent of modern, rational capitalism. Historical evidence suggests deep engagement of commercial and spiritual domains across a number of living religions. In 1969, Berger famously noted that in plural, differentiated contexts, religion "has to be marketed" and "religious traditions become consumer commodities."[31] Given a multiplicity of worldviews, Berger further argued that religion itself can be rendered "optional" and rejected rather than continue to be seen as obligatory or essential—the core of his secularization thesis. Much later on, rational choice theories of religious behavior, embedded in an economistic model of sociology, viewed individuals as "shopping for religion," selecting from a range of possible choices, driven by rational self-interest on the basis of instrumental calculation about profit and loss.[32] Iannaccone, a rational choice theorist, noted that "the logic of economics and even its language are powerful tools for the social scientific study of religion."[33] Others have argued that in a "spiritual marketplace" of religious options, religiosity and church attendance are higher as compared to contexts where there is a dominant monopolistic church and little choice for believers. Not surprisingly, these views have also been resoundingly critiqued[34] on the grounds that this theoretical paradigm is severely limited in its overemphasis on demand and supply questions and the assumption that religion is like any other commodity, and thus market forces operate exactly in the same way on religion as they do on other consumer items. Furthermore, the economistic metaphor prioritizes utilitarian and instrumental logic in religious decision making, ignoring the complexities of religious choices and the centrality of religious experience and belief. Bruce has noted succinctly:

> In a nutshell, rational choice does not work for religion because there are enormous constraints on choice and because the information required to make choice rational is not available.[35]

As religion has been viewed as a "consumer item," the comparative differences between European and American religious landscapes have brought the commodification and marketing of religion and its effect on levels of religious participation into sharp focus. Warner notes:

> In a de-traditionalized post-denominational religious marketplace, the individual consumer is king, reserving the right to relocate their religious practice according to present personal preferences. Brand loyalty is in decline and increasingly transient. Religion of choice is replacing religion of birth. . . . Congregations are becoming customers and with new found confidence are shopping around. Church goers are moving from an inherited and given denominational allegiance to an individual choice that may be provisional and transient, reserving the right to sample other religious outlets.[36]

Comparing the "religious economies of America and England," he concludes that "in both cases it is market-driven churches that show greater resilience faced with secularizing trends."[37] Other analyses of American religion confirm that religions that have creatively and strategically responded to market forces rather than retreated from them have seen dividends in terms of their capacity to draw and keep members. L. Moore's *Selling God: American Religion in the Marketplace of Culture* and J. Carrette and R. King's *Selling Spirituality: The Silent Takeover of Religion* are good examples of such reasoning. Carrette and King note that "the book examines the growing commercialization of 'religion' in the form of the popular notion of 'spirituality.' "[38] Moore notes that religious leaders as "cultural innovators"[39] have engaged not only a "market mentality"[40] but also the realm of popular culture, contributing to the commodification of religion in an increasingly competitive and aggressive religious marketplace. A decade later, using identical language, Carrette and King remark that the "market mentality" is now infiltrating all aspects of human cultural expression in (so-called) " 'advanced' capitalist societies."[41] Reginald Bibby observes a similar move in Canada, from "religious commitment to religious consumption,"[42] whereas Grace Davie has called the dominant trend in British religion "believing without belonging,"[43] so that "believers" are also "consumers" who choose the elements of religion that appeal to them and avoid the rest. Important missing elements from these Euro-American discussions are the contemporary religious landscapes of the rest of the world, such as Asia, Africa, and South America.

It would be fair to note, with some exceptions, that the interplay of religiosity and commodification has remained a marginal concern in scholarly accounts of religion in Asia. However, a handful of works explore these dimensions, focusing specifically on material features of religion and their symbolism. Some important contributions from Southeast Asia are carried in an edited volume, *Religious Commodifications in Asia: Marketing Gods*, which explores the location of religion in the interstices of capitalism and globalization, and the attendant consequences in places such as Malaysia, Vietnam, Thailand, Indonesia, and Singapore. The collection's contributors argue that it is not only material items but also "blessings," "merit," and "religion" itself that are subjected to "commodifying tactics." In her account of the trade in Buddhist talismans in Thailand, Yee notes rightly that more attention must be paid "to material objects in religious practices."[44] Yeoh's analysis of material religion at a pilgrimage shrine in Malaysia is a rare ethnographic work, which highlights how religions operate in a world dominated by market forces but without diminishing religious sensibilities.[45] In another example, the author of *Religion and Commodification: "Merchandizing" Diasporic Hinduism*, uses the lenses of "visuality" and "materiality" to gain insight into the everyday religious lives of Hindus as they strive to sustain theistic, devotional Hinduism in diasporic locations. The analysis offered in this work confirms the complex interactions of material and spiritual dimensions in everyday religious behavior. Using empirical material from Singaporean and Malaysian Hindu domains, the author argues that despite the commodification of ritual objects, their sacred sensibilities have been far from degraded.

CONSUMING RELIGION: WHAT IS AT STAKE?

The process of consumption in religious domains has occupied and engaged the intellectual energies of students of religion. I have already noticed that in the broader literature, religion itself is deemed to have become a consumer item. I now move the discussion to a different set of emphases in the scholarship on religion and commodification. To start, there has been an overwhelming prominence in this body of research on religious objects as commodities. Following from this, a related concern is with the effects of such commodification on the realm of the sacred. Interestingly, the category of "religious objects" has been identified as singularly distinct and exceptional, with the caution that its commercialization "can get a culture into trouble."[46] The preponderance of religious items in the marketplace (and their concomitant use as religious signs or otherwise), together with their popularity and the fashion trends they engender, lend weight to critics of consumption who speak of its encroachment into the religious domain, in the commercial exploitation of religious symbols, and in the assumed corollary degradation of religion. Much of this criticism emanates from the logic that the worlds of religion and commerce not only are incommensurate but should continue to be detached, although historical and contemporary evidence cited earlier in the chapter suggests otherwise. This critique has served to assert and maintain distinctions between "sacred" and "profane/secular" realms on the one hand and "spiritual" and "material" domains on the other. This insistence has been challenged through cross-cultural, comparative material, which confirms that these modalities are deeply intertwined and impact each other in complex ways.

The notions that commodification of religion and its consumption are by definition problematic in denigrating the sacred and as being self-limiting need to be queried. To begin, what is meant by "consumption of religion" and how we think about religionists as consumers both require conceptual clarity, but through a grounded, empirical discussion. David B. Clarke and colleagues, in *The Consumption Reader*, note that "consumption is a particularly tricky concept to define,"[47] not to mention that it is a "wide-ranging, contentious and contested concept."[48] They argue that it "always involves much more than simply purchasing, obtaining and using goods and services" and that it "invariably spirals out in all directions. . . ."[49] The view that consumption is wasteful, nonessential, and frivolous and that consumers are naïve, lacking agency, and thus easily swayed also defines this discourse, often emanating from neo-liberal, elite, and ethical perspectives. These moralizing strands need to be queried as they carry loaded assumptions about consumption and consumers. It is critical to ask if and how consumption of commodified religious objects and other aspects of religion negatively impacts religious sentiments and sensibilities. What does consumption mean in religious domains?

Yet the critique of consumer culture and capitalism has been sharply articulated in studies of religion. The idea here is that consumption practices invade, intrude, and threaten the sentiment of the religious domain, leading to its debasement by subjecting it to the crass banality of market forces and reckless, avid consumerism.[50] Scholars such as Daniel Bell, Paul Heelas, and Robert Bellah are among critics of consumer religion and a consumerist attitude to religion. In their assessment, the very category "sacred" is at stake in religion's location in the marketplace. Heelas, for example, argues that the sacred cannot be subjected to utilitarian consumer demands, and if this does happen, "it ceases to exist."[51] He adds:

> Utilitarian consumers assume that they have the right to turn religion to their own advantage, selecting desirable items from this domain. Such people fit religion into their own lives. . . . Such people can be said to "consume" religion because it provides them with what they happen to want.[52]

Like Heelas, Reginald Bibby has noted the "movement from commitment to consumption,"[53] signaling an altered and limited mode of engaging with the sacred. The notion of consumption is used negatively and critically in such a discourse, as entertainment and self-indulgence. Insisting on the transcendence of the sacred and placing it beyond the reach of the consumerist ideology that ultimately and justifiably everything is up for sale, Heelas asserts that "To consume religion, turning to de-traditionalized forms (New Age or others, such as "pop" Christianity) in order to satisfy the utilitarian self is to lose sight of the sacred," adding further "for religion to be religion in any significant functional sense of the term there must be limits to the extent to which it panders to the consumer. It is a contradiction in terms to speak of consuming religion; and if so, it follows that there is no such thing as post-modern religion."[54]

Bell had earlier expressed a similar view in denoting these "new age organisms ... not religious."[55] Bryan Wilson had also suggested religion had become a commodity that one could choose or not. A critical portrayal of consumption is premised on the view that consumer culture negatively changes one's relationship to religious beliefs and practices. According to D. Miller, "As consumer capitalism has expanded, corporate production has encompassed cultural goods as well as material ones,"[56] arguing that commodification in the religious domain has led to the "abstraction and fragmentation of religious traditions."[57] He offers further elaboration:

> We can offer a basic definition of consumer culture as a situation in which elements of culture are readily commodified. Cultural commodities, like literal products, are characterized by abstraction and reification; they are abstracted from their conditions of production, presented as objects valuable in themselves, shorn of their interrelations with the other symbols, beliefs and practices that determine their meanings and function in their traditional contexts.[58]

Although I agree with Miller that the context in which objects are used is crucial, I do not share his apprehensions about the negative impact of commodification in the religious sphere. If, for example, religious symbols are decontextualized and transposed to an unrelated context, there is indeed the potential for their misappropriation and abuse. Recent examples involving Hindu symbols come readily to mind: Italian designer Roberto Cavalli's depiction of the deity Rama on designer bikinis, French shoe manufacturer Minelli's shoes with the image of Rama, and Lacey's Footwear featuring the "OM" sign on shoes, to list a few prominent examples. Expectedly, all these have provoked animated but divided responses from specific clusters of Hindus. However, examples like these are also readily available in India, as Hindu imagery and symbolism have been made exotic, glamorous, and embraced by popular culture in the fashion houses of Mumbai and Delhi. Hindu icons and emblems appear on tote bags, t-shirts, lunch boxes, and as tattoos on human bodies. It is important to note that the consumers of such objects are both Hindus and non-Hindus; for the former, these items are not viewed as religious symbols and are thus unproblematic. Yet these products do draw criticism from some clusters of Hindus who object to the meaningless appropriation of Hindu icons and symbols and their representation in what are considered inappropriate media and contexts. Similar

examples from across religious traditions demonstrate the crude and irrev-
erent modes in which religious symbols and insignia have been appropriated
in popular cultural realms but which have also been firmly critiqued by
religious practitioners.

THEORIZING RELIGION'S ENCOUNTER WITH MARKET
FORCES IN LATE MODERNITY

Scrutinizing encounters of religion and the marketplace at the turn of the
twenty-first century requires one to transcend modernist frames and argu-
mentations. It is vital to consider how a context of "postmodernity" or
"late/high modernity," marked by recognizably varied and novel sociocultural formations and consciousness that have not necessarily supplanted
modernity,[59] reconfigure religious expressions and religiosity. The elements
of agency and choice, especially religious choice, have been critical in this
reconfiguration, evident in the erosion of dominant ideologies and master
narratives in all societal spheres, including the religious. Some speak of
consumers facing a "choice overload"[60] and the possibility of concocting a
"self-made," packaged notion of religion, typically associated with "New
Age religion."[61] *Where* religion is visible and *what* it looks like have become
core concerns in current approaches to making sense of the religious
domain. Others not only query the form and shape of religion but also ask
what is done in the name of religion and how individuals express religiosity.
Secularization theorists throughout the 1970s and 1980s had already noted
religion's presence outside institutional locations, seen both in its privatization and in its shift to other societal spheres. Postmodernist societal tendencies and developments have produced other sensibilities and practices in
religious domains with the rise of "do it yourself," "mix and match," eclectic,
hybrid, individualized, detraditionalized, nonauthoritarian, and noninstitu-
tional religious preferences where individuals are "seekers" rather than
"believers."[62]

From the 1970s onward, sociological and anthropological research turned
increasingly to the complex process of consumption in cultural realms by
highlighting instead its "symbolic dimensions."[63] We see the shift thus from
"use value" to "sign value" of a commodity, a phrase devised and popularized
by Baudrillard, who argued that in specific contexts "commodities are given
meanings through a logic of signs."[64] Featherstone offers three helpful perspectives on consumer culture, which shift the field discursively and complicate the binary of "good" versus "bad" effects of consumption: the first view
looks at consumer culture negatively, where consumers are seen to be
manipulated and seduced by the marketplace; the second view focuses
on how people consume, how social relationships and identities are thus

forged, and how consumption delivers satisfaction; and the third view asks why people consume—and one response is that consumption brings pleasure.[65] According to Lyon:

> If the realm of religion is restricted to institutional churches and their social reach, then consumerism could be seen as an erosive force. Featherstone's proposal is counter-intuitive; more consuming does not necessarily mean less sacred.[66]

Lyon concurs with Featherstone's conclusion that "the sacred is able to sustain itself outside of organized religion within consumer culture."[67] Given this logic, the world of markets and consumer culture and their dominance does not necessarily have sanitary and sterilizing effects on religious practices. This also compels us to rethink simplistic assumptions about religionists as consumers. Evidence suggests strongly that believers and devotees as consumers and customers are neither available for easy manipulation nor passively led to develop tastes and desires for commercialized culture. Instead, the dominant culture of consumption (including in the religious sphere) that defines a postindustrial context is mediated through a range of socially and culturally specific motifs and resonances. This recognition implies that the processes of commoditization and consumption within the religious domain have to be interpreted alternatively, that is, outside of any attempt to take the moral high ground and complain righteously about consumption based on the fear of its pernicious and toxic effects on cultural practices. Presently, the encounter of the spiritual and commercial realms is happening globally, especially in novel ways through the emergence of new technological modes and media. But this is far from always being a "troubled encounter," and so I agree with Strasser that the commodification process can be "conflicting and contradictory."[68] It is clear that religious institutions and practitioners respond to, and appropriate, the logic of the market for their own ends rather than necessarily being subjugated to it.

Among others, Miller has highlighted the contribution of such famous theorists as Mauss, Levi-Strauss, Baudrillard, Barthes, de Certeau, Douglas, and Bourdieu, rounding off the list with the decisive input from Appadurai and McCracken in accounts of materiality, consumer culture, and social relations. This list encapsulates a wide range of perspectives on the complex relationships among commodity, consumer culture, and consumption. More recently, Schor has surveyed twentieth-century debates on consumption with a call for revisiting consumer critique carried in the classical writings of Veblen, Adorno, Horkheimer, Galbraith, and Baudrillard as a much-needed corrective to subsequent micro-level, interpretive studies of consumption that are devoid of a critical edge and lack of attention to macro forces.[69]

Does consumption of religious commodities necessarily diminish the value of the sacred? Could it instead be enchanting? How does the fact of merchandising of religious objects affect (if at all) the modes in which they are consumed? For a start, it is important to recognize that religious objects are not "trapped" in a commodity state forever; in fact they have a limited "shelf life" and eventually have the potential to move out from the marketplace into a ritual domain, thus activating their other, noncommodity attributes. Douglas and Isherwood, in redefining consumption, ask the right questions, such as "why people want goods,"[70] pointing out that "what happens to material objects once they have left the retail outlets and reached the hands of the final purchasers is part of the consumption processes."[71] So what does consumption of religious objects signify for practitioners? These "things," as commodities, denote a category of items that may be objects *of* worship, objects used *in* worship, or simply those that are revered and have sacred connotations; conversely, these may be approached as having no spiritual content whatsoever but are appreciated on "purely aesthetic grounds."[72] In the everyday consumption of this set of objects, it is possible to identify at least two dimensions. One may be denoted "aesthetic consumption" by both self and other (including tourists). It suggests that individuals are attracted to merchandise that carries religious insignia and symbolism not because of its religious or spiritual value but because of its appeal to one's sense of aesthetics, artistic and visual appreciation. This is the case with clusters of Hindus who, for example, purchase a statue of a Hindu deity manufactured in China because of its artistic value and not for the purpose of performing prayers before it; such objects are secured for display, decoration, and ornamentation and thus do not find space at the prayer altar. A similar rationale applies to non-Hindus who gravitate toward goods with religious signs and motifs and who may well be fervent admirers of religious and cultural traditions and the associated craftsmanship. In framing this mode of consumption, questions can be raised about individualistic consumerism, the politics of cultural appropriation, and the exoticization of the "other" as additional factors. Bowman's second dimension may be labeled "ceremonial, symbolic consumption." Procuring objects, including from the market for a price, for the express purpose of worship sees their usage integrated into everyday religious lives. Here the idea that consumption leads to debasement of religion cannot be sustained in view of data precisely from this realm of ceremonial utilization of objects. In theorizing everyday patterns of consumption of religious objects, it is limiting to begin with the premise that individuals are driven to consume these goods for the satisfaction of temporary, superficial, restless, and worldly appetites. Drawing from her work on the "commodification of the Celt," Bowman's observation certainly is instructive across a range of religious traditions:

However, alongside and within the general market, there is a specialist clientele, for whom the commodification of the Celt is not simply commercial or aesthetic but spiritual. The worship ethos of New Age and Pagan Religiosity open up a whole new era of consumerism, in which ingenuity knows no bounds. Whether this aspect of the marketing of tradition is producing spiritual empowerment or simply Celtic kitsch is for the individual to decide.[73]

Meanwhile Grazia and colleagues suggest that

Commodification is thus not the vanishing point of the subject into the commodified object but also of the object into pure exchangeability.[74]

However, I propose that this does not necessarily happen with commodities that subsequently enter a field of religious activity, as they acquire alternative identities. Although some "prayer things" (e.g., metal statues) may be passed down to one's children, by and large they cannot be recycled, exchanged, or resold. Speaking to the "sentimentality" of objects, Festa notes:

The tales told by things transform commodities from repositories of economic value to objective correlatives of interior emotions and personal experiences. The sentimental becomes the means of revaluing commercial objects: things are coveted not because of their economic value but because of the personal bond felt between the owner and object.[75]

Extrapolating from this insight, in religious consciousness, "once upon a time" commodities have legitimacy and are appreciated and cherished because of their ritual value and are not doomed to be assessed exclusively in terms of their exchange value. Neither are they rejected nor devalued because of their association and contact with the profane world of commerce and entrepreneurship. Thus, the merchandising of religious objects does not lead to mindless, individualistic consumerism, nor is it necessarily a threat to religious and cultural sensibilities. In making these arguments, one needs to be cautious of both the pitfalls of romanticizing consumption practices and the limitations of overstating the case for seeing meaning and value in participating in consumer culture. What is critical is to map the field of religious practices, to contextualize objects as they are used, and to determine their value for users. I argue that the embeddedness of ritual objects as commodities in the marketplace need to be acknowledged and theorized. Furthermore, practitioners can and do easily transcend this commercial attribute of objects and easily forget this characteristic as the focus shifts instead to how materials enable and facilitate a style of religiosity. Indeed, ethnographic data suggest that believers appreciate that things that they saw as indispensable for their religious activities could be bought at all; merchandising of such objects and materials for them was seen as enabling and not as debilitating.[76] Following the Maussian model, James Carrier states:

> We cannot separate the objects from the people who transact them and the
> social relationships in which they are transacted, just as we cannot separate
> the relationship from the people who are in it, the objects they transact, and
> the ways they transact them. And this is as true of the personal and enduring
> relationships of the family as it is of the impersonal and transient relationships
> of the supermarket and the factory.[77]

This sentiment resonates with my argument that despite the avowed dominance of commodity relations in the present and the transaction of religious
objects in the marketplace, their consumption in a ritual domain is not con-
taminated due to their prior embeddedness with a capitalist market.
Drawing inspiration from a close reading of Marx, Ward's observations
about the effects of "marketing of religious resources" for religiosity itself
are insightful:

> I predict, on the basis of my examination of Marx, that the re-enchantment in
> contemporary Western culture that takes place in and through the marketing
> of the resources of religion (its artefacts, myths, symbols, vocabularies, cos-
> mologies, beliefs, and technologies) will only develop further. We are entering
> a profoundly post-secular age.[78]

In the language of Berman, Ward sees possibilities for the "re-enchantment
of the world." I stand with literary and cultural studies scholars cited by
Agnew, for whom "the expansive, mercurial and aleatory aspects of a
modern consumer market are sources of radical hope, not despair" and take
issue with the "romantic, republican, and moralizing strains of the critique of
consumption."[79] Certainly, commodification makes possible opportunities
for mechanical consumerist behavior even with respect to objects that may
otherwise be revered as religious. However, this also enables creativity on
the part of consumers, who often use objects in ways unintended by producers and fashion them to their own needs, and who by no means receive them
passively and relate to them in frivolous and vacuous modes. Instead, they
participate actively in this realm and often create the need for new religious
products and services through novel approaches to religiosity, and in this
sense, the market may said to be consumer-driven.

Another analytical move in rethinking consumption practices in religious
domains can turn the discussion to the complex intersections of material
culture and religion. By now, Appadurai's 1986 edited volume, *The Social
Life of Things*, and the notice that objects have biographies and move in
and out of commodity states, has become something of a classic, pioneering
text but also one whose insights have been enhanced and honed in important ways. Two recent texts that emphasize human relationships with
objects and the fluidity and mobility of things are carried in *Thinking
Through Things: Theorising Artefacts Ethnographically*, a compilation edited

by Henare and colleagues, and Costall and Dreier's edited volume, *Doing Things with Things: The Design and Use of Everyday Objects*. Students of religion have extrapolated from these ideas and applied them to how and why religious practitioners use objects and what meanings they connote. In addition to producers and consumers, the terminology of "prosumers" has also entered the discussion. The term *prosumer* was coined by Toffler in his 1980 book, *The Third Wave*. The descriptor challenges the postindustrial estrangement of the processes of production and consumption in referring to a cluster of individuals who produce what they consume. Ritzer and Jurgenson note that "*Prosumption* involves *both* production and consumption rather than focusing on either one (production) or the other (consumption)."[80] Ethnographic evidence from the field of religion and commodification suggests that this process may be highly relevant. As religious practitioners use goods and services they might themselves have produced and created, they renegotiate their meanings and resonance and compel theorists to shift the emphasis away from the politics and morality of consumption toward other modalities. Indeed, there is encouraging evidence that the latter processes are already under way. I now offer a few empirical cases by way of illustration—from the Christian and Hindu landscapes—studies that have taken seriously the idea that things connote meanings and symbolisms that become apparent when their actualization is explored. More importantly, this material steers clear of the moralizing strains of the consumer culture and consumption discourses.

I begin with King's text, *Material Religion and Popular Culture*. This book engages with the realms of material religion and popular culture and their interactions—themes that have not received the kind of scholarly attention they merit. Through a focus on the everyday religious lives of a community of Catholics in Northern Ireland, King articulates human interactions with objects *as they are used in and through* religious ritual. She details the everyday use of religious objects, in attempting to establish meanings of such items as mass-produced statues, pictures, crosses, holy water fonts, beads, and crucifixes, and theorizes the broader connections between the spiritual and the material in enactments of religiosity. These texts rightly call for placing things at the center of human, social experience, which can certainly be extended to analyses of religion. King notes that, for practitioners, religious objects encompass a sense of power, but this is not derived from their exchange value in the marketplace but rather from the sacrality and power they are seen to embody. King further demonstrates that encounters with objects of religion inspire visceral (including emotional) and sensorial responses among practitioners, experiences that typically remain unexplored in analyses of everyday religiosity. An earlier text by McDannell, *Material Christianity: Religion and Popular Culture in America*,[81] argued how material artifacts, arts, and landscapes have sustained religious worldviews and enabled everyday religiosity. In the American context, McDannell demonstrated that the sacred and profane were far from estranged, seen also in the conflation and integration of consumerism, profit, and popular piety, challenging the asserted distinctions between sacred and profane realms.

The search for new analytical guideposts can also draw usefully from students of Hinduism who have scrutinized the complex interface between visuality, materiality, and popular culture in enactment of everyday Hindu religiosity. V. Sinha's research on Hinduism and commodification from Singaporean and Malaysian contexts is an exemplar of such a focus. One area of her research is focused on the place of flowers as commodities and ritual objects in Hindu worship. She narrates the story of flowers and their consumption by Singaporean Hindus. Working backward from the realm of consumption, she asked these simple questions: where do flowers come from? How do they get to Singapore? Who brings them in and through what channels? Whose labor and efforts transform loose, fresh jasmines, marigolds, and roses into floral strings and garlands ready for sale in the five-foot way shops on a daily basis, and their eventual use in homes and temples? Answers to these questions reveal the key mechanisms and processes through which flowers are secured and the networks through which they are distributed, often traveling long distances. It is hardly surprising that flower shops are blooming in Singapore: there is money to be made, there is increased demand in the market (attributed to enhanced religiosity and financial standing of local Hindus as well as the inflow of Indian Hindus), and the profit margin is high despite the stiff but healthy competition. The empirical material is used to ask questions about the meanings of flowers in Hindu discourse—at which point are they considered sacred, and when do they display secular properties? The discussion of flowers and their place in Hindu worship make it possible to reflect on the category "sacred" as applied to objects of worship.

Despite obviously being commodified, flowers and garlands, once they are bought, are by no means considered tainted or soiled through this economic exchange. They are in fact valued even before they are used in the act of *puja,* which is why proprietors are aware that they have to observe the greatest care in treating the flowers with the respect worthy of being offered to god. They have to be "pampered"—to show customers that they appreciate the religious value of flowers, but more because it makes good business sense to do so. Of course, once they are offered to god, flowers are venerated as having being sanctified through divine contact, embodying divine grace and blessing. Just to finish the story, because flowers are organic, they do decay and rot. So what happens to them thereafter? Ideally, they should be disposed in running water, or in a garden or at the root of a tree—to be returned to nature. In urban places, this is often not possible, and the used flowers and garlands do end up in garbage bins. This raises questions about the meanings of flowers in Hindu discourse—at which point are they considered sacred, and when do they display secular properties? Clearly, this is not inherent in the objective, essential property of the flowers themselves but is rather carried in the attitudes with which they are approached by devotees. The discussion of flowers and their place in Hindu worship make it possible to reflect on the category "sacred" as applied to objects of worship. The life cycle of flowers reveals that they move in different and alternating phases of "sacredness"; they are potentially sacred before being used in worship, after which their divinity is enhanced. But what happens to this sacredness after the end of the ritual or ceremony? Do they lose their sacred quality? Most importantly, the sacred status of a flower varies with its treatment at different points in the life cycle of a ritual. Dwyer and Pinney, for example, approach "visual culture as a key arena for the thinking out of politics and religion in modern India."[82] Diana Eck's famous work, *Darsan: Seeing the Divine Image in India*, serves to focus attention on the notion of *darsan* and the two-way interaction between devotee and deity in the act of *puja*.[83] As a testament to the broader appeal of this notion of "seeing," *darsan* has been borrowed and extended to analyses of other sociocultural and political domains in Indian society, such as the world of Hindi films, the Indian political scene, and the field of consumption and public culture in India.[84] However, despite the tremendous activity and energy within this field and the burgeoning literature it has produced, the intersections of everyday Hindu religious life with processes of commodification and commercialization have yet to be comprehensively explored. Yet this lacuna is not peculiar to Hinduism, and new developments in this field are encouraging. Notable contributions, adding to earlier efforts toward theories of the interface of mass-produced religious insignia and Hindu religiosity, include Kajri Jain's *Gods in the Bazaar: The Economies of Indian Calendar Art*, Karline McLain's *India's Immortal Comic Books: Gods, Kings, and Other Heroes*, and Sumathi Ramaswamy's *The Goddess and the Nation: Mapping Mother India*.[85] The exploration of religion's location at the interstices of capitalism, postmodern consciousness, and popular culture offers exciting opportunities for creative research, but with much still to be done.

CONCLUSION

My argument here has been that exploring the encounter of religions and the processes of commodification through the lens of consumerism and consumption alone is highly problematic. Furthermore, in scrutinizing the interpenetration of religious and commercial spheres, it is limiting to approach markets, monetary transactions, and indeed money itself as contaminating and debasing to religious sensibilities. A great deal of the emphasis in the field has been on how religious objects and materials are commodified and consumed. There is a need to shift the analytical gaze toward the abstract and symbolic features of religions and their engagement with commodification processes and consumption practices. Within the sphere of religious objects, approached as cultural commodities, evidence suggests that the coterie of objects produced, circulated, and exchanged through a thriving manufacturing industry and purchased by devotees/consumers may not as a matter of fact degrade the sacred domain. It has been suggested that commodification and commercialization of religious objects along with their symbolic consumption and utilization as cultural commodities may in fact enable enactments of everyday religiosity and piety. Taking into account the earlier discussions about prosumption and prosumers (which questions the alienation of production and consumption processes) introduces tremendous scope for recognizing creative impulses on the part of religious practitioners who are producers, consumers, and devotees concurrently. The concern with generating profits and the expansion of a market share do not sit uncomfortably with the potentially and ostensibly religious or sacred nature of the commodities being traded, a view that is sometimes expressed in the scholarship. The latter is embedded in the sharp distinction that is made between sacred and profane realms (and extended to apply to commodities) and the assumption of diametrically opposed values associated with these two spheres. Ethnographic data from Hindu, Buddhist, and Catholic contexts challenge this presumption and offer alternative readings: despite their commodification, as religious objects, goods, and commodities feed back into the realm of religious practices with charged meanings, they in effect support an enchanted field of practices rather than produce mindless consumerism or a disenchanted consciousness. Some alternative analytical strategies for making sense of the field of religion, commodification, and consumerism include a turn to material culture and a focus on how and why religious objects are used and how such usage may generate a sense of religious identity, solidarity, and community. The discussion also needs to be balanced with greater comparative, cross-cultural material from across the globe and from varied religious traditions to complicate and challenge the dominant Euro-American discussion thus far in this realm. I make a case thus for more concrete, historically and empirically grounded accounts of how religious spheres interface and intersect with commercial spheres. In closing, I make a call for seeking alternative analytical guideposts in theorizing this association. This requires a fresh perspective on how the very dichotomies of "sacred-profane" and "spiritual-material" are read. For example, it is unhelpful to perfunctorily inscribe destructive and hostile attributes to profane, secular, and material dimensions of social life in terms of their capacity to authoritatively diminish if not eliminate the sacred. Nor is it feasible to judge the latter as being vulnerable and thus weakening or withering due to the assault of profane, commercial, consumerist pressures that are additionally deemed to be sacrilegious. Keenan and Arweck note that the "study of materialized spiritualities—and spiritualized materialities" has not been seriously pursued by social scientists.[86] I certainly agree with this but would add that a preliminary required step is to unpack the categories of "spiritual" and "material" and to avoid reading them as necessarily oppositional, conflicting, and irreconcilable.

GLOSSARY

Aleatory: uncertain, random, dependent on chance or luck.

Commodification: to treat something as a commodity to be bought and sold in the marketplace for a price.

Consumerism: a social and economic logic and system that encourages buying of goods and services beyond that which is required.

New Age: referring to a range of alternative spiritual approaches found in the late twentieth century and beyond which emphasize individual choice and are suspicious of institutional religion and leaders.

Prosumer/prosumption: a term coined by Toffler to describe the way in which production and consumption are no longer separated, but in contemporary (postindustrial) societies, the producer is also a consumer of what he or she produces. The term seeks to show that the two cannot be distinguished in the way we would traditionally think of them as separate spheres.

Republic: apolitical arrangement where power rests with citizenry who have the right to vote and choose leaders who will represent their interests. *Republican* is derived from this root meaning and denotes a view that favors a republic as the ideal form of government.

NOTES

1. Timothy Robinson, *Work, Leisure and the Environment* (Cheltenham, England: Edward Elgar Publishing Limited, 2006).

2. Jean-Christophe Agnew, "The Give-and-Take of Consumer Culture," in *Commodifying Everything: Relationships of the Market*, ed. Susan Strasser (New York and London: Routledge, 2003), 12.

3. Paul Heelas, "The Limits of Consumption and the Post-Modern Religion of the New Age," in *The Authority of the Consumer*, ed. RusselKeat et al. (London and New York: Routledge, 1994), 102.

4. John Benson, *The Rise of the Consumer Society*, cited in Alan Warde, "Consumption," in *The Cambridge Dictionary of Sociology*, ed. Bryan Turner (Cambridge, England: Cambridge University Press, 2006), 88–89.

5. David Lyon, *Jesus in Disneyland: Religion in Post-Modern Times* (Oxford, England: Polity Press in association with Blackwell Publishers, 2000), 76–77.

6. Ibid.

7. Ibid., 80.

8. P. Kitiarsa, ed., *Religious Commodifications in Asia: Marketing Gods* (London: Routledge, 2007).

9. Cited in S. Strasser, ed., *Commodifying Everything: Relations of the Market* (New York: Routledge, 2003), 3.

10. Cited in Lyon, *Jesus in Disneyland*, 80.

11. P. Geary, "Sacred Commodities: The Circulation of Medieval Relic," in *The Social Life of Things: Commodities in Cultural Perspective*, ed. Arjun Appadurai (Cambridge, England: Cambridge University Press, 1986); S. K. Kaufman, *Consuming Visions: Mass Culture and the Lourdes Shrine* (Ithaca, NY: Cornell University Press, 2004); and C. McDannell, *Material Christianity: Religion and Popular Culture in America* (New Haven, CT: Yale University Press, 1995).

12. J. D'Alisera, "I Love Islam; Popular Religious Commodities, Sites of Inscription and Transnational Sierra Leonean Identity,"*Journal of Material Culture* 6 (2001): 91–110; and G. Starrett, "The Political Economy of Religious Commodities in Cairo," *American Anthropologist: New Series* 97, no. 1 (1995): 51–68.

13. Kitiarsa, *Religious Commodifications in Asia*; and S. Yee, "Material Interests and Morality in the Trade of Thai Talismans," *Southeast Asian Journal of Social Science* 24, no. 2 (1996): 1–21.

14. Kajri Jain, *Gods in the Bazaar: The Economies of Indian Calendar Art* (Durham, NC: Duke University Press, 2007); C. Pinney, *Photos of the Gods: The Printed Image and Political Struggle in India* (London: Reaktion Books, 2003); Vineeta Sinha, *Religion and Commodification: Merchandizing Diasporic Hinduism* (London: Routledge, 2010); and D. H. Smith, "Impact of 'God Posters' on Hindus and Their Devotional Traditions," in *Media and the Transformation of Religion in South Asia*, ed. L. Babb, and S. S. Wadley (Philadelphia: University of Pennsylvania Press, 1995).

15. M. Bowman, "The Commodification of the Celt: New Age/Neo-Pagan Consumerism," *Folklore in Use* 2 (1994): 143–52; and N. Zaidman, "Commercialization of Religious Objects: A Comparison Between Traditional and New Age Religions," *Social Compass* 50, no. 3 (2003): 345–60.

16. D. W. Rudner, "Religious Gifting and Inland Commerce in Seventeenth Century South India," *Journal of Asian Studies* 46, no. 2 (1987): 361–79.

17. Geary, "Sacred Commodities"; McDannell, *Material Christianity*; and R. P. Weller, "Living at the Edge: Religion, Capitalism, and the End of the Nation-State in Taiwan," *Public Culture* 12, no. 2 (2000): 477–98.

18. S. K. Kaufman, *Consuming Visions: Mass Culture and the Lourdes Shrine* (Ithaca, NY: Cornell University Press, 2004), 1.

19. R. Lamb, "Sacred," in *Studying Hinduism: Key Concepts and Methods*, ed. S. Mittal and G. R. Thursby (London: Routledge, 2008), 340.

20. Ibid., 341.

21. Starrett, "The Political Economy of Religious Commodities in Cairo."

22. Rob Warner, "How Congregations Are Becoming Customers," in *Mediating Faiths*, ed. Michael Bailey and Guy Redden (Surrey, England: Ashgate, 2011), 130.

23. Warde, "Consumption," 88–89.

24. H. Lefebvre, *Everyday Life in the Modern World*, trans. Satcha Raninovich (London: Allen Lane, 1971); and D. Miller, ed., *Acknowledging Consumption: A Review of New Studies* (London: Routledge, 1995).

25. Cited in Warde, "Consumption," 88.

26. Ibid., 89.

27. Agnew, "The Give-and-Take of Consumer Culture," 12.

28. George Ritzer and Nathan Jurgenson, "Production, Consumption, Prosumption: The Nature of Capitalism in the Age of the Digital,"*Journal of Consumer Culture* 10, no. 1 (2010): 5.

29. M. de Certeau, *The Practice of Everyday Life* (Berkeley: University of California Press, 1984).

30. R. W. Hefner, ed., *Market Cultures: Society and Morality in the New Asian Capitalisms* (Boulder, CO: Westview Press, 1998), 25.

31. Peter Berger, *The Scared Canopy* (New York: Anchor-Doubleday, 1969), 138.

32. Laurence R. Iannaccone, "Religious Markets and the Economics of Religion," *Social Compass* 39 (1992): 123–31; Rodney Stark and William Bainbridge, *A Theory of Religion* (Switzerland: Peter Lang Publishing, 1987); and Rodney Stark and Roger Finke, *Acts of Faith: Explaining the Human Side of Religion* (Berkeley: University of California Press, 2000).

33. Iannaccone, "Religious Markets," 123.

34. Gregory D. Alles, "Religious Economies and Rational Choice: On Rodney Stark and Roger Finke, Acts of Faith, 2000," in *Contemporary Theories of Religion: A Critical Companion*, ed. Michael Stausberg (London and New York: Routledge, 2009); and Steve Bruce, *Choice and Religion: A Critique of Rational Choice Theory* (Oxford, England: Oxford University Press, 1999).

35. Cited in Alles, "Religious Economies and Rational Choice," 96.

36. Warner, "How Congregations Are Becoming Customers," 119.

37. Ibid., 120.

38. Jeremy Carrette and Richard King, *Selling Spirituality* (London and New York: Routledge, 2005), x.

39. R. L. Moore, *Selling God: American Religion in the Marketplace of Culture* (New York: Oxford University Press, 1994), 119.

40. Ibid.

41. Carrette and King, *Selling Spirituality*, x.

42. Reginald Bibby, *Fragmented Gods: The Poverty and the Potential of Religion in Canada* (Toronto, Canada: Stoddart, 1987).

43. Grace Davie, *Religion in Britain Since 1945* (Oxford, England: Blackwell, 1994).

44. Yee, "Material Interests and Morality," 1.

45. Seng-guan Yeoh, "Religious Pluralism, Kinship and Gender in a Pilgrimage Shrine: The Roman Catholic Feast of St. Anne in Bukit Mertajam, Malaysia,"*Material Religion: Journal of Objects, Arts and Belief* 2, no. 1 (2006): 4–37.

46. Strasser, *Commodifying Everything*, 3.

47. D. B. M. Clarke, A. Doel, and K. M. L. Housinaux, *The Consumption Reader* (London: Routledge, 2003), 1.

48. Ibid.

49. Ibid.

50. Miller, *Acknowledging Consumption*; and Clarke et al., *The Consumption Reader*.

51. Heelas, "The Limits of Consumption," 96.

52. Ibid.

53. Reginald Bibby, *Unknown Gods: The Ongoing Story of Religion in Canada* (Toronto, Canada: Stoddart, 1990), 169.

54. Heelas, "The Limits of Consumption," 101.

55. Daniel Bell, "The Return of the Sacred? The Argument on the Future of Religion," *British Journal of Sociology* no. 28 (1977): 443.

56. Miller, *Acknowledging Consumption*, 3.

57. Ibid., 10.

58. Ibid., 72.

59. Lyon, *Jesus in Disneyland*, 91.

60. Ibid., 90.

61. Heelas, "The Limits of Consumption."

62. Ibid., 107.

63. Ibid., 89.

64. Ibid., 88

65. Cited in Lyon, *Jesus in Disneyland*, 78.

66. Ibid., 83.

67. Ibid.

68. Strasser, *Commodifying Everything*, 7.

69. See Miller, *Acknowledging Consumption*; and J. B. Schor, "In Defense of Consumer Critique: Revisiting the Consumption Debates of the Twentieth Century," ANNALS of the American Academy of Political and Social Science 611 (2007): 16–30.

70. Mary Douglas and Baron Isherwood, *The World of Goods: Towards an Anthropology of Consumption* (London and New York: Routledge, 1979), 4.

71. Ibid., 36.

72. Bowman, "The Commodification of the Celt," 150.

73. Ibid., 151–52.

74. Cited in L. Festa, *Sentimental Figures of Empire in Eighteenth-Century Britain and France* (Baltimore, MD: The Johns Hopkins University Press, 2006), 116.

75. Ibid., 118.

76. Sinha, *Religion and Commodification*.

77. J. Carrier, "Gifts, Commodities and Social Relations: A Maussian View of Exchange," *Sociological Forum* 6, no. 1 (1991): 133.

78. Clarke et al., *The Consumption Reader*, 63.

79. Agnew, "The Give-and-Take of Consumer Culture," 18.

80. Ritzer and Jurgenson, "Production, Consumption, Prosumption," 1.

81. Colleen McDannell, *Material Christianity: Religion and Popular Culture in America* (New Haven, CT: Yale University Press, 1995).

82. Rachel Dwyer and Christopher Pinney, eds., *Pleasure and the Nation: The History, Politics and Consumption of Public Culture in India* (Oxford, England: Oxford University Press, 2001), 8.

83. Diana Eck, *Darsan: Seeing the Divine Image in India* (New York: Columbia University Press), 1981.

84. Rachel Dwyer and Divia Patel, *Cinema India: The Visual Culture of Hindi Film* (London: Reaktion Books, 2002); and Sandria Frietag, "Visions of the Nation: Theorizing the Nexus Between Creation, Consumption and Participation in the Public Sphere," in *Pleasure and the Nation: The History, Politics and Consumption of Public Culture in India*, ed. Rachel Dwyer and Christopher Pinney (Oxford, England: Oxford University Press, 2001).

85. Jain, *Gods in the Bazaar*; and Sumathi Ramaswamy, *The Goddess and the Nation: Mapping Mother India* (Durham, NC: Duke University Press, 2010).

86. William Keenan and Elisabeth Arweck, *Materialising Religion: Expression, Performance and Ritual* (Aldershot, England: Ashgate Publishing, 2006).

FURTHER READINGS

Alles, Gregory, D. "Religious Economies and Rational Choice: On Rodney Stark and Roger Finke, Acts of Faith, 2000." In *Contemporary Theories of Religion: A Critical Companion*, ed. Michael Stausberg. London and New York: Routledge, 2009, pp. 83–89.

Clarke, D. B., M. A. Doel, and K. M. L. Housinaux. *The Consumption Reader*. London: Routledge, 2003.

Einstein, M. *Brands of Faith: Marketing Religion in a Commercial Age*. London: Routledge, 2007.

Featherstone, Mike. *Postmodernism and Consumer Culture*. London: Sage, 1991.

Haley, E., C. White, and A. Cunningham. "Branding Religion: Christian Consumers." In *Religion and Popular Culture: Studies on the Interaction of Worldviews*, ed. D. A. Stout and J. M. Buddenbaum. Ames: Iowa State University Press, 2001, pp. 269–88.

Heelas, Paul. "The Limits of Consumption and the Post-modern Religion of the New Age." In *The Authority of the Consumer*, ed. Russel Keat et al. London and New York: Routledge, 1994, pp. 102–115.

Kaufman, S. K. *Consuming Visions: Mass Culture and the Lourdes Shrine*. Ithaca, NY: Cornell University Press, 2004.

Keenan, William, and Elisabeth Arweck. *Materialising Religion: Expression, Performance and Ritual*. Aldershot, England: Ashgate Publishing, 2006.

Kitiarsa, P., ed. *Religious Commodifications in Asia: Marketing Gods*. London: Routledge, 2007.

Schor, J. B. "In Defense of Consumer Critique: Revisiting the Consumption Debates of the Twentieth Century." *ANNALS of the American Academy of Political and Social Science* 611 (2007): 16–30.

Sinha, Vineeta. *Religion and Commodification: Merchandizing Diasporic Hinduism*. London: Routledge, 2010.

6

Terror/ism and Violence in the Name of God

Lucien van Liere

INTRODUCTION

Religious violence has recently raised enormous interest. Media reports as well as academic literature speak increasingly about the impact of religion on situations of violent conflict. Specialized institutes and think tanks calculate risk factors for terrorist threats, using data analyses and risk theory to advise governments on social policies. Often seen as related to the phenomenon of fundamentalism or to certain traits of radicalism, religious violence is difficult to comprehend from a security-focused point of view (for more on issues relating to fundamentalism, see Volume 3, Chapter 1). It is important to understand the precise role played by religion in contexts of violent conflict. Contrary to popular belief, this role is not always played by radical or fundamentalist varieties of religious traditions, nor can this role be reduced to certain features, stereotypes, and patterns that apply for all contexts where religion-related violence appears. Indeed, religious violence exceeds the boundaries of disciplines and comprises one of the most intricate challenges to present-day multidisciplinary research.

I will critically study what role religion plays in the escalation of (violent) conflicts. My focus will be not only on cases of religious violence (facts, movements, people, etc.) but on a more comprehensive approach toward the presumptions and preconditions of the phenomenon of religious violence, using research from various disciplinary fields. A few questions are foremost: what specific role can be ascribed to religion in conflict situations? How should we understand the way people use religious discourse or appropriate religious traditions (texts, rituals) to frame situations of conflict? In other words, how are religion and religious discourses used in contexts of violent conflict? Indeed, I will not pay attention to the fruitless discussion about the possibility to explain religious violence from the presumed essence of "religion." This attempt can only lead to abstract language games—interesting to play, but, in the end, leading only into dead-end definitions of presumed essences.[1] I will approach religion as a powerful social force that enables people to frame situations in the public sphere and to relate (social) issues to certain perspectives, handed down by religious traditions. Religion mediates between living traditions and present-day issues. My starting point in approaching religion will thus be the *social performance* of religion. This way, the analysis of religion-related violence and, as the title of this chapter shows, "terror/ism and violence in the name of God" should concentrate on discourses, texts, and symbols used during local and global conflicts to frame and charge (public, social) occasions as (fundamentally) religious.

MILITANTS FOR PEACE AND WAR

The question of how religion is used to frame (violent) conflict is not automatically a question about religion-related violence. Religion seems to act as a linguistic and cultural depot that is indeed used by some to inflame violence but by others to encourage moderation or even reconciliation. This phenomenon, famously coined by Appleby as the "ambivalence of the sacred,"[2] is observed by many social researchers, both empirical and theoretical. It is this phenomenon that might ring a bell about religious violence. If "religion" can do different things in the same context, on what factors does it depend to choose a violent or a peaceful path? And if religion can encourage people to go either way, does this not mean that, in studying contexts in which religion-related violence erupts, religion as such cannot unproblematically be indicated as the risk factor for violence per se? Be that as it may, religious actors can change a situation by understanding (and sometimes transforming) the actual state of affairs at (and to) a religious level. Appleby distinguishes and describes different types of so-called religious militants whose actions and discourses are informed by strongly held religious presumptions. Some of them he describes as extremists and exclusivists (i.e., the image of the religious militant that includes the religious terrorist), whereas others are militant peacemakers. These peacemakers, Appleby argues, are "no less passionate, no less 'radical' than the extremist; indeed, one could argue that the militant peacemaker's rejection of violence as a means of achieving political goals is the more strenuous and radical path."[3] Although these religious peacemakers are not studied in this chapter,[4] it is nonetheless important to note that religion can be a source for both violent and irenic performative radicalness. My interest here goes to the militant who uses religion to understand and transform the actual state of affairs (politics, economy, religion, culture) and who does not shy away from violence. On the contrary, he or she even considers violence to be a *rightful* tool in his or her hands. Such militants have entered a situation in which they prefer to obey a "higher" law than the law of the country that they inhabit. This type of violent militancy is extremely complex and knows multiple layers; it might help us understand what is at stake if we can disentangle some of these different layers.

QUESTIONING "RELIGIOUS VIOLENCE"

Why does someone commit an act of violence in the name of his or her god? Answering this as an isolated question will always be unsatisfying because the question tries to understand the subjective considerations behind the perpetrator's act of violence and reveals previous incomprehension. If we change the "why" for a "when," the context of the act becomes visible, and although things might seem to become more complex, they might become more comprehensible too. "Religion" is never isolated from its historical, economic, cultural, and political context, and neither can a single act of violence committed in the name of religion be reduced to "religious violence." There is always more than meets the eye. To understand religion-related violence, it is important to notice that there is not such a thing as a pure religious form of committing violence. Violence is a human trait, and conditions are widely discussed not only by philosophers and sociologists but also by journalists and policy makers. What makes religious violence a special branch of violence is the way in which religion is part of the contextual structure wherein people accept and justify violence.

The question then is not why but *when* do people commit acts of violence in the name of their religion. If linking religious violence to the essence of religion is a dead alley, as I argued, and religious violence cannot be reduced to the act of violence alone but needs to be contextualized to see and understand the multiple layers that are mediated in the act, under what circumstances does religious violence appear?

ELEMENTS OF CONFLICT ENHANCEMENT

Taylor argues that religious violence conceives three main elements. If religious violence appears, it (1) is excessive, (2) is purifying, and (3) has often, but not always, a ritual aspect to it.[5] Taylor calls religious violence "categorical" to distinguish between personal and impersonal violence and suggest it is based on its own agenda. Impersonal violence is violence that is committed against people belonging to a different religion, faith, ethnicity, ideology, political party, nation, and so on. Although the excessive, purifying, and ritual aspects that Taylor ascribes to religious violence cannot convincingly function as aspects distinguishing religious violence from other types of violence belonging to the categorical family, categorical violence surely is an interesting term for religion-related violence. During violent conflicts, religious groups tend to distinguish themselves from others on the basis of religious features. Opponents become framed as religious opponents. Political and economic tensions "implode" into religious divisions. The war on Ambon (Indonesia) (1999–2002) can count as an example. This war was widely labeled by journalists around the globe as a religious war in which Christians and Muslims were killing each other. After the war was ended by the Malino Treaty in 2002, more than 10,000 people had been killed. The war, however, could not have erupted without social-political tensions, a power politics of transmigration, and the Asian monetary crisis of 1997. Religion absorbed all these social tensions and transformed them into a fundamental religious clash between Christians and Muslims. In this context, religion worked as a strong category used to deal with social tensions due to economic uncertainty and fear.

Beside the fact that religious violence is categorical violence, it can also be understood as a variety of cultural violence. *Cultural violence,* a term introduced and developed by Norwegian sociologist Johan Galtung,[6] is a specification of his earlier coined term *structural violence,* which has influenced many scientists dealing with the question of violence. With structural violence, Galtung means "those aspects of culture, the symbolic sphere of our existence—exemplified by religion and ideology, language and art, empirical science and formal science (logic, mathematics)—that can be used to justify or legitimize direct violence." Galtung refers not only to symbols such as flags, images, statues, stars, and crosses but also to speeches. Cultural violence, however, he argues, "makes direct and structural violence look, even feel, right—or at least not wrong."[7] Understanding religious violence as cultural violence means that religion is a part of the affective legitimization of direct violence. In Galtung's logic, it is possible to say that religious violence explains the context in which violence is justified. In other words, it is important to trace direct violence back to the source of its justification, which, in Galtung's view, is part of the violence as well. Therefore, religion legitimating violence is called "religious violence." Interestingly, it is not the act of violence itself that is "religious," but the religious justification of and lead-up to the act of violence that is called "religious violence."

The question of *when* people commit violence in the name of their religion implicitly asks in what context religion justifies acts of violence. In what global and local context do we speak about religious violence? Most religious violence is group violence. Most group violence is violence committed by groups that feel unrepresented by (local) governmental institutions. This feeling of being unrepresented may result in social frustration and the belief that people are excluded on purpose. Fox has shown that government involvement in religion is increasing significantly worldwide.[8] This might explain why so many religion-related conflicts involve the state. It also shows that many governments use religion as a tool of repression. Related to this development, it is important to notice that most group violence erupts in contexts of economic discrimination and political disfavoring. Analysts have indicated exclusion from (institutionalized) power and economic and political discrimination as important risk factors substantially increasing the possibility of violence[9] or, in other words, increasing the willingness to justify violence as a tool for a revolt or as an instrument for self-defense.

From a different perspective, sociocultural analysts have analyzed cultural symbols and memory as determining factors in translating old grievances into new (sociotraumatic) perceptions.[10] Sometimes, groups that turn to violence do have a history of violence or are embedded into a history of negative stereotyping. These structural social and cultural elements can be discovered at the background of many conflicts, including religious ones. Religions do not exclude these elements but translate them into religious discourse. Religious groups feel that they are excluded and discriminated against because they are a *religious* group. They feel that their social identity is contested by other groups or by the state. They feel that their religion is in danger "of losing its distinctiveness and being absorbed" into secularisms, other religions, or traditions.[11] Because of this, religious actors frame perceived exclusion or discrimination as the result of a deep religious conflict, depending on the history of interreligious coexistence, the relationship with the state, and other structural, historical, and cultural aspects such as stereotyping and former violence.

The question of *when* people commit acts of violence in the name of their religion can now be more specified. People commit acts of violence in the name of their religion if they hold the idea that their religion justifies an act of violence under given circumstances. Or, to quote Galtung, if it "feels good or at least not wrong" to pass to violence.[12] Once again, the eruption of violence is preceded by a complex context. In this context, justification of violence is not an uncontested trait of religion. As most religions condemn categorical acts of violence unless the religious in-group is threatened, offended, and attacked,[13] acts of religious violence are generally justified as acts of self-defense. It is important to notice that if people feel threatened as a religious group, the threat is already felt within the social context. Responses justifying violence predominantly justify violence that has already erupted. Fox, researching the multiple contexts of religion and the state, argues that religion is seldom the sole instigator of violence in contexts of separatist revolts against governments.[14] But once religion gets involved in a conflict, it changes the conflict into a religious clash. This makes, he observes, the conflict more intense. It is important to comprehend this observation. The possibility of religious actors to deal with violent conflict based on the repository of texts, rituals, histories, memories, and interpretations of their specific traditions activates the religious frame. As a result, the present-day conflict is partly decontextualized from its political, economic, and cultural aspects and recontextualized within the religious frame. Therefore, the conflict takes on a religious meaning, which intensifies the conflict. I will deal with this issue later on.

Another important perspective on (religious) violence is presented by Girard.[15] According to Girard, conflict is the result of acquisitive imitation and rivalry. Although a society is based on what he calls *mimesis* (imitation), and *mimesis* is the basic tenet for learning, this important element of social behavior is also responsible for the eruption of social conflict, Girard argues. As desire is not individual but social, people develop their desire in the image of the other. You need, in other words, the other's desire in order to desire. It is not the object you want, but through your rivalry with the other, the object becomes more and more important. If this object becomes rare, the rivalry becomes more intense and the distance between people decreases. As a result, a crisis appears in which the rivals are contesting each others' positions and linking them to the object. Although the enemies perceive their conflict as essential, they are each others' perfect doubles. It takes a third party to channel the negative energy away from the rivals and restore the peace. This third party is the scapegoat—someone who is not involved in the conflict but nevertheless upon whom is projected all responsibility and who represents the negative stereotypes of a society. Girard's analysis can fruitfully be applied in many contexts where people, once involved in a conflict, imitate their opponents' aggression: mobs shout at each other, opponents rail against each other, and enemies frame each other with equal intensity and eagerness, accusing each other through media channels with equal accusations.

Applying Girard's notions to religious violence, is it interesting to note that religious violence is, most of the time, not about others being religiously different but about being so incredibly the same. Although actors have the idea that the others essentially differ, they are entangled in an acquisitive mimetic process; they rival with the other in the image of violence and vengeance.

RELIGIOUS TERRORISM

One of the great challenges that political analysts, journalists, and scientists face is to understand the phenomenon of religious terrorism. Again, it is important not to isolate this phenomenon but to describe its appearance in its specific, intricate context.

From a juridical point of view, a terrorist strikes terror (from *terrere*, "to make tremble") into a social situation with the purpose of destabilizing (a part of) the society. Therefore, a terrorist's action is categorical (impersonal) in such a way that his or her victims are selected at random, which increases social fear. This impersonality is exactly the difference between political violence (directed against political opponents) and terrorist violence. The *impact* of the terrorist's actions is presumed by the terrorist's perspective to be more important than the act itself. Therefore, terrorism is, in DeLillo's words, "the language of being noticed."[16] Terror is pre-eminently a public statement that claims attention.

Although terrorism is not something new,[17] since the Al Qaeda attacks on 9/11, an enormous flow of literature has been produced. Most literature, however, deals with partial understandings of terrorism, describing the phenomenon from a juridical (how to criminalize terrorism just like—for instance—"crimes against humanity")[18], historical, social, psychological (the idealization of objects),[19] or media (terrorism as partly media-framed and media-made, shaping public opinion)[20] point of view. Some analysts, like Horgan, contest the abnormality of "the terrorist," arguing that a terrorist is made under certain psychosocial circumstances and remains "unremarkable" in psychological terms.[21] This raises the discussion of whether interpretations of the terrorist are not trying to frame this phenomenon as a stereotype of barbaric otherness. All these readings, however, encounter disciplinary boundaries. As the jurist Saul shows, attempts like those of the United Nations and other efforts under international law to criminalize terrorism raise philosophical, theological, social, and other issues that exceed the disciplinary frame of legal studies.[22]

On the other hand, in many sociopolitical contexts, global Al Qaeda–style terrorism, and the war on terror in Afghanistan and Iraq, created a new perspective on international security. Asad comes up with the term *new epistemic community* to describe a new language and practice that formed new frames of what is permitted and what is not, so that governments could legitimate everything from mass surveillance and the transportation of suspects to foreign torture centers to "preemptive strike."[23] This response to terrorism, shifting what was permitted, was not without "terror" and not without religion.[24] In different international contexts, the redefinition of terrorism as a branch of Islamic extremism encouraged governments to deal accordingly with separatists and local *jihad* groups, like the predominantly Islamic rebels in Chechnya who were labeled, after 9/11, as "terrorists" by the Russian government, justifying a tough control of social space, and the Laskar Jihad, fighting a *jihad* on Ambon without international aspirations, who were suddenly engaged in "terrorist activities." During the Libyan War in 2011, Muammar Gaddafi was pointing to the Libyan rebels as "rats" and "terrorists," and in 2012, Syrian president Bashar al-Assad spoke about Al Qaeda terrorist cells, referring to the insurgents in cities like Homs.

It may be clear that "terrorism" is a difficult concept to grasp. Whether you approach the subject from a juridical, ethical, or historical point of view, the question of *who defines* what terrorism is cannot be left out of scope. The old adage that "one person's terrorist is another person's freedom fighter" remains true and forces us to jump deeper and deeper into the contextual question.

One of the historical layers of present-day Islamic terrorism is the struggle for independence and the right to live according to Islamic law (*sharia*). Modern Islamic Sunni violence (Sunni Islam is the largest branch of Islam) has its roots in radical protests against Ottoman rulers and European colonial rulers. The Wahhabi movement (a branch of Islamic radicalism based on the teachings of Muhammad ibn Abd al-Wahhab, 1703–1792) emerged during the late eighteenth century and gradually influenced other Islamic radicalisms during the nineteenth century. These radical Islamic groups were fighting for independence and the right to obey their *sharia* laws. This is important to notice because the religious violence committed by these radical groups was justified within the boundaries of their laws.

In the twentieth century, a few events encouraged Islamic radicalism to go in different directions. One direction was taken by Hassan al-Banna (1906–1949), who founded the Muslim Brotherhood in 1928, combining political activism with bottom-up charity work. The Muslim Brotherhood reinterpreted the Islamic tradition from an existential point of view, leading to a political assessment of martyrdom (by Sayyid Qutb, 1906–1966) and a strong wish to establish its own variety of *sharia* law.

Another direction was taken on the eve of and during the Iranian Revolution of 1979. This important revolution, which staggered Western media, was preceded by an existential reinterpretation of the basic sources of Shia Islam[25] (the second largest branch of the Islamic tradition, holding different perspectives on leadership and martyrdom) by influential intellectuals such as Ali Shariati (1933–1977) and Jalal Al-e-Ahmad (1923–1969).[26] These thinkers had put Islam on the political stage as a dynamic source of a new radical revolutionary politics. Parallel with the American Christian fundamentalist movement (a movement of Christian radicalism that emerged at the start of the twentieth century in the United States but was revived by Jerry Falwell, who coestablished the Moral Majority in 1979 and wanted to "resist" the "drug culture" of the United States[27]), journalists and public thinkers such as Anthony Burgess started to speak about the great dangers of political Islam, labeling the Iranian movement as "Islamic fundamentalism." Both fundamentalisms opted for more influence on national politics.

Both branches of radicalism, the Sunni Muslim Brotherhood in Egypt and the Shia revival in Iran, have bred, under specific circumstances, violence against other religious groups or against the state. Especially, the Muslim Brotherhood had great impact in many different contexts, from Lebanon to Indonesia. But although these groups share a potential not to shy away from violence if violence is needed and permitted in their legalist view, they do not contain structural elements that justify terror. Another and third branch of Islamic radicalism was, however, developed during the war between Russia and Afghanistan (1979–1989). During this war, the Taliban, assisted by the United States and influenced by Wahhabism, fought against the Russians and at the same time enforced its grip on the Afghan population. After this war ended in 1989, the Taliban implemented its own radical variety of *sharia* law, leading to a radical effort to purify the country of non-Islamic influence. After the Al Qaeda attacks in 2001, which took Sunni Islamic violence for the first time to the Western world, Afghanistan became the world's hot spot. Many *mujahedeen* (people fighting a jihad) from outside Afghanistan had joined the resistance against the Russians and—now—against the allied forces. Some of these fighters took the energy of the battlefield back "home."

One of these men was Imam Samudra (1970–2008). Samudra had learned to make explosives in Afghanistan. When he returned to Indonesia, he became involved in the Jemaah Islamiyyah, a local terrorist network responsible for several attacks in Indonesia and Malaysia. On October 12, 2002, a bomb attack on two pubs—the Sari Club and Paddy's Bar—killed at least 202 people.[28] Three people were held responsible for the attack, Imam Samudra, Ali Gufron (Mukhlas), and Amrozi Nurhasyim. They were arrested by the Indonesian police, sentenced to death, and executed in autumn 2008. What interests me here is not the violence but the justification of it. Samudra's justification entails elements that might teach us something about *when* people commit atrocities in the name of their religion. Imam Samudra said that he was inspired by stories and pictures he found on the Internet after he returned home. Through the Internet he found information about the impact of the allied attack on the ground. He recounts how he found pictures of dead children and babies without heads.[29] Samudra wrote that he wanted to avenge these children.[30] His will to kill was, oddly enough, a will to avenge the helpless. It was an attempt to make a twisted copy of the suffering and pain of these helpless unattended infants in the heart of what he considered filthy pleasure and immorality (the clubs on Bali), thus returning the violence toward (symbolic) representations of the perpetrators: "Americans," a category that also includes Australians, Balinese, and Europeans.[31] If we change the question of *when* people commit acts of violence in the name of their religion into when did Imam Samudra commit acts of violence in the name of his religion, it is interesting to see that he committed violence in a global context of violence in which information comes through digital resources. However, not only did Samudra revenge the dead children he saw on the Internet, but his religious leaders also justified revenge.

There exists an interesting correspondence between members of Al Qaeda such as Ayman al-Zawahiri, Azmiraay al-Maarek, and Osama bin

Laden concerning several hot issues, including the victims of 9/11. This correspondence was found accidentally on the hard disk of an IBM computer in Afghanistan by journalist Alan Cullison. It contains an unfinished ideological legitimation for the random killings of civilians during the 9/11 attacks.[32] Not without reason, the question within the terrorist network was raised about the killing of innocent people. The document was written by Ramzi bin al-Shibh, at the time of writing detained at Guantanamo Bay, Cuba, and accused of being the key facilitator of the 9/11 attacks. He writes in an effort to suppress feelings of doubt about the killings: "the sanctity of women, children, and the elderly is not absolute."[33] In this case they are "infidels," belonging to a country that has slaughtered millions of innocent people in Iraq. Al-Shibh is referring to the UN embargo of Iraq between 1990 and 2003 that took, according to UNICEF in 1999, an estimate of 500,000 infant lives.[34] In a democracy, al-Shibh's logic goes, everybody is responsible and there can be no innocence. Interestingly, al-Shibh says that in killing Americans, Muslim combatants (mujahedeen) must not exceed 4 million people or render 10 million homeless because, according to an Al Qaeda's count, this is the amount of Iraqi victims.

What is interesting about these accounts is the question of the justification of violence. This justification contains sociopsychological elements (revenging the innocent), anticolonial elements (the "infidels" of the West who are still after world dominance), and also religious elements (what is "sanctity"?), although religion functions more as a facilitator of violence than as an instigator. This is not to underestimate the role of religion. On the contrary, religion frames frustration, anger, and trauma in such a way that violence is justified as counterviolence. Without the enormous depot of religious texts, rituals, and—most importantly—religious leaders who have authority in translating these texts and rituals into actual frames, violence cannot become a structural element of combat but would fade away after the thirst for vengeance is quenched.

An important element of religious violence has to do with this frame or, more precisely, with the activity of framing. Imam Samudra said, "I'd only accept *sharia* law." Religion frames issues within a different space and with a different logic. This is especially true for religious militants such as Imam Samudra. It is, however, this "different space" that transforms issues through different reasonings. What appears as "illegal" in the public democratic space seems to become "legal" in the other. If you consider this logic, the public space and logic is constantly contested by this religious reframing of the same issues. What appears as "collateral damage" from one point of view (for instance, the infant deaths in Iraq) is a crime against humanity from another, and what appears as terrorist attacks from one point of view is a legal punishment from another. This disturbing upside-down logic precisely describes what is at stake: the law, on which a frame of just and unjust is based and according to which a certain act can or cannot be condemned. From a religious perspective, the law forms the divine will. In the following paragraphs, I will focus on this divine will behind the law.

THE LAW AND WHAT LIES BEHIND

Many analysts distinguish between different types of political violence, ranging from secular state punishment as the state's monopoly on violence on the one hand to rebellious, separatist, ethnic, or religious violence as "illegal" violence on the other. In earlier times, however, punishments always had to do with religion, simply because the divine was perceived as the foundation of the law. Although often forgotten or neglected, this notion shows an important element that returns in many present-day forms of religion-related conflict, where disobedience toward the state configures with obedience toward a "higher" law or where, as I have shown with Imam Samudra and Ramzi bin al-Shibh, the religious law is considered to be the only "real" law that is able to punish criminal acts.

The ancient genesis of this idea that combines the theological and the political still resonates in modern-day perceptions in which religious actors turn against the state or understand the juridical texts of their holy books at a qualitatively different level compared with contemporary state laws. Present-day fundamentalisms, in all their Christian, Islamic, Hindu, Buddhist, and other forms, do live in modern societies, with strong reservations toward the power of the state and its law. This is why fundamentalist Islamic groups in present-day Europe are perceived as disloyal by defenders of secular society. Interestingly, this reservation is related to the genesis of the religious law.

In ancient times, that is, the times in which the sacred texts were formatted, expiatory violence committed by the lawful authority always knew a metaphysical justification. The source of the law that punished the perpetrator was often understood as divine. God was, as Castoriadis explains, a shared social imaginary, giving meaning to social goods and symbols that sustained the group as a group.[35] Punishing crimes was considered important to restore the social order. Because the law was related directly to the divine, breaking the law by not punishing the destroyer of the social order was to violate the divine as well. As Blakesley argues, "in virtually all ancient cultures, metaphysics and law were merged; the social cell felt obliged to purge itself of the threat of destruction by the wrath of God or gods."[36] Punishment in this sense not only meant restoring the social order but also healing wounds inflicted by the violent acts of and on its members. A crime was not committed against an individual but against society; people had not yet developed a strong sense of individual responsibility. Punishment was doubly effective: it healed social conflict through retaliation, but it also restored the relationship with the divine, the metaphysical ground of the social cell. Therefore, punishment had to do not only with purging away the threat of chaos and crisis in the social cell but also with sacrificing to the divine and acknowledging the divine law as the constitutional element of social life.

Different religions deal differently with this process of revenge, purification, and sacrifice. Most, however, try to limit the extent of revenge, as for instance by the "eye for an eye" principle (known as the *lextallionis*) in the Hebrew Bible (Deuteronomy 19:21) that divinely orders exact expiation to limit revenge and protect both victim and perpetrator[37] or by the Hindu *Book of Manu* (Books VII, 18, 23–24; VIII, 17) that links happiness with punishment. For the perpetrator, soul-purging punishment is required to restore happiness.[38] In the Quran, a direct link between God and the law (Quran 16:90) is drawn. Punishment is understood as a "right of God." Nevertheless, God is also portrayed as the one who forgives and accepts repentance (Quran 4:16, 5:35, 39). Restoring relationships between humans is ratified by divine permission.

There seems to be a difference, however, between destroying the social order by committing crimes against your neighbor—like murder—on the one hand and contesting the divine order on the other. In the latter case, it is not the law but the source of the law that is violated, which might directly result in social crisis. This is particularly striking in Exodus 32 of the Hebrew Bible, and it surely is no coincidence that this narrative is told in the context of the origin of the Jewish law. The narrative tells about the absence of Moses and how the tribe of Israel made itself a golden bull to worship. When Moses came back, he destroyed the law that he had received from God ("he threw down the stones and broke them to pieces at the foot of the mountain," Exodus 32:19). Then he ordered, "let every man kill his brother, his friend and his neighbor" (Exodus 32:27). This phrase shows precisely a social situation in which the law failed. The absence of the law created social chaos and crisis. The confrontation between the divine and the people needed the mediation of the law. Sloterdijk reads this narrative as the triumph of a principle in which the zeal for the "One and Only" no longer solemnly defended the tribe but also killed those from the tribe who deviated from the sanctioned religious view.[39] It is precisely a situation in which this "principle" is contested and the "sanctioned religious view" is lacking that results in death and (later on in the text) disease. Without the law and its enduring metaphysical layer, the social group drops into chaos. This is why "blasphemy" in the Hebrew Bible is punished by the death penalty (Leviticus 24:16); it directly contests the legitimacy of the law. In the Quran, there is no punishment described for blasphemy, but in Islamic juridical traditions, punishments varied from fines to beheading. Religion is—as Reuven Firestone describes—about "organizing and administering human groups,"[40] bringing law and order among those groups, and binding its members together through rituals.

Of course, an enormous gap distances us now from these times, and many scientists discuss the impact of (ancient) religious laws (texts and practices) on the emergence of and gradual development of constitutionalism[41] and human rights,[42] whereas philosophers still struggle with the question of legitimacy in secular laws.[43] But many religious militants refer to "their" interpretation of the religious law as the only possible set of dos and don'ts that is allowed to shape social reality. Sometimes what is allowed and what is not does not correspond with the laws of the country, whether these laws are religious or secular. At times, this includes violence.

Dehumanization

This question of the legitimacy of violent actions shifting along different frames is raised especially within the context of secular societies. An element of religious violence contains the ethical disvaluing of imagined opponents—"imagined" because, as we saw, religious violence is categorical (Taylor) and cultural (Galtung); its victims implode into stereotypes of enmity such as "infidel," "dreamer," or "secularist" categories that are produced by the in-group. Violence against these "hostile" groups may be lawful according to religious laws. It "feels good, or at least not wrong." The victims can never be seen as real victims. Disvaluing human life is an element of all branches of categorical violence. Dehumanizing opponents to less than human (rats, cockroaches, vermin) enables people to commit atrocities without moral restraint.

In May 2004, a video was published on the Web site of Mutanda al-Ansar. The title of the video was *Abu Musab al-Zarqawi Shown Slaughtering an American*. The video showed a few masked men and a prisoner dressed in red, the color of the Abu Ghraib prison in Bagdad, Iraq. The prisoner, after identifying himself, was beheaded. What is striking about this video in the context of my argument is not only the cruel violence or the exclamations of the greatness of God before the act of killing, but the framing of this violence as shown in the title of the video. Abu Musab al-Zarqawi is mentioned. We know him as the late leader of the Iraqi subsection of Al Qaeda. But the title also mentions "an American." This "American" is not identified in the title. He stands as an example of a category. Whereas Abu Musab al-Zarqawi can only be one person, "an American" refers to millions of people. Biography and category are opposed. The biography hidden behind "an American" was Nicholas Berg's biography. It was not Nicholas they were after, however; it was "America" and the context of terror and antiterror including the Abu Ghraib humiliations, behind which Nicholas became invisible. On July 4, 1999, Benjamin Nathaniel Smith killed 11 people from minority groups in the United States before he committed suicide. Smith had been a member of the World Church of the Creator. Matthew Hale, the church's leader, mourned for the death of one white man. The 11 victims of Benjamin Smith were not grievable. They were classified as "subhuman" or "mud people."[44] Dehumanization is a process that not only enables people to "feel" blind toward the suffering of their victims (a process that is especially apparent during political and ideological genocides[45]) but also shows that the act of violence is justified as a projection of the (imagined) suffering of the perpetrator. Feeling excluded is one of the main elements responsible for this projection. Violence becomes an extreme and abstract (categorical) way of dealing with this feeling.

Although religion is accused of encouraging processes of dehumanization by dropping into categorical violence, it is extremely difficult, if not impossible, to distinguish between dehumanization as a result of the *religious* imaginary based on textual mediation and symbolic exchange on the one hand and the *national* imaginary of the state based on symbolic mediation on the other. While Matthew Hale rejected the fact that Smith was guilty of murder against black Americans (because in his view, they were "mud people," not created by God), the so-called Malmöshooter denied the accusation before the Swedish Court in May 2012 of having murdered at least three immigrants because he did not acknowledge the criminal term of "murder" to be applicable to immigrants; he only acknowledged the fact that his bullet had demolished the window of a nearby shop. The first case is quoted as an example of religious violence; the second is racist or nationalist violence. The thought frames, however, are highly comparable.[46]

RELIGION AND APOCALYPTIC VIOLENCE

Until now several features of religious violence have been discussed. The necessity but also the complexity of taking the context into account is constantly stressed as important to study the different layers of religious violence. We have seen that religious violence as such does not exist but that there are several elements of violence that, under certain circumstances, receive religious legitimacy. I have also argued that religion claims a different space and a different logic according to which religion is constantly contesting secular states. The religious memory of the divine law and its current interpretations by religious leaders make clear that the evaluative perceptions are based on a contesting logic. However, as the true law is given in the past, the lawgiver will lift up the veil of the unreal at the end of times. What was given in the past will reign in the future. Teachings about the beginning of time (*protology*) and teachings about the end of time (*eschatology*) encompass the current lie that dreamers and infidels hold for true. In this view, struggling for your religion conflates with the divine battle that goes on behind the scenes. In the end, the good God, the good principle, or enlightened goodness itself will prevail.

Juergensmeyer has coined this level of conflict with the term *cosmic war*.[47] In the article "Is Religion the Problem?" Juergensmeyer describes "cosmic war" as the interpretation that people (Juergensmeyer writes "terrorists") have about a battle as a sacred battle. If a battle is considered sacred, it becomes cosmic—"cosmic" because the battle is considered to be larger than life. "Acts of religious terror serve not only as tactics in a political strategy but also as evocations of a much larger spiritual confrontation."[48] The "ordinary rules of conduct" do not apply anymore.[49] This frame is self-evident, and as the context becomes more violent, the logic becomes more irrefutable, as Juergensmeyer argues dealing with the U.S. attack on Fallujah in 2004: "Before the fall of Fallujah, the jihad outsiders had been mistrusted; the destruction of Fallujah provided evidence in the eyes of many that the jihadi rhetoric of cosmic war was real."[50] As a consequence, if a conflict is understood at the level of a cosmic war, violence becomes inevitable (a sacred duty) and opponents necessarily inhumane. Religious symbols and traditionally handed-over and interpreted texts belong to the sphere of life people inhabit and may provide more intelligible tools to deal with a certain conflict than, say, politics or economics.

Lincoln argues that religion addresses the "more" of daily life. Religion transcends the banal or normal into an essential system of meaning. By doing so, religion "stabilizes vital human concerns by constituting them as transcendent."[51] In this realm of "more" meaning, a war needs a reason that goes beyond the banal reality of politics and economics. Religion serves this human need to understand what goes on in essential language. Religious traditions have depots and archives of apocalyptic symbols that can frame current issues. Apocalypse, revitalized in times of crisis, gives a "real" meaning to what goes on. It sees, beyond the political lies, the "real" battle that goes on, a battle between good and evil, true and untrue, real and unreal: it sees the "more" that lies beyond.

In Shia Islamic tradition, the coming of the *Mahdi* is awaited. This apocalyptic imaginary played an important role in energizing enthusiasm for the war between Iran and Iraq (1980–1990). This war was considered an apocalyptic war that would end with the coming of *Mahdi*. Christian apocalyptic imaginary, awaiting the coming of Jesus Christ and the beginning of the "Reign of the Lamb" during a millennium of peace, created sects and Christian theologies and even had its impact on political perspectives, activating apocalyptic symbols of evil that were projected on leaders such as Yasser Arafat and—later—Saddam Hussein.[52] The Japanese Aum ShinriKyo sect played out an "imagined Armageddon"[53] in the subway system of Tokyo, killing 12 people and injuring more than 5,000 in 1995, justifying its violence toward Japanese civilians with Buddhist and Christian apocalyptic language (the context of Japanese New Religious Movements is discussed further in Volume 3, Chapter 9). Apocalypse frames the longing for meaning and the wish to be at the good side. But it also intensifies (essentializes) a conflict. This "real" battle beyond the seen explains what Taylor observes as the "excessive element of religious violence" (see earlier). The "real" world behind the seen makes it difficult to negotiate with your opponents without betraying the just reason behind your battle.

Apocalypse questions the boundaries of what we call "religious violence." Do political ideologies refrain from apocalyptic tendencies? Totalitarian systems in East and West, North and South have annihilated perceptions, including the people who hold them, that diverged from the portrayed "ideal" of a perfect society. Is it possible to think about perfection or even about the "ideal democracy" without an apocalyptic "real" and—in this line—without the specter of apocalyptic violence? This issue exceeds the scope of this article, but it is interesting to ask the question of whether strong concepts of political and economic longing can be linked to apocalyptic ideas.

The Archive

Until now the complexity of religious violence is intentionally stressed. I have argued that we should study the context of religious violence to understand its different features. Religious violence is not a special way of doing violence but a specific way of justifying violence. Therefore, violence committed in the name of religion changes the conflict by framing it as a religious battle. The religious tradition delivers elements that can frame the conflict as "just" or "unjust." These elements include the archival imaginary of the religious or divine law (the beginning of social interaction) and the imaginary of the ultimate revelation of the "real" (the conflation of what "is" and what is "true"). In this last section, I will study the transition between the religious texts, rituals, and symbols and the "profane" affairs that the believers deal with or, in other words, the complex hermeneutical process of religious framing.

Religion is a practice of mediation. Texts have a special place in most religions. A text, held as sacred, mediates the imaginary of the religious social group. The practice of reading, memorizing, quoting, explaining, and interpreting the sacred text in religious spaces (churches, mosques, temples, monasteries, etc.) continually frames the present-day situation of the religious in-group. This practice contributes highly to the religious perspective on what goes on in the world and constructs in-groups, out-groups, others, and in-group heretics based on the mediating power of the sacred text. In this section, I will argue that the way people appropriate holy texts and symbols during conflicts helps them understand a conflict within, but also—in the case of terrorism—transmits a conflict into a cosmic moral conflict between representations of good and evil. If this happens, time and space collapse between textual representations of evil out-groups or evil personages and current opponents. These current opponents may become representatives of scriptural evil (see Volume 3, Chapter 3, for an example in the context of Buddhist violence in Sri Lanka). As a result, the conflict can become more intense and acts of killing morally less repugnant. Killing may even become a sacred duty.

To understand how this works, it is necessary to emphasize the "collapse" of time and space between the text and present-day affairs. This collapse induces meaning to present-day actualities in such a way that current opponents appear as negative self-representations from sacred texts mediating religious frames and present-day issues. Let me give some examples.

Horowitz has published an impressive account on the history of Jewish religious framings of antagonists, exemplifying how textual opponents, portrayed in the Jewish Bible as evildoers with extremely violent attitudes toward the Jews, were used to frame actual issues and mark a legacy of violence. Haman, the evil opponent of Mordechai who conspires against the Jews, or the Amalekites, the tribe that wages an almost continuing war with Israel in the Hebrew Bible, are mediating personages, infusing the dynamics of enmity into confronting actualities. Lieberman, chairman of the Council of Settlements, said that the "Palestinians are Amalek." Feiglin from Likud argues that the Arabs show "typical Amalek behaviour."[54] As a result, negotiating with the Palestinians, or with the Arabs, is the same as betraying Israel.

Quranic *infidels*, a word that is in the Quran particularly used for a Meccan tribe who Muhammad is often seen opposing,[55] were related to current opponents of the mujahedeen, such as Westerners, Muslims of different traditions, or Russians. During the war on terror, the "Western infidels" were also accused of a "Crusader's mentality," opening a religious and historic archive to frame the opponents during the conflict.

In the Shia Muslim tradition, *ashura* refers to the Battle of Karbala (680 CE) where the Sunni caliph, Yazeed, ordered the massacre of the family of the Prophet Muhammad (*ahl-al bait*). The split between Sunni and Shia Muslims is definitive from that day on. In Shia traditions, the battle is physically played out during *ashura*, showing men flagellating themselves to "be with" Hussayn. Since the 1960s and 1970s of the twentieth century, however, *ashura* was put into a strong political frame. Iranian intellectuals used the narrative of Karbala and the play of *ashura* to present political statements. Ali Shariati, especially, used the narrative of personages, such as the evil caliph Yazeed and the hero Hussayn, as mediating symbols to revitalize martyrdom in a strong political and economic frame. The enormous and, for the

West, surprising[56] dynamic of the Iranian Revolution in 1979 was due to this religious reframing of Karbala.[57]

During the Bosnian War (1992–1995), Bosnian Muslims were represented by Serbian nationalists not only as "traitors of the Slavic race" but also as "killers of Christ." A strong romantic Serbian literary tradition framed the Muslims as the heirs of the Turks who invaded the area in the fourteenth century. A process of dehumanization preceded the Bosnian genocide, in which Christian interpretations of the suffering Christ and nationalist perspectives went hand in hand (on religion and nationalism, see Volume 2, Chapter 10). Again, Bosnian Muslims were stereotyped with aspects that originated in a context that was (at least partly) alien to them.[58]

It is indeed complex to analyze the exact "incarnation" of the text into present-day actualities. A good analysis must take several layers into account. First, understanding the text as sacred and using it as frame is part of an imaginary that belongs to the religious self-perception. The text mediates between the symbolic religious world of good and evil and the contemporary context in which good and evil seems less obvious. Second, the "understanding" of the text can be part of an authoritative appropriation of the religious imaginary. The text mediates only if an authority works as a medium. Most of the time, such an authority is a religious, spiritual, or political leader, skillfully (re)activating powerful frames from religious texts and traditions.

The theory of Vamik Volkan on chosen trauma can be helpful to understand this specific religious framing. Volkan has researched the formation of large-group identities and how these groups imagine a shared glorious or traumatic past. However, this imaginary is always present and reveals present-day in- and out-group perceptions. This is also the case with religious framing.

Volkan puts trauma into the social sphere. A social trauma works differently compared with a personal trauma. A social trauma refers to a shared "trauma time" and thus has impact on a group's social imaginary. If a trauma does not fade away with a generation, it continues across generations (it is transgenerational). In Volkan's words, if "a traumatized group cannot reverse its feelings of helplessness and humiliation and cannot effectively go through the work of mourning, it can transfer these unfinished psychological tasks to future generations."[59] This way, a trauma is passed down to a new generation, becoming a mental representation of a historical event. This mental representation works as an emotional reference for an unfinished task. Each next generation is obliged to complete the work of the mourning of the group over the losses and, as Volkan argues, "reverse shame and humiliation, and turn passivity into assertion."[60] At this point, the meaning of the word *chosen* is explained. A trauma is chosen if "the historical image of the trauma is 'chosen' to represent a particular group."

Such a group becomes "imprisoned" by the traumatic projection. This projection is important for the self-understanding of a large group. Large groups, Volkan argues, "define themselves by ritualistically differentiating themselves from other groups." A shared past trauma on the one hand contributes to the cohesion of a large group through an imagined understanding of the suffering group but on the other hand represents contemporary enemies within the symbolic frame of a past trauma. In times of violent conflict, Volkan argues carefully, "hate speech directed toward contemporary enemies may accompany the remembrance of chosen traumas." A chosen trauma, he defines elsewhere, entails a "collective mental representation of an event that has caused a large group to face drastic common losses, to feel helpless and victimized by another group and to share a humiliating injury."[61] These mental representations can be transmitted "to subsequent generations in varying levels of identity." This way, a chosen trauma becomes a historical frame to understand current conflict. Current groups might become the mental, ethnic, or religious heirs of the brutal historical perpetrator. Present-day opponents can be represented within this mental field of the historic event, even though direct links might be vague or even nonexistent.

The crux of Volkan's interpretation is the historical image that can be chosen to represent a particular present-day group. Religious texts produce these images through the process of mediation described earlier. As a result, the negative energy that traditionally is added to these negative images sticks to these newly selected (often opposing) groups. Although religious framing does not always work the same way as Volkan's "transgenerational transgression," his remarks make clear how current opponents can be framed using "religious memory" (the negative or positive memory of textual personages). The religious archive of evil opponents (Amalek, Haman, Judas, Yazeed, and, at a more metaphysical level, infidels, evildoers, sodomites, or just sinners) works as a frame to understand current opponents at an essential level.

CONCLUSION

When do people commit violence in the name of their religion? In answering this question, several elements were discussed. As we delved deeper into this subject, the burden of answering this question became heavier. To analyze the "when" of religious violence, it was necessary to describe contexts, intentions, traditions, justifications, histories, elements of longing, and truth claims. The age-old saying that the most difficult interpretation is the strongest,[62] which made exegesis of Christian sacred texts such an intricate effort, seems to be in its place as a fundamental first rule for analyzing religious violence. The horizon can be seen but never crossed, and although the interpreter describes what he or she observes, the land-scape changes and final interpretation is lacking. Nevertheless, certain elements can be described in this unstable landscape, elements that cross contexts (although not all) and seem to contribute to a careful understanding of the phenomenon of religious violence—elements that indeed lack the power of a final word.

To understand religious violence, it is important to understand how religion works and what it does: how it interacts with and absorbs different contextual elements, and (re)frames current issues. As we have seen, religious violence is not a special way of doing violence but a specific way of justifying violence. Once religion is part of a context that justifies violence, it shows the tendency to move the conflict to a different level. At this level, the conflict is framed as a religious conflict; opponents are characterized as essentially evil opponents, the battle becomes cosmic, and the violence becomes lawful (as self-defense). As a result, the conflict becomes more difficult to analyze, and observers start to speak about religious violence, sometimes ignoring the political and economic layers that lie beneath the surface. Although religion is rarely the instigator of violent conflict, it certainly can be the magnifier of conflict due to its potential to use its alternative perspective on the law, its textual archive, and its essential interpretation of "the real" as frame. However, it is this same potential that can work the other way and, instead of promoting categorical violence, encourage peace and reconciliation. This is why in postconflict areas that have seen religious violence, the same religion that became part of the conflict can be used to demilitarize the actors.[63] In these contexts, strong religious leaders are fundamental.

Studying religious violence cannot be done without a multidisciplinary perspective. Because of the many layers of religious violence, sociological, psychological, anthropological, historical, religious studies, and philosophical perspectives all need to work together to create a diffuse and provisional image of the involvement of religion during eruptions of violence in specific contexts. This "working together" may avoid blunt statements about "religious violence," but it may also bring religion in as an important element that needs to be given attention to create a notion of what is going on. It may also create a sensibility toward what is specific about religious interpretations of the law and of "the real" and how religion reframes conflicts with the help of enormously rich and varied traditions. It may develop a sensitivity toward what religion does when it becomes part of a conflict, how it changes a conflict, and how it can help to restore peace.

An important prospect for further research is the involvement of theology and theological discourses on violence. Although many scientists (including religious studies) prefer to describe what they observe with sociological, psychological, economic, or philosophical analytical instruments, theological discourses give us a view from the inside out.[64] Meditations on truth, discourses on just wars and jihad, sermons about intricate texts, or charismatic speeches on the right to live according to the will of God are all part of the context in which conflicts can become violent,[65] and thus elucidate religion as a possible part of what Galtung calls "cultural violence." Theological discourses reflect richly (both implicit and explicit) on the history and development of religious traditions, revealing perspectives that should well be studied by people willing to understand the religious context of a specific conflict.

GLOSSARY

Al Qaeda: a militant, or fundamentalist, Islamic terrorist group with a loose organizational structure.

Apocalypse/apocalyptic: to do with the end of the world/universe in religious imagery and imagination.

Ashura: a Shia Muslim festival commemorating the Battle of Karbala when their leader was killed.

Cultural/structural violence: terms used by Johan Galtung to talk about the way violence can be made legitimate by or within a culture by reference to things such as nationalism or symbols.

Epistemic community: used in international relations to refer to any community that controls, creates, and also disseminates knowledge (epistemic being to do with knowledge, and epistemology the study of ways of knowing). It generally refers to a body of professionals (academics or bureaucrats) with the power and authority to determine what is known and who knows it.

Fundamentalism: a tendency in a religious tradition to take tradition or scripture in a literal sense, often tied to very conservative views (see Volume 3, Chapter 1).

Infidel: literally "one without faith," a historically Christian term that was sometimes used to refer to non-Christians, but when used in relation to Islam, it is often used to translate the Arabic term *kafir*, often translated as "unbeliever"; in English "infidel" has a stronger connotation as someone who actively defies or resists God rather than someone who simply does not believe.

Jihad: an Arabic term for "struggle," which can mean spiritual self-development but also refers to warfare in defense of the faith, which is how it is normally met in Western language usage.

Mahdi: a term referring to a revered teacher in Shia Islam who it is believed is now "hidden" from view but will return at the end of the world.

Mimesis: a term coined by Rene Girard to discuss the way social behavior is learned and leads to replication at the desire of the group. A simple definition is "imitation."

Mujahedeen: an Islamic soldier undertaking jihad, also applied to some specific groups, especially in Afghanistan.

Sharia: Islamic law.

Wahhabi/Wahhabism: a conservative branch of Islam going back to the eighteenth century, which has a very rigid interpretation of Islamic law and tradition.

NOTES

1. This fruitless "discussion" is keenly shown by William Cavanaugh in *The Myth of Religious Violence: Secular Ideology and the Roots of Violent Conflict* (Oxford, England: Oxford University Press, 2009).

2. R. Scott Appleby, *The Ambivalence of the Sacred: Religion, Violence and Reconciliation* (Lanham, MD: Rowman & Littlefield Publishers, 1999).

3. Ibid., 13.

4. See David Little, *Peacemakers in Action, Profiles of Religion in Conflict Resolution* (Cambridge, England: Cambridge University Press, 2007).

5. Charles Taylor, *Big Ideas: Charles Taylor on Religion and Violence*, accessed April 2012, http://ww3.tvo.org/video/173088/charles-taylor-religion-and-violence.

6. J. Galtung, "Cultural Violence," *Journal of Peace Research* no. 27 (1990): 291–305.

7. Ibid., 292.

8. Jonathan Fox, *A World Survey of Religion and the State* (Cambridge, England: Cambridge University Press, 2008).

9. Lars-Erik Cederman, Andreas Wimmer, and Brian Min, "Why Do Ethnic Groups Rebel? New Data and Analyses," *World Politics* 62, no. 1 (2010): 87–119.

10. See Vamik Volkan, *Blood Lines: From Ethnic Pride to Ethnic Terrorism* (Boulder, CO: Westview Press, 1997), and *Killing in the Name of Identity: A Study of Bloody Conflicts* (Charlottesville, VA: Pitchstone Publishing, 2006).

11. Paul Gilbert, *New Terror, New Wars: Contemporary Ethical Debates Series* (Edinburgh, Scotland: Edinburgh University Press, 2003), 68.

12. Galtung, "Cultural Violence," 292.

13. See the legacy of the so-called just war theory in Christianity and of the concept of the *jihad al-akhbar* ("Great Jihad") in Islam. See Alex Bellamy, *Just Wars: From Cicero to Iraq* (Oxford, England: Polity Press, 2006); Michael Donner, *Jihad in Islamic History: Doctrines and Practices* (Princeton, NJ, and Oxford, England: Princeton University Press, 2006); and Reuven Firestone, *Jihad: The Origin of Holy War in Islam* (New York and Oxford, England: Oxford University Press, 2002).

14. Jonathan Fox, "The Rise of Religious Nationalism and Conflict: Ethnic Conflict and Revolutionary Wars, 1945–2001," *Journal of Peace Research* no. 41 (2004): 715–31.

15. René Girard, *I See Satan Fall Like Lightning*, trans. James G. Williams (Maryknoll, NY: Orbis Books, 2002), *The Scapegoat*, trans. Yvonne Freccero (Baltimore, MD: The John Hopkins University Press, 1978), *Things Hidden Since the Foundation of the World*, trans. Stephen Bann and Michael Metteer (Stanford, CA: Stanford University Press, 1987), and *Violence and the Sacred*, trans. Patrick Gregory (Baltimore, MD: The John Hopkins University Press, 1977).

16. Cited in Andrew Sinclair, *An Anatomy of Terror: A History of Terrorism* (London and Oxford, England: MacMillan Pan Books, 2004), 327.

17. Randal Law, *Terrorism: A History* (Oxford, England: Polity Press, 2009); and Gerard Chaliand and Arnaud Blin, *The History of Terrorism: From Antiquity to al Qaeda* (Berkeley: University of California Press, 2007).

18. Ben Saul, *Defining Terrorism in International Law* (Oxford, England: Oxford University Press, 2008); and Christopher L. Blakesley, *Terror and Anti-Terrorism: A Normative and Practical Assessment, International and Comparative Criminal Law Series* (Ardsley, NY: Transnational Publishers Inc., 2006).

19. James W. Jones, *Terror and Transformation: The Ambiguity of Religion in Psychoanalytic Perspective* (London: Routledge, 2002).

20. Pippa Norris, Montague Kern, and Marion Just, eds., *Framing Terrorism: The News Media, the Government and the Public* (New York and London: Routledge, 2003).

21. John Horgan, *The Psychology of Terrorism* (London and New York: Routledge, 2005).

22. Saul, *Defining Terrorism in International Law*, 1f.

23. Talal Asad, *On Suicide Bombing*, The Wellek Lectures (New York: Columbia University Press, 2007), 29; see also, from a perspective of critical discourse analyses, Adam Hodges, *"The War on Terror" Narrative: Discourse and Intertextuality in the Construction and Contestation of Sociopolitical Reality*, Oxford Studies in Sociolinguistics (Oxford, England: Oxford University Press, 2011); and W. J. T. Mitchell, *Cloning Terror: The War of Images, 9/11 to the Present* (Chicago, IL, and London: The University of Chicago Press, 2011).

24. See Catherine Keller, *God and Power: Counter-apocalyptic Journeys* (Minneapolis, MN: Fortress Press, 2004).

25. See Haggay Ram, *Myth and Mobilization in Revolutionary Iran: The Use of the Friday Congregational Sermon* (Lanham, MD: University of America Press, 1994).

26. Ali Shariati, *Religion Versus Religion*, trans. L. Bakhtiar (Chicago, IL: Kazi Publications, 1993); and Kingshuk Shatteriee, *Ali Shariati and the Shaping of Political Islam in Iran* (Basingstoke, England: Palgrave Macmillan, 2011).

27. Gabriel A. Almond, R. Scott Appleby, and Emmanuel Sivan, *Strong Religion: The Rise of Fundamentalisms Around the World* (Chicago, IL, and London: The University of Chicago Press, 2003), 156.

28. See Kumar Ramakrishna and See Seng Tan, *After Bali: The Threat of Terrorism in Southeast Asia* (Singapore: Institute of Defence and Strategic Studies, 2003).

29. This can be compared to the argument Osama bin Laden makes to explain 9/11. He, too, speaks about the "innocent children of Palestine" and takes the killing of innocent children as a token of Pharaoh. Osama bin Laden, "Nineteen Students," in *Messages to the World: The Statements of Osama bin Laden*, ed. Bruce Lawrence and trans. James Howarth (London and New York: Verso, 2005), 147. Interestingly, bin Laden sees the killing of Israeli children by Pharaoh reflected in the Israeli killing of 12-year-old Muhammad al-Durreh in Gaza on September 30, 2000. According to an Israeli inquiry into the incident, there had been no mistake made by the Israeli forces. A French cameraman recorded the incident. See http://www.ramallahonline.com/modules.php?name=News&file=article&sid=8, as cited in Lawrence, *Messages to the World*, 147 (editor's note 5).

30. Imam Samudra says that "When I was surfing the seas of Internet, I came across pictures of babies without heads and arms, thanks to the brutality of the crusade troops of America and its allies when they bombarded Afghanistan in the 2001 Ramadan. . . . Those images are photos of what really happened, that are scanned, put into a computer, and then uploaded onto the Internet. They are immovable, without sound, numb. But the souls cried out in agony and their suffering filled my heart, taking on the suffering of their parents. . . ." Imam Samudra wrote in his diary, "Your weeping, oh headless infants, slammed against the walls of Palestine, Your cries, oh Afghani infants, all called to me; all you, who, now armless, executed by the vile bombs of hell." See Tempo, ed., "The Fires of Revenge," in *Tempo Magazine* 6, no. 4 (October 14–20, 2003).

31. Michael Sheridan, "Extracts: Michael Sheridan Interview with Bali Bomber Imam Samudra," *The Sunday Times*, March 2, 2008.

32. He published several e-mails and documents of the terrorist group in Alan Cullison, "Inside Al-Qaeda's Hard Drive," *The Atlantic* no. 294 (September 2004): 2, 55–70.

33. Ibid., 68.

34. UNICEF, "Questions and Answers for the Iraq Child Mortality Surveys," accessed May 2012, http://www.casi.org.uk/info/unicef/990816qa.html.

35. Cornelius Castoriadis, *The Imaginary Institution of Society*, trans. Kathleen Blamey (Cambridge, MA: MIT Press, 1987), 128–29.

36. Blakesley, *Terror and Anti-Terrorism*, 14.

37. The *lextallionis* is not, as J Harold Ellens suggests, "the law of the jungle" with "barbaric tones." See J. Harold Ellens, "Religious Metaphors Can Kill," in *The Destructive Power of Religion: Violence in Judaism, Christianity, and Islam*, ed. J. Harold Ellens (Westport, CA, and London: Praeger Publishers, 2007), 44.

38. See Blakesley, *Terror and Anti-Terrorism*, 14.

39. Peter Sloterdijk, *God's Zeal: The Battle of the Three Monotheisms*, trans. Wieland Hoban (Maiden, MA, and Cambridge, England: Polity Press, 2009), 26.

40. Reuven Firestone, "Divine Authority and Mass Violence: Economies of Aggression in the Emergence of Religions," *Journal for the Study of Religions and Ideologies* 9, no. 26 (2010): 222.

41. See John Witte, *The Reformation of Rights: Law, Religion and Human Rights in Early Modern Calvinism* (Cambridge, England: Cambridge University Press, 2008).

42. See Micheline R. Ishay, *The History of Human Rights: From Ancient Times to the Globalization Era* (Berkeley: University of California Press, 2008); and Michael J. Perry, *Toward a Theory of Human Rights: Religion, Law, Courts* (Cambridge, England: Cambridge University Press, 2008).

43. The most challenging account of this struggle is cited in Walter Benjamin, "Critique of Violence," in *Reflections: Essays, Aphorisms, Autobiographical Writings*, ed. Peter Demetz (New York: Harcourt Brace Jovanovich, 1978), 277–300. See also Giorgio Agamben, *Homo Sacer: Sovereign Power and Bare Life*, trans. Daniel Heller-Roazen (Stanford, CA: Stanford University Press, 1998); and Hent de Vries, *Religion and Violence: Philosophical Perspectives from Kant to Derrida* (Baltimore, MD: The John Hopkins University Press, 2002).

44. Mark Juergensmeyer, "Martyrdom and Sacrifice in a Time of Terror," *Social Research* no. 75 (2008): 424.

45. See Sönke Neitzel and Harald Welzer von Fischer, *Soldaten, Protokollen vom Kämpfen, Töten und Sterben* (Frankfurt, Germany: Suhrkamp, 2011); and Alexander Laban Hinton, ed., *Annihilating Difference: The Anthropology of Genocide* (Berkeley: University of California Press, 2002).

46. See Cavanaugh, *The Myth of Religious Violence*, 59.

47. Mark Juergensmeyer, *Terror in the Name of God: The Global Rise of Religious Violence* (Berkeley: University of California Press 2000), 149–54.

48. Mark Juergensmeyer, "Is Religion the Problem?" *Hedgehog Review* 6, no. 1 (2004): 6.

49. Mark Juergensmeyer, *Global Rebellion: Religious Challenges to the Secular State, from Christian Militants to Al Qaeda* (Berkeley: University of California Press, 2008), 181.

50. Ibid., 74.

51. Bruce Lincoln, *Holy Terrors: Thinking About Religion After 9/11* (Chicago, IL: The University of Chicago Press 2003), 53.

52. See Keller, *God and Power,* 22–23.

53. Juergensmeyer, *Global Rebellion,* 178.

54. Elliot Horowitz, *Reckless Rites, Purim and the Legacy of Jewish Violence* (Princeton, NJ, and Oxford, England: Princeton University Press, 2006), 1.

55. The Quraysh.

56. See Scott M. Thomas, *The Global Resurgence of Religion and the Transformation of International Relations: The Struggle for the Soul of the Twenty-First Century* (Basingstoke, England: Palgrave MacMillan, 2005), 1.

57. Kamran Scot Akhaie, *The Martyrs of Karbala: Shi'i Symbols and Rituals in Modern Iran* (Seattle and London: The University of Washington Press, 2004).

58. Michael A. Sells, *The Bridge Betrayed: Religion and Genocide in Bosnia* (Berkeley: University of California Press, 1996).

59. Volkan, *Killing,* 154.

60. Ibid.

61. Volkan, *Blind Trust,* 48. I have tried to apply Volkan's theory to the Ambon War (1999–2002); see also Lucien van Liere, "Fighting for Jesus on Ambon, Interpreting Religious Representations of Violent Conflict," *Exchange: Journal of Missiological and Ecumenical Research* 40, no. 4 (2011): 322–36.

62. *Lectio difficilior potior.*

63. Little, *Peacemakers in Action,* 1–12.

64. Some examples of strong theological perspectives on violence include Paul J. Daponte, *Hope in an Age of Terror* (Maryknoll, NY: Orbis Books, 2009); Lee Griffith, *The War on Terrorism and the Terror of God* (Grand Rapids, MI: William B. Eerdmans Publishing Company, 2002); and Ingrid Mattson, "Stopping Oppression: An Islamic Obligation," in *11 September: Religious Perspectives on the Causes and Consequences,* ed. Ian Markham and Ibrahim M. Abu-Rabi (Oxford, England: Oneworld Publications, 2002), 101–110.

65. For instance, see how Mario Aguilar has studied the theological frames in Rwanda before and during the genocide, in *Theology, Liberation and Genocide: A Theology of the Periphery* (London: SCM Press, 2009).

FURTHER READINGS

Appleby, R. Scott. *The Ambivalence of the Sacred: Religion, Violence and Reconciliation.* Lanham, NY: Rowman & Littlefield Publishers, 1999.

Blakesley, Christopher L. *Terror and Anti-Terrorism: A Normative and Practical Assessment, International and Comparative Criminal Law Series.* Ardsley, NY: Transnational Publishers Inc., 2006.

Cavanaugh, William T. *The Myth of Religious Violence: Secular Ideology and the Roots of Modern Conflict.* Oxford, England: Oxford University Press, 2009.

Chaliand, Gerard, and Arnaud Blin. *The History of Terrorism: From Antiquity to al Qaeda.* Berkeley: University of California Press, 2007.

Firestone, Reuven. *Jihad: The Origin of Holy War in Islam.* New York and Oxford, England: Oxford University Press, 2002.

Horgan, John. *The Psychology of Terrorism.* London and New York: Routledge, Taylor and Francis Group, 2005.

Horowitz, Elliot. *Reckless Rites: Purim and the Legacy of Jewish Violence.* Princeton, NJ, and Oxford, England: Princeton University Press, 2006.

Jones, James W. *Terror and Transformation: The Ambiguity of Religion in Psycho-analytic Perspective*. London: Routledge, 2002.

Juergensmeyer, Mark. *Terror in the Name of God: The Global Rise of Religious Violence*. Berkeley: University of California Press, 2000.

Law, Randal. *Terrorism: A History*. Oxford, England: Polity Press, 2009.

Lincoln, Bruce. *Holy Terrors: Thinking About Religion After 9/11*. Chicago, IL: The University of Chicago Press, 2003.

Little, David. *Peacemakers in Action: Profiles of Religion in Conflict Resolution*. Cambridge, England: Cambridge University Press, 2007.

Sells, Michael A. *The Bridge Betrayed: Religion and Genocide in Bosnia*. Berkeley: University of California Press, 1996.

7

Belonging, Behaving, Believing, Becoming: Religion and Identity

Paul Hedges and Angela Coco

INTRODUCTION

The way we understand ourselves, our community, and the wider world shapes not only who we think we are but also who we think those others are and affects how we relate to them. All this is about identity: the identity that we claim, the identities others attribute to us, and the identity we give to others. Scholars have conceived notions of identity and what they mean in a range of ways, perhaps most notably in philosophy, psychology, and sociology. What becomes clear through looking at identity is that it is inherently about relationship, whether it is oppositional—we often know who we are primarily by bracketing ourselves off from those we are not—or about claiming similarity to others. However, what may seem to be a relatively straightforward issue, a "hard and fast concept"[1] where we are simply a particular "I" and that identity is something you have, is actually very complex. One's identity is "always socially located,"[2] that is, built into a network of relationships, issues, and cultural factors.

In this chapter, we will look at approaches to identity across different academic disciplines before proceeding to look at some ways identity is developed, and can be analyzed, in specific religious communities.

BACKGROUND

We will begin by looking at some principle issues that have been raised in the field of identity studies. To begin, definitions of three interrelated terms are critical for our purposes in this chapter: self, identity, and role. Often self and identity are used interchangeably, but we will see there is benefit in making definitional distinctions between these words. Further, the word self is used in many ways in everyday life as well as in the social sciences, for example to mean the "person" as in "yourself" or mental behavior as in "self-reflection."

We use the term self to refer to that inner state which is able to mentally reflect on our behaviors, to reflect on the impressions gained from others, and to evaluate ways of believing and behaving. In other words, the "self" can make an object of our personality and behaviors and adjust inner and outer worlds to fit with situations in which we find ourselves.[3] The "self" can mobilize many different parts, which we call "identities." We take on different identities depending on the social situations in which we find ourselves; for example, during leisure time we might identify as a "tennis player" and others would expect us to conduct ourselves in ways that align with this identity. If we began to act like, say, a hairdresser, on the tennis court, we would not get very far in our interactions with others. This brings us to the interactional nature of the relationship between self and identity.

Whereas psychologists focus on the inner mental activities of the self, sociologists and social psychologists remind us that the self is inherently social because from birth we rely on interactions with others to know the world and our place in it. Others cannot see our "true" self as we may construct it for ourselves—for instance, we may believe ourselves to be shy, whereas others perceive us to be confident and outgoing and relate to us through the roles we assume or are assigned to us in society. We may assume many roles—parent, minister of religion, teacher, daughter, stranger—and these will change throughout our lives. Roles are related to the organizational structures of society. They are recognized by characteristic sets of behaviors and ways of interacting with others. When performing in a role, we are playing out a particular identity—we understand ourself as a teacher, son, and so on. However, as humans beings interact, they may also change characteristics of a role, bringing in personal ideas, needs, and desires. As they do this, they change society. Stets and Burke summarize the relationship between self, identity, and role well when they explain, "the core of an identity is the categorization of the self as an occupant of a role, and incorporating into the self, the meanings and expectations associated with the role and its performance."[4]

The way we think of ourselves has varied vastly throughout time and place, as Kath Woodward, a sociologist who explores issues of identity, says: "Identity matters, but how and why it matters depends on time and place and on specific historical, social and material circumstances."[5] Woodward uses the term identity in a general sense, which may refer to individuals, groups, cultures, or nations. For instance, for much of the last 200 years or so in what we may broadly term "the Western world" (northern and western Europe, North America, and Australasia), self-identity for most in that mainstream culture would have focused on the individual: who "I" am, what "I" want. This tendency emphasizes the importance of my self-becoming as an autonomous person, my difference from others, and with it behaviors that distance me from too close an identification with groups of others or particular behaviors and worldviews that would constrain me. In the various roles we play, it would be expected that we establish our individuality, for example, as a vegan in a restaurant. However, in much of the rest of the world—and traditional Chinese society is a good example—an individual's self-identity would be much more closely tied to his or her relationship within a family and community. So, for instance, you would relate to one of your uncles or aunts based not on personal names but titles given in relationship to others; you would refer, for instance, to *er jiu*, literally "second uncle," to mean your mother's second oldest brother. The paternal aunts and uncles would have different titles. This may not seem significant at first glance, but upon reflection it will be seen that your worldview will be shaped by reference not to your Uncle Tom but to someone's position within a family hierarchy, so your first point of reference to them is not to them as an individual (Tom) but to their position in a network of relationships. That is, you would conform more closely to your role as a nephew or niece and the responsibilities that go with that rather than asserting a right to "go your own way."

These two systems are sometimes termed, respectively, individualist and collectivist in relation to how people experience different identities in a culture. Indeed, although some may argue for one as preferable to the other approach, we must also realize that each needs the other. It is impossible for individualists to define themselves as different from other individuals without being, of necessity, in relationship to them, and therefore an isolated individual can only be isolated in relationship. Likewise, a more collectivist identity relies on the fact that each person is different from themselves; you cannot have a place in a hierarchy or system unless there are individual others in different positions or roles. We should not, therefore, contrast them simplistically as opposite ways of approaching this issue.

Our position in time and space also affects the identities we can have, so a contemporary scholar from the United States writes, "I cannot be a king in my society, but I could be a president. Similarly, a fifteenth century European couldn't be a president, although he could be a king."[6] The point is that much of what we use to assert our identity, our roles, or our position is not somehow "natural" but a part of a system we belong to. Developing this point, and something we pick up later, we should be aware that not just our culture but the language we speak also shapes the way we think about our relationships to individuals and others.[7] We saw this in relation to our example of Chinese society earlier where the language our culture gives us makes us more likely to relate to others in specific ways. Identity is therefore always very much shaped by our culture, as well as the roles or positions available within a specific society.

We also need to be aware that self-identity is approached in different ways across varying academic disciplines, and Giselle Walker and Elisabeth Leedham-Green outline some aspects of this, noting that "the biological self appears uncontroversial (if imperfectly known)," yet others highlight "the importance of context, exploring the difference between words and what they convey"; moreover, "I cannot know anything about *you* that is separate from myself and my standpoint." Again, approached through portraiture, we find that "portraits frequently give clues to perceived features of identity that would not be picked up by a simple passport photograph," while in law, "voice, name, appearance and so on are treated as representative of identity and thus used to imply endorsement by the owner of the identity," whereas others would emphasize a "first-person mental and physical sense" where "how *I* know who *you* are depends entirely on how I relate to you."[8] This overview only touches on some of the disciplines they discuss, whereas others are absent from their discussions. The perspectives mentioned here also do not discuss the often political and psychological issues of creating and recreating, as well as maintaining, identities. Whatever self-identity is, despite first appearances (I am *me* in this body and you are *you* in that body), it is a deeply complex and multifaceted set of relationships.

Another important factor in discussing the issue is that often we think of identity as singular, that is, we contemplate the self or another as an enclosed "thing," whereas identities are always multiple. For instance, as one of the authors, Paul, if I were to contemplate who I am, I need to take various factors into consideration. First, I am British, with a heritage that is both English and Welsh; I am also male and am an academic in a university context. Immediately, therefore, I have started to define my identity at various different levels and in different contexts—I belong, we might say, to various different identity families: British, male, academic. If I continue, I am also white, middle class (whatever that might mean these days), a father, a son, a fan of Terry Pratchett's *Discworld* novels, and so on. My self-identity is therefore something which exists in relation to all these, each of which shapes the way I experience the world and relate to others. Going back to our earlier quote that "how I know who you are depends entirely on how I relate to you," it can be seen that I will be related to, and relate to, others in different ways. Moreover, it is also important that I do not simply claim and have these identities; they exist only because of a society that makes them possible and provides these labels. This also means that my own self-identity is, partially at least, created in relation to the way others see and understand these labels. Anyone with a suspicion of intellectuals and learning may immediately have a negative reaction to me, a member of a black supremacist organization will also classify me according to his or her viewpoint, and a Malayan, female, working-class Buddhist will have her own understanding of me. Whatever I may think of my own self-identity, I must understand that I will always have that identity in relationship to others and that at certain times aspects of it will be forefronted. In the classroom, my role as an academic teacher will come forward; with certain friends discussing Pratchett's novels will be important; elsewhere the fact of my being a parent will be what drives and motivates me (although, obviously, all aspects of my identity will always be a part of this). Though we may negotiate many roles and related social identities, we acquire a self-identity that is composed of both our reflections on experiences and the sense of persisting through those experiences over time.[9]

Finally, we need to realize that self-identity, as we mentioned earlier, is often created in opposition. In other words, we often know who we are in relation to what we are not rather than what we actually are. Such oppositional identities arise at individual and collective levels. Human beings invest in belonging to and identifying with collective identities, for example sporting teams, nationalities, or activist groups. For instance, following a particular sporting team marks you out as having an identity that, to varying degrees, is always against others. If you support the New York Yankees, you want them to win and therefore their opponents to lose. On a more extreme level, especially at times in European football, this group identification leads to direct and violent confrontation with those who are defined as being outside one's group. Indeed, some theorists have primarily suggested that identity is "more the product of the marking of difference and exclusion, than they are the sign of an identical, naturally constituted unity,"[10] which is to say that we often know better what we do not stand for than what we do. However, against this, Richard Jenkins has pointed out that we need both identity and similarity to form our identity, so that we are not simply against something but also in relation to it or others. For instance, to be a socialist means that one acknowledges affinities with such political views as communism while also being against what may broadly be termed more conservative, or right-wing, stances. Jenkins, therefore, says that we need to keep similarity and difference in balance and that it is simply not logical to give one preference.[11] However, more importantly, he notes, if we assert difference as the base point, then we cannot be in communication with those we are different from, and so even to define yourself against the other implies that you acknowledge some kinship for the difference to be meaningful.[12] Therefore, we can suggest that while some identities are more clearly oppositional than others, even oppositional identities also acknowledge a relationship. Sporting teams are an example; for different teams to be in opposition, it is generally because they are playing the same game. It is an oppositional relationship but one in which a similarity exists. Moreover, differences does not necessarily imply opposition—for instance, if someone claims to be male, he does not (in most contexts) set himself against those who claim to be female, although some sense of opposition or tension can exist. Indeed, there are certainly those, particularly from religious backgrounds, but also perhaps arguing from biology, who would argue that mutuality exists—for the human species (without resort to artificial contraception), the generation of future generations relies on both male and female. This is not to say, however, that these are simple identities, and the boundaries of even such seemingly commonsense signifiers is often contested and is drawn differently in varying contexts.[13]

To conclude this section, we will touch on two matters: the first is whether we can give any final definition of identity, and the second is how this relates to religion. In this chapter, we largely follow well-established principles within sociology, and the humanities and social sciences more broadly, that personal identity development is about relationship and social involvement. As we have seen earlier, even to define oneself as an isolated individual involves distinguishing oneself from others and therefore being a social creature. We will therefore give a definition that will help us make sense of this perspective, especially as it is often used quite differently in different contexts: "The language of 'identity' is ubiquitous in contemporary social science, cutting across psychoanalysis, psychology, political science, sociology, and history. The common usage of the term identity, however, belies the considerable variability in both its conceptual meanings and its theoretical role."[14] We will therefore make use of Jenkins's definition that highlights the key aspects of social identity theory, which we are primarily employing here:

> Identity [both personal and collective] can only be understood as a process of "being" or "becoming". One's identity—one's identities, indeed, for who we are is always multi-dimensional, singular *and* plural—is never a final or settled matter. Not even death freezes the picture: identity and reputation may be reassessed after death; some identities—sainthood or martyrdom, for example—can only be achieved beyond the grave.... Bearing this in mind, for sociological purposes identification can be defined minimally thus:
>
> "Identity" denotes the ways in which individuals and collectivities are distinguished in their relations with other individuals and collectivities.
>
> "Identification" is the systematic establishment and signification, between individuals, between collectivities, and between individuals and collectivities, of relationships of similarity and difference.
>
> Taken—as they can only be—together, similarity and difference are the dynamic principles of identification, and are at the heart of the human world.[15]

In summation, identity is never fixed and static but always changing and in formation, or "becoming," even after death. It also involves our

relationship to others, both groups and individuals, in terms of similarity and difference that are always open to negotiation.

What, then, does this have to do with religion? For religious people, one of their key forms of identification is very often their religious belonging, and so alongside other identities they may claim, "I am a Hindu," "I am a Christian," "I am a practicing Buddhist," "I am a lapsed Catholic," and so on. If we follow a social identity perspective rather than seeing these labels as fixed, clear, and stable, we will realize that they fit into a network of other identities and are always open to review and change. Questions arise about claims to a religious identity such as what they mean by this identification; how they expect others to react; and how the particular terms we use for identity, and the connotations they hold, appeared. It may be objected that a religious identification carries heavier baggage than others, perhaps claiming weight as some form of "ultimacy" (I am saved; I know the purpose of life and the world), and for some people their religious identity may be seen as their primary identity eclipsing all others. Such claims are certainly worth taking seriously; however, they only exist in relationship to a society and culture where such claims are meaningful, to others who invest meanings in them, and to specific groups (collectivities in Jenkins's terminology) that similarly identify and use such identity markers to signify difference. Therefore, it does not escape the inquiry of social identity. Moreover, as has been pointed out, such identities can never exist in a vacuum, and so the Christian feminist theologian Jeannine Hill-Fletcher argues the following about identity in terms of meeting those of other religious identities:

> They [connections] will arise from the fact that each is not Muslim and Christian only (for example)—but a particular Muslim, of a particular age, from a particular background and family, meets a particular Christian whose background and experience have some hidden elements of overlap. The lifetime of being a Christian and having particular experiences has shaped the "Christian" just as a lifetime of being a particular Muslim has shaped the "Muslim."[16]

As Fletcher makes clear here, we can never be simply "Muslim" or "Sikh" or "Buddhist" but always part of a community, a family, with a certain age, gender, social class, and so on. This means that our identity will always "overlap" with those of others, even if in different ways with different people.

KEY THEORIES

In this section, we outline some principle approaches to identity from various academic disciplines that are important in the way we look at and think about identity today. We will not attempt to give a definitive account of different disciplines; rather our aim is to pull out some useful concepts and ideas from each that can be used to explore religion and religious identities. We will primarily focus on social identity theory, looking at both sociological and psychological perspectives, but also explore theories of identity in sociolinguistics and philosophy. This will involve a discussion of such areas as gender, ethnicity, culture, and class. We will also start to draw out aspects of how the theories relate to religion.

Aspects of Sociology and Identity

One important social behavior of great interest to many sociologists is narrative, or stories and storytelling. If identity, as has been suggested, is about "becoming," then it should be clear that this involves the story of who we have been, what happened to us to make us like that, and what has happened since to make us like we are now, and also what is the ongoing story—even after death. To make up such a life story, Steph Lawler, drawing upon the theorist Paul Ricoeur, talks about the three principle aspects of a narrative: character, action, and plot, where characters are the actors, both human and nonhuman, the action is the events through time, while she says of plot:

> The plot is a central feature of narrative: it is, fundamentally, what *makes* the narrative, in that it brings together different events and episodes into a meaningful whole: events or episodes are not thrown together at random, but are linked together.[17]

This is a crucial aspect of religious identity on both individual and group levels. On the individual level, people may recount their conversion narratives, what led them to become a member of their particular tradition, or they may tell the story of how a motif in their existing tradition helped bring meaning to life events. Meanwhile, the group identity is formed around specific, often founding, narratives. For many Christians, for instance, the Bible tells the story of God's relationship first with Israel and then with the church and so makes history meaningful. For Buddhists, the life story of the Buddha provides a meaningful explanation for the foundation of their tradition and also helps outline aspects of behavior and belief. The narrative is a story about the order of things, about the proper relations among individuals and between individuals and the sacred. It therefore describes the correct values and associated roles for individuals in relation to the group and brings them together into a shared religious identity. However, both individuals and groups may emphasize some parts of the story and deemphasize others, building an identity around the selected sections as they relate to their particular history. This is not simply about constructing religious identities (i.e., religious people choose the bits of their texts/narratives they like) but relating to how people always create narratives (our whole life story/self-identity is about selecting those parts of the texts/narratives that make sense to us).

Sociological analysis of narratives examines the ways one narrative interacts with other narratives, what is termed "intertextuality," or the way that texts are brought into discussion with each other (it is important to realize that "texts" here do not just mean "books" but almost any form of narrative) and also the way people emphasize certain parts of narratives (e.g., their religious tradition) at the expense of others. So Lawler tells us that sociologists see:

> A turn to intertextuality as significant: in producing a life story (one sort of text) we are always, implicitly or explicitly, referring to or drawing on other texts—other life stories, fictional and non-fictional, as well as a range of different kinds of texts. This should not to be taken to mean that the resulting narrative is "false", but simply that, in telling a life, people are simultaneously interpreting that life.[18]

A related sociological concern is embodiment, which is explored for its role in identity formation in various ways. One aspect of this is the way, in the Western world with a legacy from the French philosopher Rene Descartes (1596–1650), we have come to separate the body from the mind.[19] Increasingly, it is recognized that this division is problematic because various aspects of what we might think of as our rationality, and emotions, are embedded in our bodies (see Volume 1, Chapter 4, on aspects of this in relation to religion). It means, therefore, that to think of our identity as located in our "minds" rather than in our bodies, is difficult to maintain (we discuss related issues later in relation to philosophy). Indeed, the body is a key part of our narratives; although it is "subject to processes of birth, decay and death which result from its placement in the natural world," the events and behaviors we enact with our bodies are "also meaningful events located in a world of cultural beliefs, symbols and practices."[20] Religious narratives incorporating values, codes of ethics, and behaviors are often concerned with regulating the body and how we use it. Moreover, although Western concepts of religion have traditionally emphasized belief, it is increasingly realized that this is lopsided or unrepresentative, with many religions being more concerned with correct practice than correct belief (on issues about the definition of religion, see Volume 1, Chapter 1).

Embodiment also has additional ramifications, especially concerning gender and identity,[21] and just as those classified as having male- or female-gendered bodies within their society have different experiences of life generally (whether this be in the workplace or elsewhere), the same is often true of religion. Almost all of the world's largest religious traditions restrict certain roles to men, such that women are often unable to become a priest, bishop, imam, or monastic in their tradition. This means that a woman can never have the same experience of a religion as a man. (Not all traditions have such restrictions, but historically and still today, such segregation is enforced in many places, according to either tradition or geographical location.) Where religious narratives are concerned, feminist scholars, activists, and theologians have sought to reclaim the feminine aspects of their traditions' narratives as a means of enabling women to find their selves and identities reflected in the group's identity. (We will not dwell at length on this as such issues are discussed further in Volume 2, Chapter 1.)

The final aspect we will draw from sociology concerns culture. Culture is a very broad term and used diversely. It can have connotations of civilized life, where we would distinguish "high culture" (classical music and art, opera, literature, philosophy, etc.) and "low culture" (pop music, popular sports, music hall and fairground entertainment, etc.); such a classification has been increasingly breached in contemporary society, and it is hard to maintain to what extent it ever held. Instead, especially in sociology, it means something like, at a minimal definition, "the way of life of a group of people."[22] However, the term is more "slippery" than this, as the theologian Graham Ward suggests, who prefers a looser definition about the meaningful systems of signs "that produce shared knowledges and values amongst groups of people, constituting their beliefs about the nature of reality," or as he says, culture is "a symbolic world-view, embedded, reproduced and modified through specific social practices."[23] This latter definition is useful as it reminds us that culture, like identity, is never static but always changing, and is also not something that exists but is maintained by the members of the society as they reproduce it in their actions and have their ideas shaped through it. Our culture, which includes language, helps shape the way we perceive and receive the world around us. Our existing cultural background with its narratives is important in shaping how we relate to other narratives:

> white US college students were asked to read a Native American legend and then to recall the story as accurately as possible. Bartlett found that the students tended to forget those parts of the story that did not fit their cultural framework or expectations. Mitsztal comments,
>
> "Frames of meaning, or ways in which we view the past, are generated in the present and usually match the group's common view of the world. . . . We rely upon them to supply us with what we should remember and what is taboo [forbidden], and therefore must be forgotten."[24]

Within cultural systems, identities are created by groups that claim certain shared characteristics, for instance, social class, ethnicity, or race. Social class generally refers to people who share common socioeconomic characteristics, usually referred to as the working, middle, and upper classes.

They may develop a consciousness of their place in society: "Class-consciousness, that is the process of becoming a class for itself, is the collective process whereby a collective class grouping has the consciousness upon which to act."[25] Such class identities are subject to changing historical and social factors and vary from country to country. The idea of class is relevant for our discussion as, historically, it has been the middle and upper classes who have reinvented religious narratives and generated new religions or new forms of traditional religions.

With increasing globalization, ethnicity has also become a means of identifying groups of people by characterizing their cultural differences from other groups:

> Much of the discussion that has taken place about ethnicity and identity has focused on otherness as marked by visible difference. Even the very term "ethnic" is sometimes used to signify otherness. This suggests that some people are implicated in ethnicity and bear ethnic identities, because they are different, as if there were human beings who did not carry ethnicity; rather in the way that "ethnic food" is used to connote food from different cultures as if English or British food, for example, was not specific to a culture in any way. In this sense ethnicity has been associated with not being white. However, the concept of ethnicity has been adopted as preferable to that of race, at some points within the social sciences, as a way of marking difference, which is not tied to reductionist unchanging foundations. Ethnicity, with its focus on culture and social relations permits change and adaptation in a way that the biologically reductionist category of race does not. Ethnicity marks cultural and social differences between groups of people, rather than invoking spurious biological fixity where visible and embodied differences might be seen to determine and circumscribe identity.[26]

In this rich passage, the sociologist Kath Woodward unpacks a lot of significant points. One of them, not directly related to us here, is the way that the concept of race has become suspect for many as it is seen to be implicated in an agenda, beginning in the nineteenth century, to show clear biological and scientific differences between groups of people.[27] However, as she argues, the idea of ethnicity is not without its difficulties.[28] This opens a lot of questions beyond our immediate concern about these categories; however, we would like to take this issue about the problems of our classifications and relate it to religion.

The distinction between race and ethnicity raises a lot of questions we can relate to religion, for instance, are religious differences clearly fixed and determined (as race can be seen to be) or more fluid and capable of change (as is seen with ethnicity)? This raises questions about how we think about the categories as well: are there some essential aspects about Christianity,

Islam, Hinduism, and so on, or are the aspects of such an identity marker unstable and fluid? As has been argued, "we ... often see religious essentialism: the idea that everyone in a particular religious group shares in some essence that determines their behaviour"; however, this overlooks the way religions change over time and the vast diversity within them.[29] Indeed, it has even been suggested that where religious identities subsume all others and become the sole reference for someone, they can become dangerous.[30] Moreover, drawing on the issues within the previous quote, we need to be aware that in certain societies, with specific cultural frameworks, what is seen or encountered as "normal" religion will vary. Certainly, the idea that Christianity is the "normal" religion in Western societies still persists, and non-Christian religions in those countries may be deemed to be "ethnic" in some way—curious, exotic practices. Religion is part of the cultural discourses that shape or control our thinking and may lay behind what we normally presume;[31] that is, our sense of what is "normal" is derived from religious values such that other religions may seem strange or "exotic" simply because they come from different cultural spheres. This debate is related to discussions around the way the Western world has represented other cultures, especially of "the East/the Orient" (see Volume 1, Chapter 11).

Aspects of Psychology and Identity

Psychological approaches to identity share much in common with sociology in terms of the idea that identities are socially constructed and multiple and always in the process of becoming. However, they also highlight some specific factors, one of which is a point made by the pioneer psychologist William James (1842–1910). James proposed that the number of groups we interact with determines the number of identities that we have.[32] The famous theorist Carl Jung (1875–1961) suggested something similar, using the term *persona*, or masks, to refer to the roles we play in different situations, whether with family, friends, work colleagues, and so on; for him, though, this is a facade, a form of social identification, taken on from childhood onward that we need to overcome.[33] In religious terms, specific roles may apply in different contexts, and so a believer may adopt a different attitude in relation to the priest, other members of the community, or those outside the community.

Also, picking up from the issue of similarity and difference found in relation to sociological perspectives as well as the idea of identities created in opposition, social psychology has looked into the effects of group identification and found some interesting behaviors:

Experimental and field research do suggest that groups are willing to sacrifice large monetary gains that do not establish a positive difference between groups for smaller gains that do ..., that in-group members adopt more extreme positions after comparison with an out-group than with fellow in-group members ..., and that members prefer and selectively recall information that suggests intergroup differences rather than similarities.... This suggests that groups have a vested interest in perceiving or even provoking greater differentiation than exists and disparaging the reference group on this basis (cf. social vs. instrumental competition ...). Further, this tendency is exacerbated by contingencies that make the in-group per se salient ..., such as a threat to the group's domain or resources ... or, in Tajfel's ... terms, where the group's identity is insecure.[34]

In relation to religious identity, we will see that patterns of favoring one's own group will occur here as much as elsewhere. Indeed, the idea that there is "a vested interest in perceiving or provoking greater difference" is interesting in relation to much of the polemic and rivalry that has existed between different religious groups and that often has resulted in religious schisms. Of course, we must also acknowledge that traditional religious narratives also contain countermessages to this. Almost every religious tradition teaches some form of hospitality to those outside the tradition, with Buddhism advocating a universal compassion and the Israelite tradition of the Hebrew Bible looking to the needs of the underprivileged and stranger.[35]

Aspects of Sociolinguistics and Identity

It is fair to say that a certain overlap exists between the fields we have looked at so far, and sociolinguistic approaches draw on both mainstream sociology and psychology, especially social psychology, just as these fields will draw on sociolinguistics. However, each has a distinctive focus, and something sociolinguistics does is to look at the use and meaning of names. As a basic point, we learn the following:

> While groups' names for themselves obviously arise in many different ways— variants of "the people of the river" or "mountain-dwellers" are common, for instance—self-descriptions also often suggest that those outside the group are qualitatively different. There is a basic, if rather disturbing message in Stewart's ... observation that "many tribal names are—at least in primitive stages of culture—not formal designations, but merely equivalents of the pronoun 'we'."[36]

Moreover, many such self-identifications carry a "powerful ethnocentric bias,"[37] with groups terming themselves by such names as "outstanding people" or "real people." Cultures worldwide make such identifications, often valorizing those inside the group and demonizing those outside it. The ancient Greeks, for instance, used to classify all non-Greeks as barbarians.

The traditional native term for China literally means "Central Kingdom" (*Zhong Guo*), indicating that it is the true center of the world, and foreigners were, and still are, classified as "outside people" (*wei guo ren*), which certainly had connotations of barbarian, that is, if they did not come from the only place that was truly important, the center. We may suggest, therefore, that the "disturbing message" in the previous quote that group names have a sense of "we" is not just found in "primitive" cultures but is part of a general trend in identifying one's own groups as somehow central, normative, and foundational. Therefore, national and ethnic boundaries continue, and certainly much nineteenth-century British imperial ideology saw the spread of empire as linked to the bringing of civilization, and it continues today with the United States often presenting itself as a superpower and center of democracy and the free world.[38] Indeed, in recent decades there has been a greater emphasis on firming up and policing national boundaries with a view to excluding others, particularly refugees and asylum seekers, who often find identification with religious groups in their adopted countries. Naming is not limited to nations, ethnicities, or other groups, and we are reminded that

> Such ethnic naming conventions are also found, of course, in religiously based groups. Thus some interpretations within Islam divide the world into those within the sacred "house" and those without; and as Castoriadis . . . reminds us, the Christian Bible echoes with racism, with accounts that describe the "other" as impure, unclean, idolatrous, evil and depraved.[39]

Even if the other is not directly portrayed as "idolatrous, evil and depraved," other markers, especially in some groups, represent the world as split between those who are "saved" and "not saved," which sets up a clear demarcation that can easily create an "us and them" attitude.

Another aspect of sociolinguistics that is of interest to us is the question of representation, because language is one of the tools that helps us represent the world.[40] Continuing our previous theme, we may note that powerful or majority groups may represent others in ways that identify them as inferior and therefore lacking the necessary attributes to belong to the ingroup. However, language, as we suggested earlier, is deeply embedded into and helps shape our cultures and values, for it has both "historical and cultural associations" which relate to the way it provides "a powerful underpinning of shared connotations."[41] That is, every word is loaded with meanings, and so:

> "Outsiders" who have learned a language for practical reasons may develop a highly fluent command, but they may also find that certain deeper levels of communication remain closed to them: the technical capabilities that are more than sufficient for living and working in another speech community may not be so for a full appreciation of that culture's literature or drama.[42]

Communication involves much more than the grasp of a language. It includes nonverbal behaviors, gestures, and embodied emotional reactions, which account for at least 60 percent of the meaning in an interaction. Language and communication vary from culture to culture. This brings our discussion of identity as approached through linguistics into its relationship with communication studies and raises a variety of issues related to religion. It directs us to explore how we can understand not just the religious language of another group but also that group's inner life and motivations, as well as the full range of cultural dynamics that are transmitted through words learned through a deep immersion in that culture. Certainly, such an understanding is not impossible, but how to fully appreciate another's language and culture, and therefore their whole worldview, is something we need to consider.[43] (This links to the issues of insider/outsider debates discussed in Volume 1, Chapter 2.)

Lastly, although not a concern just within sociolinguistics, we may observe the way identity has become a prevalent concern within many academic disciplines and the effects of this. The linguistic scholar John Edwards notes that, "When I published a book called *Language, Society and Identity* in 1985, the final word in the title was not a particularly common one in the social-scientific literature."[44] Today, however, it has become a central focus, so much so that it can be said to be shaping the disciplines themselves, and one scholar speaks of "reconfiguring linguistics from the point of view of identity."[45] This is not seen as a negative, for the scholar continues by telling us that this "displaces the whole question of the basic function of language from the philosophical sphere to the political one—or more precisely, it breaks down the division between the philosophical and political."[46] This is not portrayed as a problem but as an important corrective, emphasizing the ways that things like language are not simple systems to be understood but active systems of identification with real effects in people's lives. This is important in relation to what we have said earlier, because it is those who control power who also assume the right to name who will be permitted to belong and who will not.

Aspects of Philosophy and Identity

In philosophy, discussion of identity has generally proceeded along rather different lines than in both sociology and psychology. Here, mention of identity is generally linked to a specific dispute, which may broadly be classed as the mind-body problem, and so is primarily about self-identity. That dispute asks whether we are identified with our bodies, our souls, or our minds. This argument tends to be cast primarily as a debate between materialist and dualist philosophers. Materialists argue that a physical answer is the only satisfactory one, that is, we are our bodies and nothing more: to speak of souls or some immaterial aspect of us is, they contend, simply nonsensical. On the other hand, a dualist response is that we are combined of two substances, a physical one and a spiritual one, and that to limit us simply to the first does not do justice to the way we think about ourselves nor what it means to be fully human. Such disputes may appear largely irrelevant to the dynamics of our construction as social beings that concern both sociology and psychology when they discuss identity. However, recall that we have talked about the self as that aspect of our inner being that negotiates the shape of our self-identity. Certainly, from a religious point of view, the "true" self-identity we hold may be tied to a soul or some spiritual essence rather than just seeing ourselves simply as either a body or a mind, or a combination of both. This is certainly part of claiming a religious identity.

The philosophical debates over whether we have a soul or not, and so whether we prefer a materialist or dualist answer, generally get weighed down across clear partisan boundaries and have raged for centuries. However, they have raised intriguing questions. For instance, the philosopher John Locke (1632–1704) famously argued that our sense of self-identity is primarily invested in our memories. Thus, regardless of whether we have souls or not, our self-identity, he suggested, is related to the fact that we know what we have done, who others are, and what we have done with them. Although this has a natural, commonsense appeal and relates to an awful lot of the way we do self-identify—for instance, philosophers suggest thought experiments of the type where you wake up inside somebody else's body and seek to prove that you are not the person you look like by appeal to specific memories—it has all sorts of problems. For instance, if somebody is in an accident and loses his or her memory, we do not say that he or she is no longer the same person, and we would expect the relatives to continue to care for that person. Certainly, although quite abstract, such debates often have profound ethical significance; for instance, anyone with relatives or friends with Alzheimer's or similar degenerative diseases is aware of the strains of dealing with loved ones who do not remember what they have done from day to day or may even forget who their spouse is. However, we will not dwell at length on these issues because our main concern is with the kind of concerns raised in social interaction of the type raised in sociology and psychology. Nevertheless, we must be aware that debates about identity are of many different types and can be raised in a variety of ways. Moreover, the philosophical case we have discussed here alerts us to a significant issue that identity has different facets, one of which is how we identity ourselves and another how others identify us—the case of swapping bodies or losing memories highlights this very well—identities are both achieved as a result of our reflections on personal heritage and given, that is, ascribed to us by others,[47] and these can be in conflict.[48]

SURVEY OF ARGUMENTS: IDENTITY IN CONTEXT

Taken together, the concepts of identity discussed earlier provide a powerful set of tools for analyzing identity in relation to both individuals and communities. The formation of religious identities is essentially similar to the formation of other identities, always being subject to surrounding social and cultural factors and the relationships between individuals and groups in varying ways. In what follows we will look at a range of issues and examples where identity helps us think through aspects of religion, as well as looking at ways some religions consider identity. We begin with a brief survey of three issues discussed elsewhere in these volumes before taking a closer look at some specific examples.

Approaching Religions and Identity

We begin by surveying a range of issues that are developed elsewhere within these volumes where identity is a useful factor. In the chapter on religion and nature (Volume 2, Chapter 7), the story is told of Buddhist monks in Thailand "ordaining" trees as monks, by wrapping them in the distinctive saffron robe, to protect the forests from logging. This involves a change of identity for the tree—as we saw earlier, the characters in narratives are not necessarily human—where it becomes part of a narrative around the respect for the Buddhist monastic community and links to environmental concerns. Here, cultural systems and particular symbols are at play, with identity being conferred in a specific form, the saffron robe, which because of its association with monkhood carries a marker of identity with it.

In the chapter on Jewish-Muslim relations (Volume 3, Chapter 2), we see specific words that carry weight being employed, specifically "Jew" and "Muslim." The way that an oppositional identity is set up in the minds of many simply because another person bears a particular identity marked by these words is addressed. The perception that they should be opposed is also challenged with examples of the way that at many places and times throughout history Jews and Muslims have actually lived in harmony. This example illustrates the ways that reviewing narratives can help break down the idea of difference and lead to people looking for similarities.

Finally, the issue of multiple religious identities (Volume 1, Chapter 10), where people claim a relationship with, or even a belonging to, more than one religious tradition raises questions. Seemingly antithetical to typical Western notions of religion, some form of multiple belonging, or identity, has been the norm across much of East Asia, and elsewhere, for centuries. Such an example demonstrates that the phenomenon of multiple identities can include religions ones. Although people in some traditions, such as most Christians, Muslims, and Jews, may perceive belonging to one tradition

alone as the only possibility, it is far from the only way to conceive of personal religious identities, which can be far more adaptable in specific situations. As we discussed in relation to ethnicity and race, we need to
question the categories we create and the ideologies behind them.

These three brief examples illustrate that the concept of identity and the
tools we have discussed can be brought to bear in a range of situations to
provide insight and clarity. We will proceed to discuss a few more examples
that we will develop in more depth.

Claiming Religious Identities

We develop two examples here, one from Islam and the other from
Daoism, about the way that people claim religious identities and some
aspects of this. Islam as a term means "submission," indicating submission
to the will of God ("Allah" is simply the Arabic term for God, literally "the
God"). Therefore, Muslims see anyone who submits to God's will as being
a Muslim; however, this can lead to some misunderstandings. For instance,
Muslims will identify Jesus, Moses, Abraham, and even Adam as Muslims.
To understand this claim it is necessary to realize that Muslims believe that
God has, through his prophets, always been delivering the same message to
humanity. They argue that this message has been lost or distorted in all previous cases, the one exception being the person they see as God's final
prophet, Muhammad, whose message was passed on in its purity. For
Muslims to claim identity as Muslims, therefore, places them within a narrative that is similar to the Christian one, and indeed the Jewish one too, for
they believe that the biblical texts, which these other traditions revere, are
also part of the story of God's encounter with humanity. However, they place
this in relation to the message of the *Quran*. The naming as a Muslim, therefore, carries a powerful self-identification as the true followers of God's message, which marks out both similarities and differences between themselves
and Jews and Christians. Indeed, we have alluded to some of the shared
history and the relationship of Muslims and Jews earlier. A question may
be asked, however, as to whether this identity stresses the similarity or difference. Of course, there is no simple answer, and at different times Muslims,
Jews, and Christians have stressed different aspects of this relationship. In
large part, it centers around the figure of Abraham from whom all three religions claim descent, a heritage that has both brought them together and
drawn them apart—indeed, at times it has been suggested that the bitterness
of the disputes between Christians and Muslims is because it is a family
dispute.

This example reveals how narrative histories can create both solidarity
and division, defining identities as oppositional or similar depending on the
politics of the time or situation. It is not possible to assess this debate here,

which would also distract us from the issue of identity; however, it is important to note the tensions of claiming identity inherent in this particular
claim.[49] Indeed, we may also draw on the discussion about names we mentioned earlier, and although the term Muslim in some ways acts like other
group identities to mark out those inside as superior, that is, those who submit to God against those who in some form reject him, it is not simply about
difference, as Jenkins noted, but plays strongly on issues of similarity. It is
also deeply tied in to issues of interreligious relations (see Volume 1,
Chapter 8, where we also discuss the issue of these three religions and their
family connection around Abraham). We therefore see part of the way in
which identities are complex and that we cannot rely on one aspect of identity theory alone to try to understand the various layers involved.

Our second case study is Daoism, which provides us with a useful example of the way in which a group identity is formed in a variety of ways. It is
worth noting that there is a story to tell about the roots and origins of
Daoism in China; however, our focus will be on what we may term
"Western Daoism." Most scholars suggest that the earliest tradition that we
can identify in any meaningful way as Daoist is the Celestial Masters, which
emerged in the early centuries CE in the area around modern-day Sichuan
Province in South China, an area which was then outside the growing
Chinese empire. However, most traditions of Daoism trace their origins back
to a mythical figure named Lao Zi (meaning "old sage") who is said to be an
older contemporary of Confucius, living around the sixth century BCE. This
story is, however, only partly relevant to the issue we will discuss here, which
is that since at least the nineteenth-century various Westerners have sought
to term themselves Daoists. Primarily this identification has been based on
an identification with a text attributed to Lao Zi, the *Dao De Jing* (often spelt
Tao Te Ching) and a few other philosophical texts (primarily the *Zhuang Zi*,
often *Chuang Tzu*, and to a lesser extent the *Lie Zi*, often *Lieh Tzu*). This was
linked to a set of concepts labeled "philosophical Daoism," which was
believed to be taught in these texts. Such an identity has been claimed not
only with the assumption that what Daoists did in China was irrelevant to
what Western Daoists believed about these texts but also with the
assumption that the Westerners actually understood the texts correctly
and that Chinese Daoism, as it then existed, was a corrupt and superstitious
practice hardly even worthy of consideration.[50] Indeed, the actual practice of
Daoism as a lived tradition was termed "religious Daoism" and presented as
degraded and superstitious. We cannot unpack a lot of the detailed history
behind this Western appropriation of Daoism, but it is linked to both the
nineteenth-century American transcendentalist poets reading their own
message into the Daoist texts and a later continuation of this in the hippy
movement of the 1960s; Western academics facilitated this cultural adaptation by painting a distorted and inaccurate picture of what Daoism was.

(We should note that the distinction of philosophical and religious Daoism, although tied to aspects of Chinese tradition and long upheld in the Western academy, is now realized to be an entirely false and misleading one.) Importantly, here, we see some interesting aspects of identity creation. First, there is an assumption that Daoist identity could be claimed irrespective of the tradition and culture to which it had originally belonged. A narrative was created suggesting some form of universal truth was buried in these texts that could be accessed from another cultural tradition. Second, we need to consider the way the words used were loaded with specific connotations. Here, the "pure" form of Daoism Westerners believed they found in these texts was labeled "philosophical Daoism," which was contrasted with the corrupt "religious Daoism" they believed was practiced in China. Specific labels as markers of identity were therefore employed. Third, as various studies have recently shown, what Westerners found in the Daoist text was largely what they already believed: the texts did not therefore give them some "new" or "universal" truth but were instead read to mean exactly what the readers wanted them to mean. For instance, a term such as "spontaneity," which in the original Chinese Daoist context related to the way we need to harmonize ourselves, through specific disciplines, to a higher "power" so we are not constrained by our "lower" instincts, were read to mean the spontaneity that nineteenth-century American Transcendentalist writers or twentieth-century counterculture movements like the hippies wanted, which meant freedom from all external controls, and the right to defy any authority or system of discipline. This relates to our earlier discussion about the way our cultural identities shape what we are able to take in and absorb. Ironically, perhaps, part of the appeal of Daoism is that it was not Western and represented a form of ancient Oriental wisdom. Therefore, it set up a pattern of identity as oppositional while also buying into problematic representations of the Orient (see Volume 1, Chapter 11). We can therefore see the issue of selective narratives at play, as well as the cultural formation and prejudices embedded in our identities and the way these affect the development of our becoming and taking on new identities.

Religions and Internal Foundations for Identities

So far we have discussed how theories of identity can be used to explore the ways people use religious narratives to define themselves in relation to other religions or to create new religious identities by borrowing from other traditions. What we have not asked is the way in which religions themselves view identity. Here I would like to discuss two traditions, Buddhism, especially its notion of no-self, and Christianity, especially in relationship to baptism.

When we discussed philosophical approaches to identity, we mentioned that one aspect of its concerns was the mind-body problem, and specifically within this questioning the notion of a soul, whether there is some inner "spiritual" part of our being that is essentially "us," and so defines our self-identity. Certainly many religions would sign up to some sort of concept of a soul, though often in very different ways. Buddhism, however, contests the idea of a soul or spiritual essence. As part of the Buddha's basic insight into reality, he is said to have realized that all things in this world have what are termed the three marks: impermanence, transitoriness, and no-self.[51] The last one, following the general English translation of "no-self," is what we will focus on here, although the other two are also insightful in the context of identity, as we will explain. Nothing we see in this world, the Buddha taught, has a permanent, fixed, and solid existence, rather everything is impermanent and always in a state of passing from one state to another. A chair, for instance, being made of wood, was once a tree, and will in due course rot and become something else. Buddhism therefore talks of all things as existing in a state of becoming. It could therefore be suggested that Buddhist notions actually tie in quite well with contemporary identity theory, which suggests that our identity is always in a state of becoming.[52] No-self is related to this; if everything is in a state of change, in a process of becoming, we have no permanent self, only continual becoming as we move from one form, or life, to another. The term itself, however, implies something even stronger, for the Sanskrit term is *anatman*, or "no atman," which is the denial of the term used in other Indian religious systems, such as the Hindu family of religions, to mean what we would generally call the "soul." An equally good translation is, therefore, "no-soul." This is interesting because we might commonly make the assumption that religions are tied to some notion of a solid identity linked to a claim about a spiritual or supernatural element; however, it is certainly not the case with Buddhism. Indeed, quite a lot of what we have said about identity theory in this chapter is not inherently problematic for Buddhism. (This is not to say, of course, that all Buddhists would endorse it or understand their tradition in this way; indeed, many Buddhist traditions speak of something called Buddha Nature, which can be suggested as a way to work the idea of a soul into Buddhism; certainly in popular Buddhism, especially in East Asia, the tradition operates as if there were souls.[53])

Turning now to Christianity, for many denominations identification with the tradition is linked to baptism, which is understood as an initiation into the community. In some denominations at least this is seen as linked to the creation of a new Christian identity and with it the erasure of all other identities. To quote the theologian Elizabeth Stuart, who is representing what may be said to be, broadly, a Catholic stance:

Rudy notes that it is by baptism and not biology that one enters the Church. Rowan Williams points out that baptism constitutes a ritual change of identity, a setting aside of all other identities in favour of an identity as a member of the body of Christ.[54] ... What we receive in baptism is not an identity negotiated in conversation with our communities or culture such as our sexual or gender identities ... it is an identity over which we have no control whatsoever. It is sheer gift.[55]

Such a concept has roots within the earliest texts of the nascent Christian community, in particular the words of Paul that in Christ "there is neither Jew nor Greek, there is neither slave nor free, there is neither male nor female; for you are all one in Christ Jesus."[56] From this perspective, we may suggest that Christianity has a very fixed and static notion of identity, which contrasts with Buddhism. Not only does it suggest we have an essence, the soul, which is who we truly are, but also that there is something of a monolithic and all-encompassing Christian identity compared to which all other things are insignificant. We may note, though, that for Stuart at least this is not linked to a traditional notion of a singular Christian identity as she develops a queer theology that finds a place for gays, lesbians, transgendered people, and others within the church.[57] Also, as with Buddhism, there is not a single position on this, and contemporary identity theory, with notions of multiple identities and the like, has been employed by a number of theologians; we have quoted Fletcher earlier who considers this in relation to the way Christians relate to those of other religious traditions, whereas others have related it to such things as black and feminist theologies.[58] It is also possible to question the notion that there is any form of single and fixed Christian identity and look at the ways that the narratives and language of Christianity are embedded both within its Jewish roots and in various created narratives of similarity and difference. To return to the notion of baptism, although we have seen the suggestion that it unites all Christian "in Christ," we have elsewhere shown that this very term, an identity marker for Christians, can operate as both a sign of oppositional identity and of unity between Christians:

Today, it [the term "in Christ"] is widely used to draw all Christians together, however, in the context of the phrase *"extra ecclesia nulla salvus"* [there is no salvation outside the church] its purpose would be to divide Christians. The mutual anathemas between the Roman Catholic and Orthodox churches excommunicated other Christians, declaring some to be "in Christ" and others not "in Christ".[59] Likewise, in the schisms between Rome and Protestants, or over Chalcedon, the same split was made: some Christians are "in Christ", other Christians are not "in Christ". Still today, some groups that claim Christian identity, notably the Jehovah's Witnesses and Mormons, are seen not to be part of the Christian church by most other Christians and so not "in Christ". Meanwhile, some churches, especially a number of evangelical Protestant ones, would exclude Roman Catholics, Copts, Orthodox or many other Protestants from being "in Christ". The claims and decisions about who is and is not "in Christ" is not in the realm of some supernatural, uncontested, neutral space, but part of the human dynamics that construct all theological formulae.[60]

We need to see and be aware therefore that religious identities are always constructed in various ways, and that this is always, at heart, part of a social construction about similarity and difference, sometimes operating in opposition to others, while at other times seeking to include others. Another theme we could pick up here is that of rites of passage and the way specific rituals are seen to convey new identities.[61]

CONCLUSION

Individuals and religious groups create, appropriate, and discuss identity in a variety of different ways; however, they all can be seen as part of the way in which we socially create all forms of identity. Religious, or nonreligious, identities also form part of our multiple layers of identity, can be used to claim similarity and/or difference, and can be drawn in strongly oppositional ways as well as in ways that seek peace and are more irenic. Given the way that religion is embedded into cultural systems, it is also no surprise that particular markers of identity have strong resonance in specific cultures, although these meanings can vary with time and place. The question of narrative is also important, and (as with all forms of identity creation) the stories we tell about who we are, and why we are, are important shapers of both individual and group identities. Given the prevalence of the discussion of identity in the humanities and social sciences today, the study of religion is naturally enriched by the language and tools that the study of identity bring to it.

GLOSSARY

Becoming: in relation to identity, it is suggested that we never have solid or fixed identities but that who we are (in either individual or group contexts) is always subject to social interaction, which means it changes. Therefore, identities are always in a process of "becoming" rather than "being." This has resonances with aspects of traditional Buddhist philosophy.

Buddha Nature: in Chinese Buddhist thought, all beings hold the potential to attain Awakening because we have Buddha Nature, which may be said to be the essence of ultimate reality. In much popular Buddhist thought in the Chinese cultural realm the notion of Buddha Nature acts like the notion of a "soul" or "spirit" in contradistinction to the Buddhist teaching of no-self.

Dualist: in philosophy, a position which claims that humans are composed of two aspects, a spiritual and a physical one. It is contrasted with a materialist position.

Identity: a central concept in much contemporary academic thought that can refer to either self-identity or group identity and is always multiple (we do not have just one aspect that says who we are), socially negotiated, and subject to becoming. It is often defined through roles we act out.

Materialist: in philosophy, a position that claims we are simply physical beings. It is contrasted with a dualist position.

No-self (anatman): a Buddhist teaching that both denies we have any form of "soul" or "spirit" and emphasizes that throughout our life (and lives) we continually change in relation to thoughts, feelings, experiences, and encounters with others. There is no permanent essence, which is the "I."

Role: in identity theory, it refers to specific ways we relate socially, for instance as a teacher, doctor, mother, daughter, and so on.

Self: in identity theory, it refers to the "inner" self-reflection that we see as "us" and also refers to the particular personal identity we claim, our self-identity.

NOTES

1. Giselle Walker and Elisabeth Leedham-Green, "Introduction," in *Identity*, ed. Giselle Walker and Elisabeth Leedham-Green (Cambridge, England: Cambridge University Press, 2010), 1.

2. Kath Woodward, *Understanding Identity* (London: Arnold, 2002), vii.

3. Mark R. Leary and June Price Tangney, "The Self as Organizing Construct in the Social and Behavioural Sciences," in *Handbook of Self and Identity*, ed. Mark R. Leary and June Price Tangney (New York: Guilford Press, 2000), 8.

4. Jan E. Stets and Pater J. Burke, "A Sociological Approach to Self and Identity," in *Handbook of Self and Identity*, 128–52.

5. Woodward, *Understanding Identity*, vii.

6. Craig Martin, *A Critical Introduction to the Study of Religion* (Sheffield, England: Equinox, 2012), 28.

7. Although for some time anthropologists claimed that our language creates a worldview that controls the world around us, more careful study and reflection has shown such strongly determinist views to be false; however, it is nevertheless clear that our language creates patterns, or habits, of thinking and relating that are very powerful and perhaps restrict the kind of questions we ask. See Guy Deutscher, *Through the Language Glass: How Words Colour Your World* (London: William Heinemann, 2010)—an accessible account of some main themes can be found online in the *New York Times Magazine* titled "Does Your Language Shape How you Think?" http://www.nytimes.com/2010/08/29/magazine/29language-t.html?pagewanted=all&_r=1&.

8. Walker and Leedham-Green, "Introduction," 1, 3, 4, 7.

9. Katja Crone, "Phenomenal Self-Identity over Time," *Grazer Philosophische Studien* 84(2012): 216.

10. Stuart Hall, "Introduction: Who Needs Identity?" in *Questions of Cultural Identity*, ed. Stuart Hall and Paul Du Gay (London: Sage, 1996), 4.

11. Richard Jenkins, *Social Identity*, 3rd ed. (London and New York: Routledge, 2008), 21.

12. Ibid., 21–22.

13. The classic work on this is Judith Butler, *Gender Trouble* (London and New York: Routledge, 1990).

14. Sheldon Stryker and Peter J Burke, "The Past, Present and Future of an Identity Theory," *Social Psychology Quarterly* 63, no. 4 (2000): 284.

15. Jenkins, *Social Identity*, 17–18.

16. Jeannine Hill-Fletcher, *Monopoly on Salvation?* (Maryknoll, NY: Orbis, 2005), 94. For an extended discussion on the problem of seeing Christian identity as singular and not plural, see Paul Hedges, *Controversies in Interreligious Dialogue and the Theology of Religions* (London: SCM, 2010), 31–44.

17. Steph Lawler, *Identity: Sociological Perspectives* (Cambridge, England: Polity Press, 2008), 11. We must always recall that the narrative depends on preexisting narratives within culture; see Pierre Bourdieu, "The Biographical Illusion," in *Identity: A Reader*, ed. Paul Du Gay, Jessica Evans, and Peter Redman (London and Thousand Oaks, CA: Sage, 2000 [1986]), 297–303.

18. Lawler, *Identity*, 14.

19. Ian Burkitt, *Bodies of Thought: Embodiment, Identity and Modernity* (London and Thousand Oaks, CA: Sage, 1999), 7.

20. Bryan Turner, *The Body and Society*, 3rd ed. (London and Los Angeles, CA: Sage, 2008), 55.

21. See, for an overview, Tina Chanter, *Gender* (London and New York: Continuum, 2006), 1-7.

22. Warren Kidd, *Culture and Identity* (Basingstoke, England: Palgrave Macmillan, 2002), 5.

23. Graham Ward, *Cultural Transformation and Religious Practice* (Cambridge, England: Cambridge University Press), 5.

24. Lawler, *Identity*, 18–19, citing B. A. Misztal, *Theories of Social Remembering* (Maidenhead, England: Open University Press, 2003), 82

25. Woodward, *Understanding Identity*, 4.

26. Ibid., 145–46.

27. For a discussion of this in the U.S. context, see Robert Pierce Forbes, " 'The Cause of This Blackness': The Early American Republic and the Construction of Race," *American Nineteenth Century History* 13, no. 1 (2012): 65–94.

28. Following up the argument that ethnic identity is not clear or obvious, it has been argued that it can to some degree be "chosen"; see Miri Song, *Choosing Ethnic Identity* (Cambridge, England: Polity Press, 2003).

29. Martin, *A Critical Introduction*, 43, 146–48, 150–57; and Hedges, *Controversies in Interreligious*, 31–44, where the notion of a singular and fixed or stable religious identity is challenged, primarily using examples from Christianity.

30. Bhikhu Parekh, *A New Politics of Identity: Political Principles for an Interdependent World* (Basingstoke, England: Plagrave Macmillan, 2008), 130.

31. See Nikolas Rose, "Identity, Genealogy, History," in *Identity*, 311–24.

32. Stryker and Burke, "The Past, Present and Future," 286.

33. Polly Young-Eisendrath, "Gender and Contrasexuality: Jung's Contribution and Beyond," in *The Cambridge Companion to Jung*, ed. Polly Yong-Eisendrath and Terence Dawson (Cambridge, England: Cambridge University Press, 1997), 232.

34. Blake E. Ashforth and Fred Mael, "Social Identity Theory and the Organization," *The Academy of Management Review* (14:1, 1989), 31.

35. On notions of hospitality across a range of religious traditions, see Richard Kearney and James Taylor, eds., *Hosting the Stranger: Between Religions* (London and New York: Continuum, 2011).

36. John Edwards, *Language and Identity*, Key Topics in Sociolinguistics Series (Cambridge, England: Cambridge University Press, 2009), 36.

37. Ibid.

38. On U.K. context, see Dane Kennedy, "The Great Arch of Empire," in *The Victorian World*, ed. Martin Hewitt (London and New York: Routledge, 2012), 57–72. On U.S. context, see Bernard Porter, "We Don't Do Empire," *History Today* 55, no. 3 (2005): 31–33.

39. Edwards, *Language and Identity*, 37.

40. Ibid., 15.

41. Ibid., 55.

42. Ibid.

43. The theologian George Lindbeck is especially noted for developing this interpretation; see George Lindbeck, *The Nature of Doctrine* (Philadelphia, PA: Westminster Press, 1984).

44. Ibid., 15.

45. John E. Joseph, *Language and Identity: National, Ethnic, Religious* (Basingstoke, England: Palgrave Macmillan, 2004), 23.

46. Ibid.

47. Michael T. Cooper, "The Roles of Nature, Deities, and Ancestors in Constructing Religious Identity in Contemporary Druidry,"*Pomegranate* 11, no. 1 (2009): 63.

48. On philosophical approaches, see Raymond Tallis, "Identity and the Mind," in *Identity*, 184–207; or Michael B. Wilkinson with Hugh N. Campbell, *Philosophy of Religion: An Introduction* (London and New York: Continuum, 2010), 355–67, although there are many texts covering these areas.

49. On disputes and family relations between Christianity and Islam, see Martin Bauschke, "Islam: Jesus and Muhammad as Brothers," in *Christian Approaches to Other Faiths*, ed. Paul Hedges and Alan Race (London: SCM, 2008), 191–210.

50. On the whole range of disputes discussed here, see the following: Russell Kirkland, *Taoism: The Enduring Tradition* (London and New York: Routledge, 2004), 1–19 (an accessible version of Kirkland's main thesis can be found on his Web site, "The Taoism of the Western Imagination and the Taoism of China: De-Colonializing the Exotic Teachings of the East," 1997, http://faculty.franklin.uga.edu/kirkland/sites/faculty. franklin.uga.edu.kirkland/files/TENN97.pdf); James J. Clarke, *The Tao of the West: Western Transformations of Taoist Thought* (London and New York: Routledge, 2000); and for a more positive assessment of why Western Daoists can call themselves Daoists, see James Miller, *Daoism: A Very Short Introduction* (Oxford, England: Oneworld, 2003), 16–35 (chapter on identity); this is now republished as *Daoism: A Beginner's Guide* (2008).

51. For a good overview of the Buddha's teachings in relation to this, see Rupert Gethin, *The Foundations of Buddhism* (Oxford, England: Oxford University Press), 59–68; and Donald Mitchell, *Buddhism: Introducing the Buddhist Experience* (Oxford, England: Oxford University Press), 34–38.

52. In relation to its compatibility with psychology more generally, see Caroline Brazier, *Buddhist Psychology* (London: Constable and Robinson, 2012); or David Galin, "The Concept 'Self' and 'Person' in Buddhism and in Western Psychology," http://www.rogerr.com/galin/papers/roots.htm.

53. See Jungnok Park, *How Buddhism Acquired a Soul on the Way to China* (Sheffield, England: Equinox, 2012).

54. This reference is from the original quote by Rowan Williams, *On Christian Theology* (Oxford and Malden, MA: Blackwell, 2000), 189.

55. Elizabeth Stuart, *Gay and Lesbian Theologies: Repetitions with Critical Difference* (Aldershot, England: Ashgate, 2003), 106–8. As part of the Catholic context, Stuart goes on to reference the Council of Trent in relation to what she is saying here.

56. Galatians 3:28, revised standard version.

57. Stuart, *Gay and Lesbian Theologies*, 89–116.

58. A range of representative literature on Christianity and identity would include Kathryn Tanner, *Theories of Culture: A New Agenda for Theology* (Minneapolis, MN: Fortress Press, 1997); Werner Jeanrond, "Belonging or Identity? Christian Faith in a Multi-Religious World," in *Many Mansions?* ed. Catherine Cornille (Maryknoll, NY: Orbis, 2002), 106–20; Judith Gruber, "Christian Identities: An Imaginative and Innovative Quest for Heterogeneous Unity," *ESharp* 14 (2009), accessed May 25, 2010, www.gla.ac.uk/media/media_138646_en.doc; and Judith Lieu, *Christian Identity in the Jewish and Graeco-Roman World* (Oxford, England: Oxford University Press, 2002). Fletcher represents an example from feminist theology, whereas Robert Beckford is a good example of black theology; see Robert Beckford, *Jesus Is Dread: Black Theology and Culture in Britain* (London: Darton, Longman and Todd, 1998).

59. This reference is from the original quote: "It may be objected that excommunication is a matter of church polity, simply stating we are no longer in communion with these people, not that they are not Christians. Indeed, in purely abstract theological terms this may be so, however, the actual practice and rhetoric surrounding the matter worked to place these others in the category of the damned or heathens (although periods of rapprochement did still exist). A comparable case would be to say that in 'pure' Christian theological terms all people have equality before God, however, slavery and the killing of other human beings (whether it be indigenous peoples from outside the cultural area or religious Others) has been justified and supported by the church at many times. Certainly, the idea that wrong belief or denominational allegiance equates to damnation thereby justifying violence against other Christians, has a long tradition in wars that have claimed religious justification."

60. Hedges, *Controversies in Interreligious*, 184–85.

61. Jenkins, *Social Identity*, 173–77; see also Martin, *A Critical Introduction*, 30; and Lawler, *Identity*, 110–11.

FURTHER READINGS

Dingely, James. "Sacred Communities: Religion and National Identities." *National Identities* 13, no. 4 (2011): 389–402.

Hedges, Paul. *Controversies in Interreligious Dialogue and the Theology of Religions.* London: SCM, 2010, pp. 31–44.

Hedges, Paul. "Interreligious Engagement and Identity Theory: Assessing the Theology of Religions Typology as a Model for Dialogue and Encounter" *Journal for the Academic Study of Religion* 27, 2 (2014).

Jenkins, Richard. *Social Identity*. 3rd ed. London and New York: Routledge, 2008.

Joseph, John E. *Language and Identity: National, Ethnic and Religious*. Basingstoke, England: Palgrave Macmillan, 2004.

Lawler, Steph. *Identity: Sociological Perspectives*. Cambridge and Malden, MA: Polity Press, 2008.

Martin, Craig. *A Critical Introduction to the Study of Religion*. Sheffield, England: Equinox, 2012, pp. 19–44.

Parekh, Bhikhu. *A New Politics of Identity: Political Principles for an Interdependent World*. Basingstoke, England: Palgrave Macmillan, 2008.

Stets, Jan E., and Pater J. Burke. "A Sociological Approach to Self and Identity." In *Handbook of Self and Identity*, ed. Mark R. Leary and June Price Tangney. New York: Guilford Press, pp. 128–52.

Tanner, Kathryn. *Theories of Culture: A New Agenda for Theology*. Minneapolis, MN: Fortress Press, 1997.

8

Why Are There Many Gods? Religious Diversity and Its Challenges

Paul Hedges

INTRODUCTION

Religious diversity is, arguably at least, a challenge for more people and societies today than at any time in the past. This is not to say that religious diversity is something new; many cultures and societies have lived with it for hundreds, or thousands, of years. However, today, almost every religious community has access to a wealth of knowledge about a huge array of different religions, coupled with increasingly religiously diverse societies, making this a challenge that cannot be ignored. Some of the challenges are social ones—how to live alongside people from other racial, cultural, ethnical, and religious backgrounds (for more on this, see Volume 2, Chapter 12); however, our question here is about how, internally, a religious tradition deals with these questions. Devotees may be asking questions that include: what is my understanding of these other religions? How should I behave in relation to the members of other religions (should I try to convert, understand, or ignore them)? What does it say about my religion that there are other religions in the world? And is it possible that more than one religion may be true?

In this chapter, we will address some important aspects of this debate, but first it would be useful to clarify some terms we will use in this chapter. Often when discussing religious diversity the term religious plurality or pluralism is used. However, as we shall see in due course, in making sense of religious diversity from a religious perspective there is a particular school of thought termed, variously, "pluralism", "religious pluralism", "the pluralist hypothesis", or, to reflect the variety within it, "pluralisms". To avoid confusing this theological and philosophical concept with the fact of many religions existing in multi-faith societies, we shall use the term "diversity" to refer to the latter, and reserve "pluralism" for the former.

HISTORICAL BACKGROUND AND CONTEXT

We will start by surveying a range of different historical and cultural contexts to see how religious diversity has been experienced and what it means. In these we will need to be selective and pick up on a few features in each area and historical period rather than giving a comprehensive survey of all attitudes; however, at the same time, we will attempt to give a general impression of what religious diversity meant and how it was interpreted.

Religious Diversity in the Western Christian Context

Christianity was born into a religiously diverse world; however, some writers argue our current experience is new and requires new approaches.[1] For instance, we are now surrounded by religions that, hundreds of years ago, we were in general ignorant of. We will explore these issues.

When Jesus was born, the Roman Empire constituted the known world for the majority of its inhabitants. Stretching from Wales in the west to Asia Minor and modern-day Syria in the east, and from the north of mainland Europe to northern Africa, it was one of the greatest empires the world has ever seen. Within its borders a vast diversity of religious practice could be found. The Greeks revered their gods, the Romans their own, although it was generally held that a correspondence existed between them, such that the chief of the Greek gods, Zeus, was understood to be another name for Jupiter, Rome's principal deity. A similar parity was also suggested between the Egyptian deities and deities of the Celtic peoples. Despite this, a great deal of diversity of practice existed, and local cults abounded.[2] Moreover, not everything fitted into this neat scheme. Many Romans of the higher classes spurned the popular polytheism (belief in many gods) and accepted some form of monotheism (belief in one god). Religions dedicated to particular deities also existed, such as those of Mithras and Orpheus and also Judaism. Other religions, from beyond the empire's borders were known and exerting greater or lesser influence, included Zoroastrianism (which had great influence[3]) and Buddhism. The religious world into which early Christianity emerged was clearly very diverse.

Like most religious traditions of the time, Judaism in Jesus's day was not overtly missionary. It accepted converts quite freely, although it took three generations for new converts to become full members, but it did not seek to expand aggressively into new territory. On the whole, religion was seen as linked to family, tribal, or regional customs and traditions, and therefore, conversion was not necessary.[4] Everyone had their own religious tradition that was suitable for them, although they could become part of another tradition. Some traditions, however, like the cult of Mithras, did actively seek new members, and it was this pattern that the newly emerging Christian tradition would follow. It is best to characterize the early Jesus movement as a form of Judaism that saw its fulfillment in spreading beyond the geographical and community identity of the Jewish people—the debates and arguments are recorded clearly in texts such as the *Acts of the Apostles*.[5] Therefore, what became the orthodox tradition of Christianity sought to convert others, something systematically and ruthlessly carried out when, from the fourth century CE and onward under Constantine and his successors, Christianity become first a privileged religion and then the religion of empire. From about the seventh century onward we can speak of medieval Europe as becoming the historical Christendom, a Christian world.[6] The older "pagan" traditions of Europe had been defeated through conversion and missionary energy or, at least, had disappeared underground or become enmeshed in local expressions of Christianity.[7] The only other two traditions that were known, Judaism and Islam, were interpreted as aberrant or heretical forms of Christianity. Judaism was seen as a tradition that had been transformed into Christianity with the coming of Jesus, and therefore, the continuing Jewish people were those who had refused God. It was not another religion but a failed form of Christianity—we shall say more on the implications of this shortly. Islam, for its part, was seen as a heretical form of Christianity. A tradition existed in medieval Christendom that Muhammad was a disgruntled cardinal who had set up his own church in defiance of the true church. Therefore, it was not seen as another religious tradition in its own right.[8]

For most of the medieval period, therefore, the people of Christendom lived in a world that was only self-aware of one religious tradition.[9] There were, of course, occasional heretics, but everything was centered solely on Christianity. Even with the coming of the Reformation and the emergence of Protestantism we still see different forms of only one religion, Christianity. Therefore, with the voyages of exploration and conquest that saw the European "discovery" of the world beyond Europe (the Americas, much of Africa, Asia, and beyond) there was no tradition of thinking about other religions. However, this was to change, and although the details of these explorations need not detain us, within a few centuries, Christianity, in its Western European forms, came face to face with a world full of diverse religious traditions. Therefore, the period from around the sixteenth to the eighteenth century involved a meeting with Hinduism, Buddhism, Confucianism, and a host of other religions and the growing recognition that Islam was not a heretical form of Christianity. Of course, this only applies to Western Christianity; the Christians of the Middle East have lived among different religions for centuries, as have the Christians of India and other places.

Western Christians[10] now find themselves (once again) in a religiously diverse setting. Increasingly, this means any notion of Christendom or "Christian nations" makes little sense: in many countries, Christians, at least active ones, are in a minority.[11] It is also a different context from the religious diversity that early Christianity found itself in. For one thing, our understanding of what religion is has changed greatly, and we tend no longer to see religion entwined with the pathways and traditions of one's ancestors. In the West, at least, choice is seen to be the determining factor for belonging—although, in some large sections, tradition and culture determine belonging as well[12]—while there is greater awareness and understanding of the various religious traditions.

Religious Diversity in the Chinese and Far Eastern Context

The Chinese cultural world extends over many other Far Eastern countries, most especially Japan and Korea. Here, the traditional understanding of "religion" has always been very different. Never faced with the dominance of a single tradition, as was found in medieval Christendom, the different religions have lived alongside one another in a greater degree of harmony. This is not to say that interreligious intolerance, rivalry, and bitterness has not existed, because there have certainly been persecutions and enmity.[13] Nevertheless, a place for other religious traditions alongside one's own has often been acknowledged.

In Japan, for instance, because the indigenous religious tradition of Shinto has taboos against both blood and death, it has been normal for the business of funerals to be placed in the hands of Buddhist monks and priests (although, in most cases, it is correct to speak only of Buddhist monks and nuns, the existence of married "monks" makes the term priest suitable in the Japanese context). Shinto, on the other hand, has been central in the marriage service, while various coming-of-age ceremonies (often known as rites of passage) are also within its remit. In at least some senses, Buddhism is the religion of the Japanese at birth and death (the blood associated with childbirth also violates the Shinto taboo, and so the blessing of babies lies with Buddhism), whereas Shinto fills the life in-between. Therefore, for most Japanese to ask whether they are Shinto or Buddhist simply makes no sense. They are both, but without, necessarily, a sense of belonging explicitly to one or the other in terms of a commitment to belong—the Western sense of commitment to a specific set of beliefs, principles, and traditions is alien to many people: you simply partake of the local, or appropriate, religious services as part of your everyday life. However, this is not to deny that some people do commit to just one or that some traditions have been less understanding of other religions at different times.

In China itself things are slightly more complicated. Here, we may talk of four religious traditions as the mainstream of Chinese religion: Confucianism, Buddhism, Daoism, and folk religion. It is often disputed whether Confucianism is a religion or philosophy, and certainly in some manifestations it is more clearly the latter; however, through most of its history it has operated and had the institutions of a religious tradition.[14] Most Chinese people throughout the last thousand or more years have engaged, at some point of their lives, with all these traditions.

Many popular presentations explain the interaction with the three traditions (*sanjiao*, i.e., Buddhism, Daoism, and Confucianism) in something like the following way: Confucianism provides sets of codes for morals and behavior and so provides a code of living for public life; Daoism is understood as a tradition of self-transformation providing personal spiritual exercises; and Buddhism's rites and rituals provide ceremonies for events such as funerals and displays of devotion.[15] Each is seen as part of a harmonious whole where, depending on where one is, at what time, or for what purpose, there is seen as being no conflict between them as each has its own distinct sphere and role, and certainly some people have lived within such a worldview, and there are certainly important religious thinkers who have integrated each tradition into one system as complimentary strands. The twelfth-century Daoist thinker Wang Zhe consciously blended Confucian and Buddhist elements into his Daoist tradition.[16] However, this is not the only, or even the primary, way of understanding the traditions and their relationships: at various periods, Daoists and Buddhists vied with each other for supremacy and hurled insults at the other; Confucian scholars, meanwhile, derided the other two traditions.[17] To give one example of the interaction, we can consider local gods. For much of Chinese history, the country was run by a civil service of scholars trained in Confucianism. By this means, Confucianism provided a state cult, with civic ceremonies for city gods and earth gods in its remit and Confucian scholars being the official "priesthood." Therefore, in some collective sense, Confucian acts of religious observance were the mainstay of religion. However, the dry Confucian ceremonies lacked popular appeal, and many city gods would also be in temples that could be identified as Daoist, with Daoist priests presiding over the worship of the same divinities for the people.[18]

It is fair to say that throughout most of the last thousand and more years (since Buddhism became a widespread tradition) the Chinese have (on the whole) lived in a world of religious diversity where it has not been seen as incompatible to "belong" to several religious traditions. There have been cases where adherents of one particular tradition have had an exclusive viewpoint that suggested other religions were lower or unsuitable (note a distinction here with some other views: it is not that the other religions are false, although sometimes such a view was heard, but just at a "lower" level than one's own). For instance, many Confucians saw Buddhism as superstitious, or a religion of the masses.

Religious Diversity in the Southeast Asian Context

Many scholars today use Southeast Asia to refer to the area around India, which includes countries such as Pakistan, Nepal, Sri Lanka, and other neighboring places; although, today, each is politically, and sometimes culturally, distinct, at least historically they have shared traditions and ideas, and peoples have moved back and forth across the often new political borders. It has also been an area marked by religious diversity. This diversity includes both a host of traditions that have developed in the area, such as Hinduism, Buddhism, Jainism, and Sikhism, not to mention various local and tribal traditions, and religions from elsewhere, most significantly Islam and Christianity, although Judaism and Zoroastrianism have been found there for centuries, indeed probably millennia.

It is impossible to adequately survey this diversity and approaches to it. What is important is that for much of the last 3,000 years or so it is hard to speak of a dominant religion. Although almost very book you will ever read will tell you that Hinduism is and has been the main religion of India, the idea of there being a single religion under this name is a very recent phenomena, going back primarily to Western descriptions of the religious traditions in the nineteenth-century, or in some degree back a few centuries before to the Muslim invasions and the distinction they made between the local traditions and themselves (for further discussion on how we define "religions," see Volume 1, Chapter 1). Before that, and largely today, those we term "Hindus" would identify by belonging to a specific tradition associated with a deity, caste, teacher, and so on. The religious diversity was approached in various ways, for instance, in one ancient text, the *Rig Veda*, the following pronouncement is made: "truth (or reality) is one; the wise (or learned) term it variously."[19] This quote expresses an understanding that there are many religious traditions; however, it also implies these have one source—we will return to this again. We also find a lively tradition of debates between traditions that has gone on for millennia termed *shastrarth*. Often quite fierce, and designed to show the truth of one point of view over another, these public debates could be found between advocates of different traditions seeking to prove their interpretation of sacred texts was better than those of their rivals.

In recent times, many significant Hindu thinkers have been involved with questions of the relationship between religions, such as Mohandas "Mahatma" Gandhi (1869–1948) and Vivekananda (who we will discuss later) who have helped shape a popular impression that Hinduism is extremely tolerant of other religions and accepts diversity as part of its understanding that truth is known in many ways.[20]

KEY TERMS, PEOPLE, AND DEBATES

We will consider both the contemporary period and important historical figures who are often looked to in today's debates. Our focus is the Western Christian tradition because, at least today, it provides the key theories and debates; however, we maintain our global focus. Space permits us to only choose a few examples.

According to Justin Martyr (c. 100–165 CE), the early Christian church needed to define itself in relation to the surrounding culture, and his text *Dialogue with Trypho* was influential in this. Like many books of its time and since, it took a dialogue format, where two or more characters were seen in debate. Here, Justin tries to explain why it is that noble ideas such as justice, compassion, and wisdom are found in the great Greek philosophers like Plato. His answer is that Jesus as eternal word of God is the inner spirit dwelling in all people. Therefore, the philosophers' wisdom comes not from following Jesus as found as a human being on earth but from Jesus seen as the divine word present in all creation. This meant that Christian use of Greek philosophy was justified, but this was not the only early Christian answer, and the North African theologian Tertullian famously asked, "What has Athens to do with Jerusalem?"[21]—here "Athens" means Greek philosophy and "Jerusalem" means Christianity.

Despite being aware primarily of one religious tradition (as discussed earlier), the medieval Christian world was much inspired by other religions and cultures, and Thomas Aquinas (1225–1274) is a fine example. Drawing upon Aristotle, whom he called "the philosopher," Thomas utilized much Greek thought. However, his source for this was Aristotle as understood and transmitted through Islamic philosophical theology, which influenced him in many ways. His arguments on God and God's existence were greatly inspired by this source, and indeed, it was only due to Islamic thinkers that Greek philosophy and science, which by this time were supplemented by new insights, came to western Europe and utterly transformed its thought. Thomas also helped define the distinction between natural theology and revealed theology. The latter was the truths made known through Jesus and found in the biblical texts and Christian tradition. The former, however, was what any person could come to know without this, which was that there was a God and that certain moral behavior was required. In terms of thinking about religious diversity, Thomas therefore argued that all people in the world could come to God through their own instincts and observing the world around them.[22]

Wang Zhe (also known as Chongyang) (1113–1170) was the founder of the Complete Realization School of Daoism (Quanzhen Dao) and consciously incorporated Buddhist, Confucian, and Daoist elements together. To this end, he instructed his followers to recite scriptures that belonged to each of the three traditions (*sanjiao*) as part of their practice: the Confucian *Classic of Filial Piety*, the Buddhist *Heart Sutra*, and the Daoist *Daodejing* and *Qingjingjing* (a text still used as part of the school's morning and evening rituals).[23] This was a very conscious blending of these three traditions to stress their essential compatibility, while Confucian and Buddhist elements had already been incorporated into Daoist thinking over the previous few hundred years.[24]

In sixteenth-century northern India, a new religious movement emerged which is exceptionally interesting in terms of religious diversity. For several centuries, a movement that blended Islamic Sufi traditions (often termed "Islamic mysticism" it refers to movements that often emphasize a strong personal connection between the devotee and Allah) and Hindu *bhakti* traditions (devotional movements that seek a close and loving relationship between the devotee and their chosen deity, or *ishta devata*) had been developing, known as the Sant tradition, which characterized northern Indian *bhakti*. Figures who exemplified this such as the poet Kabir have always been seen as holy figures within both Islamic and Hindu traditions, and both Sufi and *bhakti* devotees revere his religious poetry and example as one who sought passionately after God.[25] Into this context came Guru Nanak (1469–1539), who founded his own religious tradition which explicitly stated that, "There is no Muslim and there is no Hindu." For Nanak, God was called by many names, and there were many legitimate paths by which he could be sought. Therefore, anyone who sought division based on different sectarian belonging or terms was simply failing to understand devotion to God: "God is One" (*Ek Onkar*) is a fundamental tenet of the movement. For many who claim that it is purely a modern Western idea that God is called by many names and that there are many paths to seek the divine, Nanak and his Sikh community provide a strong corrective.[26] Indeed, a favorite Sikh metaphor for religious diversity, of many blind men feeling an elephant, is also ancient. According to this metaphor, a king assembles many blind men together so they can find out what an elephant is like. One touches its trunk and says it is like a snake, another touches its leg and says it is like a tree trunk, and another touches its tail and says it is like a fly whisk. The blind men, of course, represent the limited human conceptions of the divine, which is always present beyond all human understanding, and their disputes are those of people in different religions who do not understand that they have only a partial and limited grasp of what, if known correctly, is One.[27] This, of course, reminds us of the saying we encountered earlier, that although we have different names for the truth, there is only one source of truth.

Here we move from ancient and medieval thinkers to the modern age—Vivekananda (1863–1902), although in part our interest in him stems from his following of the renowned saint Ramakrishna, who is sometimes said to have been the final medieval saint of India. The part of Ramakrishna's message that concerns us is his series of religious experiences when he spent time investigating Christianity and Islam. His visions and experiences when paying devotion to figures in these religions convinced him that all religions were, at heart, the same—he recognized in each, he claimed, a central core. This was a message that Vivekananda was to take to the world, and the World Parliament of Religions held in Chicago in 1893 gave him the opportunity. Articulate and handsome, Vivekananda was one of the stars of the event, and his message that all religions had a common core was one which, it seems, many were ready to hear. He followed up this event with successful tours of the United States and Europe and returned to India as a national hero—this was, of course, the period of colonial rule by Britain, and instead of receiving Christian missionaries to their shores in a one-way process, many Indians now believed that they had sent their own missionary to the West. For our purposes, we should note that although Vivekananda taught all religions were paths to the same end, he was, nevertheless, very clear that there was a definite hierarchy of teachings with his own school of monistic Vedanta (the teaching that God and humanity are in essence one) at the top.[28]

We have not mentioned any female thinkers so far, partly because in most religions the lineages of "great" figures have been formed by men (see Volume 2, Chapter 1). However, as we come to the twentieth century, we start to see many influential female commentators on religion, and a good number are concerned with religious diversity. A popular writer on "mysticism," Evelyn Underhill (1875–1941), helped to define and popularize modern conceptions. Part of this involved the notion that a common "spiritual/mystical" core lay at the heart of all religions. We will discuss this idea more in the next section, but for the moment it is useful to note that as an early twentieth-century Christian scholar and popular theologian her writings were influential in spreading ideas about the common essence shared by all religions.[29]

A Dutch missionary theologian, Hendrik Kraemer (1888–1965) vehemently opposed the idea that all religions led to the same path. He emphasized a discontinuity between revelation, for him the truths of Christianity, and sin or falsehood, the teachings of all other religions. For Kraemer, if knowledge of God could only come from God himself, then without revelation (i.e., the person, life, and work of Jesus) we would only be able to follow our own sinful ways.[30] Although, especially today, some suggest that this approach is the normative Christian teaching, we should stress that it is certainly not the case as we see in figures such as Justin Martyr and Thomas Aquinas, whereas others such as Augustine of Hippo believed we could "mine" the "'treasures" of other religions and philosophies for truths that Christians could learn. The excessive emphasis on other religions as "sinful" or "demonic" is far from universal in Christianity, especially among those often counted the "great theologians."[31]

John Hick (1922–2012) was the most important theorist and proponent of what is often termed the pluralist hypothesis in Christian theology. We discuss this in due course, but for now we can say that a pluralist will argue that we cannot be sure that one religion alone is true and, more than this, that it seems most plausible to suggest that there are in fact many "true" religions, which is to say many traditions may all be talking about the same God/real/absolute in some form and offer ways of relating to it. Hick began life, though, as an evangelical who thought other religions were false, but his experience of meeting and living alongside those of other religions convinced him that their depth of commitment, life of prayer, and ethical living were at least equal to his own or those of any Christian. Therefore, Hick was led to affirm and defend a pluralist theology of religions, which he did in many works over the years.[32]

Tenzin Gyatso (1935–), the fourteenth Dalai Lama, maybe the most famous and widely respected religious figure in the world today. He has shot to international prominence as a result of his exile from his native homeland in Tibet. An inspiration for many because of his passionate and sustained calls for peace and understanding in his homeland, for which he has won the Nobel Peace Prize, his position as a global spokesperson for Buddhism (at least for his own Tibetan tradition), makes his views on religious diversity important. He teaches that all religions are paths to truth and that following any one of them will lead you to the same end. Although often sounding like, or being claimed as, a pluralist, the Dalai Lama actually holds that his own Buddhist tradition is the best guide to knowing ultimate reality. Indeed, it is partly because of these Buddhist teachings with the understanding of reincarnation, so that a good Christian, Muslim, or Sikh will perform meritorious actions leading to a better rebirth, that he can teach that all religions are paths to truth. Notably he has described Jesus as a *bodhisattva*, a term for an enlightened, or awakened, religious teacher or even a manifestation of ultimate reality within his tradition.[33]

Diana Eck (1945–) is a famous contemporary religious scholar. She leads the pluralism project at Harvard University in the United States, which seeks to map the country's religious diversity. She is also personally committed to promoting tolerance and understanding. More than this, Eck is best understood as a pluralist thinker whose engagement with religious others has led her to move beyond seeing her own Christian tradition as the right way alone. In this, her stance can be said to be similar to that of John Hick who we have discussed earlier; however, like many other feminist theologians, Eck sees her pluralism as inspired by a feminist concern and understanding. Indeed, many feminist theologians in the area have suggested that an engagement with women across religious boundaries leads to a point of solidarity that emerges from a shared experience as women (often from a situation of oppression). Eck has also spoken about finding the other tradition familiar, that is, finding things within it that you recognize from your own tradition, something she suggests that points to, or drags you toward, a pluralist stance because you come to know, she holds, that each religion responds to a common core.[34]

We have already mentioned the theology of religions typology and its terms. First proposed by the British Anglican pluralist Christian theologian, interfaith activist, and priest Alan Race, the typology originally suggested that Christian approaches to other religions could be categorized as exclusivism, inclusivism, and pluralism and is now a standard part of the academic discussion. Today, it is often rendered in the plural (to emphasize that each is a range of approaches, e.g.,exclusivisms) and with a further paradigm, particularities, attached.[35] It should also be mentioned that although originally intended to describe Christian positions, many have found it useful to describe the attitudes of different religions.[36] The typology is not without its critics, though, and the idea that it can be applied across religions is perhaps controversial for some; nevertheless, even its critics tend to use it or something very similar, and in broad terms it is most probably useful to help frame debates across traditions.[37] I will provide a brief overview of each term here in a generally Christian context but with some notes on its use in other contexts.[38] First, exclusivisms are the position that there is only one true religion and that others are false. We can place Hendrik Kraemer within this camp. An exclusivist is likely to suggest that other religions may even lead people away from God, and often that its adherents will go to hell. Sometimes, though, an exclusivist will take a "universalist" stance suggesting that although their religion is false, because of his great mercy God wants to save all people and that nothing can stop this. Karl Barth is often cited as a representative of this style of exclusivism. In general, exclusivisms can be said to typify an approach that stresses radical discontinuity, that is, there is a chasm between true and false religion; one is from God and the other is not: therefore, they stand forever opposed. Second, inclusivists are those who believe that their religion is true but that other religions contain some elements that point to this truth. Justin Martyr, Vivekananda, and the Dalai Lama can all be said to be inclusivists. That is, they think all people may be heading toward God or the truth in some way, but this is best understood from their own religion. For instance, for Justin Martyr, those who were not Christians but nevertheless taught morality or other good principles responded to the spirit of Jesus as the heart of creation. Vivekananda, like-wise, represented a position in which people could come to know God through their own tradition; however, unless they understood that God and the human soul were ultimately one, they had not yet realized the high-est truth. Inclusivisms can be set to typify an approach of radical fulfillment, which is to say that whatever is good in another tradition finds its comple-tion, true understanding, or fulfillment within one's own tradition. Third, pluralisms, as we discussed in relation to John Hick, deny that any single reli-gion alone has the legitimacy to be termed the only truth. Employing the elephant metaphor used in Sikhism, pluralists often suggest that as limited human beings we can never know everything about God, or the real, to use Hick's phrase; therefore, all our traditions can at best provide glimpses of that truth, which may even complement each other. Many pluralists will argue that we simply have no basis to judge truth beyond asserting our own tradition's claims (which for most people in the world today is the one they were born into), and so when we meet people of other religions whose depth of spiritual life and devotion of justice equals our own, we lack any rea-son to suppose that our way is the only true one. Pluralisms can be described as typified by radical openness, that is, they wish to break down boundaries of competition so that they are open to hearing what other religions claim. Fourth, particularities suggest that we are actually wrong to suggest that each religion really relates to others at all. To say one is false or all are true assumes that each is at some deep level alike. Disputing the claims of figures such as Justin Martyr, Guru Nanak, Vivekananda, or Evelyn Underhill, the particularist will say that each so-called "religion" is actually a network of terms and practices that only make sense in relation to itself. To ask how Buddhism and Christianity relate, for instance, would be a bit like asking how wrestling and hockey relate—they may both be sports but so different that we cannot talk meaningfully about whether one is better, or how to explain wrestling through the rules of hockey. Radical differences typify the particularist approach because each tradition is held to be fundamentally of a different kind.

SURVEY OF ARGUMENTS

Elephants or Sports?

It can be argued that whether religions are best understood by something like a pluralist, particularist, exclusivist, or inclusivist response is at heart a theological judgment—something wedded to a particular religious view-point that a scientific study of religion cannot discuss. In her provocative book, *The Invention of World Religions*, the historian of thought Tomoko Masuzawa argued that the modern conception of many religions as in some ways comparable and valid is best seen as a relic of Christian theological views inherited from the nineteenth-century and evolved in the early twentieth-century rather than being a neutral judgment on these many different traditions (she is discussed further in Volume 1, Chapter 1).[39] Certainly she is right that a lineage links much contemporary Western thought, even of a supposedly secular leaning, with Christian theology. However, this is true of almost any area of thought: philosophy, sociology, and even sciences such as physics and biology all stem from what is a fairly solid Christian heritage.[40] An awareness of this inheritance is useful to understand the way we think about religious diversity and our preconceptions when we come to it. With this in mind we will try and keep our discussion of the issues based on philosophical and empirical grounds. It will be philosophical in that we will try and think through and discuss the arguments. It will be empirical in that we will keep attention to the evidence. We will also base it around the four options in the typology: particularities, pluralisms, inclusivisms, and exclusivisms.

The particularist stance claims that it is the most theoretically secure and morally sound position: the former because it accepts what it sees as recent thinking in the social sciences that understands all religions as expressions of separate cultural islands, and the latter because, unlike the other paradigms, it does not attempt to place another belief system within its own system (which it suggests even the pluralist does, as we will discuss later). However, the former claim, when examined, turns out to be extremely dubious. A basic familiarity with religious history will inform someone that many traditions are deeply interrelated. For instance, Judaism, Islam, and Christianity as discussed earlier have common foundations as Abrahamic religions, even explicitly affirming that they believe in the same God, the God of Abraham. Meanwhile, Hinduism, Buddhism, Jainism, and Sikhism grow from roots within South Asia. Moreover, as we have discussed earlier, the Sant tradition fused aspects of Islamic and Hindu thought, while in the contemporary world various movements such as inter-monastic dialogue see monks from various traditions, often Christian and Buddhist, meeting to share their traditions of prayer and meditation.[41] Clearly, empirically speaking, the particularist stance rests on very shaky grounds. As to the claim of ethical respect, this is also dubious philosophically, because one part of the claim that each "religion" is different is tied to another claim that "my religion" is true. Now, if a Christian says that Buddhists and Muslims are doing something that does not equate in any way to what Christianity does, there is a big claim being made: one leads to salvation, the others do not! That might be a legitimate theological claim; however, it is clear that the often-vaunted ethical superiority of stressing difference is not so simple.[42] We may also mention that some critics have suggested that the particularist

204 Controversies in Contemporary Religion

system, a very recent theological movement, is also very bad theology, but that lies beyond the scope of our investigation.[43]

Turning to pluralisms, we have to say whether all religions are paths up the same mountain is a distinctly theological claim that we cannot approach empirically or philosophically. This argument rages over whether it represents a legitimate theological stance within the Christian tradition.[44] Empirically, we can say that it is very recent and that many stances that are often held to represent pluralism actually conceal an inclusivist position, as we saw was the case with the Dalai Lama (though, as far as I am aware, he has never claimed to be a theological pluralist in the sense used here). Whether anyone can be seen as a pluralist before the late twentieth century is an interesting question. Guru Nanak certainly approached it but is divorced from us in space and time, making an accurate assessment difficult, whereas parts of the *Hebrew Bible* contain interesting claims that God worked in and through those beyond Israel, but this may well represent an inclusivist stance—although probably not in the same way this would be understood in contemporary Christian theology. Arguably, though, we find it expressed in an ancient Indian saying about truth being one but variously expressed.[45] However, an interesting philosophical critique is that pluralism is actually an impossibility because every stance, pluralisms included, actually involves denying the religious claims of others, making it a form of inclusivism (some have suggested exclusivism, but this seems to stretch the point too far).[46] The critique is that pluralism tells many religious people that their beliefs are wrong: they are not possessors of the unique truth revealed from God but must instead understand their beliefs as but one of many partial and always limited expressions of human searching for the divine. Certainly, Hick has argued that he finds, in the situation of religious diversity, pluralism the most credible option. There is clearly then a tricky problem. One response, advanced by Perry Schmidt-Leukel, is that the argument is too imprecise in its terminology. For words to mean anything, he argues, we need to have clearly in mind what we mean. For example, if we say Spain is the greatest country in the world, we are clearly making a claim that all other countries are of less worth, which makes a specific point. If, however, we say people from Spain are Spanish but French people are not, we also make a specific point. Both such claims, Schmidt-Leukel tells us, are exclusive in nature: the former in making a claim that one alone is the greatest and the latter that only people of one nationality have that nationality. However, he argues, to describe both of these as "exclusivist," if we use the term to mean the same thing, is clearly inaccurate. Likewise, he points out the inclusivist claim—that one religion is ultimately true, others partially so—and the pluralist one that many religions are potentially true are clearly distinguishable claims. Therefore, he suggests it is simply bad philosophy to say we should categorize them as identical.[47] This is a partial answer, however; it does not avoid the larger claim that a similar move is made in pluralist theologies that it "fulfills" others' claims and so is not truly pluralist: that is, any other religious viewpoint is best expressed by the pluralist view that every religious standpoint is only partial. As an analogy, if we use the first statement that Spain is the greatest country, and somebody else says that actually no country is the greatest but all countries are very good, we can see that this latter claim does involve a denial of the first claim. A potential answer to this critique is suggested, however, by the title of John Hick's major work in the area, *An Interpretation of Religion*, in which he makes it clear that he is not, as those who advance this critique often argue, proposing a kind of super-religion that encompasses all others; rather he is making a tentative proposal that makes sense of religious diversity from his perspective without the claim that this is necessarily true. Certainly such a modest statement does not propose a new master narrative that fulfills all others but merely suggests what seems to be, in light of the available evidence, a good way of making sense of this without asserting one's own tradition as necessarily and definitely true of all. However, on a personal level, Hick, like many other pluralists, seemed to accept this not just as a proposal, which is what it is at the philosophical level, but as a belief system to live by. Therefore, it can be said that this does not give an absolute answer to the critique. I would suggest, though, that a modified form of Schmidt-Leukel's response may be found adequate. The pluralist position generally asserts that although no one religion in itself can be said to encapsulate the truth of the Real, each one may be said to be a legitimate path to the Real. Therefore, it is not a denial of the truth, or truths, found within each religion. Although to some degree it can be said that affirming pluralism as a belief system necessarily intends that you believe, or think it most likely, that an inclusivist or exclusivist position is wrong or inadequate, it is not a denial of the claims that each religion makes about its ability to lead people to the Real. Here, there is clearly a difference between the inclusivist position and the pluralist, because for the former there is only one final way to approach the Real; either another religion is included or fulfilled within the religion affirmed or it does not reach toward the Real. This move is not made by the pluralist; the potential that each religion fully, and of itself, offers a root to the Real is found within the pluralist stance. As Schmidt-Leukel argues, for any statement to be meaningful, it must exclude something else, and as such pluralism would be meaningless if it did not set out a position, which means that if it is correct, other positions are incorrect, but that does not mean that it is therefore the same as an inclusivist or exclusivist claim. Each one is different, and the differences are substantial. This does not mean, of course, that the pluralist position is more likely to be true; it simply shows that it is not unfeasible.

Turning to inclusivisms, understood in a broad sense, this is perhaps the most widespread option in almost all religions throughout time, at least when a clearly defined theology in relation to religious others has been attempted. We have already discussed some notable Christian cases and have mentioned Islam's traditional view, which can arguably be seen as a form of inclusivism. (It is worth noting that, traditionally at least, it can be argued that Islam is not setting out a theology of religions because there is only one religion and other teachings have simply fallen away from this.) Buddhism likewise, although extremely diverse, can generally be seen to suggest that its teachings are the one sure root to attaining awakening, although any path that promotes ethical behavior (akin to the ethical codes of Buddhism) will lead people to better rebirths and so toward the potential for attaining awakening[48] in a future life. Empirically, we can simply say it is widespread. Philosophically, although it has been accused of being patronizing or offensive, these are value judgments, and so it must be left to theological debates within traditions to determine what is made of its claims.

Finally, exclusivisms are again widespread in many religions. Generally, exclusivists argue that their views are founded solidly in their scriptures and traditions, although Christian exponents of inclusivisms and pluralisms also argue that their interpretations are better founded within scripture and tradition.[49] Here we enter into difficult questions on the interpretation of scripture (hermeneutics), for we must remember that texts do not have a simple meaning that can be read out neutrally but must be read within context and understood in terms of the tradition (see Volume 1, Chapter 3). However, these are mainly theological issues, although philosophical reasoning can be brought to bear. For instance, if, as many religions claim, God is supremely good and all-loving (omnibenevolent), can it really be that most people who have ever lived are destined to eternal damnation, without hope of salvation, simply because they would never have heard of the one religion that could save them? Although exclusivists may argue that God's ways are beyond human comprehension from a strictly philosophical standpoint, it does seem to involve a contradiction. Also, from a strictly empirical stance, in relation to Christianity at least, the number of references in the Biblical text that imply that people beyond those we can call Jewish or Christians are saved, blessed by God, or found worthy in God's sight make an exclusivist Christian stance something which needs far more robust defense than it is normally given.[50] Many other religions, such as Judaism and Islam, likewise seem to hold resources that make an exclusivist position far from coherent in many senses.

The Abrahamic Religions and Internal Religious Diversity

Although we often think of each religion as different, many traditions share a history of development. One instance of this is what are called the three Abrahamic religions, Judaism, Islam, and Christianity; the term "Abrahamic" coming from the fact that they all look to the biblical patriarch Abraham as a foundational prophet. This is important because each explicitly says that their God is the God of Abraham, and all three therefore believe in the same deity—while some Christian polemic says that the Islamic God is called "Allah," this is a misapprehension, as it is not the name of a deity but simply Arabic for "the God."[51] Further, Islam explicitly claims that Jesus, Moses, David, Abraham, and Adam (among others) are all prophets within their tradition.[52] It must be recognized here that there is a sense in which both Christianity and Islam are developments from Judaism, which means that Judaism is placed within the worldview of these two religions. We will briefly say something about the understanding of religious diversity, especially in relation to the other two, in each tradition.

Judaism, as the first of the three Abrahamic religions, does not have a "built-in" attitude toward the other two. Although Judaism as it exists today, what is termed Rabbinic Judaism came into existence at the same time as Christianity, both were coming from what is usually termed Second Temple Judaism.[53] For its part, the Rabbinic tradition did not accept Jesus as the Messiah—indeed, he was just one of many around this period who claimed this title and was of little consequence for the tradition as a whole—but was concerned with reformulating itself in relation to the destruction of the temple in Jerusalem by the Romans. However, as time went on, Judaism had to define itself in relation to what became its more powerful cousin, but its concern was often more for protection than theological reflection on what Christianity might mean. In general, though, Judaism has always accepted other religions. Although understanding themselves as God's chosen people, this did not mean that God was not present elsewhere or in communication with others; rather it just meant that Jews were charged with a special task of following the laws and commandments that had been given to them in a specific covenant.[54]

We have already discussed earlier, to some degree, Christianity's relationship to both Judaism and Islam. It is worth saying something more about each case. Christianity understands itself as superseding Judaism, for the Messiah was seen as having come, and therefore the Christian position suggested the older tradition was outdated and, in effect, illegitimate once Christianity came into existence. This position is known as supercessionism—the belief that Christianity completed and fulfilled the Jewish religion. More recently, a number of Christian churches have rejected this position, partly in reaction to the horrors of the Holocaust—and the recognition that

Christian theology had played a large part in allowing and legitimating the ideas that the Nazi regime developed to, arguably, their ultimate conclusion—but also, and alongside this, partly from moves in interfaith dialogue, which we will discuss later. We have spent longer discussing the Christian position on Judaism than the Jewish position on Christianity, but this in part reflects the fact that it is the Christian tradition that has spent far more time positioning itself in relation to the other.[55] Next is Islam, and here Christianity has always had a problem because Islam both comes later than it (many other religions predate Christianity, and it has frequently employed the notion of "fulfillment," to be discussed more later, which it used in relation to Judaism) and explicitly rejects it. As discussed earlier, a very influential early Christian interpretation saw Islam as a heresy, but once it came to understand that it was another religion it had to come to terms with it. One extreme view, found in medieval works and in some "fundamentalist" approaches today, is to see Islam as demonic; however, anyone who has met Muslims normally finds this impossible, and so Christians have had to discuss what this religion may mean for it, and there is no single answer.[56]

Turning to Islam, we find that just as Christianity could easily place its older sibling Judaism, so Islam finds it easy to place both its earlier cousins. As we mentioned earlier, the great biblical prophets, including Jesus in this category, are seen as prophets sent by God to teach people. Therefore, we can speak of Islam as having a supercessionist approach to both Judaism and Christianity. Moreover, Islam does not understand itself as a "new" religion beginning with Mohammad; rather Muslims believe that God has always sent the same essential message, but until the last prophet, Mohammad, this had been misunderstood or had become distorted in its transmission. Here it is important to understand that "Islam" is not so much the word for a set of religious teachings but simply means "surrender" (to the will of God). Therefore, Muslims claim that Adam, Moses, David, and Jesus were all people who had surrendered to Allah and so were Muslims. In relation to Christianity in particular, Muslims claim that Jesus's followers had distorted and lost his original message such that instead of understanding Jesus as just a prophet who had taught the oneness of God, they had misunderstood him as being divine and also proclaimed a form of polytheism in seeing God as the trinity.

The differences between Muslims and Christians on the nature of God and on Jesus's role have been long-standing areas of tension between the traditions, although they also offer areas of hope for contact in that both explicitly declare belief in the same God and have high respect for the figure of Jesus. One final aspect of the relationship that should be mentioned is that Islam put both Judaism and Christianity in a special category, that of People of the Book, meaning that they like Islam had a revelation from God delivered via a prophet (Muslims believe that Jesus himself wrote a book, the *Injil*, and that the Christian *Gospels* are a corrupted version of this). The *Quran* and Islamic tradition put them in a special status in relation to Islam, and so Christians and Jews are allowed to follow their own religions within Islamic societies and not be subject to conversion—although, today, there seems to many to be a natural enmity of Jews and Muslims, this has not historically been the case, and many Jews welcomed the expansion of the Islamic empire in its early days as it gave them greater freedom and protection than living in many Christian lands.[57] However, the *Quran* also stated that God had sent prophets to every nation, even suggesting that 124,000 had been sent (*Quran* 26:207), and so as the Islamic empires expanded, other religious traditions were fitted into the category of People of the Book, including Zoroastrianism and Hinduism—the latter was held by many of the Muslims who encountered it to have the *Vedas* as its original inspired text.

Fulfillment

Sometimes seen as another name, or an important element, of an inclusivist stance on other religions, in the context of the theology of religions a fulfillment theology implies that another religious tradition finds its ultimate conclusion in one's own religion.[58] Although as a term "fulfilment theology" has a specific Christian history and association, the concept is, arguably at least, found much more widely across many religions; indeed, many people who are presented as pluralist often seem to propound some form of fulfillment ideology, whereby they say that other people's religions are true, or valid, but nevertheless hold that this truth or validity must be interpreted in terms of their own beliefs.[59]

Interreligious Dialogue

An important recent innovation in the relationship of religious traditions is interreligious dialogue. Although religions have met and debated for centuries (for instance, Daoists and Buddhists contested in medieval China, and Mughal emperors organized debates between proponents of different religions in India), the concept of all religions being able to come together to talk and work without any agenda of triumph, or contestation, or one side being privileged is seemingly new. Many date the symbolic beginnings of the dialogue movement to the World Parliament of Religions in 1893, referred to earlier. That year a great world exposition was held in Chicago, giving the United States a chance to show off its engineering and technology, as well as bringing advances from around the world to be displayed. To coincide with this, some forward-thinking Christians decided to have a religious exposition that would showcase all the world's religions at the event.

To this end, a call went out to leaders and representatives of every major religion, as it was reckoned then (notably, no Native Americans were called while a list of 10 major religions was drawn up for invitation). Brought together and allowed equal time and authority to present their point of view, the Parliament, as suggested earlier in relation to Vivekananda, did much to spread a message of religious tolerance and appreciation. Notably, though, its principle organizer, Rev. Charles Bonney, presumed that Christianity's superiority would naturally be displayed by this arrangement, but this was clearly not the case with the great stars being Vivekananda as well as two Buddhists.[60] Whether the Parliament actually began a movement is debatable, but it was clearly a landmark. By the time, 100 years later, that a follow up was held in 1993, again in Chicago, dialogue had clearly become a major movement in many places, often inspired by what was seen as an ideal set by 1893, whereas the latter event saw a whole series of follow-up events, including an ongoing program of parliaments around the world.[61]

As it has developed, interreligious dialogue has taken various forms; some of these stress theological meeting and the comparison of ideas, while at other times the concern is social activism or community cohesion in multireligious societies. Generally it is considered that there are four potential types of dialogue: the dialogue of theological exchange, the dialogue of life, the dialogue of action, and the dialogue of religious experience.[62] The first is concerned with ideas and doctrines and is generally conducted by religious or educated elites. The second is not an organized form of dialogue but refers to the simple day-to-day activity of meeting and getting along with neighbors of other religions in the course of life. The third occurs when religious communities or groups join together for a specific cause, often of shared ethical concern. The last refers to activities of shared prayer or meditation. It should be stated that none of these are mutually exclusive and in some cases may lead on from one another, while several may be part of one event or project.

Within Western societies and elsewhere, dialogue has come to replace mission, conversion, or hostility as one of the primary means of encounter among at least the major religious traditions and groups. This is a move that, in many places, has intensified since the events of 9/11 and the attack on the twin towers of the World Trade Center. Since then, partly in government-sponsored initiatives and partly through grassroots activism, many religious communities have come together in acts of interreligious solidarity and in organized groups to promote religious integration and tolerance.[63] Indeed, in much of today's world it seems we should heed the words of the German theologian Hans Küng that "there will be no peace in the world unless there is peace amongst the world's religions."[64] In this, interreligious dialogue at local, national, and international levels may play a key role.

CONCLUSION

Religious diversity has been a fact throughout history in almost every society, and different ways have been found to negotiate this. Here we have looked at some of the possible responses to this situation in various different religious and historical contexts. Far from being the case that other religions have generally castigated others as "false" or "demonic," there has often been an attempt to explain other religions in relation to one's own in ways that seek to show that it is "fulfilled" or properly understood only by one's own religious narratives. In this sense, how to understand religious diversity becomes a deeply theological question within each tradition. Moreover, this reflection and even positive engagement with the religious other is not simply a new or modern response in our contemporary world but something deeply embedded within the history and internal resources of many religious traditions. What is, arguably, a new innovation is what is known as religious pluralism, the idea that not just one religion has the absolute truth, but that many religions may all be responding to "truth" (variously termed God, the Real, *absolute reality*, etc.) in different ways and that in our terms we cannot tell if one or another does this more adequately, and so adopt a stance that many religions are equally valid paths to this truth. However, even here we find precursors for this in various religions and scriptures, and the Christian theologians who have largely pioneered this approach today, such as John Hick, Paul Knitter, Alan Race, Diana Eck, Ursula King, and Perry Schmidt-Leukel, see it as something that they are led to out of their own Christian tradition rather than being (as might be supposed) a denial of that tradition. Meanwhile, many Hindus or Sikhs will suggest such an approach has always been part of their tradition (it is doubtful, though, that they were fully pluralist in the way it is understood today, but they are certainly significant precursors).

We have, in this chapter, dealt with the question from religious viewpoints in a descriptive and analytic way. Of course, as we have mentioned, this leaves out questions of truth. Meanwhile, atheist or humanist accounts would give alternative suggestions, often that the very diversity of religions and beliefs shows that none of them can be considered true—every religion asserts its own miracles, cosmologies, and so on, and so they may cancel each other out.[65] However, as we have seen for many religions, they would not deny other religions—and so cancel each other out—but see the other's truth claims as partial or distorted versions of a higher truth, while pluralists would suggest that in responding to something that lies beyond human knowledge, it is inevitable that different cultural and philosophical attempts to make sense of this will arise at the human level and will inevitably be partial and even contradictory as human terms are applied to something beyond human understanding.[66] Therefore, we give various religious answers to the question, "Why are there many gods?" These include those who suggest demonic forces are trying to lead us away from truth through false gods; others see the many gods as distorted or partial reflections of truth, while some suggest they represent different human responses to one divine reality, or others that the divine appears in different ways appropriate to human needs. Although many suggest this last concept may be most commonly associated with Hinduism, it is not unknown elsewhere, and so we end with an Islamic injunction from the *Quran* that can be understood to suggest that Allah intended there to be many cultures and religions, so that people could learn from dialogue with one another:

> To each of you We prescribed a law and a method. Had Allah willed, He would have made you one nation [united in religion], but [He intended] to test you in what He has given you; so race to [all that is] good. To Allah is your return all together, and He will [then] inform you concerning that over which you used to differ.[67]

GLOSSARY

Allah/the God: although sometimes mistaken as a term for the Islamic deity, Allah is actually an Arabic term meaning the God and is consciously understood by Muslims to be the God of Abraham, that is, the same deity worshipped by Jews and Christians. Arabic-speaking Jews and Christians say "Allah" to refer to God as well.

Bhakti: Hindu devotional traditions.

Bodhisattva: a Buddhist term referring, in Mahayana Buddhism, to beings who have attained the necessary spiritual attainment for awakening, or liberation/salvation, but who choose to remain close to the world to help all other beings to be liberated from suffering. It also refers to the historical Buddha before he attained awakening.

Christendom: a term that is chronological, geographical, and ideological, referring to Europe during the middle ages (c. 500–1600) when it was a self-consciously Christian arena.

Exclusivisms: the belief that only one religion is true, others are false.

Fulfillment: in the theology of religions, this relates to the idea that one religion is the supreme, or best, representation of divine truth, whereas other religions are only partial representations of it. Therefore, the lesser truths find their completion or full expression (fulfillment) in the greater truth.

Globalization: although often envisaged as a contemporary process, the bringing together of cultures and peoples in mutual awareness has been going on for hundreds, if not thousands, of years, and the contemporary context of globalization is a process that directly links back to the period of European colonialism beginning around the sixteenth century. It refers to the processes (in communication, transportation, media, and other technologies), knowledge (of others), and access to those others that make the world "smaller."

Inclusivisms: the belief that although one religion is ultimately true, other religions may be partial truths, best understood in relation to one's own religion. Fulfillment can be seen as a key aspect of this.

Multiculturalism: a term used in various ways to refer and with different referent points, but in general it means to the way that many different cultural and religious forms live alongside one another in contemporary societies, each being respected in its own right without any expectation to adapt to the norms of a dominant cultural group.

Mysticism: a very problematic term in contemporary academic studies. It had been used to refer to internal spiritual experiences, often of a deep nature and associated with the "saints" or "spiritual masters" of various religions. It was suggested by many twentieth-century theorists that all religions shared a common mystical heart; however, the way that all religious experience and discourse is shaped by cultural, political, and social factors has made such a notion suspect. Nevertheless, it remains a viable theological or religious proposition in many circles.[68]

Particularities: a contemporary stance in Christian theology that argues that religions should not be compared but seen as radically different things—it would even dispute whether we should even speak of them as the same type of thing, that is, "religions" at all.

Pluralistic hypothesis: the idea that many religions (not necessarily all) provide equally valid and viable paths to seek what may be variously termed God, absolute reality, or the Real. It is commonly associated with the writings of the Christian philosopher of religion John Hick.

Sant tradition: a medieval Indian tradition that blended elements primarily from Hindu devotional and Islamic mystical traditions as part of a syncretic whole. Many of its great figures were, and still are, revered by both Hindus and Muslims. Sikhism emerged from this tradition.

Sufism: a term that refers, generally, to Islamic traditions of asceticism and spirituality that seek to bring the devotee close to God, often called Islamic mysticism.

Supercessionism: it refers to the way that Christianity understands itself to have replaced Judaism as God's chosen religion—it represents a form of fulfillment theology. Under this ideology, Judaism was no longer a way to God and so anyone remaining in it did so wrongly. The history of Christian anti-Semitism that saw Jews suppressed throughout almost 2,000 years and ultimately resulted in the Holocaust is part of a direct consequence of this theological attitude. Many churches and theologians have renounced this position in the late twentieth century.[69]

Theology of religions typology: first proposed by Alan Race in 1983, it suggested that Christian approaches to other religions can be "exclusivist," "inclusivist," or "pluralist." Most recent studies also include "particularities" as a fourth category, at least in Christian thought.

Universalism: within the theology of religions, a stance that argues not only that God desires that all people will be saved but that actually all people will be saved because God's love and mercy is so overwhelming. It has ancient roots in Christian thought and continues to this day. As a term in the debate, though, it is often seen as being an expression of an exclusivist theology of religions stance.

NOTES

1. Hugh Nicholson, *Comparative Theology and the Problem of Religious Rivalry* (Oxford, England: Oxford University Press, 2011), 33.

2. On Greco-Roman religion, see John Wacher, ed., *The Roman World*, 2nd ed. (London and New York: Routledge, 2001), Part 10.

3. Scholars generally accept that a great number of beliefs were adopted either directly or indirectly from Zoroastrianism into Judaism, Islam, and Christianity (see Mary Boyce, *Zoroastrians: Their Religious Beliefs and Practices* [London and New York: Routledge, 2000]). These beliefs may include monotheism, heaven and hell, apocalypticism, messianism, and resurrection.

4. For early Christianity and Rome, see Linda Woodhead, *An Introduction to Christianity* (Cambridge, England: Cambridge University Press, 2004), 9–10.

5. A good example is Acts 10:1–11:18 where Peter accepts a gentile (non-Jew) into the Jesus movement and then gives an account of this to others in Jerusalem who opposed this asking, "Why did you go to uncircumcised men [i.e. gentiles] and eat with them?" (11:3 RSV).

6. Missionaries actively spread Christianity throughout what we now call Europe and beyond, such that by about the seventh century CE the whole of mainland Europe and the British Isles were largely Christianized, while Christianity had also spread throughout the Middle East, into much of North Africa and as far afield as India and China in Asia.

7. See Ronald Hutton, "How Pagan Were Medieval English Peasants," *Folklore* 122, no. 3 (2011): 235–49.

8. Martin Bauschke, "Islam: Jesus and Muhammad as Brothers," in *Christian Approaches to Other Faiths*, ed. Paul Hedges and Alan Race (London: SCM, 2008), 192.

9. This was not universally true, of course, and a greater appreciation of what religious diversity existed was encountered in the crusades, in medieval Spain, and in a few significant thinkers.

10. By this term we can understand western Europe, North America, Australia, and New Zealand as exemplar cases—the term *Western* being more ideological than geographical in this context. It should also be noted that especially in the "new world" contexts religious diversity was there even before the "Westerners" arrived, whereas in the "old world" more diversity existed than was generally admitted (see Paul Hedges and Anna Halafoff, "The Development of Multifaith Societies," *Studies in Interreligious Dialogue*, special edition: "Multifaith Societies" (2015).

11. On the U.K. context, see Paul Weller, *Religious Diversity in the UK* (London: Continuum, 2008), Chapter 1.

12. For instance, much of the so-called Bible belt of the southern United States where Christianity is normative, while in many immigrant communities it is assumed that everyone will follow the religious tradition of their parents.

13. For a brief account of the disputes, see Xinzhong Yao and Yanxia Zhao, *Chinese Religion: A Contextual Approach* (London: Continuum, 2010), 67–68.

14. The classic work on the religious aspects of Confucianism is Rodney Taylor, *The Religious Dimensions of Confucianism* (Albany: State University of New York Press, 1990). For a discussion on different perceptions of Confucianism as religion, philosophy, or humanism, see Xinzhong Yao, *An Introduction to Confucianism* (Cambridge, England: Cambridge University Press, 2000), 38–47.

15. See Paul Hedges, "China," in *Religion and Everyday Life and Culture*. Vol. 1, *Religion and the Practice of Daily Life in World History*, ed. Richard Hecht and Vincent Biondo (Santa Barbara, CA: Praeger, 2010), 48–49; see also Yao and Zhao, *Chinese Religion*, 65–68.

16. We will discuss him later.

17. On some of the complexities of Confucianism's relationship with Buddhism and Daoism, see Yao, *An Introduction to Confucianism*, 223–37.

18. Hedges, "China," 64.

19. *Rig Veda* 1.164.46 (*ekam sat vipraa bahuda vadanti*).

20. For discussion on various Indian responses, see Harold G. Coward, ed., *Modern Indian Responses to Religious Pluralism* (Albany: State University of New York Press, 1987).

21. For more on Justin Martyr and the concept of logos in relation to Christian views on other religions, see David Cheetham, "Inclusivisms: Honouring Faithfulness and Openness," in *Christian Approaches to Other Faiths*, 66ff.

22. For more on Aquinas and his relationship to Greek philosophy and Islamic thought, see Wayne Hankey, "Thomas Aquinas," in *The Routledge Companion to the Philosophy of Religion*, ed. Chad Meister and Paul Copan (London: Routledge, 2010), 128–37.

23. Stephen Eskildsen, *The Teachings and Practices of the Early Quanzhen Taoist Masters* (New York: State University of New York Press, 2004), 14.

24. It is worth noting that in some ways suggesting that there were clear and distinct traditions is not always applicable in the Chinese context, especially between Daoism and Confucianism, and especially in the period before the Christian Era, and in much of the next thousand years, it is often anachronistic to distinguish some elements as simply belonging to one or the other. On the complications of understanding Chinese traditions, see Hedges, "China," 49–61.

25. Although Kabir himself held views that would not necessarily be distinctively identified with other Sufis or bhakti thought.

26. Although the Sikh notion of God as a universal spirit may differ from other conceptions of God, this way of thinking nevertheless is significant.

27. For more on Guru Nanak and Sikh views on other religions, see W. Owen Cole and P. S. Sambhi, *Sikhism and Christianity: A Comparative Study* (Basingstoke, England: Macmillan, 1993), 191ff.

28. For more on the views of Ramakrishna, Vivekananda, and their movement toward other religions, see R. W. Neufeldt, "The Response of the Ramakrishna Mission," in *Modern Indian Responses to Religious Pluralism*, ed. Harold G. Coward (Albany: State University of New York Press, 1987), 65–83. The Parliament of World Religions will be discussed later.

29. For more on Evelyn Underhill's ideas, see her classic work *Mysticism: A Study in Nature and the Development of Spiritual Consciousness* (Oxford, England: Oneworld, 2000), http://www.ccel.org/ccel/underhill/mysticism.pdf.

30. As a Calvinist/Reformed theologian, he was strongly influenced by the doctrine of original sin through the lineage of Augustine of Hippo, John Calvin, and Karl Barth. For more on Kraemer and some of these other thinkers, see Dan Strange, "Exclusivisms: 'Indeed Their Rock Is Not Like Our Rock,'" in *Christian Approaches to Other Faiths*, 41, 43–44.

31. For more discussion on this theological heritage, see Cheetham, "Inclusivisms," 63–74. Notably, Strange in "Exclusivisms" (p. 39) suggests the theological heritage Cheetham refers to runs against an "exclusivist monopoly," which he suggests categorizes the biblical writings and more core teachings of the Christian heritage; however, such a "monopoly" is often assumed rather than proved, and the testimony Cheetham cites shows a list of the major thinkers in the tradition, although this tradition sees the bible as its

"bedrock" and looks to many biblical texts that are indicative of such a standpoint (Paul Hedges, *Controversies in Interreligious Dialogue and the Theology of Religions* [London: SCM, 2010], 23), even a pluralist stance can be argued from the biblical basis (see Hedges, *Controversies*, 133–44; and Perry Schmidt-Leukel, *Transformation by Integration: How Inter-faith Encounter Changes Christianity* [London: SCM, 2009], 146–58).

32. Writings by and on Hick are voluminous; particularly important among his works are *An Interpretation of Religion* (Basingstoke, England: Macmillan, 1989), and *The Rainbow of Faiths* (London: SCM, 1995). For secondary literature, see Perry Schmidt-Leukel, "Pluralisms: How to Appreciate Religious Diversity Theologically," in *Christian Approaches to Other Faiths*; Hedges, *Controversies*, 113–29; and David Cheetham, *John Hick: A Critical Introduction and Reflection* (Aldershot, England: Ashgate, 2003).

33. For more on Tenzin Gyatso's views, see *Towards the True Kinship of Faiths: How the World's Religions Can Come Together* (London: Abacus, 2010).

34. For more on Eck, see Diana Eck, *Encountering God: A Spiritual Journey from Bozeman to Banaras* (Boston, MA: Beacon Press, 1993); and Jeannine Hill Fletcher, "Feminisms: Syncretism, Symbiosis, Synergetic Dance," in *Christian Approaches to Other Faiths*, 144.

35. Race's original typology is outlined in Alan Race, *Christians and Religious Pluralism* (London: SCM, 1993). For recent developments, see Paul Hedges, "A Reflection on Typologies: Negotiating a Fast-Moving Discussion," in *Christian Approaches to Other Faiths*, 17–33; or in brief, Hedges, *Controversies*, 17–20.

36. See Hedges, *Controversies*, 19–20.

37. See Hedges, "A Reflection," 17 and 31, n. 4.

38. The account that follows draws upon Hedges, *Controversies*, 20–30.

39. Tomoko Masuzawa, *The Invention of World Religions* (Chicago, IL: The University of Chicago Press, 2005), 327.

40. For a discussion of, for instance, the way science developed in relation to Christian thought, see Nancy Morvillo, *Science and Religion: Understanding the Issues* (Chichester, England: Wiley-Blackwell, 2010).

41. On the failings of the particularist notion, see Hedges, *Controversies*, 174–96; or Paul Hedges, "Particularities: Tradition-Specific Post-modern Perspectives," in *Christian Approaches to Other Faiths*, 120–30 (each paper upholds a similar case though emphasizing some different elements).

42. See Hedges, *Controversies*, 194–96; and Hedges, "Particularities," 127–30.

43. For a discussion of this, see Hedges, *Controversies*, 177–89, 193–94, 228–37.

44. For a view that argues that it is not, see Strange, "Exclusivisms," 46–8; for the contrary view, see Schmidt-Leukel, "Pluralisms."

45. I am grateful to Professor Jaranape Makarand for suggesting this; however, scholars debate whether it is truly pluralistic.

46. The best-known statement of this viewpoint is that of Gavin D'Costa, "The Impossibility of a Pluralist View of Religions," *Religious Studies* 32 (1996): 223–32; for a response, see Hedges, "A Reflection," 19–20.

47. Schmidt-Leukel, *Transformation*, 59.

48. Although often translated as "enlightenment," the Buddhist term *nirvana* (the ultimate realization, or experience, of the Buddha) is more accurately translated as "awakening," both literally and as an expression of what it means.

49. For some statements of each position see, on exclusivisms, Strange, "Exclusivisms," 37–44; on inclusivisms, see Cheetham, "Inclusivisms," 64–74; and on

pluralisms, see Schmidt-Leukel, "Pluralisms," 85–86, 88–89; and Hedges, *Controversies*, 137–43.

50. Various examples can be mentioned, and to start with the Hebrew scriptures, Schmidt-Leukel ("Pluralisms," 88) refers to *Amos* 9:7, Joseph Osei-Bonsu mentions the fact that the covenant with Noah is made with all nations (*Gen.* 10), something affirmed in relation to Abraham (*Gen.* 28.14) (J. Osei-Bonsu, "Extra Ecclesiam Nulla Salus: Critical Reflections from Biblical and African Perspectives," in *Christianity and the Wider Ecumenism*, ed. Peter Phan [New York: Paragon House, 1990], 136), while Cyrus II, the Persian king who released the Israelite exiles in Babylon and allowed the rebuilding of the temple in Jerusalem, is almost unconditionally praised. In both *II Chronicles* and *Ezra*, God is seen to work through him (*II Chron.* 36:22–23, *Ezra* 1), whereas *Isaiah* (45:1) goes as far as to call him God's Messiah—the term literally means "anointed [with oil]" and was used to refer to prophets and, of course, became the Christian term for Jesus as the one through whom God acted and who acted in accordance with God's will. Given that as Persian king Cyrus was a Zoroastrian, this shows a biblical passage which asserts that God's chief agent on earth, at that time, is someone who is neither Jewish nor Christian. For the New Testament, many examples could be cited; for some discussion, see Osei-Bonsu, "Extra Ecclesiam," 137–40; Schmidt-Leukel, *Transformation*, 146–58; Hedges, *Controversies*, 137–41, 231–37 (which deals also with Hebrew Bible references); and Durwood Foster, "Christian Motives for Interfaith Dialogue," in *Christianity and the Wider Ecumenism*, 21–33.

51. Indeed, Arabic-speaking Christians call the Christian God "Allah"; this is simply how to say God in Arabic!

52. Clinton Bennett, *Understanding Christian-Muslim Relations: Past and Present* (London: Continuum, 2008), 92.

53. Ronald Miller, "Judaism: Siblings in Strife," in *Christian Approaches to Other Faiths*, 176ff.

54. Dan Cohn-Sherbok, "Judaism and the Universe of Faiths," in *Multi-Faith Britain: An Experiment in Worship*, ed. David A. Hart (Winchester, England: O Books, 2002), 1ff.

55. There are many excellent works examining the history and relationship of Christianity and Judaism. As an initial source, I would strongly recommend Miller's "Judaism," which references many other useful works in the area. On the way Christian theology today can deal with Judaism; see Hedges, *Controversies*, 33–36.

56. Bauschke "Islam" provides a good overview of the debates.

57. For a general overview of this status as "People of the Book" (*dhimmi*), see David Waines, *An Introduction to Islam* (Cambridge, England: Cambridge University Press, 2003), 52–53; and Reuven Firestone, *An Introduction to Islam for Jews* (Philadelphia, PA: Jewish Publication Society, 2008), 56–57, 152–56. The ideal of protection was sometimes violated (see F. E. Peters, *The Children of Abraham: Judaism, Christianity, Islam* [Princeton, NJ, and Oxford, England: Princeton University Press, 2004], 64).

58. The theologian Paul Knitter when setting out the typology calls "inclusivisms" the "fulfillment model" (see Paul Knitter, *Introducing Theologies of Religions* [Maryknoll, NY: Orbis, 2002]), whereas the current author has argued that inclusivisms have a motif of "radical fulfillment," whereby the whole of the other religion is subsumed into one's own inherent in them (Hedges, *Controversies*, 30). On fulfillment as a type within inclusivisms, see Cheetham, "Inclusivisms," 66ff; and Hedges, *Controversies*, 24–26.

59. The classic study of fulfillment theology as a school is Paul Hedges, *Preparation and Fulfilment: A History and Study of Fulfilment Theology in Modern British Thought*

in the Indian Context (Oxford, England; Bern, Switzerland; and New York: Peter Lang, 2001), 17–43 (for its background and an analysis of it).

60. On the Parliament and its agenda, see Justin Nordstrom, "Utopians at the Parliament: The World's Parliament of Religions and the Columbian Exposition of 1893,"*Journal of Religious History* 33, no. 3 (2009): 351–53.

61. On the past and current work of the parliament, see Council for a Parliament of the World's Religions, "A History of the Parliament," accessed July 11, 2012, http://www.parliamentofreligions.org/index.cfm?n=1&sn=4.

62. Alan Race, "Interfaith Dialogue: Religious Accountability Between Strangeness and Resonance," in *Christian Approaches to Other Faiths*, 161–63.

63. Anna Halafoff, "Netpeace: The Multifaith Movement and Common Security," *Australian Religion Studies Review* 24, no. 2 (2011): 143.

64. Hans Küng, *Global Responsibility: In Search of a New World Ethic* (London: SCM), xv.

65. As a humanistic response, this answer goes back at least as far as the seventeenth century and the Scottish philosopher David Hume (see Terence Penelhum, "David Hume," in *The Routledge Companion to the Philosophy of Religion*, ed. Chad Meister and Paul Copan [London: Routledge, 2010], 138–47).

66. The way in which every major religion speaks of God or ultimate reality as ultimately unknowable and claims that ultimately its own language is partial and flawed is particularly picked up and emphasized by Schmidt-Leukel in his presentation of the pluralistic hypothesis (Schmidt-Leukel, "Pluralisms," 85–86).

67. This is certainly not the only interpretation of this passage (*Quran* 5:48, Sahih International translation), and various other translations are available; see http://quran.com/5/48-48.

68. For two different stances on this, see, on the one hand, Nicholson, *Comparative Theology*, 71, 194, and 284 n. 105, n. 106, and, on the other, Hedges, *Controversies*, 178–79.

69. See Miller, "Judaism," 86–87.

FURTHER READINGS

Bharat, Sandy, and Jael Bharat. *A Global Guide to Interfaith: Reflections from Around the World*. Winchester, England: O Books, 2007.

Cheetham, David, Douglas Pratt, and David Thomas, eds. *Understanding Interreligious Relations*. Oxford, England: Oxford University Press, 2013.

Cornille, Catherine, ed. *The Wiley-Blackwell Companion to Interreligious Dialogue*. Chichester, England, and Malden, MA: Wiley-Blackwell, 2013.

Eck, Diana. *Encountering God: A Spiritual Journey from Bozeman to Benaras*. Boston, MA: Beacon Press, 2003 [1993].

Hedges, Paul. *Controversies in Interreligious Dialogue and the Theology of Religions*. London: SCM, 2010.

Hedges, Paul, and Alan Race, eds. *Christian Approaches to Other Faiths*. SCM Core Text Series. London: SCM, 2008.

Meister, Chad. *The Oxford Handbook of Religious Diversity*. Oxford, England: Oxford University Press, 2011.

Race, Alan. *Interfaith Encounter: The Twin Tracks of Theology and Dialogue*. London: SCM, 2001.

Sharma, Arvind, and Kathleen Dugan, eds. *A Dome of Many Colors: Studies in Religious Pluralism, Identity and Unity*. Harrisburg, PA: Trinity Press International, 1999.

9

Is Religion Dying? Secularization and Other Religious Trends in the World Today

Jayeel Serrano Cornelio

INTRODUCTION

Is religion dying? The significance of this question to many is immediately demonstrated by the fact that it generates a long list of Google results, ranging from online forums to blog accounts. And apart from passionate critics, those who have something to say about the question include religious leaders, academics, and policy makers. Media outfits also devote attention to this question by providing space to experts in the study of religion. A very recent entry comes from Bass, who argues that religion is at a crossroads today whether it dissipates or reinvents itself.[1] To her, either way is a choice for religion, with the succeeding generations looking back to ours as a watershed with far-ranging consequences.

Bass' attitude reflects a sense of urgency over the future of religion. Perhaps resonating with her are those who mourn what they see as the consequences of religious negligence: moral breakdown, the disintegration of the family as a social institution, pornography, and materialism.[2] This lamentation, however, runs in contrast to the triumphalism of a particular brand of secularism that calls for the eradication of the religious in public life.[3] Casanova describes this as "secularist secularity" whose lobbyists believe that "being liberated from 'religion' [is] a condition for human autonomy and human flourishing."[4] Reinforcing this is the increasing prominence of "New Atheism" that champions a militant attitude against those who profess religion (see Volume 2, Chapter 5).[5]

Rightly or wrongly, the question "is religion dying?" readily unravels the tensions in the public sphere. No wonder those who wish to address it objectively have to carefully explain themselves.[6] Herein lies the main controversy or "discontent" concerning the supposed dying state of religion.[7] Sentiments toward religion are surfaced by the question.

Without doubt, the question is important—and controversial—to the public and also to students of religion who have engaged the question from various angles and disciplines. The central idea that this question underpins is secularization, which broadly argues that religion is expected to fade away from social significance as societies undergo modernization. From this perspective, religion, in other words, is dying a natural death.

It is not, however, as forthright as it seems. For many observers, the geographic relevance of secularization is a crucial source of controversy. The question on the death of religion appears, for example, to be rather a public concern in advanced societies, mostly in the West, where cathedrals are increasingly empty. In the non-West, perhaps the main problem of the public sphere, if any, is that it may be too religious. This distinction is verified by Norris and Inglehart's recently updated work on "global religiosity."[8] Although belief in God is very high across societies around the world, there are statistically significant variations between agrarian, industrial, and post-industrial societies with regard to religious participation, values, and beliefs. Agrarian societies are consistently high in these areas. Therefore, as opposed to the experience of the West, the rest of the world appears to be, in the words of Peter Berger, "furiously religious."[9]

The controversies manifested in these incessant debates clearly demonstrate to us that the question remains far from being answered with finality. Claims by social scientists that secularization, as a theory, needs to be put to rest once and for all may not be giving due credit to the merits of divergent analyses.[10] Also, there is a tendency for both the supporters and refuters of the death-of-religion thesis to accuse each other of hiding their ideologies behind purported sociological facts. In another work, Casanova, for example, has questioned the value judgment that sees secularization as "normal" and "progressive."[11] In discussing secularization, then, Wilson has felt the necessity of articulating the sociologist's position of neutrality: "To put forward the secularization thesis as an explanation of what happens in society is not to be a secularist, nor to applaud secularity; it is only to document and to illustrate social change."[12]

This attempt at clarifying matters informs, too, the thrust of this chapter. In what follows, I wish to unravel for the reader the layers of complexity of the concept of secularization. The idea of secularization has a long history, and so generations of scholars have tried to define, describe, and comment on it. I have tried to the best of my ability to include in this chapter the many thinkers in the study of secularization from the classics to the contemporary. As a result of their scholarship, we are in a better position now to assess the merits of secularization and in so doing be able to define our own convictions over the fate of religion in the world today. So as to avoid redundancy with other theoretical overviews of secularization, I have drawn from the most recent scholarship of some of these thinkers. Also, the other contribution that this chapter makes is that it reflects on the limitation of the question above and offers an alternative to it. To ask whether religion is dying limits the potential answers we can get and may in the end be ideologically infiltrated.[13]

Before I proceed, I need to make clear here that the ideological infiltration may be due to the confusion between secularism and secularization. As Taylor puts it, "we think of 'secularization' as a selfsame process that can occur anywhere. . . . And we think of secularist regimes as options for any country."[14] Secularism is not a neutral word, and its definition is historically and politically contingent, with varying attitudes toward the presence of religion in civil and public life.[15] Suffice it to say that secularism is a framework by which institutions are established and governed using a "secular imaginary" of being without recourse to religion.[16] Social space may be afforded in a secularist regime but with careful management of religious presence. Secularization, which is the topic of this chapter, speaks mainly of an empirical trend concerning the decline of religion; thus the question, is religion dying?

The first section offers a brief historical overview of the concept of secularization and how it has become a master narrative in thinking about religion and modernization. The master narrative, however, can be problematic and has been contested in terms of what secularization really means and whether it is indeed a linear process. To address these problems, I then present the different nuances by which the concept of secularization has been clarified and explained. But again, because of its status as a master narrative, its relevance to the vibrant state of religion in other societies has been called into question. From there on, I would suggest that perhaps the question "is religion dying?" needs to be rephrased to allow other analytical possibilities. The last section deals with the "coexistence thesis" in which secularization is just one of the trends concerning religious change in the world today.

HISTORICAL OVERVIEW

The concern about the fate of religion in the hands of modernity has been, from its origins, one of the key tenets of sociological thought. Although the forerunners of sociology all anticipated the decline of religion, they did not offer a clear definition of secularization. What they did was to describe the condition of a decline in religion that paralleled social change in terms of urbanization and industrialization.[17] In this section, I will discuss the ways in which secularization pervaded the thought of early sociologists and how even among contemporary observers it continues as an inherited model.

Secularization as Master Narrative

We can discern from their writings that what the early sociologists generally observed is the weakening significance of religion to social institutions
and the life of individuals. It is this association between processes of modernization and secularization that has served as a master narrative in the
sociology of religion.[18] Comte, Marx, Weber, and Durkheim are considered
here.

Although they were observing the same phenomenon, their attitudes
toward religious decline were varied. As a discipline of the Enlightenment,
sociology could be expected to actively entertain the removal of religion.
Indeed, August Comte, the "father of sociology," has argued that history
has arrived at a positive stage whose empirical-scientific paradigm replaces
theology and metaphysics. As an Enlightenment thinker, Comte celebrated
the looming death of religion as he also saw the key role of sociologists in
shaping the secular future of society.[19] In this manner, sociology was envisioned to be in opposition to theology.[20] Marx could also be said to have
adopted a militant posture against religion but with a different motivation.
Given his critical view of capitalism, Marx called for a conscious eradication
of religion as the "opium of the people" for being a massive obstruction to
genuine class consciousness. One, however, can argue that Marx had dis-
cernible sympathies for the role of religion in social life in describing religion
as "the sigh of the oppressed creature, the heart of a heartless world, just as it
is the spirit of spiritless situation."[21]

It is perhaps this sympathetic stance that seems more evident in the works
of Weber and Durkheim. In the *Protestant Ethic and the Spirit of
Capitalism*, Weber also lamented society's imminent disenchantment.[22]
Although its virtues of hard work and industriousness facilitated the rise of
capitalistic enterprise, the transcendence of religion (in particular,
Calvinism) no longer had any central role to play in the process of modernization: "In the field of its highest development ... the pursuit of wealth,
stripped of its religious and ethical meaning, tends to be associated with
purely mundane passions."[23] For Weber, however, the decline of religion
entailed the dehumanizing tendencies of "iron cage rationality." In describing the people of this stage, Weber here resonates with Marx's rhetoric:
"Specialists without spirit, sensualists without heart."[24] Put differently, the
intensification of instrumentality and bureaucracy as the guiding principle
of social life could only mean that the space for aesthetics, emotions, and
the subjective is shrinking.

A similar sense of apprehension is evident in Durkheim although for a different reason. Given his interest in social order, Durkheim saw religion as
the underpinning value for society's cohesion.[25] But as society became more
complex because of structural differentiation, the influence of religion over

the different institutions of society could only be expected to wane. Durkheim's attention therefore was on the moral force of religion that could only be found in the collective. And now Durkheim's dilemma is as to what will serve as the social foundation of shared morality: "There can be no society which does not feel the need of upholding and reaffirming at regular intervals the collective sentiments and the collective ideas which make its unity and its personality."[26]

The decline of religion was critical to both Weber and Durkheim. Whereas Weber was concerned about the increasing control of instrumental rationality over social life, Durkheim was anxious about the loss of a moral imperative. Whereas Weber was concerned that the cost of modernity was the subjective human experience, Durkheim saw that the subjective might be gaining too much of a foothold—the problem of anomie. In other words, the decline of the religious necessarily entails the decline of the collective, leaving the individual to the personal and subjective.[27] Transpiring here is a crucial paradox, which might offer some sense of hope to Durkheim. As society becomes more complex, the decline of religion would have to be replaced with a new form aligning with the modern mind-set, which could be in the rituals of the nation-state, for example: "A day will come when our societies will know again those hours of creative effervescence, in the course of which new ideas arise and new formulae are found which serve for a while as a guide to humanity."[28]

Secularization as the Inherited Model

Regardless of the attitudes, it is this general anticipation of the decline of religion that seems to have been "inherited," as Wilson puts it, by generations of sociologists who succeeded the classics.[29] Reflecting these points, the inherited model pertains to the waning significance of religion to politics, the economy, and other aspects of the social system. In this elaboration, whether religion will continue to be important to individuals is not of paramount concern to the sociologist. What matters is that secularization in terms of the loss of the influence of the religious institution over the affairs of society is a general pattern in various places, however gradual or fast it might be: "As the degree of technical, economic, and political changes occurring in Western societies is experienced elsewhere and comes to characterize other cultures, we can expect to see a recession of the influence of religion there."[30] It is in this manner that the inherited model becomes a key master narrative for the study of religion.

Historical accounts are typically invoked, for example, to illustrate the standard model. In discussing this, Martin refers to what he considers as a "handy historical tripod" with the legs of the Middle Ages and the Victorian period as the historical peaks of religiosity.[31] From these periods, one could only see decline in terms of religious beliefs and practices. Indeed, a historical approach, as will be seen later, has been the attempt of many sociologists and historians to demonstrate the validity of the thesis. What is different about the standard model, however, is that it has attempts at linearity, and this is what makes it a master narrative. As Vincett, Sharma, and Aune demonstrate, the correlation between secularization and industrialization is taken to have universal applicability.[32] It is noteworthy that this "one-directional" rendering of secularization parallels the evolutionary thinking of the Enlightenment, which is also responsible for such developmental processes of industrialization,[33] modernization, and urbanization.[34] And because the rest of the world is adopting the developmental model of the West, the global decline of religion, so the narrative goes, can then be anticipated.

The master narrative that is the secularization thesis informs several key thinkers in the sociology of religion, but in varying degrees: the young Peter Berger, Bryan Wilson, and Steve Bruce. Although they approach secularization in different ways, they resonate with each other in terms of their views on the general tendency for the social significance of religion to decline.

Writing in the mid-twentieth century, the young Berger described religion as a "sacred canopy" whose ideas and practices serve as legitimating mechanisms for the operations of everyday life.[35] In the mind of an individual, religion is the worldview that makes social life manageably coherent and possible. Continuous religious socialization is that which keeps the canopy from falling apart. The frailty of the canopy, however, is gradually unraveled by the pluralistic conditions of modernity wherein, because of migration, scientific advancement, and the spread of alternative ideas, a claim to a monopolistic religious worldview is no longer tenable.

It is important to note here, however, that Berger has recanted this position at the turn of the century. Seeing the global resurgence of religion in the form of conservatism and revivalist movements, for example, Berger admits that modernization can also provoke "powerful movements of counter-secularization."[36] He argues, for instance, that religion affords "certainty" in a religiously diverse environment.[37] In contrast to the claims of secularization, what happens, therefore, is that although diversity undermines the taken-for-grantedness of religious beliefs and practices, it remains possible "to hold beliefs and to live by them," as Berger puts it in a festschrift in his honor.[38]

Bruce, a staunch defender of the secularization thesis, finds Berger's recantation to be "curious" and "unnecessary."[39] He asserts that what he subscribes to, which he finds in the original thought of Berger, is that that there is a pattern that suggests that institutional religion is bound to be insignificant. It is in this manner that Bruce echoes Wilson. And it is an irreversible pattern insofar as "the conditions required to construct, sustain, and reproduce across generations a shared supernatural word-view are destroyed by individualism and pluralism."[40] In a very recent and highly readable work, Bruce[41] argues that such processes of modernization as industrialization, social and structural differentiation, and increasing diversity are not hospitable to the sustained presence of institutional religion. The decline of religious power in society can only lead to the decline in the importance of religion to the modern individual. As a result, religious socialization becomes difficult to accomplish, and hence, the perpetuation of religion for the next generation is ultimately threatened. That is why Bruce is more convinced than Wilson that privatized religion "fails to make the group lost by . . . traditional religion."[42]

What these statements suggest is that even if Bruce may not be claiming the universality or inevitability of secularization, he is instrumental in reinforcing to a certain degree the master narrative: if modernity involves pluralism, structural differentiation, and even increased individualism, then religion in the context of modernity will be increasingly insignificant. It is a qualified master narrative, as it were. True enough, a claim he makes about the rest of the world is that as it modernizes, religious life is merely undergoing transition whether it is the United States or Asia. The idea is that "*if other places modernize* in ways similar to the European experience, then we can expect the nature and status of religion also to change in similar ways."[43]

Although this claim might be controversial , a compelling study by Norris and Inglehart does demonstrate the seeming reliability of the master narrative.[44] Drawing from global surveys spanning decades, they claim that modernization, which increases levels of human security in terms of finding education, health care, and general welfare, "greatly weakens the influence of religious institutions in affluent societies."[45] For these authors, human security is the critical condition that makes demand for the religious untenable in the long run. Conversely, levels of religiosity in terms of church attendance and beliefs are very high in poorer societies where human security is evidently challenged. Echoing Bruce's qualifier, they point out that global religion, however, is not fading away in the foreseeable future because of demographic trends that show, for example, high fertility rates in poorer and thus religious societies. Even now, the total number of those who profess religion outweighs those who do not.

NUANCING SECULARIZATION

The previous section recounts various ways by which the death of religion, in varying degrees, occupies the theoretical articulation of key thinkers in the sociology of religion. The inherited model, so to speak, argues that with modernization comes the weakening significance of religion. However, as seen earlier, divergences between the thinkers are evident with regard to its pace, its fundamental cause, its impact on the individual, and even its desirability. Although secularization is now considered by many as an "unfashionable theory," as the title of Bruce's recent work puts it, its validity and significance have not been fully quashed in the literature.[46] This is even if specific empirical evidence has been lodged against the theory, a point I will return to in a later section.

It is important to recognize that as a master narrative, the "death-of-religion" thesis disregards divergent experiences. That secularization narratives disregard difference according to gender, for example, has been tackled by Vincett, Sharma, and Aune in their landmark text on women and religion.[47] They argue that attendance figures demonstrating religious decline are predominantly masculine. They show that women have exhibited high religiosity and are even engaged in contemporary alternative spiritualities. Also, the master narrative has the tendency to explain away the sustained presence of religion or of new religious forms as final gasps for transcendental air. Contesting this tendency, Hervieu-Léger offers an astute discussion on the nature of modernization as in effect not hostile at all to religion.[48] The tension inherent to modernity between an envisioned ideal future and the ways to get there affords space for the religious imagination. The presence of religion, then, is not necessarily antimodern or a tragedy waiting to happen.

Such a critical attitude toward secularization does not have to reject the idea completely. In another important work, Hervieu-Léger herself, for example, attempts to explain the various processes that have led to the dismantling of traditional community formations in France that has led to the decline of Catholicism.[49] She does not argue, however, that religion as a phenomenon is bound to be completely insignificant. Along similar lines, Turner argues that secularization remains an applicable concept in spite of the prominence of fundamentalism and religion in the public sphere.[50] In the context of the "differentiation of spheres of activity in modern societies between religion, the economy and the polity," religion will always have to compete with other agencies in articulating, explaining, and dealing with reality.[51] Hence, religion becomes commodified in popular culture, for example.

What these statements suggest is that religion, whether in terms of institutional leadership or everyday practice, can sometimes lose or otherwise. Here, the narrative is no longer master and it is in this light that other thinkers elaborate the nuances of secularization.[52] In this section, I spell out the different ways in which the idea of secularization has been elaborated by seminal thinkers. Although adopting different approaches, these thinkers share a common denominator in not giving a straightforward answer to the question, "is religion dying?" Instead, what they offer are nuanced ideas that have direct implication on the secularization narrative: the definition of religion,[53] levels of analyses,[54] and historical contingency.[55]

Defining Religion

One crucial matter that has not been discussed in this chapter so far is what we mean by religion. Having a clear definition of religion will allow us to be more or less clear, too, about its condition in the world today. If it is indeed dying or otherwise, how do we know?

In his introductory book on religion and everyday life, Hunt calls attention to two broad approaches in defining religion: substantive and functional.[56] A substantive approach generally revolves around the essential aspects or what religion is mainly about. In this sense, religion is about beliefs, practices, and traditions grounded in a conviction that a transcendental or supernatural reality exists. The thinkers discussed earlier have clearly dealt with religion in this manner. Adopting a substantive definition provides a narrow scope to assess religious decline. By looking at such indicators as religious attendance, belief in doctrines, participation in rituals, or frequency of prayer, the observers recounted earlier have been able to say that there is a general trend of decline.

This is not easily the case though when one follows a functional approach. This approach pays attention to what religion fundamentally does. Functionally, religion is an experience of shared beliefs and ideals that form and reinforce group solidarity. Societies and small communities, even if nonreligious in the substantive sense, have to subscribe to and enact shared values if they are to survive. State rituals and community festivals demonstrate this. From a functionalist view, one can then argue that even if institutional religions may no longer be relevant, individuals are still perpetuating the religious. Hence, secularization in terms of the death of religion is not even a question in this framework.

The point here is that to be able to assess the contemporary state of religion, one has to be clear about what exactly is being referred to. Different definitions offer different depictions. However, this does not mean that the substantive approach, which Hunt supports, is necessarily superior.[57] The substance of a religion can also cover many aspects and dimensions. And a decline in a specific practice, for example, may not be seen in another. With this in mind, the question "is religion dying?" now becomes "which aspects of religion are dying?" In this view, religion cannot be taken as a whole. This is another issue that the master narrative overlooks.

The other point that these definitions implicitly deal with concerns the origin or source of religion. If one begins from the assumption that to be religious is an inherently human desire, then religion—whether in its substantive or functional form—will prevail, but perhaps in transformed patterns. This has been the argument of Luckmann, who reflects on human aspirations for the transcendent as seen not just in the desire for a higher being but also in one's experiences of personal limitations, relationships, and life transitions.[58] With the decline of institutional religion, the emergence of deinstitutionalized forms of exploring the transcendent such as the New Age makes sense. But transformed religious patterns may not entirely be religious in a traditional (or substantive) fashion. A recent book by Benthall draws from the anthropological argument that "religious inclination, the need for a framework of orientation or object of devotion, is a human universal."[59] This inclination, he argues, is necessary to the stability of society, which explains why even if the world may be in a secular age, activities or social arrangements resembling religion are still coming to fore. He then makes the connection of religion to faith-based organizations, environmentalism, and the humanitarian movement. Interestingly, the demand for the religious as a constant is an assumption, too, that will be invoked by a rational choice approach, which I will revisit later.

But if one assumes that human beings are not inherently religious, then the process of secularization can be anticipated. This, of course, has informed the evolutionary model of the Enlightenment thinkers who perceived scientific thinking as superior to all forms of explaining the world. This, too, is invoked heavily by the New Atheist movement in the West. The argument is that religion is merely a social construct and the sustained reliance on it amounts to delusion and creates hostility against other people.[60] In contrast to the previous anthropological claim, religion is viewed in the end as detrimental to social stability.

Levels of Analysis

For Dobbelaere, secularization can be analyzed at three levels: societal, organizational, and individual.[61] Societal secularization refers to how religion, in the process of modernization, has lost its influence over how the social system is to be run. This is the same as the process of functional differentiation discussed by sociologists such as Bruce and Wilson. Reflecting its trajectory in the West, the religious institution has been replaced by secular institutions with specific functional mandates over health, welfare, and education, for example. That the social system has become secular does not mean the end of religion. The same can be said about organizational secularization. Religious transformation can take place within religious organizations, and certain processes can be described as secularization without necessarily implying decline. In terms of ethos, for example, Dobbelaere suggests that religious institutions and even new religious movements have adopted a this-worldly approach by encouraging their members to exercise social justice or to be in touch with the inner self. The transformation lies in the deemphasis of a high divine being and in the appeal to universal values. Finally, individual secularization pertains to how individuals no longer feel obliged to follow a set of doctrines or be subject to institutional religious practice or membership. Transformation is seen not in terms of the loss of the importance of religion to the individual but in how people can fluidly construct their religious identities.

The value of Dobbelaere's analysis is in demonstrating first that the processes of secularization are different at each level. But collectively they can be related to each other. Societal secularization, for example, has an effect on how people think and go about their daily lives to the effect that some areas do not have to be decidedly religious. Second, Dobbelaere demonstrates that secularization is not necessarily tantamount to religious decline. In fact, he argues that "secularization and sacralization are the result of actions by collective actors and not mechanical evolutionary processes."[62] At the very least, these processes suggest the transformation of religion taking place in different ways.

It is these two themes concerning secularization that Casanova picks up in thinking about the increasingly public character of religions in the modern world.[63] He suggests that secularization became a loaded concept because the experience in Europe has been that the three levels of secularization seemed to have taken place all at the same time.[64] The differentiation of social institutions coincided with the decline of religious beliefs and practices and the privatization of religion away from the secular and democratic processes. Although these three levels may be connected to each other, they cannot be taken to mean the overall decline of religion. In particular, Casanova challenges the view of secularization as the privatization of religion in that history has seen the public engagement (or deprivatization) of religion in the experience of Christianity in the United States and Poland, for example.

Here we see that although neither Dobbelaere nor Casanova rejects secularization, they do not subscribe to its general applicability or linearity concerning the death of religion. Instead, they reconfigure the concept to present its heuristic value as multidimensional. They also agree that because secularization at its core is about societal differentiation, they welcome the possibility that religious institutions can contest their privatization and that individuals can remain religious in novel ways.

Historical Contingency

Secularization as a model has been widely developed in the discipline of sociology. Observers from other disciplines such as history, theology, and anthropology, however, have challenged its reliability to assess and describe the general trajectory of religion. These nuances have challenged secularization as a general model in various ways.

To treat secularization as a linear process fails, in the first place, to recognize that processes between secularization and sacralization exist. Martin, who draws from the history of ideas, does endorse the irreversibility of structural differentiation.[65] But, to him, this does not mean that religion is relegated to social insignificance. He argues that the contestations over nature, nation, and the autonomy of religion reveal the dynamic processes of secularization and sacralization. Although secular discourses are used to explain nature and nationhood, metaphors of religion have still been employed by poets, for example in admiration of nature, and by civic leaders to speak of national renewal. Finally, the autonomy of religion is contested by the example of Evangelicalism. Although it emphasizes interiorized forms of piety, the evangelical ethos, as seen in the United States, enters the various spheres of health care, leisure, and even entertainment. Secularization, then, is not necessarily a unidirectional process. Interestingly, this, too, is a view shared by Smith, who offers a controversial claim that the observed levels of religiosity in the West today are in fact very similar to those in the Middle Ages.[66] He challenges the view that secularism is fundamentally devoid of religion. Smith highlights the sustained belief in God and the renewed interest in ethics, charity, and doing good to argue that "secularism in the West is a new manifestation of Christianity."[67] In other words, a religious transformation—and not decline—is taking place. This then directly counters the claim that the Christian character of Britain has effectively died.[68]

To adopt secularization as a master narrative disregards, too, particular geographic and historical conditions shaping religious change. This is why Davie contends that the propositions of secularization and its various levels, for example, need to be worked out "case by case and country by country."[69] Brown's claim that Christianity in Britain has effectively died, for example, is based not only on declining indicators of piety but also on changing moralities, especially since the 1960s.[70]

Although it may be valid in Britain, this story, however, is not indicative of the fate of religion elsewhere. Turning the master narrative on its head, Berger, Davie, and Fokas argue that the condition of religion in Europe is not in fact the model.[71] In view of what they consider to be the religiosity of the rest of the world, Europe becomes the exception. To them, the United States clearly demonstrates that modernity is not inimical to religious life. They suggest that competition among religious groups and the importance of churches as social spaces for immigrants are two important conditions keeping religion alive. Indeed, this sense of competition is what Stark and Finke believe to be the main driver of religious vibrancy in the United States.[72] Adopting a rational choice approach, they point out that the abundance and diversity of religious supply ensure that demand is being addressed. The assumption is that demand for the religious is constant. In view of this, religious vibrancy necessarily thrives in a milieu of religious diversity.

Asia, too, becomes interesting as it is now the site of exemplary projects of modernity that employ a secularist agenda adopted from the West. But as Bubandt and van Beek show in their recent volume, a secularist agenda that disregards the presence of religion is not always successful.[73] What becomes evident in Asian societies is that secularism has varieties in which religion plays roles in shaping politics, governance, and the national imagination. An urban community in Bangkok, for example, uses Buddhist rituals and the defense of sacred sites to challenge attempts of the state, which invokes Buddhist values too, to evict its households.[74] In the Philippines, in contrast to the experience of Catholicism in some European societies, the Church has been instrumental in the democratizing process. It is behind, for example, the successful attempt to depose the authoritarian regime of Marcos in the 1980s. Records show, too, that the Catholic Church has been partnering with civil society organizations in encouraging human empowerment.[75] Another interesting case is Singapore, which for a long time has been ranked the most globalized country in the world in terms of such indicators as trade, capital movements, and technological advancement.[76] The Singaporean state has taken a strong stance against the presence of religion in the public sphere. Because of conflicts engendered along ethnic and religious lines, religion has been viewed as necessitating public management. But in spite of this sense of antagonism, religious life tends to be vibrant in Singapore, with more than 80 percent of its population adhering to a religion, for example.[77] Paradoxically, the state is also ready to obtain the support of religious institutions "to inculcate good citizenship, temper the rough edges of secular life by providing a moral anchor, and encourage industriousness. . . ."[78]

In discussing the sustained presence of religion in other parts of the world such as Asia, one has to be wary about the problem of Orientalism (see Volume 1, Chapter 11).[79] Orientalism assumes the backwardness of Eastern societies (the Orient) from the perspective of Western history.[80] In this view, religious life does not suggest premodern sensibilities. More than anything, the earlier illustrations indeed suggest that secularism has varied trajectories in other societies where religion plays an important role.[81]

In his influential text on the relationship between religion and modernity in India and Britain, van der Veer takes the historical problem further by arguing that other religions have different understandings of their relationship to the state and society.[82] Indeed, secularization presupposes that the religious can be separated from the secular in the first place. But this is a uniquely Christian discourse derived from Latin Christendom's distinction between the spiritual/religious and the temporal/secular/profane. That is why until today religious priests are those who are in the monastery or a particular congregation while their secular parish-based counterparts are with the ordinary laity. In the wake of the Protestant Reformation, secularization meant leaving the monastic life to serve in the world or giving up monastic properties.[83] Islam, in contrast, does not have this dyadic distinction, which explains its influence in economic life such as banking and in everyday life in terms of dietary restrictions, for example. In addition, other religions have different forms of piety, which makes measuring religiosity more problematic. Church attendance or frequency of prayer do not necessarily reflect piety in, for example, Buddhism or Hinduism. Without regard for religious particularities and sociohistorical conditions, using secularization as a theoretical lens commits the Orientalist problem of imposition. Here it pays to be reminded that "religion" is a concept exported to the rest of the world as a colonial category with specific cultural baggage from Christianity.[84] Clearly then, these views challenge the attempts of Norris and Inglehart to come up with a global picture of secularization based on varying levels of human security.[85]

ALTERNATIVE INTERPRETATIONS: RELIGIOUS TRENDS

In discussing ways in which secularization has been nuanced (in terms of definition, level of analysis, and historical validity), the previous section has already touched on some of the problems of employing the death-of-religion thesis as a master narrative. The master narrative becomes irrelevant in light of social and geographic specificity, the different trajectories of secularism, and the multidimensionality of secularization itself. But generally, these analyses still welcome the usefulness of secularization as a descriptive idea. A common denominator, for example, is what we may consider their minimalist view that it is first and foremost about structural differentiation.

At this point, one can imagine that the death-of-religion thesis has been losing its influence. In fact, Bruce, who remains to defend it, admits that it is unfashionable.[86] Broadly, I see two possible explanations for this.

First, discussions on secularization have been generally confined to the West and among Western observers. In this case, the question "is religion dying?" may in fact be of interest only to these scholars. One case after another from the United States and Europe is employed to support and refute the conventional secularization thesis. As Casanova puts it, "an impasse has been reached in the debate" and one needs to "adopt a more global perspective."[87] For this, one is easily reminded of, for example, the rise of Pentecostalism in Latin America and Africa,[88] the emotionally charged expressions of Islam in different parts of the world,[89] the demographics of Roman Catholicism shifting to the Global South,[90] and the growth of reformist Buddhism in East Asia.[91] This does not include the surge of interest in religion brought about by religious violence and 9/11. Indeed, my observation is that for researchers embedded in the non-West, the vibrancy of religion in the media, public life, schools, government, and other social institutions makes it impossible to even think about the question at hand.

Second, secularization is a concept derived from the historical experience of Christianity in Europe. Therefore, it is too limited to capture the dynamic ways by which religions are unfolding in other societies. Globalization appears to be a key process here, with religions having to face challenges of increasing diversity, migration, urbanization, and conflict.[92] Drawing from Wilson, Tschannen suggests that the survival of religion depends on its ability to foster communities.[93] In a globalizing world, community formation is not hampered at all. The rise of online religion, for example, shows that mediated piety is possible, seen in the participation of connected individuals from different continents. New forms of online evangelism demonstrate the virtualization of spiritual experience.[94] As a process, globalization also means the spread of ideas, issues, and ethical problems. Indeed, Casanova is right in suggesting that the need for religious responses to global issues will be greater.[95] On one hand, the forms of religious response we see can reek of pessimism. Robertson, for example, feels that as a result of 9/11, the world has entered what he calls a "millennial phase" in which the theme of imminent disaster has pervaded religious and political rhetoric at a global scale.[96] But on the other hand, global issues are engendering coordinated humanitarian responses, too. Today, we are seeing the emergence of transnational religious philanthropy, exemplifying the feasibility of global communities forming around specific causes.[97] Also, because of global conflict involving religious groups, there will be a greater need for policy makers to engage religion as a resource for concerted action.[98]

These considerations unravel for us the limitation of secularization as a concept to capture the complexity of religious transformation in the world today. Demerath captures this sentiment very well in arguing that "focusing on the fate of old forms of religion may deflect attention from new forms of the sacred."[99] Here, I suggest that "is religion dying?" which is a question steeped in the historical specificity of the condition of religion in Europe, must be modified to entertain other analytical possibilities. Instead, we must ask a broader question: *what can we say about the condition of religion in the world today?* With this question, secularization becomes only one of the possible answers. Here I adopt the coexistence thesis proposed by Woodhead and Heelas in suggesting that different religious transformations are taking place parallel to each other.[100] Whereas Martin suggests that secularization is not a linear process with tensions existing between secularization and sacralization (or the return of religion), the coexistence thesis proposes that various trends are operating simultaneously in the world today.[101] Apart from secularization, the other three discussed here are as follows: *sacralization, detraditionalization*, and *universalization*.

Sacralization

Sacralization, a concept that has cropped up a few times above, turns secularization on its head by arguing that religion is in fact experiencing, more than anything, resurgence in modern times. In fact, this could be the default situation for global religion. Although it might indeed be the case that indicators of religiosity vary depending on levels of human security as Norris and Inglehart contend, they also admit that because of demographic conditions, there are by default more religious people in the world than there are otherwise.[102] But this is a banal point to argue sacralization.

Sacralization, as a trend, can be more interesting in how its varied processes encourage religious upsurge. Three processes have been identified by Woodhead and Heelas: *growth, dedifferentiation*, and *intensification*.[103] *Growth* takes place because of conversion, especially among those without previous religious affiliation. This may be the case in particular among women converting to Islam in the West. Islam's appeal lies in how it encompasses various spheres of everyday life and fosters community.[104] Facilitating sacralization by conversion, too, is online religion, which I briefly mentioned earlier. Indeed, the new face of online evangelism lies in the ability of the Internet to bring together seekers and online missionaries through which conversion can take place.[105] *Dedifferentiation* is what Casanova considers deprivatization, in which religious institutions are finding a role once again as actors in civil society.[106] Religions, in other words, can resist their marginalization brought about by structural differentiation. They see themselves as having important contributions to make in policy-making or community mobilization, for example. In the twentieth century, liberation theology in Latin America has demonstrated the Catholic Church's potential in shaking political structures.[107] This, of course, has had lasting impact on Catholicism in other developing societies in Asia. Finally, sacralization also involves the process of *intensification*. Broadly, this refers to how individuals with nominal religious affiliations are imbibing a more committed outlook with implications on their religious behavior or piety. In their study of American religion for the post-Boomer generation, Flory and Miller have noticed that there are young people who are reclaiming or rediscovering emotional affinity with traditional religiosity associated with orthodox forms of Anglicanism, for example.[108] The shift is triggered by disillusionment with what they feel to be the ephemeral nature of contemporary religions in the form of "megachurches," for example.

Detraditionalization

Another trend shaping religion today is detraditionalization, which, broadly speaking, is the process by which religious authority is transferred from traditional sources that are normally external to the individual to the authenticating mechanism of the self.[109] The traditional sources of authority include the scriptures and the religious institution itself as having the official promulgating and interpretive entity. The view, too, of God or a divine being as high and unreachable reflects the external authority of religious tradition. In the context of detraditionalization, individuals do not feel constrained to submit to such forms of authority. I mention three possible varieties of detraditionalization: the "weakening" of tradition, the "consumerization of religion," and religious "individualization."[110]

Some of the key facets of liberal Christianity include the way it challenges scriptural authority and the transmitted knowledge concerning God and his ways. In many ways, liberal Christianity is in direct contrast to the evangelical view that the Bible is to be taken literally and as the final authority over one's life. It is in this sense that liberal Christianity "weakens" the tradition as known and received in conservative Christianity. This disposition overlooks the exclusivist claim of traditional Christianity in terms of, for example, Christ's unique role in salvation history.[111] Megachurches are an interesting case of the consumerization of religion. At one level, they can be seen as conservative in theology, and this is to be expected since many of them align with Evangelicalism.[112] But at another level, megachurches tend to be very detraditionalized and contemporary with their approach to "doing church." In the United States, for example, Miller documents how these "new paradigm" churches downplay theological language to make Christianity understandable to the public.[113] In Singapore, whose megachurches harbor thousands of members, individuals are drawn to spectacular forms of worship in huge auditoriums that make use of an ensemble of light and music.[114] In South Korea, which is home to the biggest churches in the world, preachers, while conservative in orientation, are invoking prosperity theology and political power.[115] All these examples point to how even conservative institutions can employ detraditionalization in the form of religious consumerization. Finally, religious individualization clearly reflects the process of detraditionalization in that here one sees the self as the final arbiter of what is authentic. Here the distinction between religion and spirituality begins to make sense. Religion can be distinguished as that which embodies traditions and the institution tasked to maintain them. Spiritualities of life, on the other hand, are heavily deinstitutionalized forms of connecting to the inner self. In the West, such Eastern practices as yoga and meditation appeal to a small but still significant proportion of individuals.[116] Individuals are moving away from religious traditions toward alternative forms of spiritual experience. I note here, however, that religious individualization does not have to take place outside religious institutions. In my research, I have argued that "indwelt individualization" is possible in which religious actors can reflect on their faith and see the importance of certain beliefs and practices depending on how they surface authenticity within them.[117] That is why it is possible to encounter young people professing to be Catholic without necessarily going to Mass because to them participating in a voluntary initiative demonstrates their religion better.

Universalization

The final religious trend discussed by Woodhead and Heelas is universalization, primarily grounded in the "ethic of humanity," which is "premised on the idea that ethnic, gendered or national differences should not be allowed to disguise the fact that—essentially—we are all humans."[118] In a way, this development is also a form of detraditionalization. Traditional religions, by invoking an authority external to the human being, tend to be exclusivist. With universalization, differences are downplayed in favor of that which unites us all—our humanity.

Interestingly, this sense of inclusivity is how religion can contest diversity. As argued earlier, diversity can be detrimental to religion as it fosters different ways of viewing reality (see Volume 1, Chapter 8).[119] In this light, the monopoly of truth by a religion is irrevocably challenged. Universalization, however, presents itself as a creative way of transcending difference by emphasizing what is common to all. Perhaps the fact that this resonates with Buddhist ideals makes Buddhist organizations in East Asia successful.[120] The temples, for example, are becoming instrumental in administering welfare, and there are other movements such as *Soka Gakkai* and *Tzu Chi* whose appeal to the diasporic Chinese lies in their humanitarian efforts in the region.[121]

Universalization as a trend, interestingly, is not only reshaping religious institutions. Even at the level of everyday religion, the ethic of humanity appears to be a conviction more important than fundamental beliefs that separate religions from each other. In the United States, for example, Ammerman observes that the pervading understanding of Christianity among many Americans (and liberals in particular) sees the Golden Rule as the most important principle of religious life.[122] In this regard, Golden Rule Christianity rejects exclusivism based on specific doctrines that consider Christianity, for example, as the only true religion. The ethical turn is also seen in the emergence of religious nongovernment organizations such as World Vision and Christian Aid, which see their primary purpose in caring for the needy around the world. There is no strong ethos of proselytism in such organizations. Finally, under universalization can also be included activist organizations that fight for human dignity, environmentalism, and even animal rights. Even if they may not have a substantively religious foundation, these organizations imbibe a para-religious morality that shapes their worldview and social action.[123] It will be remembered in the earlier discussion that the functional aspects of religion are sustained under the premise that religious inclination is a human universal. From this vantage point, the ethical turn toward humanity is the pinnacle of humanity's search for the transcendent, which, paradoxically, rests within us. Benthall, hence, is justified in challenging the critics of religion as follows: "You hold that religions are products of the human mind that have done much harm through dividing people from one another. Will you also concede that they have also done good, through uniting people and through inspiring outstanding creativity?"[124]

CONCLUSION

So, is religion dying? In view of the earlier comprehensive discussion, any straightforward answer will not do justice to the complexity of the presence of religion—in its various forms—in the world today. A careful answer, I believe, would be: it depends. Answering this controversial question depends on several factors recounted earlier: what we mean by religion and which one we are dealing with, its historical and geographic conditions, the level of analysis being employed, and even whether such variables as gender and age make any difference to the observations we offer. Indeed, the thorough nuancing of secularization made by generations of scholars clearly points to the controversies generated by the theory concerning its validity and historical veracity.

But it also has normative tendencies. The concept of secularization has been controversial as it served as ammunition between secularists and religious devotees engaged in what appears to be an endless and exasperating exchange of "facts." Historical and statistical data have been read in different ways to refute each other's claims. This reveals the discontent some people may have about secularization.[125] Social scientists, therefore, have carried the burden of justifying their role and presence in studying religion in the most neutral manner possible (see Volume 1, Chapter 2).[126] This attempt, of course, is not always successful, as when researchers are treated with suspicion by religious individuals, for example.

The endlessness of the controversies surrounding the supposedly dying state of religion can mean, at least to me, that perhaps the question is constraining. The earlier discussion has recounted how the idea that religion is dying has predominantly confined its articulation within the experience of religion in the West. Well known, for example, has been the debate as to which one is anomalous to the secularization thesis—Europe or the United

States.[127] Furthermore, the question "is religion dying?" is also limiting with regard to the answer it elicits—either yes or no. Religions are necessarily complex and their fortunes throughout history cannot be simply reduced to a simple linear process implicit to this question.[128] As mentioned earlier, one has to take into consideration processes of globalization, the unfolding of novel global ethical dilemmas, the continuing significance of religion in the public sphere, the transformations of religious institutions, the emergence of New Religious Movements, and even the development of alternative forms of individual religiosity. Perhaps, a question that welcomes other analytical possibilities be asked instead: what can we say about the condition of religion in the world today?

For this, I have drawn from the work of Woodhead and Heelas, who suggest that there are at least four trends concerning contemporary religious change.[129] Secularization is only one of them. The others, as elaborated earlier, include sacralization, detraditionalization, and universalization. Manifesting themselves in varying degrees, each of these trends may be present at the various levels of the religious institution and everyday religion. And they take place parallel to each other—the coexistence thesis.

But this question on the condition of religion is important not only because it entertains new ways of understanding the religious life in the here and now. If secularization is simply one of the trends coexisting with the others, researchers can also entertain the possibility of seeing the sustained (but yet again transformed) presence of religion in the future. Two analytical directions crop up: one concerning the social nature of religion itself, and the other its future.

Following Wilson's train of thought, Tschannen suggests that the continuity of religion depends on the "continuity of community."[130] On one hand, religious communities can still be formed as spaces within highly rationalized and individualistic societies. But they will be marginal relative to the mainstream. On the other hand, religion can maintain social significance if societies can maintain strong communal culture as they undergo technological advancement. The Durkheimian assumption is that religion is necessarily of a communal nature where religious socialization takes place and for religion to proceed in this manner is an uphill battle given the individualizing tendencies of modernity.

This dilemma, as we have seen, is gradually being entertained in the emergent literature on detraditionalization and spiritualities of life.[131] And one quick answer might be to speak of contemporary religion as being that of the individual alone, as in Sheilaism.[132] But the question also concerns the changing social aspect of religion. In other words, how is the nature of religion as a communal activity changing relative to individualization? I have touched on these issues in my work on the virtualization of spiritual experience[133] and on the reflexive spirituality of Catholic youth.[134]

Other emergent areas needing exploration include the religiosity of transnational movements, migrants and their religious rootedness, the religiosity of the socially excluded, and religious socialization outside religious institutions.

The other analytical direction resulting from the coexistence thesis concerns the very future of religion. Although the social sciences do not have the privilege of absolute accuracy, being able to ask and theorize about the future of religion is a worthwhile endeavor especially because of the implications on governance, religious leadership, social welfare, and public morality.[135] Indeed, the diversity and uneven presence of religious persuasions around the world is accompanied by tensions over what cultural values are to prevail within a religion itself and the society at large.[136] Battles, for example, are being fought over the traditional issues of homosexual marriage (see Volume 2, Chapter 3), abortion, and divorce and the new bioethical issues engendered by scientific advancement in procreation, medical treatment, and the possibility of living forever (see Volume 3, Chapter 4).[137] Another issue, of course, is the formation of communities in an increasingly multicultural environment.[138] To say that these matters are purely secular in the future would be a mistake.[139] Both students and followers of religion today are therefore called upon to reflect on the future of religious leadership and membership, the institution, theology, practice, and religion's ultimate relevance.

NOTES

1. Diana Butler Bass, "Is Religion Dying—or Reinventing?" *The Washington Post*, March 7, 2012, http://www.washingtonpost.com/blogs/guest-voices/post/is-religion-dying—or-reinventing/2012/03/07/gIQApziWxR_blog.html.

2. Graeme Smith, *A Short History of Secularism* (London and New York: I.B. Tauris, 2008).

3. David Voas and Abby Day, "Secularity in Great Britain," in *Secularism and Secularity: Contemporary International Perspectives*, ed. Barry Kosmin and Ariela Keysar (Hartford, CT: Institute for the Study of Secularism in Society and Culture, 2007), 95–112.

4. Jose Casanova, "The Secular, Secularizations, Secularisms," in *Rethinking Secularism*, ed. Craig Calhoun, Mark Juergensmeyer, and Jonathan van Antwerpen (Oxford, England: Oxford University Press, 2011), 60.

5. Amarnath Amarasingam, "Introduction: What Is the New Atheism?" in *Religion and the New Atheism: A Critical Appraisal*, ed. Amarnath Amarasingam (Leiden, Holland, and Boston, MA: Brill, 2010), 1–8.

6. Bryan Wilson, "Secularization: The Inherited Model," in *The Sacred in a Secular Age: Toward Revision in the Scientific Study of Religion*, ed. Philip E. Hammond (Berkeley and Los Angeles: University of California Press, 1985), 9–20.

7. Rob Warner, *Secularization and Its Discontents* (London and New York: Continuum, 2010).

8. Pippa Norris and Ronald Inglehart, *Sacred and Secular: Religion and Politics Worldwide*, 2nd ed. (Cambridge, England, and New York: Cambridge University Press, 2011).

9. Peter Berger, "The Desecularization of the World: An Overview," in *The Desecularization of the World: Resurgent Religion and World Politics*, ed. Peter Berger (Washington, DC, and Grand Rapids, MI: Ethics and Public Policy Center and W.B. Eerdmans Pub. Co., 1999), 2.

10. Jeffrey Cox, "Towards Eliminating the Concept of Secularisation: A Progress Report," in *Secularisation in the Christian World: Essays in Honour of Hugh Mcleod* (Farnham, England: Ashgate, 2010), 13–26; and Rodney Stark, "Secularization, R.I.P.," *Sociology of Religion* 60, no. 3 (1999): 249–73.

11. Jose Casanova, "Rethinking Secularization: A Global Comparative Perspective," in *Religion, Globalization and Culture*, ed. Peter Beyer and Lori Beaman (Leiden, Holland, and Boston, MA: Brill, 2007), 111.

12. Bryan Wilson, *Religion in Sociological Perspective* (Oxford, England: Oxford University Press, 1982), 148.

13. Charles Taylor, "Western Secularity," in *Rethinking Secularism*, 31–53.

14. Ibid., 31.

15. Craig Calhoun, Mark Juergensmeyer, and Jonathan van Antwerpen, "Introduction," in *Rethinking Secularism*, 3–30.

16. Ibid., 10; and Charles Taylor, *A Secular Age* (Cambridge, MA, and London: Belknap Press of Harvard University Press, 2007).

17. Grace Davie, *The Sociology of Religion*, Bsa New Horizons in Sociology (London: Sage, 2007).

18. N. J. Demerath, III, "Secularization and Sacralization Deconstructed and Reconstructed," in *The Sage Handbook of the Sociology of Religion* (London and Thousand Oaks, CA: Sage, 2007), 57–80.

19. Inger Furseth and Pal Repstad, *An Introduction to the Sociology of Religion* (Aldershot, England: Ashgate, 2007).

20. Wilson, "Secularization."

21. Karl Marx and Friedrich Engels, *On Religion* (Moscow: Foreign Languages Pub. House, 1957), 42.

22. Max Weber, *The Protestant Ethic and the Spirit of Capitalism* (Mineola, NY: Dover, 2003).

23. Ibid., 182.

24. Ibid.

25. Emile Durkheim, *The Elementary Forms of the Religious Life*, trans. John Ward Swain (London: George Allen and Unwin, 1915).

26. Ibid., 427.

27. Bryan S. Turner, "Talcott Parson's Sociology of Religion and the Expressive Revolution: The Problem of Western Individualism,"*Journal of Classical Sociology* no. 5 (2005): 303–18.

28. Durkheim, *The Elementary Forms of the Religious Life*, 427–28.

29. Wilson, "Secularization," 19.

30. Ibid., 16.

31. David Martin, *On Secularization: Towards a General Revised General Theory* (Aldershot, England: Ashgate, 2007), 124.

32. Giselle Vincett, Sonya Sharma, and Kristin Aune, "Women, Religion and Secularization: One Size Does Not Fit All," in *Women and Religion in the West: Challenging Secularization*, ed. Giselle Vincett et al. (Aldershot, England: Ashgate), 1–19.

33. Wilson, "Secularization."

34. Phillip E. Hammond, "Introduction," in *The Sacred in a Secular Age*, 1.

35. Peter L. Berger, *The Sacred Canopy: Elements of a Sociological Theory of Religion* (Garden City, NY: Doubleday, 1967).

36. Berger, "The Desecularization of the World," 3.

37. Ibid., 11.

38. Peter Berger, "Postscript," in *Peter Berger and the Study of Religion*, ed. Linda Woodhead, Paul Heelas, and David Martin (London and New York: Routledge, 2001), 194.

39. Steve Bruce, "The Curious Case of the Unnecessary Recantation: Berger and Secularization," in *Peter Berger and the Study of Religion*, 87–100.

40. Ibid., 100.

41. Steve Bruce, *Secularization: In Defence of an Unfashionable Theory* (Oxford, England, and New York: Oxford University Press, 2011).

42. Bruce, "The Curious Case of the Unnecessary Recantation," 48.

43. Ibid., 201 (italics in the original).

44. Norris and Inglehart, *Sacred and Secular*.

45. Ibid., 25.

46. Bruce, *Secularization*.

47. Vincett, Sharma, and Aune, "Women, Religion and Secularization."

48. Danièle Hervieu-Léger, "Religion and Modernity in the French Context: For a New Approach to Secularization," *Sociological Analysis* 51 (1990): S15–S25.

49. Daniele Hervieu-Leger, *Religion as a Chain of Memory* (Cambridge, England: Polity Press, 2000).

50. Bryan S. Turner, *Religion and Modern Society: Citizenship, Secularization and the State* (Cambridge, England, and New York: Cambridge University Press, 2011).

51. Ibid., 150.

52. Martin, *On Secularization*.

53. Stephen Hunt, *Religion and Everyday Life* (London and New York: Routledge, 2005).

54. Jose Casanova, *Public Religions in the Modern World* (Chicago: University of Chicago Press, 1994); and Karel Dobbelaere, *Secularization: An Analysis at Three Levels* (Brussels, Belgium: P.I.E.—Peter Lang, 2002).

55. Martin, *On Secularization*; and Smith, *A Short History of Secularism*.

56. Hunt, *Religion and Everyday Life*.

57. Ibid.

58. Thomas Luckmann, *The Invisible Religion: The Problem of Religion in Modern Society* (New York: Macmillan, 1967); and Thomas Luckmann, "Shrinking Transcendence, Expanding Religion?" *Sociological Analysis* 51, no. 2 (1990): 127–38.

59. Jonathan Benthall, *Returning to Religion: Why a Secular Age Is Haunted by Faith* (London and New York: I.B. Tauris, 2010), 1.

60. Amarasingam, "Introduction."

61. Dobbelaere, *Secularization*.

62. Ibid., 192.

63. Casanova, *Public Religions in the Modern World*.

64. Casanova, "The Secular, Secularizations, Secularisms."

65. Martin, *On Secularization*.

66. Smith, *A Short History of Secularism*.

67. Ibid., 3.

68. Callum Brown, *The Death of Christian Britain: Understanding Secularisation 1800–2000* (London and New York: Routledge, 2002).

69. Davie, *The Sociology of Religion*, 51.

70. Brown, *The Death of Christian Britain*.

71. Peter Berger, Grace Davie, and Effie Fokas, *Religious America, Secular Europe? A Theme and Variations* (Aldershot, England: Ashgate, 2008).

72. Rodney Stark and Roger Finke, *Acts of Faith: Explaining the Human Side of Religion* (Berkeley: University of California Press, 2000).

73. Niels Bubandt and Martin van Beek, "Varieties of Secularism—in Asia and in Theory," in *Varieties of Secularism in Asia: Anthropological Explorations of Religion, Politics and the Spiritual*, ed. Niels Bubandt and Martin van Beek (London and New York: Routledge, 2012), 1–28.

74. Michael Herzfeld, "Secularity and Religiosity: Holy Spaces and the Battle for Administrative Control over Land in Bangkok," in *Varieties of Secularism in Asia*, 231–49.

75. Antonio F. Moreno, *Church, State, and Civil Society in Postauthoritarian Philippines: Narratives of Engaged Citizenship* (Quezon City, Philippines: Ateneo de Manila University Press, 2006).

76. "Singapore Ranked Third Most Globalized Economy," *Singapore Business Review*, February 8, 2012, http://sbr.com.sg/economy/news/singapore-ranked-third-most-globalized-economy.

77. Department of Statistics, *Census of Population 2010 Statistical Release 1: Demographic Characteristics, Education, Language and Religion* (Singapore: Ministry of Trade and Industry, 2011).

78. Eugene K. B. Tan, "Keeping God in Place: The Management of Religion in Singapore," in *Religious Diversity in Singapore* (Singapore: Institute of Southeast Asian Studies and the Institute of Policy Studies, 2008), 71.

79. Peter van der Veer, *Imperial Encounters: Religion and Modernity in India and Britain* (Princeton, NJ, and Oxford, England: Princeton University Press, 2001).

80. Edward Said, *Orientalism*, 25th anniversary ed. (New York: Vintage Books, 2003).

81. Bubandt and van Beek, "Varieties of Secularism."

82. Van der Veer, *Imperial Encounters*.

83. Casanova, "The Secular, Secularizations, Secularisms."

84. Talal Asad, *Genealogies of Religion: Discipline and Reasons of Power in Christianity and Islam* (Baltimore, MD: Johns Hopkins University Press, 1993).

85. Norris and Inglehart, *Sacred and Secular*.

86. Bruce, *Secularization*.

87. Casanova, "Rethinking Secularization," 103.

88. David Martin, *Pentecostalism: The World Their Parish* (Malden, MA, and Oxford, England: Blackwell Publishing, 2001).

89. Gabriele Marranci, *Understanding Muslim Identity: Rethinking Fundamentalism* (Basingstoke, England: Palgrave Macmillan, 2009).

90. Philip Jenkins, *The Next Christendom: The Coming of Global Christianity* (Oxford, England: Oxford University Press, 2002).

91. Khun Eng Kuah-Pearce, *State, Society, and Religious Engineering: Towards a Reformist Buddhism in Singapore*, 2nd ed. (Singapore: Institute of Southeast Asian Studies, 2003).

92. Robert W. Hefner, "Multiple Modernities: Christianity, Islam, and Hinduism in a Globalizing Age," *Annual Review of Anthropology* no. 27 (1998): 83–104.

93. Oliver Tschannen, "The Evolutionary. Principle in the Study of Religion and Society," in *Predicting Religion: Christian, Secular and Alternative Futures*, ed. Grace Davie, Paul Heelas, and Linda Woodhead (Aldershot, England: Ashgate), 41–50.

94. Jayeel Serrano Cornelio, "The New Face of Global Evangelism: Virtualizing Spiritual Experience," in *Mediating Piety: Technology and Religion in Contemporary Asia*, ed. Francis Khek Gee Lim (Leiden, Holland, and Boston, MA: Brill, 2009), 183–207.

95. Casanova, "Rethinking Secularization."

96. Roland Robertson, "Global Millenialism: A Postmortem on Secularization," in *Religion, Globalization and Culture*, 9–34.

97. Tun-jen Cheng and Deborah A. Brown, "Introduction: The Role of Religious Organizations in Asian Democratization," in *Religious Organizations and Democratization: Case Studies from Contemporary Asia*, ed. Tun-jen Cheng and Deborah A. Brown (Armonk, NY, and London: M.E. Sharpe, 2006), 3–40.

98. Linda Woodhead, Paul Heelas, and Grace Davie, "Introduction," in *Predicting Religion*, 1–14.

99. Demerath, III, "Secularization and Sacralization Deconstruction and Reconstructed," 69.

100. Linda Woodhead and Paul Heelas, *Religion in Modern Times: An Interpretive Anthology* (Malden, MA: Blackwell Publishers, 2000).

101. Martin, *On Secularization*.

102. Norris and Inglehart, *Sacred and Secular*.

103. Woodhead and Heelas, *Religion in Modern Times*.

104. Karin van Nieuwkerk, "Introduction: Gender and Conversion to Islam in the West," in *Women Embracing Islam*, ed. Karin van Nieuwkerk (Austin: University of Texas Press, 2006), 1–16.

105. Serrano Cornelio, "The New Face of Global Evangelism."

106. Casanova, *Public Religions in the Modern World*.

107. David Tombs, "The Church in a Latin American Perspective," in *The Routledge Companion to the Christian Church*, ed. Gerard Mannion and Lewis S. Mudge (Oxon, England, and New York: Routledge, 2008), 306–25.

108. Richard W. Flory and Donald E. Miller, *Finding Faith: The Spiritual Quest of the Post-Boomer Generation* (Brunswick, NJ: Rutgers University Press, 2008).

109. Woodhead and Heelas, *Religion in Modern Times*.

110. Ibid., 344.

111. John Hick, *The Metaphor of God Incarnate* (Louisville, KY, and London: Westminster John Knox Press, 2006).

112. Jayeel Serrano Cornelio, "New Paradigm Christianity and Commitment-Formation: The Case of Hope Filipino (Singapore)," in *Religion and the Individual: Belief, Practice, Identity*, ed. Abby Day (Aldershot, England: Ashgate, 2008), 65–77.

113. Donald E. Miller, *Reinventing American Protestantism: Christianity in the New Millennium* (Berkeley: University of California Press, 1997).

114. Joseph Nathan Cruz, "A Spectacle of Worship: Technology, Modernity and the Rise of the Christian Megachurch," in *Mediating Piety*, 113–38.

115. Ju Hui Judy Han, "The Urban Ecology of Religious Growth in Seoul: Megachurches, Microchurches, and the Politics of Scale," paper presented at the Doing Asian Cities: A Workshop on Urban aspirations, Singapore, June 5–6, 2012.

116. Paul Heelas and Linda Woodhead, *The Spiritual Revolution: Why Religion Is Giving Way to Spirituality* (Oxford, England: Blackwell, 2005).

117. Jayeel Serrano Cornelio, *Religious Identity and the Isolated Generation: What Being Catholic Means to Filipino Youth Today* (Quezon City, Philippines: Ateneo de Manila University Press, forthcoming).

118. Woodhead and Heelas, *Religion in Modern Times*, 386.

119. Berger, *The Sacred Canopy*.

120. Cathy Cantwell and Hiroko Kawanami, "Buddhism," in *Religions in the Modern World: Traditions and Transformations*, ed. Linda Woodhead, Hiroko Kawanami, and Christopher Partridge (London and New York: Routledge, 2009), 67–102.

121. Kuah-Pearce, *State, Society, and Religious Engineering*.

122. Nancy Ammerman, "Golden Rule Christianity: Lived Religion in the American Mainstream," in *Lived Religion in America: Toward a History of Practice*, ed. David D. Hall (Princeton, NJ: Princeton University Press, 1997), 196–216.

123. Benthall, *Returning to Religion*.

124. Ibid., 171.

125. Warner, *Secularization and Its Discontents*.

126. Wilson, *Religion in Sociological Perspective*.

127. Berger, Davie, and Fokas, *Religious America, Secular Europe?*

128. Tschannen, "The Evolutionary Principle in the Study of Religion and Society."

129. Woodhead and Heelas, *Religion in Modern Times*.

130. Tschannen, "The Evolutionary Principle in the Study of Religion and Society," 49.

131. Heelas and Woodhead, *The Spiritual Revolution*.

132. Robert Neelly Bellah et al., *Habits of the Heart: Individualism and Commitment in American Life* (Berkeley: University of California Press, 1985).

133. Serrano Cornelio, "The New Face of Global Evangelism."

134. Jayeel Serrano Cornelio, "Being Catholic as Reflexive Spirituality: The Case of Religiously Involved Filipino Students," *Asia Research Institute Working Paper Series* (2010).

135. Woodhead, Heelas, and Davie, "Introduction."

136. Norris and Inglehart, *Sacred and Secular*.

137. Bryan S. Turner, *Can We Live Forever? A Sociological and Moral Inquiry* (London and New York: Anthem Press, 2009).

138. Calhoun, Juergensmeyer, and van Antwerpen, "Introduction."

139. Casanova, "Rethinking Secularization."

FURTHER READINGS

Berger, Peter, ed. *The Desecularization of the World: Resurgent Religion and World Politics*. Washington, DC, and Grand Rapids, MI: Ethics and Public Policy Center and W.B. Eerdmans Pub. Co., 1999.

Bruce, Steve. *Secularization: In Defence of an Unfashionable Theory*. Oxford, England, and New York: Oxford University Press, 2011.

Davie, Grace. *The Sociology of Religion*, BSA New Horizons in Sociology. London: Sage, 2007.

Demerath, III, N. J. *Secularization and Sacralization Deconstructed and Reconstructed.* London and Thousand Oaks, CA: Sage, 2007.

Furseth, Inger, and Pal Repstad. *An Introduction to the Sociology of Religion*. Aldershot, England: Ashgate, 2007.

Hunt, Stephen. *Religion and Everyday Life*. London and New York: Routledge, 2005.

Norris, Pippa, and Ronald Inglehart. *Sacred and Secular: Religion and Politics Worldwide*. 2nd ed. Cambridge, England, and New York: Cambridge University Press, 2011.

Stark, Rodney, and Roger Finke. *Acts of Faith: Explaining the Human Side of Religion*. Berkeley: University of California Press, 2000.

Warner, Rob. *Secularization and Its Discontents*. London and New York: Continuum, 2010.

Woodhead, Linda, and Paul Heelas. *Religion in Modern Times: An Interpretive Anthology*. Malden, MA: Blackwell Publishers, 2000.

10

Christian and Hindu, Jewish and Buddhist: Can You Have a Multiple Religious Identity?

Rose Drew

INTRODUCTION

In the West, we tend think of religious identities as falling into clearly distinct, even contradictory, categories. One is a Christian *or* a Hindu, a Buddhist *or* a Jew. Yet greater knowledge of other religious traditions and growing interreligious interaction is increasingly yielding multiple religious identities that challenge this way of thinking. Take, for example, the declarations of well-known theologians Raimon Panikkar and Paul Knitter. Upon returning from India, Panikkar famously claimed that he had "left" as a Christian, "found" himself a Hindu, and "returned" a Buddhist, without having ceased to be a Christian.[1] And Knitter recently stated that, although still a Roman Catholic, he is now also "a card-carrying Buddhist."[2] What sense are we to make of such claims? Is it really possible to belong to more than one tradition, to be, say, a fully committed Christian *and* a fully committed Buddhist, or is partial belonging and commitment to a second tradition as much as can be justifiably claimed?

The phenomenon of multiple religious belonging has only in the last decade or so become a focus of sustained sociological and theological scrutiny. The questions it generates are proving controversial: does religious belonging imply a surrender of one's will and judgment that is incompatible with the exercise of personal choice implied by participating in more than one tradition? Can the belief systems of distinct traditions be reconciled sufficiently to allow simultaneous adherence to more than one? If religious commitment must in some sense be singular, does this rule out multiple belonging, or is religious commitment ultimately to something or someone beyond one's religious tradition or traditions? Do different religions have distinct goals and, if so, can those goals be pursued simultaneously? Does thoroughgoing religious commitment entail taking one's tradition to be superior to all others, and even if one thinks not, what if the authority within one's tradition disagrees? In this chapter, we will take a closer look at these questions and at the debates they generate.

But let us begin by getting the phenomenon of multiple religious belonging into clearer focus.

HISTORICAL BACKGROUND AND CONTEXT

When we look at both the historical record and contemporary religious trends, we find a range of different kinds and degrees of multiple religious participation in various contexts. We will take a look at a few of the most common contexts so as to begin to hone in on the phenomenon that will be our focus and to distinguish it from some of the more common, softer forms of multiple religious identity.

Cultural Identity and Particular Religious Functions

In contrast to the West, there are Asian societies in which multiple religious identities have long been the norm and more a matter of cultural identity than personal choice.[3] Being Chinese, for example, has tended to involve being shaped by Confucian, Daoist, and Buddhist ideas and practices. And Japanese identity has been similarly shaped by Buddhist, Shinto, Confucian, and sometimes Christian ideas and practices. In these contexts, different traditions are often seen as fulfilling distinct ritual functions, hence many Japanese, for example, visit Shinto shrines on auspicious occasions, Christian churches for weddings, and Buddhist temples for funerals. Thus, diversity constitutes a kind of unified system, in which each tradition has its allocated function.[4] Yet precisely because limited ritual function is assigned to each tradition, it is debatable whether we should think in terms of multiple belonging here. As Cornille points out, Buddhism, for example, is not merely about funeral rituals. Likewise, Christianity is not just about weddings. Hence, while religions may sometimes concede to fulfill a limited ritual function, "this always entails a certain degree of compromise, or in some cases a distortion of the tradition."[5]

Dual Religious Upbringing

Religiously mixed families present another context in which multiple religious participation occurs because children of parents who belong to different religious traditions may grow up participating in both. Some parents choose not to strongly promote either tradition but hope that children will, in time, make their own choices.[6] Others choose to raise their children predominantly within one or the other tradition. Children of a Christian mother and Sikh father might, for example, attend a church on a weekly basis and a gurdwara only on festival days. In other cases, children participate regularly in both traditions. Arwick and Nesbitt have carried out research on the religious formation of children in mixed-faith families. Although that research does not point to a typical profile, one recurring feature identified is the apparent ability of young people to retrieve different aspects of their identity depending on the context.[7] In this sense, their religious identities appear fluid, taking the form most appropriate to the situation. Over time, some children may come to identify more strongly with one tradition than the other, and others may reject both. But there may also be cases in which a strong and roughly equal sense of belonging to both traditions develops and endures, and participation in both continues. Such cases would be clear instances of multiple belonging.

Occasional Ritual Participation

One of the most prevalent forms of multiple religious participation found around the world is the occasional visiting of the temples, shrines, or saints of other religious traditions in response to particular needs, especially the need for physical healing. Examples include African converts to Christianity or Islam who seek the services of native religious healers and Japanese people from various religious traditions who participate in the healing rituals offered by new religious movements in Japan.[8] In such cases, identification with the religious tradition in question is limited in scope and apparently lasts no longer than the duration of the particular need with respect to which help is sought. Given this, it is not clear that this occasional participation should be viewed as multiple belonging. For as Cornille points out, these are not cases in which another religious tradition is embraced wholesale but rather cases of tapping the "services" of another tradition in times of crisis.[9]

Adoption of Particular Practices or Ideas

There are also cases in which individuals are immersed in and committed to one tradition but engage with a particular aspect of another tradition in a more sustained way rather than merely in response to occasional needs. Today it is not uncommon to come across, for example, Christians who practice yoga or Jews who practice a form of Buddhist meditation. There are also those who integrate certain beliefs from other traditions into their own belief system, such as Christians who believe in rebirth. In these cases, a certain aspect of another tradition is adopted, but there is no wholesale immersion in—or identification with—that tradition. So, again, it is not obvious that we should see this kind of selective engagement with another tradition as *belonging*. Or, at least, if we do, this belonging should be regarded as secondary or partial.

Contemporary Bricolage Religiosity

Cases in which individuals draw selectively on ideas and practices from a range of traditions without being immersed in or committed to *any* present us with yet another contemporary form of multiple religious participation, sometimes referred to as New Age or postsecular religiosity. Many in the West today are not satisfied with materialism, but neither are they satisfied with traditional religious institutions and authority structures. Hence, they choose to construct their own personal package of beliefs and practices on the basis of what they find meaningful and helpful.[10] This kind of bricolage —or patchwork—religiosity can be related to the modern "shift to the subject," a cultural shift, originating in the European Enlightenment, which has led to a suspicion of external authorities and an emphasis on the individual as the sole arbiter of truth and value and as the appropriate director and shaper of his or her life.[11] This emphasis on individual autonomy is combined, moreover, with today's increased awareness of religious diversity. Geffré links contemporary bricolage religiosity to the process of globalization and the emergence of a "supermarket of beliefs and practices," catering for the growing number of "consumers." He suggests that because many people "are no longer fixed to a normative tradition with regard to questions of truth and practice, they can accumulate practices derived from very different traditions without contradiction."[12] Rather than referring to such cases as instances of multiple belonging, both he and Cornille suggest, instead, the application of Davie's well-known phrase "believing without belonging."[13]

Inculturation and Interreligious Dialogue

One of the contexts in which the phenomenon of multiple religious belonging first came into focus within the Christian tradition was that of inculturation, such as, the attempt to make Christianity intelligible and relevant to new cultural contexts. For some Christians, this involved immersing themselves in the thought and practice of other religious traditions to better understand them. In the course of the twentieth century, this process began to occur systematically. Pioneers of this phase of Christian engagement included such figures as Jules Monchanin (1895–1957), Henri

Le Saux (Abhishiktananda) (1910–1973), Bede Griffiths (1906–1993), Hugo Enomiya-Lassalle (1898–1990), and Raimon Panikkar (1918–2010). For some of these pioneers, their immersion in Hindu or Buddhist thought and practice changed their own religious identities profoundly as they came, increasingly, to identify with the religious context in which they were immersing themselves.

Increasing interreligious interaction and growing openness toward other religious traditions means that, today, opportunities for personal interreligious encounters are more widely available. Such encounters take various forms from participation in formal or informal interreligious dialogue to studying another religious tradition in depth or living with another religious community and sharing in its observances. Some find that in the process of this encounter their identification with that other tradition becomes so strong that it is no longer perceived as "other" but becomes, instead, a second home. If a strong sense of belonging and commitment develops, unaccompanied by a corresponding weakening commitment to their original tradition, such individuals may feel unable to relinquish participation in either tradition, and so dual belonging emerges. To take some Buddhist Christian examples, Thompson writes: "I have come to a point in my life where I feel I owe both faiths a kind of unconditional allegiance ... without denying the real differences between them."[14,15] And King explains that she perceives profound truth in both Quaker Christianity and Buddhism and feels that she *needs* both, despite the fact that she does not see them as entirely reconcilable.[16]

KEY TERMS, PEOPLE, AND DEBATES

What we see from this brief survey is that there are various different types of multiple religious participation, leading to different kinds of multiple religious identity, but that not all cases seem to warrant the term *multiple belonging*. It is likely that in most cases of multiple religious participation one tradition remains dominant and another or others are drawn upon only selectively. One might, then, be said to belong fully to one's primary tradition and, at most, only in a partial or qualified way to another or others. And in cases in which individuals draw on beliefs and practices from a range of traditions without being firmly grounded in any, it is not clear that it makes sense to speak of belonging at all. In rare cases, however, participation in the thought and practice of more than one tradition (usually no more than two) appears to be thoroughgoing, and the traditions in question influence the thought and practice of the individual so profoundly that it is no longer clear which, if any, is dominant. It is here that terms such as *multiple belonging*—and, usually, *dual belonging*—are most aptly applied. Let us reserve these terms for cases in which there appears to be a deep and sustained immersion in the thought and practice of the traditions concerned and a strong identification with each of them. In the most unequivocal cases of dual belonging, individuals identify with both traditions, practice within two communities, and have made a formal commitment to both. By using the terms *multiple belonging* and *dual belonging* here, I do not mean to suggest at the outset that there are no problems with these categories. Rather I am simply using these terms to refer to people who practice within, and understand themselves as belonging to, two or more traditions. Whether or not that understanding can in the end be vindicated is precisely the question on which we will focus.

One of the most well-known cases of dual belonging is that of Christian Benedictine monk Henri Le Saux, or Swami Abhishiktananda, to use his Indian name. After travelling to India in 1948, Abhishiktananda immersed himself in Hindu thought and practice and, in so doing, came to identify strongly with the experience of nondualist Hinduism (*Advaita Vedanta*), where the true self of a being (its *atman*) is seen to be identical to the divine ground of all being (*Brahman*). Yet this did not lead to a renunciation of his Christian commitment, despite the acute tension he sometimes experienced between the two: "I cannot be at the same time Hindu and Christian, and I cannot either be simply Hindu or simply Christian," reads one of his diary entries.[17] Another, contemporary, example is provided by Habito, whose dual belonging is to Christianity and Buddhism. In accordance with new guidelines from the Second Vatican Council on the imperative of interreligious dialogue,[18] Habito (then a Jesuit priest) was sent on a mission to Japan in 1970 to study Buddhism. There, he took up Zen meditation and *koan* study[19] in the *Sanbo Kyodan* tradition, quickly becoming one of the first Roman Catholics to have what is called *kensho* (the initial awakening experience in Zen) confirmed by a Japanese master. For many years he continued to study and teach Buddhism, to practice meditation, and to study koans. Habito explains that through this immersion in the Buddhist tradition he came to an increasingly profound "understanding and appreciation of Buddhist perspectives on the world, on human existence, on spiritual practice."[20] He is no longer a priest, but today he remains a practicing Roman Catholic and is also the director of a Zen center in Dallas. He explains that he takes refuge in the Buddha, the *Dharma*, and the *Sangha*[21] and intends to live as a Buddhist "through and through." Yet he also continues to aspire to "live thoroughly in the Spirit of Christ Jesus" and to identify with all those who take Jesus as their model in life.[22]

Such cases make clear that we are not dealing here with the more superficial forms of multiple religious participation discussed in the fifth category earlier. Hence, multiple belonging escapes some of the complaints concerning "pick and mix" religiosity, including the criticism that people select from various traditions only the elements they *like*, ignoring the more demanding aspects of the traditions, and that extracting *any* elements from their traditional contexts drains those elements of their original meaning and value, yielding a superficial mixture of ideas and practices that bears limited resemblance to any of the traditions drawn upon. Bäumer, for example, criticizes approaches in which certain elements of a tradition are selected by individuals who do not understand the context that gives those elements meaning. She complains that most "imitations" of Eastern religious practices in the West lack the background against which those practices make sense.[23] Hinduism is not merely a way of meditation taken out of context, and Zen meditation not just a particular way of sitting, insists Bäumer; on the contrary, spiritual life is a totality.[24] She compares the common Christian approach to the integration of Eastern practices to "somebody wanting to bathe in a river without getting wet!"[25] Yet Bäumer recognizes that her criticism does not apply to multiple belongers, given their immersion in the traditions from which they derive nourishment. Indeed, she speaks favorably of dual belonging as an alternative approach: "One may sincerely and fully accept another spiritual tradition, without giving up one's own roots," contends Bäumer. "This vocation may be rare, and it is not easy, but it can be pioneering also for others."[26]

Similarly, Phan denounces what he sees as a postmodern form of syncretism in which various religions are looked upon as a "supermarket" or a "smorgasbord of . . . beliefs and practices."[27] Yet he too recognizes the possibility of deeper and more fruitful approaches that are based on firm rootedness in the home tradition, ongoing and serious engagement with the doctrines and practices of the other tradition, cognizance of the danger of facile syntheses of ideas and practices, and willingness to live with irresolvable tension.[28] Dual belongers such as Abhishiktananda and Habito appear to meet these criteria, showing great concern to protect the integrity of the traditions and to preserve the distinctiveness of each, even where this means living with tensions. Indeed, Abhishiktananda explicitly rejects what he calls "facile syncretism,"[29] and Habito is at pains to emphasize that he is not interested in creating "a hodgepodge of Christian elements and Buddhist elements" and is critical of approaches in which "people just take this or that from this or that other tradition and . . . build their own little supermarket kind of spirituality." He explains that he is concerned to protect the integrity of the traditions and, in this regard, emphasizes the necessity of *thoroughly* practicing a tradition rather than simply taking elements from it without an appreciation of their context.[30]

Yet, even if multiple belongers escape some of the criticisms that beset more superficial forms of multiple religious participation, it is precisely the *thoroughness* of their immersion in more than one tradition that makes the phenomenon so challenging and controversial. To begin to understand what is at stake, we must recognize that questions of religious identity have an objective as well as a subjective dimension. Authentic Christian identity, for example, requires more than simply identifying oneself as a Christian; one must additionally be recognized by others who belong.[31] And if one claims to be Christian *and* Buddhist, this claim must be tenable from Christian and Buddhist perspectives. *Selective* engagement with a second tradition can be easily dismissed from within that tradition as not amounting to belonging and fairly readily accepted from within the *primary* tradition (if there is one) as complementing rather than compromising identity. For example, when Jesuits such as Enomiya-Lassalle began practicing Zen meditation in Japan in the 1940s, eventual Vatican sanction of their practice *depended* on Zen being drawn on selectively; Zen was understood as a neutral practice technique, devoid of all doctrinal implications, and therefore unthreatening to Christian identity. Many Buddhists would question whether practicing Zen meditation with this attitude would amount to belonging to the Buddhist tradition, and many Christians see no threat in Christian participation in Zen meditation when understood in this way. More difficult to dismiss from a Buddhist perspective, and to accept from a Christian perspective, is the practice of those Christians who do *not* extract Zen meditation from its doctrinal context. Habito, for example, explains:

> . . .as I continued to study Buddhism and continued to appreciate the richness of this tradition, I realized that I cannot prescind from the Buddhist dimension or from the Buddhist fruits of *Zen* . . . I am now less inclined to just detach it from its Buddhist roots but precisely appreciate . . . the Buddhist background of *Zen* and I employ that also in my own verbal formulations of the *Zen* tradition; not prescinding from it but rather . . . enabling it to come into full play.[32]

It is this more thoroughgoing immersion in a second tradition that presents the greatest challenge to the traditions implicated.

Controversy centers on the question of whether it is possible to belong fully and equally to more than one tradition at the same time, or whether being religious is, to quote Griffiths, "a monogamous affair"—and so-called multiple belonging therefore is impossible, or at least undesirable.[33] Cornille has been the most vocal skeptic. She likens religious belonging to complete surrender to another person in marriage, insisting that most religious traditions regard "full and exclusive membership" as the ideal and generally conceive of religious belonging in terms of "an unreserved and undivided commitment."[34] As far as she is concerned, it is impossible to give this commitment to more than one tradition. It is at most possible to belong fully and authentically to one tradition and only partially to another, and such partial identification does not count as belonging.[35]

Let us look at a few of the arguments on each side of this exciting debate.

SURVEY OF ARGUMENTS

Religious Individualism

Although the thoroughgoingness of multiple religious belonging means it escapes some of the concerns surrounding "pick and mix" or "supermarket" spirituality, there is an aspect of this critique that may yet apply. For some worry that drawing on more than one tradition necessarily implies giving priority to one's own will and judgment and that this is at odds with the submission to a tradition that religious belonging requires. The criticism is that multiple belongers prioritize their own experience and preferences rather than surrendering to a tradition. The theologian Tanaka, for example, suggests that "multiple allegiances" become possible only when "the individual rather than the tradition becomes the primary standard for determining what is correct and important."[36] And Cornille argues that "simultaneous belonging to various religions implies a discriminating and self-sufficient subject that is precisely what needs to be left behind in the pursuit of the highest levels of spiritual and religious attainment."[37] As far as she is concerned, "multiple religious belonging bypasses the very purpose and dynamics of religious belonging," which should be "about the complete surrender of one's own will and judgment to a truth and power that lies beyond or beneath one's own rational and personal judgment."[38] She argues that most religious traditions emphasize the importance of total self-surrender, based on the common understanding that it is pride or the ego that presents the greatest obstacle to spiritual growth. It is, says Cornille, "[s]urrender to one particular teacher or teaching" that facilitates the necessary self-surrender.[39] Buddhist scholar Thurston, commenting on King's Quaker and Buddhist practice, makes similar objections. She points out that "tradition" comes from the Latin *traditio*, meaning "the action of handing over or surrendering."[40] "What pleases, assuages, comforts, or 'works for' me is manifestly not the point."[41] As far as she is concerned, there is insufficient evidence of this surrender in the lives of multiple belongers such as King.

Such criticisms tend to assume, first, that multiple belongers exercise a subjective choice that single belongers do not and, second, that exercising this choice runs against the grain of religious belonging. But is either of these assumptions correct? Arguably, exercising personal choice with respect to one's religious tradition is inevitable. For one thing, one has to decide to *which* truth and power to surrender: diversity both within religious traditions and among them makes choice inescapable, even if one does not choose consciously.[42] For another, if all knowledge of truth and power comes through the limited and fallible understanding of human beings, the exercise of personal judgment *remains* essential. Defending her approach to religion, King acknowledges her own fallibility and, therefore, the danger that exercising personal choice will lead her into error, but contends that there is no alternative available to her or anyone else.[43]

The theologian Schmidt-Leukel offers a more positive perspective on the multiple belongers' engagement with several traditions, linking it not to a refusal to commit but to a growth in spiritual maturity. He acknowledges that in Eastern traditions, especially, spiritual progress is frequently assumed to depend on submitting to the guidance of just one religious guru or master, but he asks: "is not the aim of every education, whether spiritual or ordinary, that the disciple shall eventually become a master and that the child shall not remain a child but reach its own maturity with the capacity of making its own decisions and choices and of listening, in the course of that process, quite deliberately and increasingly so to more than just one voice?"[44]

For Cornille, however, the question is not merely whether it is possible or desirable to learn from the wisdom of more than one tradition, but whether it is possible to fully submit to more than one tradition, or whether multiple belonging "always implies a certain holding back, an inability to fully accept some form of heteronomy."[45] She contends that multiple belongers grant themselves too much autonomy when it comes to deciding which elements of the traditions they are willing to embrace.[46] Simultaneous belonging to two or more traditions is made possible, thinks Cornille, only by withholding full commitment.[47] So-called multiple belonging, therefore, usually amounts to "a process of selective engagement with more than one religion in which one holds back from complete surrender to any," preventing one "from experiencing the fullness and depth of any particular teaching."[48]

One reason one might agree with Cornille's assessment is the problem of conflicting truth claims. So let us attend next to this most obvious potential obstacle to multiple belonging.

Doctrinal Tensions

If two sets of teachings are, in significant respects, incompatible, then Cornille would seem to be right when she says that, "ascendancy to the truth of one would necessarily exclude simultaneous belonging to the other."[49] What the tensions are—and how severe they are—will depend on the particular combination of traditions. But let us take the combination of Christianity and Buddhism as an example. If Christians believe in God and Buddhists do not, or if Christian teachings entail that the Buddha is inferior to Jesus Christ, which Buddhists clearly cannot accept, then complete fidelity to both traditions looks impossible. Such tensions may lead one to conclude that the very idea of being a fully committed Christian and a fully committed Buddhist is both logically and psychologically something of a nonstarter. Yet we do well to avoid hasty conclusions regarding questions of doctrinal compatibility. Searching interreligious dialogue frequently reveals levels of compatibility that are not immediately apparent. Religious traditions are, moreover, internally diverse: there are inconsistencies not only *between* but also *within* them. Crucially, each tradition contains numerous strands of thought about how various doctrines should be understood and interpreted. Hence, the extent of compatibility between Buddhist and Christian teachings very much depends on *which* strands of thought in each tradition are emphasized. To illustrate this, let us take the apparent conflict between Christian and Buddhist teachings over the question of God.[50]

As far as Cornille is concerned, "[i]f one religion affirms the existence of a personal God and another religion denies it, one cannot logically claim to equally belong to the two religious traditions at the same time."[51] But whether or not she is right will depend heavily on precisely how one understands the *nature* of God. And within the Christian tradition we find a range of possibilities. Christians who strongly affirm the mystery and transcendence of God (affirming that God is somehow beyond the universe as we know it and beyond all that we can think of or put into words) will have an easier time reconciling their theism with Buddhist teachings about the nature of ultimate reality than will Christians who think of God as "a being" who literally possesses all the classical attributes—omnipotence, omniscience, and so on (such a being would, from a Buddhist perspective, be just another being in need of liberation). There are traditional strands of theology that present God as a radically transcendent, ultimate reality that "surpasses every form that our intellect reaches," to quote Aquinas,[52] or strands in which "God" is a symbol that reminds us of the existence of that ultimate unspeakable mystery, as Rahner puts it.[53] Such conceptions of God contrast much less starkly with Buddhist conceptions of ultimate reality.

Indeed, similar Buddhist conceptions mean it is possible to see Buddhism and Christianity as concerned with one and the same ultimate reality, which is experienced and spoken of differently in each (as "God" in Christianity and as "nirvana" or "the dharmakaya" in Buddhism). This possibility has been famously argued for by Hick, among others, though not in connection with the question of multiple belonging.[54] In this context, the supposition that Buddhism and Christianity are concerned with one ultimate reality not only dissolves the appearance of a fundamental incompatibility between Christianity and Buddhism but also speaks to the concern expressed by Dupuis, when he asks:

> To what extent is it possible to make each of the two objects of faith one's own and to combine both at once in one's own religious life? Even apart from any

interior conflict that might arise in the individual, every religious faith constitutes an indivisible whole and calls for a total commitment of the person. It
may easily seem a priori impossible that such an absolute engagement might
be divided, as it were, between two objects.[55]

If both traditions are assumed to be concerned with one and the same transcendent, ultimate reality, then dual belonging need not be taken to require a
problematic division of absolute engagement between two distinct objects,
because the dual belonger has just one ultimate orientation. On this understanding, the singularity of wholehearted and unambiguous religious
commitment depends not on commitment to a single tradition but on
commitment to one ultimate reality; multiple belongers simply orient
themselves toward that reality *through* more than one tradition.

Cornille agrees that religious belonging involves "abandonment to a transcendent reality mediated through the concrete symbols and rituals of a particular religion." She insists, however, that surrender is "not to the ultimate
as such" but "through—and in the end—*to* the teachings and practices
embedded in a concrete religious tradition."[56] But should the teachings
and practices of a person's religious tradition be understood as the object
of their faith or as expressions of and means of fostering that faith?
Submission to ultimate reality is, indeed, mediated through particular concrete symbols and rituals. But one could argue that precisely because of their
symbolic nature, the teachings and rituals of a tradition direct that submission beyond themselves toward the reality they mediate. In this sense, then,
religious traditions are not ends in themselves. Cantwell Smith emphasizes
this point strongly and warns that we fall into idolatry when we make the
mistake of:

> ...identifying with the divine, with the truth, with the final, with transcen-
> dence, the particular form in or through which we have been introduced to
> it, by way of which It or He or She has come into our particular lives—rather
> than relating that form to It/Him/Her, subordinating it, relativising it in
> relation to the Absolute that it serves.[57]

This reflection throws the question of doctrinal tensions into a new
light. Are we right to assume that in order to belong thoroughly to two
traditions their teachings must be consistent in every regard? Provided
multiple belongers take both sets of teachings seriously and continue
to grapple with both, having mutually challenging perspectives might
actually help them to preserve the symbolic function of both. King's reflections appear to confirm this; "I do feel it's very useful to have two in order
to not slip into idolatry ... into thinking the words one was using ... were
really adequate," says King. She reflects that she has "one faith" in that which
is "before Buddhism and Christianity"; "I *most* identify with that,"

she explains. King does admit doctrinal tensions between the traditions to which she belongs, and at times these tensions are a source of spiritual struggle for her, but she does not experience them as amounting to a major division in her faith commitment because she sees both traditions as relative to the object of that commitment; "My basic commitment is to the place before there's a Buddhism and before there's a Christianity," says King, "that's my deep commitment and I *know* that neither Buddhism nor Christianity nor anything else is ever going to perfectly express that ultimate reality. So that's alright: if neither of them is going to perfectly express it, it doesn't really matter if they're not perfectly reconcilable." Buddhism and Christianity "just offer ... tools. They offer languages for me to try to speak."[58]

King is agnostic with respect to those Buddhist and Christian teachings which really seem to her to conflict—the question of rebirth, for example. She explains that she does not reject either the Buddhist teaching that we are reborn or the Christian teaching that we have just one earthly life, but keeps both in mind as possibilities and is constantly investigating both, a questioning attitude she takes to be sanctioned by both Buddhism and Quakerism. Cornille would no doubt argue that keeping teachings in mind only as possibilities amounts to holding back from complete commitment, but is it possible to take a more positive view of King's agnosticism with respect to certain issues? She explains that one of her most fundamental commitments is to be honest with herself about what she knows and what she does not know[59] and that due to this she would *anyway* reserve judgment about whether there is one life or many because this is something that cannot be resolved on the basis of her experience so far.[60] One could argue that this epistemic humility is precisely what needs to be developed within religious traditions if dogmatism is to be put aside and space made for mutual learning. Cornille herself argues that a degree of humility regarding one's own tradition's doctrines is a prerequisite for receptivity to the insights of others and that, without this humility, "there seems little prospect for mutual religious transformation and growth."[61] Such an acknowledgement surely offers grounds for a more positive reading of King's approach.

Whether or not one endorses this more favorable reading, however, one could argue that the pressing question when it comes to multiple belonging is not so much whether one can simultaneously assent to two sets of teachings at an intellectual level, nor whether reserving judgment with respect to some specific tensions between them is justifiable, but, rather, whether one person can live the life prescribed by those teachings. If different sets of teachings make mutually exclusive demands on adherents, then it will not be possible to meet the demands of both. Let us turn then to this more practical concern.

Mutually Exclusive Ways?

Even if one takes two traditions to be concerned in different ways with one ultimate reality, if those traditions orient adherents toward that reality in mutually exclusive ways, then belonging simultaneously to both would mean being pulled in different directions. Cornille thinks dual belonging does indeed involve being "divided and torn between religious traditions,"[62] and that the dual belonger's chances of attaining the spiritual objectives of either tradition are thereby jeopardized. As a Japanese proverb puts it: "He who chases two rabbits will catch neither." Single belonging is, thinks Cornille, "necessary to attain the highest religious or spiritual goals of a religion."[63] In the final analysis, the problem with multiple belonging is "not merely one of conflicting truth claims or theological incompatibility," she concludes, "but rather one of arrested spiritual development and growth."[64] One reason one might agree is if one thinks that different religious traditions orient their adherents toward different salvific or liberative ends. For this would imply that multiple belongers try, in vain, to follow distinct paths to distinct destinations.

The hypothesis that adherents of different traditions pursue different ends has been argued for by a number of contemporary thinkers, most notably Heim. Heim offers a theory of multiple religious ends that depends on the notion that ultimate reality is complex and, therefore, capable of supporting this diversity of ends. For example, Christians hope for communion with God, says Heim, and this end is attainable; Buddhists hope for nirvana, and this end is also attainable.[65] But, as *final states*, these goals "exclude each other."[66] One's religious thought and practice can condition one for the achievement of *one* of them, thinks Heim, but not *both*. In this sense, the logic of the faiths is radically disjunctive.[67] If Heim is right, then practicing within two traditions looks likely to hinder spiritual progress, as Cornille claims. As Bosworth Burch puts it, multiple religious belonging would lead to "religious frustration,"[68] for "a person can plant his two feet on two mountains only at the lowest point of the valley."[69]

Certainly there are tensions between the ways in which the ultimate goal of the spiritual life is characterized in different traditions. Christian and Muslim characterizations of heaven, for example, tend to assume that individual personhood is retained, as distinct from God and other persons, whereas Buddhist—and certain Hindu—characterizations of the "ultimate state" tend to assume that individual personal identity and interrelationships are transcended. But there are also similarities. Buddhist Christian dual belonger Habito reflects that attaining nirvana involves the "complete extinction of ignorance, hate, and greed," and that heaven is the "complete end to sin and complete happiness"; "[s]o how can we still qualify those states; if they are the same or if they are different?" asks Habito; "[t]hey're described differently but, to me, personally, they seem to point to the same reality."[70] Similarly, Habito insists that Buddhism and Christianity do not lead in "two different directions":

> Buddhists use the term "nirvana" and Christians use the term "heaven" but, if we get stuck on the conceptual imagery of these terms, then we will be limiting ourselves . . . [I]t's something that keeps pointing beyond . . . [I]t is . . . a way of expressing ultimate destiny.[71]

Perhaps it will turn out that the differences in Buddhist and Christian characterizations of ultimate destiny relate to real differences in the ends toward which these traditions orient people and that one of these ends will prove the lesser of the two. (Heim, for example, takes the Christian end to be the only genuinely salvific religious end, and Makransky takes the Buddhist end to be "uniquely liberating.")[72] Should this transpire, dual belongers may reach a point at which one of these traditions becomes the more adequate vehicle for facilitating further spiritual progress. But for as long as both traditions are experienced as beneficial and as orienting them in a single direction for the time being, what is to prevent dual belongers from committing fully to the practice of both in the here and now?

For Griffiths, this is not a rhetorical question. He is skeptical about whether one can practice two traditions adequately, arguing that religions bear the relation of "noncompossibility" to each other, prescribing courses of action that cannot be executed by one and the same person.[73] But whether or not this conclusion is justified very much depends on which combination of traditions one has in mind and what one takes the requirements of each to be. Corless, for example, while feeling it was performatively possible for him to practice in both the Roman Catholic and Tibetan Buddhist traditions, reflects that some combinations would present more of a challenge: "If one were to take something like orthodox Judaism and orthodox Hinduism, it would be more difficult, and I leave others to speak about that, but it seems one would have a difficulty in knowing what to eat in that situation."[74] If one cannot observe the demands of both traditions, then one's participation in one or both will necessarily be incomplete or piecemeal, and as Cornille contends, "such lukewarm participation is hardly the ideal of religious belonging."[75] But there might not be more viable combinations in which full participation is possible?

The testimony of Buddhist Christian dual belongers, for example, suggests that at a fundamental level the demands of these two traditions are existentially compatible, because both call for the replacement of egotistical, selfish ways of being with loving, wise, and compassionate ways of being. "[T]hey're not two different paths pulling away and tearing me apart," insists Habito, for example, but "[o]ne path, informed by those two traditions."[76]

This is not to say that dual belongers, such as Habito, do not admit differences in salvific or liberative emphasis. Buddhists take ignorance and attachment to lie at the root of our predicament, hence Buddhism's primary emphasis is on the development of wise nonattachment, whereas Christians take sin—or broken relationship with God and others—to be at the root of our troubles, hence Christianity's primary emphasis is on the development of love. These emphases might initially be thought to compete: how can one throw oneself fully into loving involvement with one's neighbors while at the same time remaining nonattached? Yet deeper interrogation reveals that from a Christian *and* a Buddhist perspective, both love *and* nonattachment are necessary, because nonattachment is what makes love undiscriminating and unconditional and love is what protects nonattachment from indifference. For this reason, a number of thinkers have argued that the salvific or liberative emphases of these two traditions are complementary.[77] Maintaining the creative tension between them can be a struggle for dual belongers.[78] But, far from constituting an obstacle to spiritual progress, this struggle is experienced as a catalyst for it. Habito, for example, reflects that although Buddhism and Christianity challenge each other, "in that mutual challenge, there's also a mutual enrichment and a mutual transformation." And King reflects similarly that the areas in which the traditions challenge each other are areas of growth for her.[79]

The Assumption of Superiority

Yet there is another potential obstacle to consider. For even if one takes the prescriptions of two traditions to be compatible and even complementary, one might still think being religious is a monogamous affair if one believes that belonging fully to a religious tradition requires taking that tradition to be uniquely superior to all others. Were this assumption correct, belonging fully to *two* traditions would be impossible. Cornille, for example, apparently equates fidelity to nonnegotiable convictions with the assumption that the truth of one's own tradition is superior to that of others[80] and argues that "[c]ommitment to the truth of one religion logically excludes recognition of the equal truth of others."[81] Hence, as far as she is concerned, the most that religious belonging allows is the affirmation of an *asymmetrical* complementarity between traditions. This asymmetry makes possible only a certain kind and degree of belonging to a second tradition, inasmuch as that tradition must be reinterpreted by the lights of the primary tradition.[82] This qualified appropriation of a second tradition would, of course, not be recognized as genuine belonging by the lights of the tradition concerned.

But can one really be a fully committed Christian only if one views Christianity as superior to Buddhism, and vice versa? If one's growing knowledge and experience of another tradition leads one to question this superiority, must this questioning be interpreted as a "loosening of commitment"[83] to one's home tradition or as being "torn between two traditions."[84] It surely must if the teachings of those traditions *entail* superiority. In the Christian case, for example, the superiority claim often arises from the belief that Jesus Christ is *uniquely* divine and that his death and resurrection *constitute* salvation. But what if one embraces interpretations of those teachings that do not entail superiority? There are contemporary Christologies that construe Jesus's divinity noncompetitively and his death and resurrection as *demonstrating* rather than *constituting* salvation. Haight's "Spirit Christology," for example, affirms Jesus as the Christ "in a way that does not construe Christianity as the one and only true faith and way of salvation uniquely superior to all others."[85]

The question is whether seeing Jesus as an embodiment of God and demonstrator of salvation is sufficient for Christian identity, or whether a further requirement is that one sees Jesus as the *only* embodiment and demonstrator. Cornille acknowledges that, through the process of dialogue, Christian self-understanding is informed and enhanced by the teachings of others[86] and that one may come to realize "that at least some of what was previously thought to be unique turns out to have any number of correlatives elsewhere." She even concedes that Christian belief in the uniqueness of Jesus can receive "new accents, connotations, and even full-fledged conceptions."[87] Yet she is apparently unwilling to accept any such development that results in a rejection of the claim to Christian superiority. Christian pluralists see things differently, however. They reject the notion that Christianity is superior to all other traditions but do not see this rejection as weakening Christian commitment. From their perspective, it is far from obvious that a construal of Jesus as "truly," but not "only," savior expresses a lack of strong convictions.[88] Hence, Knitter, for example, trusts that he can be a faithful follower of Jesus, even though he does not believe that Jesus is the "one and only" for all people.[89] But what if the *authority* within one's tradition disagrees? Knitter, as a Roman Catholic, provides a case in point. The Vatican has vigorously rejected any interpretations of Jesus's nature that undermine the Christian claim to superiority. So where does this leave Knitter's claim to belong?

This brings us to the more general question of where the authority to interpret doctrines and to decide who is "in" and who is "out" resides. Let us take a closer look at this issue, focusing on the Roman Catholic context.

The Question of Authority

One could easily argue as follows: in Roman Catholicism, it is up to the Vatican to make judgments about which theological interpretations are faithful to Christian revelation, and if one's own interpretations are at odds with the "official line," then one cannot claim to belong fully and authentically to the Roman Catholic tradition. There may, however, be good reasons to resist this line of reasoning.

First, studies show that the theological views of self-identified Catholics diverge in all sorts of ways from official teachings.[90] Therefore, to insist that belonging fully and authentically to the Roman Catholic tradition means endorsing every tenet of the Vatican's teachings is to render the self-understanding of self-identified Catholics irrelevant to the question of what faithfulness to the Roman Catholic tradition consists in. It is, moreover, to risk imposing a criterion that might very well rule out the *majority* of self-identified Catholics. We should also keep in mind that the "official line" has *changed* in various respects over the centuries. And while certain doctrines are unquestioned in one time and place, those same doctrines can be contested or forgotten in other times and places.[91] A more inductive approach, then, would suggest that what it is to belong fully and authentically to the Roman Catholic tradition is not a question that is ever answered definitively by the current Vatican. Rather the answer is negotiated and renegotiated in a continuous conversation between the Vatican and all those people who self-identify as Roman Catholic. Given that this conversation is always in progress, the boundaries of Catholic identity are always broader and fuzzier—hence, more accommodating of diversity—than the boundaries of orthodoxy inscribed in current Vatican pronouncements.

Second, if it is accepted that Christian revelation must be constantly interpreted afresh in light of new historical circumstances, then, paradoxically, a certain amount of *discontinuity* with tradition is in fact essential to the *continuity* of the tradition because the context in which doctrines must be interpreted is constantly changing.[92] In this sense, then, faithfulness to a tradition may be more a matter of protecting its dynamic ability to integrate new insights than of preserving its current stage, like a snapshot. Regarded from this perspective, the emergence of doctrinal interpretations that diverge from the official "party line" can be seen as an indicator of a healthy, dynamic tradition striving to refresh its witness to truth for a new generation. Increased knowledge of and interaction with other religious traditions present every tradition with one of the greatest challenges and opportunities of our day. And, in response to dialogue with—and growing understanding of—religious others, many Christians have come to feel that a rethinking of certain aspects of the Christian tradition are in order and that at this point in the church's history, there are elements of its heritage of which, in faithfulness to Christian revelation, it is time to let go.

As far as Knitter is concerned, the superiority claim is an aspect of the church's theological baggage of which we should now dispose.[93] He explains that a central concern for himself, as a "Buddhist Christian," is that the "theological genes" he is passing on are still Christian. He believes that his reinterpretation of Christian belief, "though really different, is not *totally* different from what went before" and that he is "creating something new that is rooted in and nourished by the old."[94] He states that he is looking for the validation of his Christian community and hopes that his "hybrid identity" places him not on the "outer edge" of that community but on the "*cutting edge*"—on an "edge" that "is leading to what some call 'a new way of being church'—a church that lives and finds life through dialogue."[95] What will eventually receive validation cannot easily be judged at the moment in history at which a change is taking place, but insofar as dual belongers are contributing to Christian explorations of ways of rearticulating Christian revelation in light of the insights of others, they can be seen as helping to foster any transformations that prove necessary.

CONCLUSION

We began by distinguishing multiple religious belonging from some of the more common, softer forms of multiple religious identity. Borrowing certain ideas and practices from another tradition does not amount to multiple belonging, nor does occasional participation in another tradition in response to particular needs. Multiple belonging also differs from contemporary bricolage religiosity in which there is no rootedness in any tradition. Skeptics such as Cornille, although recognizing this more thoroughgoing form of multiple religious identity, doubt whether complete and undivided commitment to more than one tradition is possible. Cornille questions the coherence of the category "multiple belonging," arguing that the supposition of its possibility is based on a subjective conception of religious belonging that clashes with the objective conception implicit in the self-understandings of the religions in question.[96] Yet our investigation suggests that things may not be so straightforward, for it is not as if any tradition exhibits a single self-understanding, speaking with one voice on the questions most pertinent to this issue. Rather each contains a multitude of perspectives, some of which are more hospitable to recognition of multiple belonging than others. There is, of course, much more to be said on both sides of the debate. But we have at least glimpsed some key skeptical concerns and some possible responses that cast this phenomenon in a more favorable light.

To summarize, it is true that multiple belongers exercise personal choice, but this does not distinguish them from single belongers. Moreover, their engagement with more than one tradition could be an indicator of a mature spirituality rather than a juvenile promiscuity. Doctrinal tensions between traditions do exist, even if these are not always as severe as they first appear. Multiple belongers must, therefore, be prepared to live with tensions if they are to avoid distorting the traditions by interpreting one in light of the other or creating a new religion out of elements selected from each. How severe these tensions are will depend on the combination of traditions and on how particular doctrines are interpreted. Yet if religious teachings are thought to be relative to an ultimate reality beyond them, then even significant tensions can be viewed positively as reminders of the inadequacy of all verbal formulations. Reservation of judgment on points of conflict might also foster the kind of doctrinal humility that needs to be developed in religious traditions if they are to be open to the insights of others. Multiple belonging does not necessarily involve being torn in different directions by one's religious commitments, for there are combinations of traditions that do not appear to make mutually exclusive demands on adherents, and which are even complementary. Some rule out the possibility of authentic multiple belonging because they assume that belonging fully to a tradition requires taking it to be superior to all others. Yet there are also those who do not consider the assumption of superiority to be an essential aspect of religious identity and who interpret traditional doctrines in a way that does not entail this superiority. These interpretations may not always reflect official teaching, but we should pause before dismissing claims to belong on this basis, not least because traditions are constantly in flux and must be so if their witness to truth is to remain constant in a changing world.

Although softer forms of multiple religious identity are likely to become increasingly common, multiple religious belonging seems too spiritually, intellectually, and practically demanding a vocation to ever become widespread. Yet the phenomenon may, nevertheless, have positive effects on the traditions beyond the impact on the individuals concerned. Multiple belongers serve as mediators between communities, encouraging mutual openness and understanding. And inasmuch as interreligious dialogue is internal to their own spirituality, they embody both its fruits (in their integrated comparative understandings and cross-fertilizing practice) and its remaining disagreements and questions (in their agnosticism on certain issues and their experience of tension and ongoing internal debate). Their religious lives and reflections may, therefore, point toward—and help foster—some of the theological and practical transformations that interreligious encounter will yield, as each tradition uncovers forgotten strands and assimilates beneficial new insights and practices. If this is so, the presence of multiple belongers, rather than weakening religious traditions, may instead help strengthen and preserve them.

GLOSSARY

Bricolage religiosity: drawing selectively on a range of religious traditions to construct a personal package of beliefs and practices.

Christology: theological reflection on the person of Jesus Christ.

Inculturation: the attempt to make Christianity intelligible and relevant in new cultural contexts by allowing those contexts to influence the presentation and interpretation of Christian teachings.

Koans: riddles and paradoxes passed from Zen master to student which admit no conceptual solution but invite the student to a direct awareness of ultimate truth.

Multireligious identity: a religious identity formed under the influence of more than one religious tradition.

Pick and mix spirituality: a superficial form of multiple religious participation in which individuals select elements from different religious traditions solely on the basis of what appeals to them while ignoring the fuller contexts that give those elements their meaning.

Quakers: Quakers, or Friends, belong to a family of Protestant Christian movements known collectively as the Religious Society of Friends. A key doctrine to which Quakers adhere is the priesthood of all believers.

Religious individualism: a stance that emphasizes the value of the individual's experience, goals, and choices and opposes submission to any external religious authority.

Supermarket spirituality: an approach to spirituality in which religious traditions are treated like a supermarket from which individual elements can be selected on the basis of personal tastes and preferences. See also "pick and mix spirituality."

NOTES

1. Raimon Panikkar, *The Intra-Religious Dialogue*, rev. ed. (New York: Paulist Press, 1999), 42.

2. Paul F. Knitter, *Without Buddha I Could Not Be a Christian* (Oxford, England: Oneworld Publications, 2009), 216.

3. See Catherine Cornille, "Multiple Religious Belonging and Christian Identity," *The Santa Clara Lecture* (2011): 2–3 (text kindly provided by the author).

4. See Jan Van Bragt, "Multiple Religious Belonging of the Japanese People," in *Many Mansions? Multiple Religious Belonging and Christian Identity*, ed. Catherine Cornille (New York: Orbis, 2002), 7–19.

5. Cornille, *Many Mansions?* 17.

6. This was true of most of the parents in Arweck and Nesbitt's study. See Elisabeth Arweck and Eleanor Nesbitt, "Close Encounters? The Intersection of Faith and Ethnicity in Mixed-Faith Families," *Journal of Beliefs & Values* 31, no. 1 (2010): 39–52, http://wrap.warwick.ac.uk/3295/1/WRAP_Arweck_Close_Encounters.pdf.

7. Ibid., 12–13.

8. See Cornille, "Multiple Religious Belonging and Christian Identity," 3–4. For further examples, see Selva Raj and Corinne Dempsey, *Popular Christianity in India: Writing Between the Lines* (Albany: SUNY Press, 2002).

9. Cornille, "Multiple Religious Belonging and Christian Identity," 4.

10. See Kajsa Ahlstrand, "Boundaries of Religious Identity: Baptised Buddhists in Enköping," in *Converging Ways? Conversion and Belonging in Buddhism and Christianity*, ed. John D'Arcy May (Klosterverlag Sankt Ottilien, Germany: EOS, 2007), 155–64. See also Paul Heelas and Linda Woodhead, *The Spiritual Revolution: Why Religion Is Giving Way to Spirituality* (Oxford, England: Blackwell, 2005).

11. See Charles Taylor, *Varieties of Religion Today: William James Revisited* (Cambridge, MA: Harvard University Press, 2002), 101; and Heelas and Woodhead, *The Spiritual Revolution*, 4, 126.

12. Claude Geffré, "Double Belonging and the Originality of Christianity as a Religion," in *Many Mansions?* 94.

13. Ibid.; and Cornille, "Multiple Religious Belonging and Christian Identity," 4.

14. Ross Thompson, *Buddhist Christianity: A Passionate Openness* (Winchester, England, and Washington, DC: O Books, 2010), 4.

15. John Malcomson, "Not One, Not Two: Being a Christian Buddhist (Part 1)," See Rose Drew, *Buddhist and Christian? An Exploration of Dual Belonging* (London and New York: Routledge, 2011), 33–34.

16. Sallie B. King, "The Mommy and the Yogi," in *Beside Still Waters: Jews, Christians, and the Way of the Buddha*, ed. Harold Kasimow, John P. Keenan, and Linda Klepinger Keenan (Boston, MA: Wisdom, 2003), 170. The Quakers ("The Religious Society of Friends") are a branch of Protestant Christianity. Not all Quakers understand themselves as Christians, though King does. See Rose Drew, *Buddhist and Christian? An Exploration of Dual Belonging* (London and New York: Routledge, 2011), 33–34.

17. Abhishiktananda, *Ascent to the Depth of the Heart: The Spiritual Diary (1948–73) of Swami Abhishiktananda (dom Henri Le Saux)* (Delhi: ISPCK, 1998), 19.

18. The Second Vatican Council (1962-1965) concerned the relationship between the Roman Catholic Church and the modern world. Among the changes brought about by Vatican II was a new openness to the good, the true, and holy in other religious traditions.

19. Koans are riddles and paradoxes passed from master to student which admit no conceptual solution but invite the student to a direct awareness of "ultimate truth."

20. Ruben L. F. Habito, "Being Buddhist, Being Christian: Being Both, Being Neither," in *Converging Ways?*, 168.

21. Taking refuge in the "three jewels" (the Buddha, the Dharma, and the Sangha) is traditionally what defines one as a Buddhist. The Buddha is the teacher of the Dharma (the truth about the way things are as well as how to act in accordance with this truth) and the community of accomplished disciples established by him is known as the Sangha.

22. Habito, "Being Buddhist, Being Christian," 178–79.

23. Bettina Bäumer, "A Journey with the Unknown," in *Spirituality in Interfaith Dialogue*, ed. Tosh Arai and Wesley Ariarajah (Geneva: WCC Publications, 1989), 40.

24. Ibid., 38.

25. Ibid., 37.

26. Ibid., 41.

27. Peter C. Phan, *Being Religious Interreligiously: Asian Perspectives on Interfaith Dialogue* (New York: Orbis, 2004), 62, and "Religious Identity and Belonging Amidst Diversity and Pluralism: Challenges and Opportunities for Church and Theology," in *Passing on the Faith: Transforming Traditions for the Next Generation of Jews, Christians, and Muslims*, ed. James L. Heft (New York: Fordham University Press, 2006), 181. See also Geffré, "Double Belonging," 94.

28. Phan, "Religious Identity and Belonging Amidst Diversity and Pluralism," 181–82. See also Peter C. Phan, "Multiple Religious Belonging: Opportunities and Challenges for Theology and Church," *Theological Studies* 64 (2003): 495–519.

29. Abhishiktananda, *The Further Shore: Two Essays by Abhishiktananda* (Delhi: ISPCK, 1975), 25.

30. See Drew, *Buddhist and Christian?* 198–200.

31. See Raimon Panikkar, "On Christian Identity: Who Is a Christian?" in *Many Mansions?* 123.

32. See Drew, *Buddhist and Christian?* 181–82.

33. Paul Griffiths, *Problems of Religious Diversity* (Oxford, England: Blackwell, 2001), 35.

34. Catherine Cornille, "Double Religious Belonging: Aspects and Questions," *Buddhist-Christian Studies* 23 (2003): 48; and Cornille, *Many Mansions?* 10–11.

35. Ibid., 18.

36. Kenneth K. Tanaka, "The Individual in Relation to the Sangha in American Buddhism: An Examination of 'Privatized Religion,'" *Buddhist-Christian Studies* 27 (2007): 125.

37. Catherine Cornille, "Introduction: The Dynamics of Multiple Belonging," in *Many Mansions? Multiple Religious Belonging and Christian Identity*, ed. Catherine Cornille (Maryknoll, NY: Orbis, 2002), 3.

38. Cornille, "Double Religious Belonging," 48.

39. Cornille, *Many Mansions?* 14.

40. Bonnie Thurston, "A Christian Response to Joint Buddhist-Christian Practice," *Buddhist-Christian Studies* 14 (1994): 179.

41. Ibid.

42. See Sallie B. King, "On Pleasure, Choice, and Authority: Thoughts in Process," *Buddhist-Christian Studies* 14 (1994): 190–91.

43. Ibid., 192.

44. Perry Schmidt-Leukel, *Transformation by Integration* (London: SCM Press, 2009), 53.

45. Cornille, "Double Religious Belonging," 49.

46. Cornille, "The Dynamics of Multiple Belonging," 3.

47. Cornille, *Many Mansions?* 17.

48. Ibid., 14–15.

49. Ibid., 12.

50. For a detailed discussion of this doctrinal tension and its bearing on the question of dual belonging, see Drew, *Buddhist and Christian?* 41–85.

51. Cornille, *Many Mansions?* 12.

52. *Summa contra Gentiles* I:14, in Saint Thomas Aquinas, *On the Truth of the Catholic Faith: Summa contra Gentiles, Book One: God*, trans. Anton C. Pegis (New York: Image Books 1961 [1955]), 96.

53. Karl Rahner, *Foundations of Christian Faith: An Introduction to the Idea of Christianity*, trans. W. V. Dych (London: Darton, Longman and Todd, 1978), 21.

54. See John Hick, *An Interpretation of Religion: Human Responses to the Transcendent* (New Haven, CT: Yale University Press, 2005 [Macmillan, 1989]).

55. Jacques Dupuis, "Christianity and Religions: Complementarity and Convergence," in *Many Mansions?* 64.

56. Cornille, "Double Religious Belonging," 44 (my italics).

57. Wilfred Cantwell Smith, "Idolatry in Comparative Perspective," in *The Myth of Christian Uniqueness*, ed. John Hick and Paul Knitter (New York: Orbis, 1987), 59.

58. Interview with King, quoted in Drew, *Buddhist and Christian?* 211, 208.

59. Ibid., 132.

60. Ibid., 154.

61. Catherine Cornille, *TheIm-Possibility of Interreligious Dialogue* (New York: Herder & Herder, 2008), 11.

62. Cornille, "Multiple Religious Belonging and Christian Identity," 11; and Cornille, *Many Mansions?* 18.

63. Cornille, *Many Mansions?* 14–15.

64. Ibid., 14.

65. S. Mark Heim, *Salvations: Truth and Difference in Religion* (Maryknoll, NY: Orbis Books, 1995), 151–52.

66. S. Mark Heim, *The Depth of the Riches: A Trinitarian Theology of Religious Ends* (Grand Rapids, MI, and Cambridge, England: William B. Eerdmans Publishing Company, 2001), 288.

67. Heim, *Salvations*, 169.

68. George Bosworth Burch, *Alternative Goals in Religion* (Montreal, Canada: McGill Queen's University Press, 1972), 102.

69. Ibid., 111.

70. Interview with Maria Reis Habito, quoted in Drew, *Buddhist and Christian?* 129.

71. Interview with Habito, quoted in ibid.

72. See, for example, S. Mark Heim, "The Depth of the Riches: Trinity and Religious Ends," *Modern Theology* 17, no. 1 (2001): 31; Heim, *Salvations*, 163, 165; J. Makransky, "Buddha and Christ as Mediators of the Transcendent: A Buddhist Perspective," in *Buddhism and Christianity in Dialogue*, The Gerald Weisfeld Lectures 2004, ed. Perry Schmidt-Leukel (London: SCM Press, 2005), 191–92; and J. Makransky, "Buddhist Perspectives on Truth in Other Religions: Past and Present," *Theological Studies* 64, no. 2 (2003): 358–59.

73. Griffiths, *Problems*, 34–35.

74. Roger J. Corless, *Profiles in Buddhist-Christian Dialogue: Roger Corless* (1996), accessed July 2012, http://innerexplorations.com/catew/9.htm.

75. Cornille, "Multiple Religious Belonging and Christian Identity," 9.

76. Interview with Habito, quoted in Drew, *Buddhist and Christian?* 161.

77. Aloysius Pieris, for example, argues that "[i]t is the dialectical interplay of wisdom and love that ensures a progressive movement in the realm of the human spirit" and that these are "complementary idioms that need each other to mediate the self-transcending experience called "salvation." See A. Pieris, *Love Meets Wisdom: A Christian Experience of Buddhism* (New Delhi, India: Intercultural Publications, 1988), 9–10, 111.

78. See Drew, *Buddhist and Christian?* 141–45.

79. Interview with Habito, quoted in ibid., 161; and interview with King, cited in ibid., 221.

80. See, for example, Cornille, *TheIm-Possibility*, 89.

81. Ibid., 84, 88.

82. See ibid., 87; and Cornille, *Many Mansions?* 13.

83. Cornille, *TheIm-Possibility*, 61.

84. Cornille, *Many Mansions?* 18.

85. Roger Haight, "Pluralist Christology as Orthodox," in *The Myth of Religious Superiority: A Multifaith Exploration*, ed. P. Knitter (New York: Orbis Books, 2005), 151.

86. Cornille, *TheIm-Possibility*, 205–206.

87. Ibid., 206.

88. P. Knitter, *Jesus and the Other Names* (Maryknoll, NY: Orbis, 1996), 72–73.

89. G. D'Costa, P. Knitter, and D. Strange, *Only One Way? Three Christian Responses on the Uniqueness of Christ in a Religiously Plural World* (London: SCM, 2011), 211.

90. A case in point is the attitude of American Catholics to official superiority claims. In a recent survey, only 18 percent of the American Catholics surveyed strongly agreed that "Catholicism contains a greater share of truth than other religions." See Paul Lakeland, *Church: Living Communion (Engaging Theology: Catholic Perspectives)* (Collegeville, MN: Liturgical Press, 2009), 136.

91. See Panikkar, "On Christian Identity," 123.

92. Haight argues this case persuasively. See Roger Haight, *Dynamics of Theology* (New York: Paulist Press, 1990), 223–25.

93. "While we have to be aware that we bring our theological baggage to the journey of dialogue," writes Knitter, "that doesn't mean that during the journey we may not have to rearrange, or even dispose of, some of that baggage." See P. Knitter, *Introducing Theologies of Religions* (Maryknoll, NY: Orbis, 2002), 236.

94. Knitter, *Without Buddha*, xiv.

95. Ibid., 216–17.

96. Cornille, "The Dynamics of Multiple Belonging," 4; and Cornille, *Many Mansions?* 16–18.

FURTHER READINGS

Cornille, Catherine, ed. *Many Mansions? Multiple Religious Belonging and Christian Identity*. New York: Orbis, 2002.

D'Arcy May, John, ed. *Converging Ways? Conversion and Belonging in Buddhism and Christianity*. Klosterverlag Sankt Ottilien, Germany: EOS, 2007.

Drew, Rose. *Buddhist and Christian? An Exploration of Dual Belonging*. London and New York: Routledge, 2011.

Goosen, Gideon. *Hyphenated Christians: Towards a Better Understanding of Dual Religious Belonging*. Bern, Germany: Peter Lang, 2011.

Kasimow, H., J. P. Keenan, and L. Keenan Klepinger Keenan, eds. *Beside Still Waters: Jews, Christians, and the Way of the Buddha*. Boston, MA: Wisdom, 2003.

Knitter, Paul F. *Without Buddha I Could Not Be a Christian*. Oxford, England: Oneworld, 2009.

Scheuer, J., and D. Gira, eds. *Vivre de Plusieurs Religions: Promesseou Illusion?* Paris: Les Éditions de l'Atelier/Les Éditions Ouvrières, 2000.

Schmidt-Leukel, Perry. *Transformation by Integration*. London: SCM Press, 2009.

11

Empires and Religions: Colonialism, Postcolonialism, and Orientalism

Clinton Bennett

INTRODUCTION

This chapter argues that while religious studies self-consciously attempts to correct past misinterpretation, distancing itself from earlier attitudes and assumptions, it remains focused on European, and North American, perspectives. Religious studies is taken to be the multidisciplinary, neutral academic inquiry, research, and teaching about religion and religious phenomena in public higher education from the late 1960s (see Volume 1, Chapter 2). Attempting to present plural perspectives, religious studies also claims to give credence to believers' views. Beginning with relevant terms, namely *imperialism, colonialism, postcolonialism, neocolonialism,* and *Orientalism,* this chapter identifies important people, events, and debates. It suggests five features that are characteristic of much Western writing about Others. Two interlinked studies, the contributions of William Jones (1746–1794) and Ernest Renan (1823–1892), provide in-depth analyses of European constructions of Hinduism and Islam. The first study has important background for the second, on the Indo-Aryan concept. The conclusion indicates several future directions and unresolved issues, including public and popular caricatures of religions and their followers who contribute to clash-of-civilizations phobia, to distrust of religious minorities, and even to policy making in some areas, such as immigration and security. It also proposes five possible correctives against bias and misrepresentation.

BACKGROUND, TERMS, PEOPLE, AND DEBATES

Imperialism

Imperial power over subject people creates polarities. Those who exercise power govern the lives of Others, who are usually racially, culturally, and religiously different. Inequality, an "us–them" dichotomy, and ideas about "our" superiority and "their" inferiority inevitably follow the fact of political subordination. It is important to note that histories of political subjugation of other peoples, accompanied or driven in part by religious bigotry, are not the legacy only of the Western world but also, for instance, of Islam. This poses a challenge to the discipline of religious studies, which, on the one hand, wants to avoid contributing to Islamophobia but, on the other hand, needs to take a critical view of religious practices, including fanaticism and religious oppression. Psychological processes work to produce juxtapositions. Others are effectively dehumanized, sometimes demonized. Psychologically, there is probably a human tendency toward justifying colonial power. Imperial powers often represent themselves as occupying moral high ground by civilizing, mentoring, or even enabling subject people to fulfill their supposed natural, innate servitude, vide Aristotle: "The lower sort are by nature slaves, and it is better for them as for all inferiors that they should be under the rule of a master."[1]

Empires can be defined as political systems governing territory or colonies stretching beyond the metropole, whose peoples have limited rights and little or no participation in governance. Metropole, from "mother city" refers to a colonizer's original state. A detailed analysis of imperialism lies beyond this chapter's remit. Empires have risen, declined, and fallen throughout recorded human history. Historians try to understand this dynamic. Empires often begin when an emerging commercial power defends or protects its interests, although sometimes an ambitious leader decides to conquer the world, or as much territory as possible. Conquest is often represented as part of a civilizing mission—which applies to such projects as Alexander the Great's, Rome's, and, if not initially, at least by the nineteenth century, modern European empires. European powers modeled themselves on Rome's idea of a "civilizing mission."[2] Rome's task, according to Virgil, was to spare the meek, humble the haughty, and bring peace and law to conquered spaces:

> You Roman, remember to govern
> The peoples with power (these arts shall be yours), to establish
> The practice of peace, spare the conquered, and beat down the haughty.[3]

Racist assumptions of superiority over subject people is not new; depending on who held power in ancient Egypt, those with darker or lighter skins were seen as evil and degraded.[4] The Greeks, Chinese, and Japanese were all "civilized," whereas others were "barbarian." Greece's mission was to civilize Iran, which was seen as badly governed and immoral. This dichotomy helped polarize the West (Occident) and the East (Orient). The idea of a Western self opposed by Eastern Others, whose influence had to be resisted, appears in Herodotus (d. 425 BCE), Thucydides (d. 395 BCE), and Xenephone (d. 354 BCE); Plato, though, rejected as absurd any division of the world into Greeks and barbarians,[5] even suggesting that Persians may be culturally superior to Greeks.[6] This ancient making other of the East, despite Plato, continued.

After the rise of Islam, Europe saw itself as irreconcilably different from the Muslim-majority world, which it perceived as a threat. There may not be a "straight line" between ancient Greek attitudes and contemporary assumptions of East–West difference, but "classical Greek affirmations of a political contrast to the East" can be seen as a prototype of "later trends."[7] More recently, Rudyard Kipling (1865–1936), whose poetry expressed Britain's imperial ideals, put it that "east is east, and west is west, and never the twain shall meet."[8] He also famously expressed the notion of a civilizing mission; "take up the White Man's burden, send forth the best ye breed, go bind your sons to exile, to serve your captives need."[9] Kipling's attitude toward Indians is more complex than this popular line conveys; he admired the so-called military races (Pathans, Sikhs, Rajputs) but despised Bengalis as "effeminate and cunning . . . only fit to be lower grade clerks."[10] Imperialists invariably devalue almost everything encountered in their colonies: indigenous peoples' intellectual abilities, moral characters, values, art, languages, cultures, and religions. Minorities in the metropole may also develop such notions—for example, concepts of black power and supremacy in the United States. Earlier, colonized people may have had colonies too. Empires are frequently governed by absolute rulers, although metropoles may be democratic and republican. Empires may provide pathways to citizenship, seeing the acculturated and assimilated among subject peoples as equal or nearly equal. France, at times a republic during its imperial period, went further than many in granting rights, although early attitudes about equality and "universal citizenship" gave way to ideas about "separation" or "association" (rather than "assimilation"). How genuine affirmations of universal equality and rights were is subject to debate; they may have been sincere or never anything more than imperial apologetic, a way to justify imperialism to themselves and to subject peoples.

Colonialism

Colonialism and imperialism are more or less synonymous, although a colony is always occupied, while imperialism may work without occupation; thus, colonialism may be considered a special form of imperialism. A colony is usually defined as territory governed by an imperial or colonial power. The term is from the Latin *colonia*. Many ancient colonies were founded as trading or agricultural outposts (*colonus* means farmer). This pattern repeated itself when commercial companies such as the British East India Company (founded 1600), the Dutch East India Company (founded 1602), and the Imperial British East Africa Company (formed 1885) established settlements and concessions that later morphed into larger imperial possessions. However, imperial power can also extend over legally sovereign territory. Such power is called hegemony; for example, Britain and Russia more or less ruled Iran in the early twentieth century, yet Iran was never colonized. Foreign powers, including the United States, exercised hegemony over China from 1842 through the Nanjing Treaty: Britain gained Hong Kong; China had to pay punitive reparations for trying to end the opium trade. European powers exercised control of Ottoman finances from 1878 and ran many utilities, as in Iran. From 1500, when France obtained the first "capitulation," European powers enjoyed near sovereignty over trading posts in Ottoman space. The controversial term *American imperialism* describes the United States's role in projecting power globally, having governed relatively few territories as actual colonies (still controlling several). Discussion of American imperialism is linked with the idea of "exceptionalism"—the United States's overseas involvement would promote democracy, freedom, and equality and protect human rights. This idea has roots in the revolution itself:

> Our beliefs in liberty, equality, constitutionalism, and the well-being of ordinary people came out of the Revolutionary era. So too did our idea that we Americans are a special people with a special destiny to lead the world toward liberty and democracy.[11]

The Soviet empire in Eastern Europe was a hegemony; communist states were theoretically sovereign. The term neocolonial also describes power exercised in this way, referring especially to how the developed world fosters dependency of developing states through loans, control of international agencies, and other mechanisms. Actual reasons why an imperial power succeeds in obtaining other people's land vary. Sometimes, they possess more lethal weapons. Duplicity, stealth, and unequal or misunderstood treaties between imperialists and colonized all play a part. Indigenous cultures were almost universally condemned as worthless. Artifacts were dismantled or smelted for component parts, not valued as art.

Europeans failed to recognize as advanced cultures that minimized waste, conserved nature, or valued smaller-scale communities. Even when their own medicine was mediocre, they ignored or destroyed others' equally effective or better systems. Seeing Africa as the "Dark Continent" with no culture or civilization at all, Europeans were blind to what existed before their arrival, which included "participatory and direct democracy, free village markets and free trade" and "freedom of expression."[12] Sometimes, superiority follows from accidental advantages—for example, when China suddenly ended overseas ambitions (1424), turning in on itself at the exact time that world domination was easily within reach Europeans benefited.[13] Decimation of indigenous populations by the unforeseen spread of European disease greatly aided Spanish and Portuguese imperialism in the Americas.

Ferguson is right to point out that "some empires were worse than others." Relatively speaking, the French Empire was more "liberal," the Belgian empire "the worst in Africa," and the short-lived German overseas empire (1884–1920) "the worst of all."[14] Germany experimented with eugenics and genocide in its African possessions. However, Ferguson's claim that, while not flawless, Western civilization "still seems to offer human societies the best available set of economic, social and political institutions" capable of solving "the problems the twenty-first century world faces" is open to challenge.[15] The elevation of profit over everything else, how big displaces the small, begs questions about values and priorities. How states were created by departing colonial powers, ignoring local loyalties, ethnic, religious, linguistic boundaries, and traditions of governance and imposing a "one-model-fits-all" system lies behind current problems in many former colonies. Some departing colonial powers left more infrastructure, such as schools and hospitals, behind than others. However, what they did leave mainly served their own interests, even when rhetoric said otherwise.

The taking of land was often justified as a necessary aspect to the civilizing mission, perhaps blessed by the church (e.g., the Treaty of Tordesillas, 1493, which divided all territory outside Europe between Spain and Portugal— Europe's two major colonial powers at that time), or because indigenous people had no concept of sovereignty, so what was regarded as unclaimed land could be occupied without purchase or treaty (which Australia upheld as a legal fiction until a 1991 High Court decision). Infamously, Juan Ginés de Sepulveda (1489–1573) argued that American Indians were natural slaves (citing Aristotle), "Born for servitude, not for civil life," and their land could be legally confiscated as they were non-Christians.[16] When European powers divided Africa among themselves, notions of Europe's advanced civilizational status versus others' retardation, informed by theories of evolution and progress, were firmly established. From 1885, they simply "sliced up" Africa "like a cake."[17] The only legal restraint was that if a power failed to engage in economic activity, it forfeited territory.

Postcolonialism

Postcolonialism refers to the social, cultural, political, and psychological realities and experiences of colonialism and their study. It is concerned with relationships between former colonizers and former colonies, with issues surrounding identity, nationality, race, and ethnicity (see Volume 1, Chapter 7, "Religion and Identity"). Postcolonial writers may be citizens of former colonies or of former metropoles. Postcolonial literature highlights the iniquities of economic exploitation, cultural genocide, and political disempowerment but also analyzes how colonialism impacts the metropole. It is concerned with constructing a future that learns lessons from the past; it is not restricted to historical retrospection. Characteristically, whatever justification was cited to defend colonialism, it is seen as exploitative and immoral, raising questions about apologies and reparations. There is little doubt that making a profit was colonialism's fundamental rationale. Imperial powers claimed to bring peace, but as one writer put it, the reality was "tax" not "pax," making a pun with the notion of *Pax Britannica* (the British Peace), which was also often an "axe Britannica" destroying forests and other natural spaces.[18] Some literature produced during colonialism can be classed as "postcolonial," for example, E. M. Forster's *A Passage to India* (1924) and earlier writings by Anti-Imperial League members in the United States. Many critics regard postcolonialism as a means for some academics from previously colonized countries to find jobs in metropoles at the cost of indigenous scholars. This leads into what is sometimes termed neocolonialism, which is the way formerly dominant powers through means like global capitalism continue to exert dominance (hegemony) around the world. It is sometimes linked to the way that academic power is also controlled, with "experts" now in the former colonizer's metropoles speaking on the colonized countries and their situation rather than allowing scholars within such places to exert their voices.

Orientalism

Orientalism has two somewhat polarized meanings. From the seventeenth century on, it referred to European study of the East, whether of fauna or religions. Geographically speaking, "Orient" denoted a large portion of the globe stretching across North Africa, through the Middle East, to South Asia, East Asia, and the Far East. Following Edward Said's 1978 book *Orientalism*, it refers to postcolonial criticism of that scholarly enterprise as biased, shaped by attitudes of racial and religious superiority. Said (1935–2003) defined Orientalism as "the corporate institution for dealing with the Orient—dealing with it by making statements about it, authorizing views of it, describing it, by teaching it, settling it, ruling over it: in short, Oriental as a Western style for dominating, restructuring and having authority over the Orient."[19] He describes a system of information and control. Knowledge, whether produced by scholar-officials, missionary-scholars, or university teachers, provided colonial authorities with data they needed to exercise power. Behind this lay the assumption that colonizers knew the colonized better than they knew themselves and so governed for their moral good and improvement. The Orient was seen as passive and inert, waiting for Europeans to possess it, improve it, and govern it. It was almost always seen as static, unable to progress without outside intervention. Responses to Said tend to point out that colonialism was more variegated than he suggests, that actual motives of scholars differed, and that despite bias and misrepresentation, much useful classificatory and translation work was carried out that should not be devalued. The degree to which Oriental scholarship was "inextricably bound up with the fact of domination" is challenged by, among others, Albert Hourani (1915–1993) and Bernard Lewis (b. 1916).[20] People's motives varied. Lewis recognizes that bias existed and exists, thus "scholarly criticism of Orientalist scholarship is . . . legitimate and . . . necessary," but says that the more important question is, "the validity . . . of Orientalist findings."[21] Some scholars had little or no link with empire. European encounters with, indeed discovery of, Hinduism (a term coined by Europeans in the nineteenth century) were almost entirely a result of colonial expansion, and much of Said's argument withstands scrutiny in this context. Islam, though, was "known" and studied in Europe long before the colonial period, as Lewis points out.[22] Also, as the historian of thought J. J. Clark has made clear, the flow of ideas was not simply one way, and the East also changed thought and ideas in the West.[23]

On the other hand, what was written about Islam *before* colonialism led to more extended encounter *reinforced Orientalist attitudes.* Earlier scholars did not justify imperial power; they did write to defend Europe against a perceived, threatening rival. When Vasco Da Gama reached India in 1498, he tried to deport Muslims—recently expelled from Iberia—from Calicut and attacked their ships.[24] On the one hand, this may have had as much to do with wanting to dominate maritime trade as with religiously motivated hostility. On the other hand, his actions were consistent with set European ideas about Muslims. Centuries of opposition to Muslims in Iberia following the Moorish conquest, depictions of Muslims as devil worshippers, and other popular myths shaped these ideas; for example, the *Song of Roland* (late twelfth century) has dogs and pigs trampling an idol of Muhammad.[25] In fact, apart from the *Quran*, hardly any significant Muslim texts were translated or widely used in the West until the colonial period. Another issue relates to different types of Orientalism. Trautmann distinguishes between what he calls Orientalism^{1}, "knowledge produced by Orientalists, scholars who knew Asian languages" from Orientalism^{2}, "European representations of the Orient, whether by Orientalists or Others."[26]

Some, such as Charles Grant (1746–1823) and Thomas Babington Macaulay (1800–1859), opposed early Orientalists who promoted Sanskrit. They wanted only English-medium instruction yet "were also involved in the production of knowledge of a kind Said calls Orientalism." Another criticism is that Said did not deal much with German scholarship. Links with colonialism (given the short life of German's overseas empire) cannot explain this significant enterprise.[27] It did, though, serve national purposes, helping construct the myth of German-Aryan superiority, which built on Jones's concept of an "Indo-European" past and on Renan's more racist ideas. During the Third Reich, oriental studies was a "strategically important science."[28] Nazi Orientalism appropriated aspects of an earlier tradition of German Indology for its own purposes, distorting its theories and findings. Said fell short of claiming that what Orientalists produced had no foundation in reality. His point was not that no correspondence exists between Orientalist portrayals and a "real Orient" but that the former reduced the latter to certain essential, immutable norms, which fell short of European counterparts. The East, he says, was *always subject* to European domination; Europeans never lost "the upper hand." Ideas about European progress and the Other's inability to advance permeate colonial discourse. Adam Smith's idea that China was static or stationary and Europe was progressive was more or less applied universally to non-European contexts:

> China has long been one of the richest, that is, fertile, best cultivated, most industrious, and most populous, countries in the world. It seems, however, to have been long stationary. Marco Polo, who visited it more than five hundred years ago, describes its cultivation, industry, and populousness, almost in the same terms in which they are described by travellors in the present times.[29]

Colonialism and Religions

Attitudes toward subjects' religions vary from context to context. Some imperial powers are reluctant to interfere in religious matters, assuming that this might further alienate and anger their subjects. However, many also set out to substitute existing religions with their state-sponsored or majority religion, sometimes destroying places of worship, artifacts, and texts as pagan. From Greece to the Far East, statues, images (so-called idols), and objects of representational art have been systematically destroyed, vandalized, disfigured, or desecrated. Muslims and Christians have both engaged in the destruction of images. Hardly an ancient image from Greece or India has survived intact; most are broken or disfigured, the shortest form of which is snipping off the nose. Such images, housed in museums around the world, give silent testimony to an aspect of history that is often ignored yet which, regrettably, is permanently etched in stone.

Efforts to convert indigenous populations may be state supported or, at least theoretically, independent of colonial authority. Sometimes, conversion to the colonizers' or conquerors' religion resulted in privileges, such as better employment or paying less tax. Despite popular notions of forced conversion to Islam, Muslim conquerors often made little effort to convert non-Muslims; partly, this was because they paid more tax than Muslims. Over time, attracted by economic and social advantages as well as by Islam's religious appeal, people converted. Muslim teachers also often adapted and acculturated to local contexts, thus attracting converts.

In the nineteenth century, many Christians rejected Darwin's theory, but social evolution was widely affirmed. Religions, many believed, evolved from primitive forms (worship of tree and animal spirits, or animism), through worship of many gods (polytheism), to the highest form of monotheism (worship of one god; perhaps through the intermediate stage of henotheism, coined by F. Max Müller, where one great god was worshipped without denying the existence of other gods), just as civilizations evolved through such phases as savagery and barbarism, according to Lewis H. Morgan (1818–1881).[30] Polytheism, said E. B. Taylor (1871–1958), is found among "lower races," and monotheism develops "among higher nations."[31] Terms such as polytheism and monotheism are not neutral. They dated from the seventeenth century, coined to distinguish Christianity from rival or false religions, judged inferior. Indeed, "Monotheism is self-description; polytheism is construction of the other."[32] Most so-called polytheistic religions, however, conceive an "ultimate unity of the divine world." Deities may be "clearly differentiated and personalized by name, shape, and function" but belong within "a common semantic universe."[33] Jews and Muslims actually regard Christian monotheism with suspicion, raising questions about what the term means.

Missionaries were often among first invaders and settlers. Priests accompanied Columbus on his second cross-Atlantic voyage (1493) and Vasco Da Gama to India in 1498. Sometimes, missionaries explored new territories, preceding conquest or settlement. Sometimes, colonial authorities discouraged or even prohibited them. Often, colonial rulers actively promoted Christianity, regarding missionaries as allies in the civilizing task. Similarly, Islamic conquests were often preceded or accompanied by Sufi settlements or hospices from which useful information about prospective lands for conquest could be relayed to invaders; at the same time, many of these shrines served as a refuge to those outcast by their own societies or recently converted by the conquerors. At times, missionaries defended the rights of indigenous people, opposed colonial policies, and ended up being banned. One example is dramatically depicted in the film *The Mission*, set in Paraguay in the 1770s.[34] Bartolomé de las Casas (1484–1566) defended the rights and humanity of indigenous Americans.[35] Early missionaries in India and China were actually sympathetic toward the religions they encountered, representing them as containing parallels with Christianity that might point people toward the true faith. Jesuit Matteo Ricci (1552–1610), a missionary in China, introduced "Confucianism" to the West. Ricci saw Confucian rites as civil observance. Hostile toward Buddhism, which he thought had corrupted Confucian tradition, he identified parallels between Christianity and Chinese thought, which can prepare the ground for Christian faith. He defended using Chinese terms in the liturgy. What he failed to recognize was that the "Three Ways" (Confucianism, Buddhism, and Daoism) supplement each other and that people participate in all three without seeing this as problematic (known as multiple religious identity; see Volume 1, Chapter 10). Religions were not conceived as rival, closed systems. This is relevant for the first case study; different paths and schools in India were not rigidly separate or perceived as rivals. Some people participated in more than one. Defining Hinduism, similarly, continues to be debated, including whether it only exists as an abstract scholarly construction. Embracing many paths, always open to new developments, it is perhaps more a matrix than a system. Europeans would often see Confucianism and Buddhism as "philosophies," not religions, which impacted how they were explored, described, and taught in the academy (see Volume 1, Chapter 1).

The position of missionaries in India was ambiguous. Until the 1813 East India Company charter, missionaries were not officially permitted, fearing that interference in subjects' religion might provoke revolt. However, the Anglican Church was part of the colonial infrastructure, and some chaplains engaged in outreach. Baptists, too, established a mission in Danish territory north of Calcutta before 1813. After 1813, missionaries were admitted to promote "religious and moral improvement," but the official policy remained "neutrality."[36] Charles Grant, whose *Observations* of 1792 saw nothing worthwhile in Indian culture, past or present, had campaigned with others for this "pious clause." Many colonial officials were staunch Christians (including Jones, although he valued India's past literary legacy); some enthusiastically supported missions. Whatever their official status, missionaries created "interests," which, alongside military, communicational, commercial, and cultural, could be protected.[37] After British control was established around the 1820s, missionary activity was encouraged, with some calling for a massive Christianizing of India. One of the main causes of the 1857 revolt was a large-scale reaction to this. After 1858, the religious agenda was once again muted, but the northeastern hill tribes, many of which were neither Hindu nor Muslim, were rapidly converted. Continued support of Christians in this region by Western agencies attracts criticism that they are encouraging separatism there as part of a neocolonial strategy to dismantle India. Some had secular motives in supporting a conversion agenda; they thought that Christians would be more English-like. Renan, a humanist, did not share ideas about Christianity's merits but championed Europe's innate superiority; if others were primitive, having failed to progress up the ladder of social and religious advancement, this must be due to inferior racial characteristics or perhaps inferior climate.

Five Features

Various schemes developed to analyze colonial discourse include David Spurr's list of "rhetorical features" employed to "construct a coherent representation out of" what he describes as the "strange and . . . often incomprehensible realities confronted in the non-European world."[38] This chapter proposes five features that typify European bias and misrepresentation of others, derived from Spurr and Said. First, most colonial constructions of others were *paternalistic.* The European "knew" and the native did not. Europeans assumed that texts were key to learning about laws, religious beliefs and practices, privileging philology and linguistics over other disciplines. Partly, this served to enhance scholarly authority over journalists, travel writers, and amateurs, who could claim to "know" because they were "there" but rarely acquired classical or vernacular languages.[39] This assumption followed Christianity's location of authority within texts.

Jones and Renan, who both feature in Said's work, were instrumental in placing philology center stage. Jones especially contributed to the idea that what is of interest in India is historical; studying India's ancient past involves learning about our own. He had less interest in contemporary Indian culture and religion, which he saw as corrupt. Europeans and Indians shared ancient origins; subsequently, Europe progressed and India decayed. This is also why so-called primitive religion was studied; Europeans assumed that European religion had long ago evolved from similar origins. While social science methods were used in that study, given the absence of texts, the study of both Indian religion and Islam was almost exclusively textual. Although insiders were sometimes involved in the translation process, they were far from equal partners. When insider voices were heard, these were inevitably male, not female. Texts and people were "objects," lacking any authentic voice of their own. Paternalism also assumes a familial relationship; the colonial authorities in India were often called *mai-baap* (mother-father) by Indian peasants. The aim of exterminating people, which applied in some contexts, went beyond paternalism, which has some regard for the other's welfare. Outside expertise trumped insider knowledge, reinforced by a whole set of our second feature, assumed *polarities.* Others were irrational, dishonest, and immoral, thus they could not be trusted to interpret their own texts. At best, they were childlike, in need of parental supervision. Until they matured, they needed Europe's guiding hand. Jones and Renan both believed that Europeans were naturally logical and others were incapable of rational thought. Everything found in the Orient became a European *possession*, to be exhibited, owned, displayed, and described in a manual.[40] European knowledge and expertise was *privileged* over everything non-European. Finally, behind paternalism, polarities, possession, and privilege lay the fact of *power*, which always gave Europeans the "upper hand." The conclusion offers five remedies to these tropes, namely *partnership, pluralism, provisionality, politicization*, and *personalization*.

SURVEY OF ARGUMENTS

In this section, we will look at some of the origins of the way we think of religion today; this will mean going back to the nineteenth century, but in doing so making reference to our contemporary situation and context.

William Jones and the European Construction of Hinduism

Jones played a seminal role in the European construction, some say invention, of Hinduism and in establishing oriental studies as an academic field. Interestingly, like many other significant contributors to oriental learning, he was employed outside the academy, although it can be argued that the academy as such did not exist then; until the late nineteenth century, British university posts were restricted to celibate teachers, or Fellows, who did not necessarily see their role as researchers. Much knowledge was produced by well-to-do amateurs, who could afford to fund their research interests. The pay structure of the East India Company's employees was so unequal that they could easily hire scores of native scholars, not to speak of dozens of servants. There were other perks of the job, too, that came from commissions, graft, or plain plundering; virtual paupers such as Robert Clive (1725–1774) went to make their fortunes in the East, returning to Europe in vastly different circumstances from how they left. As Chief Justice of the colonial Supreme Court in Calcutta, a very important position indeed, Jones used this post in the service of gathering texts and promoting scholarship. With regard to European constructions of Hinduism, Jones pioneered the tendency of privileging text over practice and some texts over others, and of homogenizing Indian religion. He was one of the earliest Europeans to write extensively on Hinduism, writing around about the time that the term "Hinduism" first appeared in English. Jones's proposal that Latin, Celtic, German, Greek, Sanskrit, and various other languages developed from a single, original Indo-European tongue flowed into ideas about an Aryan people, who may have invaded (AIT) or migrated (AMT) into India from elsewhere, with whom Europeans have a shared ancestry. Thus, he believed, Hindu origins lay outside, not inside India.

Thinking of Indians as immature gained support from many otherwise liberal quarters. John Stuart Mill (1806–1873), who worked for the East India Company in London, championed liberalism at home while arguing that "liberty" could "not be extended to children nor to those backward states of society in which the race itself may be considered in its nonage."[41] Mill's writing was influential in Britain's decision to rule India directly after the 1857 revolt, because "150 millions of Asiaticks" could "not be trusted to rule themselves."[42] Mill's father's 1817 book attacked Orientalists (i.e., those who studied it), arguing that lack of languages was an advantage, allowing impartial scholarship, while Orientalists such as Jones were too romantic; his "imagination on the accomplishments of the orientals delighted to gild, and hardly set any limit to its glittering creations."[43] Obviously, both Mills did much to construct ideas about the Orient, fitting Said's Orientalist category (the creation of the "Orient" as Europe's "Other" in negative terms). The British parliament, where Grant, J. S. Mill, and other India hands sat, also debated these two positions, with official policy and legislation favoring the latter.

What follows discusses William Jones's role in the European construction of Hinduism, focusing on debates between European scholars. Indians did take part in discussion. However, their voices had either little or no impact on European contributors, because they were ignored or they were less interested in refuting what Europeans said than in reforming Indian society.

Born in London, Jones was educated at Harrow and University College, Oxford, gaining his Fellowship (1766), BA (1768), and MA (1773). In 1772, he became a Fellow of the Royal Society. He qualified as a barrister in 1774. A love of languages saw him acquire Latin, Hebrew, Greek, Arabic, Farsi, and a range of European tongues. His translations of Arabic and Farsi poetry and legal and political writing (including a text on Muslim inheritance law) made him a public figure. In 1780, he applied unsuccessfully for an Oxford chair in Arabic, was passed over due to his political views, and failed in a bid for parliament. In 1783, he was knighted and appointed to the Supreme Court in Calcutta, serving until his death (1794). In 1784, he founded the Asiatic Society of Bengal to promote oriental learning. Known as "Oriental Jones" and as "Biblical Jones," his enthusiasm for Indian history and ancient texts did not please everyone. Grant's *Observations* can be seen as a counterpoint to Jones's ideas about the value of studying India's history.

In the late eighteenth century, the British were "discovering" Hinduism. They already thought they knew about Islam, as had Da Gama. Adopting the term "Hindu" (used in ancient Iran for those who lived beyond the Indus river) to describe the non-Muslim population, which they realized was a majority, they soon developed the ideas that Hindus and Muslims were rivals. Initially taking power from Muslims, the British tended to employ and privilege Hindus. It was also the case that Hindus embraced the English language and modernity with greater, almost eager, enthusiasm; in Bengal, most of the middle classes who supported British rule were Hindu—the displaced aristocracy was Muslim, as was the dispossessed peasantry. Britain's divide-and-rule policy dealt separately with each community, driving them further apart. With the civilizing mission, maintaining peace was used to justify colonialism; were the British to leave they claimed Hindus and Muslims would exterminate each other. This reflected their conviction that Islam was Europe's enemy—having occupied Spain and the Balkans, twice threatening Vienna, Islam was the enemy Europe *most feared* for *many centuries*. For some in the West, Islam still is the most feared enemy (some issues dealing with this can be found in Volume 3, Chapter 5).

Arguably, ideas about European identity developed over and against the Muslim world, creating the belief that their "whole history, culture and social-economic" systems were incompatible.[44] Europeans often forget that relations with Muslims have been complex, involving not only conflict but diplomacy, trade treaties, and peace accords. Many prefer the idea of an all-but-inevitable conflict with Islam: Huntington's clash thesis.[45] In India, too, while Muslim–Hindu conflict is a fact, this was not the whole story. The ancestors of most Muslims in the subcontinent embraced Sufi-flavored Islam. Initially, they were probably "Hindu-Muslims." Conversion required the simplest of affirmations of faith, with two witnesses, but took generations for Arabization to "finish" the process, something we still see in states such as Assam. What can be said is that along with a history of conflict, there was an even more powerful, more complex history of coexistence, syncreticism, cooperation, and exchange between the two communities. The reality was closer to China's pattern of multiple religious identity (see Volume 1, Chapter 10, and also Volume 1, Chapter 8). Christians in Kerala, who credit Saint Thomas with evangelizing their ancestors in the first century (which may or may not be mythical), melted into the prevailing caste system (as *Brahmins*); Jainism may historically have been seen as a "Hindu" path, not as a separate religion. For legal purposes, Jains, Buddhists, and Sikhs are still classified as Hindus in India. In the census of 1881, many respondents recorded their "sect or caste" in the religion column, a "problem of definition" that "haunted the census authorities until at least 1901."[46] India's partition in 1947 exacerbated the Hindu–Muslim question, making it impossible to depoliticize it. The "two-nation" theory sees harmony as impossible; this is the opposite of the "peaceful coexistence" thesis associated with M. K. Gandhi (1869–1944) and others. These examples should help to clarify that the kind of definitions of Hinduism and the nature of other religious communities debated by nineteenth-century scholars still affect us today.

Jones's interest in India's history and religion began as result of his legal responsibilities. Governor-General Warren Hastings (1732–1818) wanted to govern Indians by their own laws. To do so, they had to be identified. Like the Mughals (1526–1757), whose power they usurped, the British used Farsi as the official language (until 1837). However, they were becoming aware that Indians spoke Hindi and Bangla, whose acquisition would aid governance. N. B. Halhed (1751–1830), who wrote *Bengali Grammar in English* (1778), produced "the first sketchy account of the structure of Sanskrit," Bangla's "grand source," noting similarities with Greek.[47] This stimulated Jones's study of India's ancient language, which led to his "Indo-European" concept, that is, the languages of India and Europe were related.[48] Pragmatically, to catalog Hindu and Muslim laws, he needed sources for the former (the latter were more easily available). Hindu scholars (known as *pundits*) helped him master Sanskrit, suggesting *The Laws of Manu* as an appropriate legal text, named after a mythic figure. However, it probably had no widely accepted usage in practice, and so this obscure 2,000-year-old text suddenly became, and remains, a defining Hindu text.[49] Moreover, by using this single text as the basis for legal construction, ignoring other sources, Jones invaded and manipulated "the textual space of the colonized," effectively replacing the Sanskrit original with his English translation.[50] He took *possession* of *Manu*, thereby dispossessing Hindus. Distrusting Hindu interpretations, he *privileged* his own. The point is not that *Manu* lacked authority but that *we do not know* whether it was literally or widely applied, or to what extent "textual prescriptions" described "reality."[51] Doniger suggests, for example, that constant prohibitions against women and lower castes studying the *Veda* proves that they did, "whenever the pundits weren't looking."[52] Jones thought his codification of law would prevent Indians from "tampering with it."[53] Believing that, as they stood, laws "lacked coherence" and "needed improving," he set out to do this. Sugitharajah says that "for Hindus, the meaning of a text is not confined to nor firmly entrenched in the written word" but conveyed through oral repetition, including such forms as "story-telling, dance, music and drama," none of which Jones, and other scholars, studied.[54]

Jones believed that Adam and Eve were humanity's common progenitors. He may or may not have argued this for reasons of faith, although Henry Morris describes Jones as "a thoroughly devout man" who strove in all things to "be guided and directed by God."[55] However, convinced that the Biblical version of history is true, he dated Adam at 4004 BCE, identifying Adam with Manu. Dismissing Hindu notions of cyclical time and long eons, he fitted what he understood as vedic history into biblical chronology. With others, he was anxious to link Greece, India, Egypt, and Iran, all revered as precursors of modern civilization, and so argued that these people spoke a single language. The flood, which he found in Sanskrit literature as well as in the *Bible*, occurred in 2350 BCE. India's origins as a civilization was soon after that event, making it ancient but younger than many Indians believe; B. G. Tilak (1856–1920) proposed 10000 BCE.[56] From a common point of origin, three races (from biblical precedent descended from Shem, Japheth, and Ham) migrated. With others, Jones linked Ham (who was cursed) with black people. Muslims placed Hindus in this category. Indo-Europeans were descended from Japheth. Jones thought that all people were originally primitive monotheists; thus primitive or original monotheism lies buried in the *Vedas*, which validated the biblical record. Where many Europeans saw only polytheism, he saw monotheism as well as "seeds of polytheism and idolatry" in the *Vedas*. Numerous texts declare the unity of the "godhead."[57] Later, Müller saw the *Vedas* as barbaric; exposing their inferiority would aid Christian purposes. He knew their true meaning; Hindus did not. It is, though, unclear whether Müller used a term such as *barbaric* to appease his critics, who thought he was too sympathetic toward Indian religion. The Hindu right has tried to discredit Müller by concocting letters and sources to suggest that he was part of some huge Christian conspiracy.

Aryan invasion theory (AIT) and Aryan migration theory (AMT) explain both linguistic similarities between Indian and European languages and their ancient religious narratives as well as differences between India's north and south. Jones believed that Sanskrit was the most sophisticated of classical languages, articulating this in his third Asiatic Society anniversary discourse, on February 2, 1786.[58] He proposed his Aryan concept both as a linguistic theory and to reduce distance between English and Indians, who became cousins. This probably did not mean equality—else he would have trusted Indians. He may not have anticipated that his theory would be given a racist twist, or Indian objection to the claim that Hindu origins lie outside India. AIT was hugely influential in theorizing Hindu origins; page one of what was perhaps the first textbook on Hinduism, by Monier Monier-Williams (1819–1899), begins with Aryans migrating from Central Asia "through mountain passes into India," as if this were established fact.[59]

AIT–AMT has many permutations and versions. Some argue for an "out of India" alternative; some for "out of Germany"; some for "out of Lithuania." Some distance modern Indians from contemporary Europeans, arguing that despite common origins, only the latter retain their superior status; Indians lost theirs through intermingling with lesser races.[60] Doniger and Flood have excellent summaries;[61] Bryant is a book-length, carefully nuanced treatment of a wide range of alternative views.[62] Ideas about the danger of mixing races are relevant here; it was as recent as 1967 that the U.S. Supreme Court ruled laws prohibiting cross-race marriage unconstitutional. Renan developed ideas about racial distinctives, drawing on the Aryan concept.

Jones may not have intended to begin a trend. However, what followed in European constructions of Hinduism was a tendency toward uniformity, ignoring diversity, local customs, the role played by non-vedic languages and texts—considered equally sacred by some. Several Tamil texts are regarded as vedic, which European scholars ignored.[63] Europeans produced, some say invented, "Hinduism" as a great tradition, of which Monier-Williams's book may be the first example. It became the model for "a host of later historical summaries of Hinduism."[64] Here, the four *Vedas*, four stages in life, four ages, and four cases (*varna*) are set out as a systematic scheme. Hinduism in this construct is a textual tradition—a priest-dominated *Brahmanical* tradition. Texts that Europeans liked or even disliked, once translated, were assumed to be seminal for all Hindus.[65] The issue is not that many such texts were unimportant; rather, their new iconic status was disproportionate to the role they played in Hindu life. There is no real evidence that either *The Laws of Manu* or the *Bhagavad-gita* previously enjoyed the primacy they do in post-English translation.[66] Therefore, in various ways the current image we have of "Hinduism" is, at least partially, a creation of British (and also German) scholorship, as scholars, often associated with, and certainly enabled by, the imperial power created a vision of that religion that fitted various purposes of their own. What these constructions ignored was the diversity of India's religious landscape, conveniently labeled "Hinduism."[67] Even the term *sanatama dharma*, preferred by many Hindus, tends to represent a supposed normative tradition.

Jones did not develop a racial theory in any detail; he thought that various races, speaking a common language, probably migrated from "a central country," possibly Iran.[68] However, his ideas lie behind later developments, including those about a subsequent decline. Sugitharajah says that although he supported greater political and civil liberty at home, he did not "apply the same principles" in India. There, he believed that without European help, Indians were too immature to appreciate such rights.[69] He liked Indians and was genuinely interested in their welfare but was *paternalistic* in his attitudes toward their ability to administer their own laws. India's past was interesting; the India he saw was "degenerate and debased."[70] Thus, Jones subscribed to the *polarizing* view of "us" and "them," seeing Indians as immature, good at imagination (hence their prolific stories), but lacking much reasoning ability, similar to Renan's idea that Islam hinders rational thought.[71] While not as central for Jones as for Renan, this represents another similarity between their thinking.

Jones never wrote, though, about Indians in the insulting way that Grant could, who described all Bengalis as lacking "truth, honesty, and good faith, in an extreme of which European society furnishes no example." Grant attributed this to Hinduism's baneful influence, which only Christianity's triumph could counter. Hindu government's only principle was "despotism"; justice was nothing more than a "traffic in venality," with money securing "acquittance even for murder."[72] Hinduism is eclectic. Aryans or people who entered India from outside and the indigenous culture probably both contributed to what became Hinduism, which fused two cultures, although in "some places," it resembled a "tossed salad, a multiplicity."[73] Nonetheless, AIT–AMT remains a theory which should be taught as such, not as proven fact.

As a term, *Hinduism* is here to stay, despite ongoing debate about definition. Hindus have used the term since at least 1816, when Ram Mohun Roy
(1772–1833) pioneered this, according to Wendy Doniger.[74] Others say that
Hindus had an "identity" before the British reached India.[75] Lorenzon suggests that there is enough "family resemblance" across "variegated beliefs
and practices" to identify what can be called Hinduism, which probably
developed later rather than earlier, possibly during centuries of Muslim
rule.[76] King, though, thinks it anachronistic to project the term back into
precolonial times.[77] Jones's example of looking at India's past while seeing
the present as degraded (though he was not as vocal on this as others were)
impacted "reformers," who looked at the same ancient texts and said that
nothing there justified practices Europeans condemned, which were indeed
corruptions. *Varna* is described; however, membership is not defined exclusively as a birth right. Decline could also be explained by the ancient idea
that, in the age of *Kali*, religion would decay. Almost all representations
of Hinduism perpetuate a bible-derived chronology that owes much to
Jones and Müller's work, whose date for the writing down of the *Vedas*
(1200 BCE) is widely cited. Given religious studies' claim to take believer's
views seriously, this sits oddly with traditional Hindu chronology, which
many texts simply ignore. Even excellent texts refer to AIT–AMT as if it
were fact; for example, Markham's "Fact Sheet" on Hinduism and Hopfe
and Woodward's section, "The Coming of the Aryans" (a 12th edition),
which claims to take note of new scholarship but states, "it seems clear that
the Aryan invaders of India brought with them a polytheistic religion. . . ."[78]

What we *do not find* in Jones is total disdain for everything Indian. In fact,
while he did speak about lack of reason, of "whimsical imagination" distorting truth, he found pleasure in Hindu poetry, which he thought could
reinvigorate European literature.[79] He especially loved female deities. This
went against the trend, which saw Indians as effeminate, in need of mascu-
linizing.[80] William Ward (1769–1823), Jones's contemporary, author of a
four-volumed work on "the Hindoos," describes Hindus as "destitute of
generosity . . . grossly impure, false, litigious, cruel, treacherous, covet-
ous. . . ."[81] India's climate produced effeminate men, while "integrity" is associated with "climates where men are more robust."[82] Müller thought that to
win Hindus, Christianity would have to present a less masculine version.[83]

Ernest Renan and the European Construction of Islam

Ernest Renan (1823–1892) gave significant impetus to the philological
bias of Islamic studies, helping pioneer a French tradition that overlapped
with, and informed, German scholarship. Renan drew on Jones's Aryan concept; considered the father of modern philology by some, Jones's role in

making philology central to Hindu studies, and Renan's for Islamic studies, also links the two, although Renan was born after Jones's death. For Renan, philology substituted for religion; it represented the "spirit of the age." The modern world would "not be what it is without philology," an ally of reason and progress. If philology perished, "criticism would perish with it ... all supernaturalism will receive its deathblow by philology."[84] Philology can teach us "about the origins of humanity, civilization and language."[85] Language launched civilization. Before language, humanity was silent. Language results in creativity, innovation, and science: "language in the whole of its construction dates from the first days of man."[86] One of the first people to *polarize* Aryans (Euro-Indians) and Semites (Jews and sometimes Arabs), he contributed to ideas about racial superiority. American Indians, blacks, and Semites were inferior, Aryans superior, possessing "creative ability, discipline and a capacity for independent political organization" which others lacked.[87] His ideas about Islam shutting down critical and rational thought represent his chief contributions to a European construction of Islam. He thought that Islam was entering a period of decline and so did not subscribe to the threat thesis. Islam would die out. Semitic thought produced monotheism because it lacked the necessary imagination to create "mythology which is the mother of polytheism," but this is all it has contributed to the world.[88] Ideas about a normative Islam, as described by Orientalist scholars, opens up anything that differs or varies from this to the charge of being *not Islam*. Renan and others focused on Arab Islam, but Islam had adapted culturally to many contexts, often challenging Arab Islam's ideas about gender, minority rights, even mosque–state relations.

Born in Brittany, Renan attended a local college before studying for the priesthood in Paris, but he abandoned Christianity in 1845. Disillusioned with philosophy and theology, he found mathematics more satisfying, but it was languages that most attracted him. He studied Arabic, Hebrew, and Syriac at seminary, at the School of Oriental Languages, and at Collège de France (1844–1849), winning prizes. He formally abandoned his priestly vocation and Christianity in 1845. He attained his doctorate in 1852, submitting a Latin thesis derived from his Syriac studies, arguing that Muslim knowledge of Aristotle and "anything else possessed by the medieval Arabs, was wholly derived from Syriac translation," and his famous French essay on Ibn Rushd (d. 1198).[89] From 1850 he worked for the French National Library before becoming Professor of Hebrew at the Collège de France. Like Jones, he stood unsuccessfully for parliament (1867). Dismissed after publishing his *Life of Jesus* (1863), he was reappointed in 1870, becoming Director in 1879. He continued to travel, spending 1864–1865 in Asia Minor, described in his 1878 book.[90] In Egypt (1864), his ideas about the "mediocrity" of Arab culture were confirmed.[91] Jones pursued his most acclaimed work in a colony; Renan visited the Muslim-majority world but mainly worked in the metropole.

Renan's thought was shaped by ideas about Europe's civilizing mission in the world, with France at the helm. Non-Europeans might advance, but only under European tutorship. Renan's conviction that philology was the key that led him to conclude that Semitic languages were inferior to Indo-European. According to Renan, Arabs lack "imagination and curiosity" and so neglect philosophy and the creative arts.[92] They could not reach the heights attained "by the Indo-Germanic races."[93] Said characterizes Renan's constructions as laboratory-generated; his construction of both an Islam that cannot progress or think creatively and of the progressive, creative, imaginative Indo-German took place within a space he controlled.[94] Like Jones, Renan *privileged* his expertise over Muslims—the idea that they might participate in the enterprise of studying Islam was preposterous. France had occupied Algeria in 1830, which it saw as an extension of itself across the sea. Settling it, the French also set out to "Frenchify" their possession. Arab culture and Islam had no value. Increasingly, "Islam" was seen as a "catastrophe for Africa and France's most dangerous enemy," influenced by Renan's ideas.[95] For Renan, Arab inferiority was scientific, "grounded in the same order of things that was responsible for, and assured the continuance of, Aryan superiority and progressiveness."[96]

German scholars enthused about Renan's ideas on race and languages, regarding German as superior, even if among classical tongues Sanskrit was best. In his essay on Ibn Rushd, he concluded that after the philosopher's death, rational thought disappeared in Islam, ensuring the triumph of the *Quran* over free thought. He described al-Ghazali (d. 1111) as the enemy of philosophy, widely blamed for shutting down critical thought in Islam.[97] With many contemporaries, he saw Islam as "moving toward a dead end." Muslim societies were "doomed to stagnancy," their "beliefs and practices ... survivals from the past" that "hindered development."[98] In an 1883 lecture, Renan said that "a thousand leagues" separated Islam from reason and science.[99] This provoked a response from reformist thinker Jamal al-Din al-Afghani (1838–1897), whom Renan had met, who argued that there was no antagonism between Islam and science.[100] Some point to what they describe as intolerance of dissent in many Islamic societies to support Renan's view; legal rulings are routinely passed against varieties of nonconformists. On the other hand, close examination of specific Islamic contexts shows debate and differences of interpretation, while some call for an end to such legal rulings as contrary to the principle that permits diversity of opinion in many areas.[101]

Renan took *possession* of his subject, reducing it to a definite "norm" that *could not change*. He *privileged* his authority. There could be no "future" for "Muslims and their societies outside of the colonial relationship."[102] Renan was only interested in Islam as a "postscript," that is, an example of a late religion lacking legitimate vitality, doomed to die. His ideas had a direct impact on several Muslim reformers, especially in Egypt. There, opposing reform, the British Consul-General, administrator-scholar Lord Cromer (1841–1917), influenced by Renan, magisterially declared, "Islam reformed is Islam no longer" but "something else." In a typically "us–them" juxtaposition, he stated that the "chief characteristic of the Oriental mind" is "want of accuracy" while Europeans are "close reasoners," even if untrained in logic.[103] Islam must remain what Renan and Cromer said it was; Muslims had no right to interpret their own tradition. Ideas that Islam is incapable of change are patronizing. Religious studies should not privilege one expression of Islam over others; all are valid contextualizations of Islam's values, beliefs, principles, and legal guidelines to specific cultures, localities, and regions for those who formulate them.

Renan was *paternalistic* in relation to colonial subjects. His negation of Islamic creativity, his view that Islam shuts down rational thought, had a wide impact on European scholars, who routinely claim that Islam and rational thought are incompatible. Less surprising than similar statements in works by contemporaries, they surface in recent writing. There has been vitriolic debate, at times, about whether Muslims merely copied from Greek and other sources, passing this knowledge onto Europe via Spain, for example, where Christians studied at Islamic centers of learning before 1492, or whether they added to scientific, medical, and other learning. Ferguson, in his analysis of why Europe rose to power, acknowledges that the West owes a "debt to the medieval Muslim world, for both its custodianship of classical wisdom and its generation of new knowledge" but says that Muslims "fell behind." However, he dates this later than Ibn Rushd's death (1198) to the Ottoman period, when like China the Ottomans turned inward and "became focused exclusively on theology" exactly when European universities expanded "the scope of their scholarship."[104] Attempts to account for the rise of the West inevitably contrast this with the decline of others. Is this actually the case, or a biased and subjective analysis?

Racist interpretations of the Indo-Aryan concept, such as Renan's, are *ideological*. There may have been a single people speaking a common tongue who migrated in various directions. Given that "out of Africa" is widely held for all human origins, perhaps they had first traveled north to a central Asian location.[105] Movement in different directions to find suitable land would have been easier for smaller groups. Europeans, Iranians, and others embraced by this theory could take pleasure in shared ancestry, in many shared values. The racist claim that some people progressed while others did not is exactly that—racist ideology. Throughout history, cultures and religions have borrowed, cross-fertilized, and thrived. Ideas about the illegitimacy of traditions because they borrow from elsewhere, or arrived from elsewhere, deny a common humanity.

CONCLUSION: FIVE REMEDIES TO THE FIVE FEATURES

Use of the term *remedy* here is not meant to imply that all previous scholarship is tainted or redundant; in fact, many scholars, including Jones, anticipated aspects of what this chapter advocates. However, the following may help guide future efforts to represent others; most of these "remedies" actually already characterize much contemporary work. Religious studies today should embrace *pluralism*, which means using many methods to scrutinize religion, including lived experience. It involves listening to many voices, of women, men, skeptics, insiders and outsiders, those who might be labeled deviant, and those who self-define as orthodox. It avoids imposing terms and categories from the outside.

Religious studies should become increasingly *participatory*, involving insiders, outsiders, skeptics, agnostics, atheists, and people from across the college campus and beyond. It enters the "field" as well as the library.

It should be aware that scholarship can and often does serve *political* ends. Funding may serve national agendas, to which it might even be linked. Neutrality, recent thought suggests, may be an elusive goal. Declaring perspectives, rather than hiding these, and making your presence explicit by reflecting on how this impacts conclusions, changes perceptions, and challenges earlier findings should be encouraged. Representations of Islam as incompatible with Western values can inform immigration policy; the threat thesis has security implications. Caricatures about Islam denying creativity or shutting down scientific thought may impact how Muslim citizens are perceived and treated, perhaps limiting their opportunities in education and employment. Is it intellectually credible to perpetuate ideas that oppose some segments of humanity against others, or speak about East and West as essentially, innately different? Muslims and Hindus live in every Western state. There are dangers here. Scholarship could easily become a subcategory of the political; this would conflate "good scholarship" with what is judged to be "politically correct." Politicization has negative and positive aspects; critically, scholars ought to be aware of political realities, not naïve that their work is somehow independent or neutral. Religious studies needs to recognize that researching religion has a *personal* dimension. In fact, whatever else religion is, faith or belief has personal meaning for believers. Studying religion involves reading texts, observing external rites and practices, and attempting to enter people's hearts and heads. It should deal with subjective meanings that are interior to people, with emotions, feelings, and personal (including spiritual) experience.

Finally, *provisionality* means that what we produce is never final; our findings are determined by the people we *did* meet, the texts we *did* read. If women's voices were neglected (neither Jones nor Renan read what women wrote, at least not about religion), our work may have an androcentric bias. A European and North American bias that tends to see "religions" as primarily textual, homogenous, and reducible to definitive descriptions should not be replaced by alternative centrisms. Instead, religious studies needs to critique a wide range of perspectives. If constructing "us–them" polarities is a universal human tendency, it is possible that this also applies to ideas that equality and justice are innate ideals within human nature, as proposed by Plato (d. 347 BCE) and Rene Descartes (d. 1650). Recognizing that the task of producing "authorative" accounts of others is problematic and challenging and that stereotypes may impact the thinking of the most self-critical and cautious scholar is also part of the solution. The real remedy is for the Western academy to move beyond merely professing values such as pluralism and participation to producing the kind of scholarship that actually embodies them.

GLOSSARY

Aryan: in nineteenth linguistic and racial classification, a term that links the European and Indian peoples and languages. It derives from a term generally seen as referring to "lighter skinned people" of India, sometimes linked with an invading group who became Hindus, to be distinguished from native Indians. Such theories continue to be controversial and contested.

Colonialism: colonialism and imperialism are more or less synonymous, but a colony refers to an occupied territory.

Hegemony: an overwhelming power over another; in relation to imperialism, colonialism, and postcolonialism, it refers to the way one country, civilization, or culture can exert power over another without actual political or military control.

Imperialism: colonialism and imperialism are more or less synonymous, though imperialism refers to any attempts to exert power over another state or territory, while colonialism refers to directly ruling another territory.

Metropole: referring to a "mother city," the term refers to the original state or nation from which a colonizer comes; that is, a British imperial official in India during the British Empire would have the United Kingdom as their metropole.

Neocolonialism: the continuation of domination after the end of political or military colonialism, for instance through trade or knowledge control.

Orientalism: originally meant people who study the "East" or "Orient," but after Edward Said's book *Orientalism* it is often used to mean the methods and means, whereby the "West" controlled knowledge of and power over the "East," creating an image of the "Orient" as the "other."

Polytheism/monotheism/henotheism/animism: worship of many gods (polytheism); worship of one god alone (monotheism); worship of a supreme deity among other deities (henotheism); worship of animal and plant spirits (animism).

Postcolonialism: refers both to the period after colonialism and to the critique of systems of colonial control and their after effects.

Semite: often used to categorize Jews alone (as in the modern usage of anti-Semitic), Semites more broadly, and technically in some usages, cover the Jewish and Arabic peoples, languages, and cultures of the Middle East.

NOTES

1. Aristotle, *Politics* (New York: Cosimo, 2008), 34.

2. Antonie Anghie, *Imperialism, Sovereignty and the Making of International Law* (Cambridge, England: Cambridge University Press, 2007), 84.

3. Publio Virgilio Maron and L. R. Lind, *The Aeneid: An Epic Poem of Rome Publius Vergilius Maro, Known as Vergil,* trans. L. R. Lind (Bloomington: Indiana University Press, 1963), 860.

4. Thomas F. Gossett, *Race: The History of an Idea in America* (New York: Oxford University Press, 1997), 4.

5. Thorsten Pattberg, *The East-West Dichotomy* (New York: LoD Press, 2009), 1; and Plato, J. B. Skemp, and Martin Ostwald, *Plato's Statesman* (Indianapolis, IN: Hackett Pub. Co., 1992), 12.

6. Plato and Benjamin Jowett, *Alcibiades I and II* (Teddington, England: The Echo Library, 2006), 30.

7. Johann P. Arnason, "East and West: From Invidious Dichotomy to Incomplete Deconstruction," in *Handbook of Historical Sociology,* ed. Gerard Delantry and Engin F. Isin (London: Sage, 2003), 220–34.

8. Rudyard Kipling, *Ballads and Barrack-Room Ballads* (New York: Macmillan, 1897), 3.

9. Rudyard Kipling and Charles Wolcott Balestier, *The Writings in Prose and Verse of Rudyard Kipling* (New York: C. Scribner's Sons, 1897), 78.

10. Khushwant Singh, *Kipling's India* (New Delhi, India: Roli Books, 2001), 15.

11. Gordon S. Wood, *The Idea of America: Reflections on the Birth of the United States* (New York: Penguin Press, 2011), 2.

12. George B. N. Ayittey, *Africa Betrayed* (New York: St Martin's Press, 1992), 18.

13. Niall Ferguson, *Empire: How Britain Made the Modern World* (California: Penguin, 2004), 26–33.

14. Ibid., 190–91.

15. Ibid., 324.

16. Juan Ginés de Sepúlveda, excerpt from "The Second Democrats," *Digital History,* 1547, accessed July 2012, http://www.digitalhistory.uh.edu/learning_history/spain/spain_sepulveda.cfm.

17. Thomas Pakenham, *The Scramble for Africa: White Man's Conquest of the Dark Continent from 1876 to 1912* (New York: Avon Books, 1992), xxi.

18. John Keay, *India: A History* (New York: Harper Collins, 2000), 415.

19. Edward Said, *Orientalism* (New York: Penguin, 1978), 6.

20. Albert Hourani, *Islam in European Thought* (Cambridge, England: Cambridge University Press, 1991), 63; and Bernard Lewis, *Islam and the West* (Oxford, England: Oxford University Press, 1993), 117.

21. Lewis, *Islam and the West,* 118.

22. Ibid.

23. James J. Clark, *Oriental Enlightenment: The Encounter Between Asian and Western Thought* (London and New York: Routledge).

24. Ferguson, *Empire*, 39.

25. Gerald J. Brault, *The Song of Roland: An Analytical Edition*, Volume II (University Park: Pennsylvania State University Press, 1981), 159.

26. Thomas R. Trautmann, *Aryans and British India* (New Delhi, India: Yodi Press, 2004), 23.

27. Lewis, *Islam and the West*, 108.

28. Ekkehard Ellinger, *Deutsche Orientalistik zur Zeit des Nationalsozialismus 1933–1945* (Edingen-Neckarhausen, Germany: Deux Mondes, 2003), 70.

29. Adam Smith, *The Wealth of Nations: The Economics Classic: A Selected Edition for the Contemporary Reader* (Chichester, England: Capstone, 2010), 83–84.

30. Lewis Henry Morgan, *Ancient Society: Or Researches in the Lines of Human Progress from Savagery Through Barbarism to Civilization* (Chicago: Charles H. Kerr, 1910).

31. Edward Burnett Taylor, *Primitive Culture: Researches into the Development of Mythology, Philosophy, Religion, Language, Art and Custom* (London: Murray, 1903), 304.

32. Jan Assman, "Monotheism and Polytheism in Ancient Religions," in *Ancient Religion*, ed. Sarah Iles Johnston (Cambridge, MA: The Belknap Press of Harvard University Press, 2007), 17.

33. Ibid., 24.

34. Robert Bolt et al., *The Mission* (Burbank, CA: Warner Bros, 2003) (DVD).

35. Bartolome de las Casa and Nigel Griffin, *A Short Account of the Destruction of the Indies* (London: Penguin Books, 1992).

36. Brian Stanley, *Christian Missions and the Enlightenment* (Grand Rapids, MI: Eerdmans, 2005), 55.

37. Said, *Orientalism*, 100.

38. David Spurr, *The Rhetoric of Empire: Colonial Discourse in Journalism, Travel Writing and Imperial Administration* (Durham, NC: Duke University Press, 1993), 3. He uses surveillance, appropriation, aestheticization, classification, debasement, negation, affirmation, idealilization, insubstantialization, naturalization, eroticization, and resistance.

39. Trautmann, *Aryans and British India*, 32–33.

40. Said, *Orientalism*, 41.

41. J. S. Mill, "On Liberty," in *Utilitarianism, Liberty and Representative Government*, ed. J. S. Mill (New York: Everyman's Library, 1968), 73.

42. John Stuart Mill, *A President in Council the Best Government for* India (London: Penny), 1.

43. James Mill, *The History of British India, Vol. I* (London: Baldwin, Crasddock and Joy, 1817), xiii, 368.

44. Mary Anne Perkins, *Christendom and European Identity: The Legacy of a Grand Narrative Since 1789* (Berlin: Walter de Gruyter, 2004), 263.

45. Samuel P. Huntington, *The Clash of Civilizations and the Remaking of World Order* (New York: Simon & Schuster, 1996).

46. Sekhar Bandyopadhyay, *From Plassey to Partition: A History of Modern India* (New Delhi, India: Orient Longman, 2004), 245.

47. Trautmann, *Aryans and British India*, 31.

48. These studies have indicated that, arguably, the most ancient but still existing written Indian language, Sanskrit, was an influential root behind Greek, Latin, and therefore modern English as spoken in the United Kingdom, the United States, and elsewhere.

49. Believed to contain words of Manu's mythical "father," the god Brahma, this sets out rules for conduct, penalties, duties, and responsibilities. *Manu* is very widely cited in religious studies texts, assumed to be the most important source of Hindu ethics. *Manusmṛti*, according to some, is a sociological text; no village or region's laws were derived from it.

50. Sharada Sugitharajah, *Imagining Hinduism: A Post-Colonial Perspective* (New York: Routledge, 2003), 36.

51. Ibid., 25; see Wendy Doniger, *The Hindus: An Alternative History* (New York: Penguin Press, 2009), 596.

52. Doniger, *The Hindus*, 36, 39–40.

53. Sugitharajah, *Imagining Hinduism*, 27.

54. Ibid., 47.

55. Henry Morris, *Heroes of Our Indian Empire: The Friends of William Wilberforce*, Volume 2 (London: Christian Literature Society for India, 1908), 80.

56. Edwin Francis Bryant and Laurie L. Patton, *The Indo-Aryan Controversy: Evidence and Inference in Indian History* (New York: Psychology Press, 2005), 427.

57. Wiliam Jones and Asiatick Society. *Asiatick Researches, or, Transactions of the Society Instituted in Bengal, for Inquiring into the History and Antiquities, the Arts, Sciences, and Literature of Asia* (Calcutta, India: Asiatic Society, 1801), 279.

58. William Jones, "The Third Anniversary Discourse," in *Complete Works*, Volume 3, ed. William Jones (New York: New York University Press, 1993), 24–46.

59. Monier-Williams, *Hinduism* (London: SPCK, 1890), 1.

60. Trautmann, *Aryans and British India*, 211

61. Doniger, *The Hindus*, 89–99; and Gavin Flood, *An Introduction to Hinduism* (Cambridge, England: Cambridge University Press, 1996), 31–34.

62. Edwin Bryant, *The Quest for the Origins of Vedic Culture: The Indo-Aryan Migration Debate* (Oxford, England: Oxford University Press, 2002). Much debate centers on the relationship, if any, between the Indus Valley civilization (IVC) and the supposed Aryan people. This civilization was discovered in 1920. Technologically advanced; it flourished from about 2500 BCE (Jones's date for the flood) to about 1500 BCE. It was probably abandoned rather than conquered—theories credit invading or migrating Aryans (light-skinned people) pushing supposedly darker-skinned, non-Indo-European speakers (*Dravidians* or *Dasas*) into southern India, usually dated about 1500 BCE. Speculation based on female figurines posits that the female divine was the focus of worship; this contrasts with the*Vedas*, where male deities dominate. One artifact has been linked with the Hindu deity Shiva or Indra. Climate change may have ended the culture. Seals (yet to be deciphered) also attract speculation. Doniger suggests that the seals might actually "not record any language at all" but represent "random symbols of ownership" (Doniger, *The Hindus*, 81; and Edwin Bryant, cited in Ramesh Chandra Majumdar, "Rigvedic Civilization in the Light of Archeology," *Annals of the Bhandarkar Oriental Institute* 40 [1959]: 6). Several writers comment that we have texts but no artifacts for ancient Vedic culture, artifacts but no texts for IVC (see, for example, Doniger, *The Hindus*, 86). One issue involves horses and chariots; central in the *Vedas*, there is no evidence that either existed in the IVC, which for some supports the theory

that Aryans entered India from elsewhere *after IVC's demise*. Also, vedic texts are ignorant of many technologies present in IVC. There might, though, be no trace of a small-scale Aryan settlement.

63. Sugitharajah, *Imagining Hinduism*, 49–50.

64. See David N. Lorenzen, *Who Invented Hinduism? Essays on Religion in History* (New Delhi, India: Yoda Press, 2006), 13.

65. No one would deny the importance of the *Vedas*, but translator Müller saw them as exclusive, that is, no later texts mattered (Sugithrarjah, *Imagining Hinduism*, 49). This was partly driven by the classical distinction between *sruti* (revelation) and *smṛti* (remembered). However, while an elite may have seen the *Vedas* as far superior to *smṛti* texts (which technically includes *Manu*), the latter (*Puranic* texts, 500 BCE to 500 CE) inform the lives and praxis of many more Hindus (ibid., 47).

66. Doniger, *The Hindus*, 596. As another example, although Doniger's work has been criticized for reading sex into everything; however, she describes the *kama-sutra* (first translated 1883) as being rescued from obscurity; a puritanical streak in India, probably influenced by British attitudes, had banished it to decaying libraries (ibid., 596).

67. King argues that orientalists also represented *Vedanta* in a way that exaggerated its place within Hinduism; choosing to emphasize a "particular strand" (*Advaita*), they represented this as "the paradigmatic example of the mystical nature of the Hindu religion," effectively conflating *Vedanta*, and *Advaita Vedanta*. Richard King, *Orientalism and Religion: Post-Colonial Theory, India and "The Mystic East"* (London: Routledge, 1999), 128.

68. Jones, *The Collected Works of Sir William Jones*, 189–90.

69. Sugitharajah, *Imagining Hinduism*, 24.

70. William Jones, *Asiatick Researches*, Volume I (Calcutta, India: Asiatick Society, 1799), 421.

71. Sugitharajah, *Imagining Hinduism*, 4.

72. Charles Grant and Christian Frederick Swartz, *Observations on the State of Society Among the Asiatic Subjects of Great Britain, Particularly with Respect to Morals, and on the Means of Improving It* (London: East India Company, 1813), 26, 44, 27.

73. Doniger, *The Hindus*, 99.

74. Ibid., 615.

75. Lorenzon, *Who Invented Hinduism?* 24.

76. Ibid., 23.

77. King, *Orientalism and Religion*, 107. He also questions applying the term *Hindu reform* to movements that reacted to European criticism, especially on such issues as "idol worship," caste (*jat*, a subset of class), gender roles, belief in many deities, not to mention *Sati* (widow-immolation, allegedly widely practiced but exaggerated by European writers), and lack of social consciousness. These movements, ranging from Roy's *Brahmo Samaj* (founded 1830), through the *Arya Samaj* (founded 1875), to the less formally organized Gandhian movement, clearly responded to Christian criticism, adopted some Christian ideas (e.g., proselytizing, seminal texts, congregational worship), and organizationally resemble denominations, but if Hinduism was itself in flux, they were alternative expressions or interpretations rather than reformist. Grant and Ward, perhaps Jones too, would be astonished to see European members of such movements as the Vedanta Society and the International Society for Krishna Consciousness. Ideas about India's spiritual wealth, popular among these movements, though, had strong support among Theosophists.

78. Ian S. Markham and Christy Lohr, eds., *A World Religions Reader*, 3rd ed. (Oxford, England: Wiley-Blackwell, 2009), 65; and Lewis M. Hopfe and Mark R Woodward, *Religions of the World* (Boston, MA: Pearson, 2012), 77.

79. Sugitharajah, *Imagining Hinduism*, 32.

80. Ibid., 34.

81. William Ward, *A View of the History, Literature, and Mythology of the Hindoos; Including a Minute Description of Their Manners and Customs, and Translations from Their Principal Works*, Volume 1 (London: Printed for Kingsbury, Parbury and Allen, 1822), xvi.

82. Ibid., 290.

83. Sugitharajah, *Imagining Hinduism*, 65.

84. Ernest Renan, *The Future of Science* (Boston, MA: Roberts Brothers, 1893), 128, 135.

85. Said, *Orientalism*, 134.

86. Renan, *The Future of Science*, 235.

87. William Brustein, *Roots of Hate: Anti-Semitism in Europe Before the Holocaust* (Cambridge, England: Cambridge University Press, 2003), 118.

88. Francis Espinasse, *Life of Ernest Renan* (London: W. Scott, 1895), 210.

89. Ibid., 62–63.

90. Ernest Renan, *Mélanges d'histoire et de Voyages* (Paris: Calmann-Lévy, 1878), 187.

91. Espinasse, *Life of Ernest Renan*, 120.

92. David Semah, *Four Egyptian Literary Critics* (Leiden, Holland: E. J. Brill, 1974), 77.

93. Said, *Orientalism*, 149.

94. Ibid., 145.

95. Pessah Shinar, *Modern Islam in the Maghrib* (Jerusalem: Hebrew University of Jerusalem, 2004), 183–84.

96. I. Gershoni and James P. Jankowski, *Egypt, Islam, and the Arabs: The Search for Egyptian Nationhood, 1900–1930* (New York: Oxford University Press, 1986), 102.

97. Ernest Renan, *Averroès et Laverroisme: Essai Historique* (Paris: Michel Lévy frères, 1866), 2, 32.

98. Jean Jaques Waardenburg, *Muslims as Actors: Islamic Meanings and Muslim Interpretations in the Perspective of the Study of Religions* (Berlin: Walter de Gruyter, 2007), 146.

99. Ernest Renan, "Islamism and Science," in *Readings in Orientalism*, Volume 1, ed. Bryan S. Turner (London: Routledge, 2000), 201.

100. Jamal al-Din al-Afghani, "Jamal al-Din al-Afghani Answers Ernest Renan's Criticism of Islam, May 18, 1883," in *Sources in the History of the Modern Middle East*, ed. Akram Fouad Khater (Boston, MA: Wadsworth/Cengage Learning, 2011), 25–31.

101. In Islamic thought, the legal rulings are called *fatwas*, the principle of diversity of opinion, *Ikhtilaf.*

102. Waardenburg, *Muslims as Actors*, 146.

103. Evelyn Baring Cromer, *Modern Egypt* (New York: Macmillan, 1916), 229, 146.

104. Ferguson, *Empire*, 51, 68.

105. Following the chronology in Flood, *An Introduction to Hinduism*, 21–22.

FURTHER READINGS

Clarke, J. J. *Oriental Enlightenment: The Encounter Between Asian and Western Thought.* London: Routledge, 1997.

Curtin, Martin. *Orientalism and Islam: European Thinkers on Oriental Despotism in the Middle East and India: Thinkers on Muslim Government in the Middle East and India.* Cambridge, England: Cambridge University Press, 2009.

Dube, Saurabh. "Postcolonialism." In *Studying Hinduism: Key Concepts and Methods*, ed. Sushil Mittal and Gene Thursby. London: Routledge, 2008, 289–302.

Iwamura, Jane. *Virtual Orientalism: Asian Religions and American Popular Culture.* Oxford, England, and New York: Oxford University Press, 2011.

King, Richard. *Orientalism and Religion: Post-Colonial Theory, India and "The Mystic East."* London: Routledge, 1999.

Lewis, Bernard. *Islam and the West.* Oxford, England: Oxford University Press, 1993.

Lorenzen, David N. *Who Invented Hinduism? Essays on Religion in History.* New Delhi, India: Yoda Press, 2006.

Said, Edward. *Orientalism.* New York: Penguin, 1978.

Sugitharajah, Sharada. *Imagining Hinduism: A Post-Colonial Perspective.* New York: Routledge, 2003.

About the Editor
and Contributors

ABOUT THE EDITOR

PAUL HEDGES, PhD, is Reader in Interreligious Studies at the University of Winchester, UK. He has previously worked for other British, Canadian and Chinese universities. His published works include *Controversies in Inter-religious Dialogue and the Theology of Religions, Christian Approaches to Other Faiths* (edited with Alan Race, Textbook and Reader), and *Preparation and Fulfillment.*

ABOUT THE CONTRIBUTORS

CLINTON BENNETT received his PhD in Islamic Studies from Birmingham University in 1990. Especially interested in how we construct images of Others, he teaches at SUNY New Paltz, USA and has authored a dozen books in his field.

ANGELA COCO is senior lecturer in the School of Arts and Social Sciences at Southern Cross University, Australia. She is author of *Catholics, Conflicts and Choices: An Exploration of Power Relations in the Catholic Church* published by Acumen, 2013.

JAYEEL SERRANO CORNELIO has been recently appointed Director of the Development Studies Program at the Ateneo de Manila University (Philippines). He was a postdoctoral research fellow at the Max Planck Institute for the Study of Religious and Ethnic Diversity (Göttingen, Germany).

RENÉE DE LA TORRE is Professor of Social Anthropology at Centro de Investigaciones y Estudios Superiores en Anthropologia Social in Mexico.

ROSE DREW manages a new interfaith project for charity, Interfaith Scotland. Since completing her doctorate in 2008, she has also lectured in interfaith studies and Buddhism at the University of Glasgow and in 2011 held a research scholarship at Uppsala University, Sweden.

ANNA S. KING is University Reader in Peace and Conflict Studies, Winchester Centre of Religions for Reconciliation and Peace. A social anthropologist, her current research interests include religious traditions and modernity, contemporary spiritualties, conflict transformation, and peace-building.

LUCIEN VAN LIERE is assistant professor at the Department of Philosophy and Religious Studies at Utrecht University. His research focus is on profiles of religions in violent conflicts.

VINEETA SINHA is Associate Professor of Sociology at the National University of Singapore. Her research includes the critique of concepts and categories in the social sciences, sociological theory, sociology and anthropology of religion, the Hindu Diaspora, and the political economy of health care in medically plural societies.

CHRISTINA WELCH, PhD, has a particular research interest in the representations of religions in popular culture, and especially the material and visual representation of North American Indians and their spiritual traditions. She lecturers in Religious Studies at the University of Winchester.

Index